HUMAN INSTINCTS, EVERYDAY LIFE, AND THE BRAIN

HUMAN INSTINCTS, EVERYDAY LIFE, AND THE BRAIN

A paradigm for understanding behavior

Volume Two

Specific behaviors in response to instincts, or feelings

> Conserving time and energy
> Protecting self and resources
> Removing physical discomfort
> Taking precautions
> Trying to get what others have

Case examples: #1156 - #2272

A research series by

Richard H. Wills, University of Prince Edward Island

ISBN: 0-9684020-1-1

Distributed by

The Book Emporium
169 Queen Street
Charlottetown
Prince Edward Island
Canada C1A 4B4

Telephone: 1-902-628-2001

To everyone who participated in this research

CONTENTS

Prince Edward Island

North Cape

Tignish

Alberton

PRINCE
COUNTY

O'Leary

West Point

Lennox Island

Mont-Carmel

Miscouche

Summerside

Borden

Kensington

Cavendish

North
Rustico Beach

Brackley
Beach

Stanhope
Beach
Complex

Mount
Stewart

QUEENS
COUNTY

York

Cornwall

Crapaud

Victoria

Stratford

Charlottetown

Brudenell
Park

Dundas

KINGS
COUNTY

Souris

Georgetown

Panmure
Island

Montague

Murray
Harbour

Wood Islands

mi. 0   15
km. 0   25

N

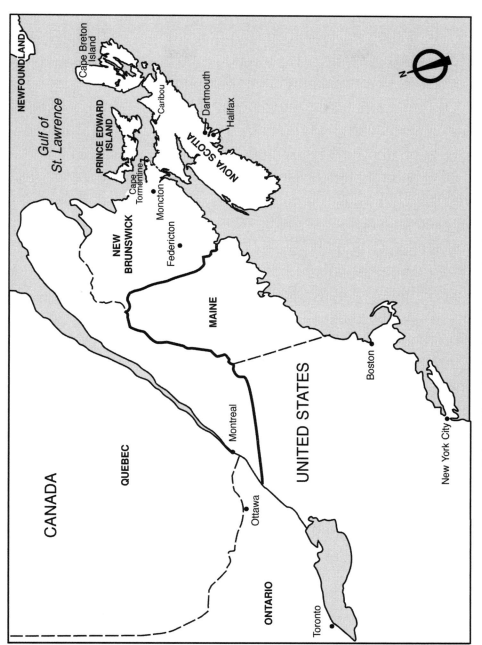

Prince Edward Island relative to other locations

1. INTRODUCTION

Volume One

Volume One, the previous volume in this series, contains a list of implications; photographs; a theoretical introduction; five chapters on specific behaviors in response to instincts, or feelings; and a discussion of a) the study of behavior, and b) human perception of nonhumans. The five chapters on specific behaviors deal with seeking positive reactions; avoiding embarrassment, criticism, and rejection; and not hurting others. A short summary of Volume One is provided in the next few paragraphs.

Feelings act as instincts in humans and other species. Feelings are designed to help us obtain and protect resources. Feelings are a more reliable means of directing our behavior than are learning, memory, culture, and conscious thought. Instead, we use learning, memory, culture, and conscious thought as means to satisfy our feelings. We seek positive feelings and avoid negative feelings. Positive feelings occur in the form of pleasure, which is provided by a variety of sources, including positive reactions from others, pleasant stimulation, the achievement of goals, and sex. Negative feelings include loneliness; anxiety; envy; anger; and hurt from criticism, rejection, embarrassment, and self-criticism. Feelings involve an increase of tension or a release of tension. Tension and the increase of tension are experienced as hurt, and the release of tension is experienced as pleasure. People engage in specific behaviors in response to positive and negative feelings. The five behaviors which are dealt with in Volume One are seeking positive reactions, avoiding embarrassment, avoiding criticism, avoiding those who reject us, and trying to help others. Each of these is considered in turn below.

People want positive reactions from others, and try to get them in a multitude of ways. People seek positive reactions in order to avoid loneliness and to experience pleasure. When people receive the kinds of positive reactions they want from the individuals they want them from, they feel pleasure and they cease to feel lonely. People establish relationships in order to obtain a steady supply of positive reactions. Those who provide a person with positive reactions usually provide the person with resources. Resources include food, shelter, protection, help, money, stimulation, and sex. Those who do not provide a person with positive reactions usually do not provide the person with resources. Therefore, the ability to get positive reactions from a person serves as an early indicator that one is likely to get resources from the person. People provide others with positive reactions and resources in order to get both positive reactions and resources from them. When people experience pleasure they smile and laugh. Smiling and laughing are desired positive reactions, and people do things for others in order to receive smiles and laughs.

People are embarrassed when others know they have done something that is disapproved of. Embarrassment is a punishing experience because it hurts. People try to avoid embarrassment in order to avoid hurt. In order to avoid embarrassment, people a) avoid doing the things that others disapprove of, and b) try to keep others from finding out what they do that others disapprove of. When a person is disapproved of, others are less willing to give the person resources. Embarrassment acts as an early warning system. It notifies us that we are in a situation which is likely to cause others to cut off our resources. When we avoid embarrassment we avoid alienating others and losing resources.

People try to avoid criticism from others. Criticism hurts, and people avoid criticism in order to avoid hurt. When a person is criticized, other people are already reducing that person's resources or making plans to do so. Therefore the more sensitive a person is to criticism and the possibility of receiving it, the more the person tries to avoid criticism, and the better the person protects his or her resources.

People reject others because their own resources are limited. If they give their resources to everyone who wants them, they will not have them available for themselves and those they want to give them to. People usually do not experience hurt when they reject others. However, those who are rejected do experience hurt. Because of this hurt, people normally avoid those who reject them. This enables them to stop wasting time and energy continuing to try to get resources from those who are unlikely to provide them. Instead, people seek resources from those who do not reject them and are much more likely to provide them with resources.

When people hurt others, cause them to lose resources, or fail to help them, they often criticize themselves. Self-criticism, or guilt, is a punishing feeling. It hurts. Therefore people try to avoid hurting others in order to avoid feeling hurt themselves. People spend most of their time with a small number of people and receive most of their resources from them. It is very much in their interest that they do not damage these people or alienate them. When they take good care of their human resources they are likely to continue receiving resources from them. It is an expensive process to try to establish relationships with new people in order to receive the same resources that one was already receiving. When people feel hurt, they cry, cry out, or want to do so. When they cry they notify others that they are being hurt and need help. When they cry they are more likely to cause those who are hurting them, or who could help them, to feel guilty. Therefore crying helps people protect themselves from being hurt and enables them to get help.

Volume Two

Volume Two, this volume, contains chapters on five other specific behaviors in response to instincts, or feelings. The behaviors which are dealt with are conserving time and energy, protecting self and resources, removing physical discomfort, taking precautions, and trying to get what others have. This volume also contains photographs and an updated and expanded list of implications.

Numerous quotes are given in the volumes in this series. These quotes were gathered from people on Prince Edward Island. A small percentage of the material deals with experiences that people on Prince Edward Island have had in other provinces and in other countries. The person quoted is not identified by age and occupation because in most cases the person would not want this information known. Given the small size of the province, the amount of information that people know about each other, and the effort they put into learning more about others, facts such as age and occupation would confirm the identity of many of those quoted.

Unimportant details in the quotes and case studies are sometimes changed to protect the identities of the subjects. Specific amounts of money are mentioned in a number of examples. In a few cases is it possible to identify the year that the amount of money refers to.

In this volume case examples are numbered consecutively starting with #1156 and ending with #2272. Volume One contained case examples #1 through #1155. An index of case examples is provided at the end of each volume. There are two exercises in this volume for the reader to do. Please do these exercises. They will make it easier to understand the subject matter.

2. IMPLICATIONS OF THIS RESEARCH

Contents

continued on next page

Implications of this research

Introduction

This is a partial list of ideas, or models, which have been produced by the research to date. These ideas result from the research reported in Volumes One and Two and from the research which is currently in process which has not yet been published. This is a working list which will certainly change as the research proceeds. There will be alterations, deletions, and additions to this list.

Feelings as instincts

1. Humans have biologically programmed feelings.

2. These feelings are present in all members of the species.

3. Feelings act as instincts.

4. Most instincts in humans and other animal species are experienced as feelings.

5. Responses to feelings in nonhuman animal species have been interpreted as instincts.

6. Feelings explain most of the behavior in humans and other animal species.

7. Feelings provide the motivational system of a species with voluntary movement.

8. Evidence that a species responds to any feeling, such as discomfort (hunger, thirst) or anxiety (running from threats, hiding from threats), indicates that the species responds to other feelings too.

9. Our behavior is directed by feelings, rather than by reason and learning. Reason and learning are used to help us satisfy our feelings. They serve as handmaidens of feelings.

10. Feelings encourage the individual to get and keep resources. Discomfort encourages us to find resources, such as food, water, and shelter, which will remove specific discomforts. Loneliness encourages us to establish relationships with friends and mates, who help us get resources, share their resources with us, and help protect us. Envy encourages us to get the same resources that others are getting. Anxiety helps us avoid threats to ourselves and our resources. Anger helps us defend ourselves and our resources. Guilt encourages us to take care of our human resources. The hurt produced by criticism, rejection, and embarrassment encourages us to avoid doing things which alienate other people, who provide us with most of our resources.

11. Feelings are activated at the first signs that resources are available or threatened.

12. Individuals act in response to feelings, or they act in advance of feelings to avoid or promote the feelings.

13. The three major types of feelings are the pleasures, the hurts, and the bothers.

14. The individual pursues pleasures while avoiding hurts and bothers.

15. Our lives are dedicated to trying to obtain pleasant feelings and avoid unpleasant feelings. Pleasant feelings are provided by the pleasures. Unpleasant feelings are provided by the hurts and bothers.

16. The pleasures are produced by sex, positive reactions, and stimula-

tion. In addition, the removal of hurts and bothers releases tension and produces pleasure.

17. The hurts are produced by physical and mental effort; negative reactions from others (criticism, rejection); loneliness; threats (anxiety); envy; self-criticism, or guilt; pain; and physical discomforts, such as hunger and not breathing.

18. The bothers are produced by phenomena which are not categorized, inconsistency, phenomena which are not oriented, and differences between models and reality. The bothers hurt also, but usually to a lesser degree than the hurts.

19. Humans can experience and act on feelings without being consciously aware of them. For example, humans take each breath in response to the feeling of increasing discomfort that they experience when they do not take a breath. Humans are not normally consciously aware of this discomfort or of their decision to act and take a breath in order to get rid of it.

20. A considerable amount of excess behavior occurs in response to specific feelings which fails to obtain and conserve resources.

21. Individuals respond to current feelings and live in the present.

22. Human feelings and responses are constant in different cultures and in different historical periods.

23. There is a common set of feelings which is shared by different animal species. For example, in many species individuals associate together in order to obtain positive reactions from each other. Their desire for positive reactions is so strong that they engage in efforts to obtain positive reactions which attract the attention of predators.

24. Various animal species employ different behaviors in response to common feelings. For example, humans smile, cats purr, and dogs wag their tails to express pleasure.

25. Specific feelings are tied to specific muscle groups. For example, humans feel anxiety in their diaphragms, hurt in their lower eye sockets, and pleasure at the raised corners of their mouths.

26. Different feelings are experienced at different locations on the body.

27. Feelings which are experienced at separate locations on the body are separate feelings.

28. Feelings which are experienced at the same locations on the body are the same feeling.

29. The same feeling can be tied to different muscle groups in different animal species. For example, humans feel pleasure where they smile, cats feel pleasure where they purr, and dogs feel pleasure where they wag their tails.

Individuals

30. An individual is designed to a) get and keep resources, b) compete with other individuals for resources, c) cooperate with other individuals to get and keep resources, and d) exchange resources with other individuals.

31. Feelings encourage individuals to get and keep resources, compete for resources with others, and cooperate and exchange resources with others. An individual is encouraged to get resources by the feelings of discomfort, loneliness, and envy. Discomforts, such as hunger, thirst, and feeling hot or cold, encourage one to obtain resources which will remove the discomforts. Loneliness encourages one to seek the company of others, who provide protection and other resources. Envy encourages one to obtain the same resources that others are getting. An individual is encouraged to keep resources by

the feelings of anxiety and anger. Anxiety encourages one to take precautions. Anger enables one to aggressively protect oneself and one's resources. Also, the hurt produced by effort encourages one to avoid exertion and conserve time and energy. Because individuals experience their own feelings rather than the feelings of others, they try to satisfy their own feelings. As a result, they compete with others to obtain resources. Individuals are encouraged to cooperate with each other and exchange resources by the desire for positive reactions and the desire to avoid both negative reactions from others (criticism, rejection, and embarrassment) and guilt (self-criticism).

32.   An individual experiences his own feelings. He learns about the feelings experienced by other individuals, but he does not experience them firsthand. Therefore an individual experiences his own feelings far more vividly than he experiences the feelings of other individuals. As a result, each individual spends most of his time acting for himself, thinking about himself, and trying to communicate about himself to others.

Communication of feelings

33.   The members of an animal species share a well-developed means of communicating certain of their feelings to each other.

34.   Such feelings are communicated to each other through the action of the specific muscle groups associated with each feeling.

35.   Simulating the actions of these specific muscle groups will enable humans to better communicate with other animal species.

36.   Indicating one's feelings to others is costly in terms of a) the biological systems required to be able to do so, and b) the time and energy expended when one does so. Nevertheless, individuals

frequently make their feelings known to others by various means, including sounds, facial expressions, and the movement and position of body parts. Therefore, it must be advantageous to indicate what one is feeling to others.

37. Because feelings determine behavior, it is important to let others know what you are feeling in order that they can correctly predict how you will act and coordinate their behavior with your own. When others correctly recognize what you are feeling, they are more likely to act in an appropriate way at the appropriate time. When others correctly coordinate their behavior with your own, you have to exert less time and energy trying to get them to do so.

38. Because feelings determine behavior, it is important to know what others are feeling in order that you can predict how they will act and you can coordinate your behavior with their behavior. When you correctly coordinate your behavior with the behavior of others, you expend less time and energy dealing with them. Appropriate behavior expends less time and energy than does inappropriate behavior, and is more likely to be successful.

39. Signs of specific feelings carry specific messages which provide advantages. Signs of happiness (smiling, purring, tail wagging) provide others with positive reactions and enable one to obtain positive reactions and resources from them. Signs of discomfort and unhappiness, such as crying, enable one to obtain help and resources from others. Signs of anger warn others that one will aggressively protect oneself and one's resources. Signs of fear notify those one depends on for resources and protection that there are threats present. Signs of interest notify those one depends on about the presence of threats and opportunities.

40. Individuals experience their own feelings, but not the feelings of others. Therefore it is easy for individuals to fail to take into account the feelings of other individuals. When individuals show others what they are feeling, they notify others that they have feelings, they remind others that these feelings need to be taken into account, and

they reveal precisely what these feelings are. Only by revealing feelings can others take them into consideration.

41. In many species a tail is a device for communicating both visually and physically what one is feeling to others. Cats use their tails to indicate alertness, interest, enthusiasm, irritation, affection, fear, discouragement, and relaxation. Humans and apes use facial expressions instead of tails for this purpose. Tails are particularly noticeable because they are a distinct appendage, move independently of the rest of the body, make pronounced movements, are frequently banded in contrasting colors, and hit against other individuals.

42. Both tails and faces indicate the nature and degree of the tension that the individual is experiencing.

Activators

43. Individuals have *activators*, or specialized behaviors which activate specific feelings in other individuals. Crying, smiling, and anger are three examples of activators in humans.

44. Different animal species use different activators to achieve a common purpose. For example, humans smile, cats purr, and dogs wag their tails as activators to obtain positive reactions from others.

45. Activators are the first social behaviors expressed by the infants of many animal species. Mewing and purring are two examples of activators in kittens.

46. Individuals cheat, or use an activator without experiencing the feeling which produces the activator, in order to get others to respond appropriately. Cheaters employ various activators, including crying, smiling, and anger.

47. The presence of activators can be used to trace the presence and evolution of certain feelings in various animal species.

Behavior

48. The regular use of a specific social behavior by members of a species indicates that the behavior frequently evokes a specific feeling and a specific response in other members of the species.

49. The Parallel Feelings Hypothesis: If two different species a) use the same social behavior, and b) produce the same response in others, then c) the feeling which is evoked in others by the social behavior is the same in both species. For example, because infant humans and infant birds a) both "cry," and b) in both cases their parents respond by feeding them, then c) the same feeling is evoked in both sets of parents, i.e., a desire to avoid self-criticism, or guilt.

50. In accordance with The Parallel Feelings Hypothesis, when we can identify the feeling that is evoked in one of the two species, we can assume the same feeling is evoked in the other species. Therefore, when we know what the feeling is in humans (when humans are one of the two species), we can assume that the same feeling is present in the other species.

Association and extension

51. An individual recognizes what he thinks, does, says, and owns as extensions of himself.

52.　An individual recognizes a positive reaction by others to anything he thinks, does, says, or owns as a positive reaction to himself.

53.　An individual recognizes a negative reaction by others to anything he thinks, does, says, or owns as a negative reaction to himself.

54.　An individual considers the other individuals he is associated with to be extensions of himself.

55.　An individual treats negative reactions to those he is associated with as negative reactions toward himself.

56.　An individual views the behavior of those he is associated with as though it is his own behavior. As a result, actions which would embarrass the individual if he did them himself, embarrass him when they are done by other people he is associated with.

57.　When a person is familiar with another individual's experiences, he does not experience them as the other individual experiences them. Instead, the person experiences them as he would feel if the experiences had happened to himself.

58.　People "adopt" others as an extension of themselves. Thus they adopt characters in novels and films, individuals in the news, and sporting teams and players. When something happens to someone or something that a person has "adopted," the person responds as though it is happening to himself. This is the case when those who are adopted (or their resources) are threatened, or when those who are adopted succeed and receive positive reactions. People have difficulty adopting a character when the character does things which they would not do themselves, such as things which they consider bad, incompetent, immature, self-centered, selfish, foolish, stupid, rude, inconsiderate, narrow minded, or a result of bad judgment.

Tense and release

59. Feelings involve an increase of tension or a release of tension.

60. Tension is experienced as hurt.

61. An increase in tension produces a corresponding increase in hurt.

62. Difficulty releasing tension, or the inability to release tension, prolongs hurt.

63. We try to minimize physical and mental effort because they involve tension and hurt. When we conserve time and energy, we avoid effort, and we avoid tension and hurt.

64. The release of tension is experienced as pleasure.

65. When we complete a task or achieve a goal, we release the tension that was driving us, and we feel pleasure. Therefore we feel pleasure when we complete a paper we are writing, pay off a mortgage, complete our income tax return, win a sporting competition, or get the positive reactions we want.

66. Sources of stimulation, such as movies, novels, amusement-park rides, and certain sports, produce entertainment by providing tension and releasing it. People seek out these sources of stimulation in order to experience tension, its release, and the resulting pleasure. The more tension experienced and the greater its release, the more successful the entertainment.

67. The more tension released, and the more easily tension is released, the more pleasure experienced.

68. Humans and other animal species seek to a) avoid tension, b) release

tension, and c) increase tension in order to release it and experience pleasure.

69.   Warmth releases muscular tension, and this release of tension provides pleasure. Therefore humans like lying in the sun, hot showers and baths, hot tubs, whirlpools, saunas, hot drinks, hot food, smoking, heat lamps, hot-water bottles, and electric heating pads.

70.   Many other species like lying and relaxing in the sun, which indicates that the release of tension also provides them with pleasure. This indicates that their bodies and minds operate on the same tense and release principles that human bodies and minds do.

71.   Massage is pleasurable to humans and other species because it releases tension.

72.   A living organism consists of an organized system of tense and release mechanisms. These tense and release mechanisms are able to perform respiration, circulation, movement, digestion, reproduction, nervous control, mental operations, and other activities, such as yawning and sneezing.

73.   It may prove possible to explain all physiological phenomena and the origin of life with tense and release models.

74.   The brain evolved to coordinate tense and release mechanisms.

Effort

75.   People avoid physical and mental activity because activity requires tension. People experience tension as hurt. In order to minimize hurt, individuals a) tense as little as possible, and b) release tension as

soon as possible. As a result they exert themselves as little as possible, and conserve as much energy as possible.

76. People engage in physical and mental activity in response to their other feelings. They act when a) the pleasure they obtain from the activity, or b) the hurt they feel from other sources when they do not engage in the activity, outweighs the hurt they feel from exerting themselves.

77. People avoid activities in which the hurt they feel from exerting themselves is greater than the pleasure they experience from the activity.

78. People avoid activities in which the hurt they feel from exerting themselves is greater than the hurt they feel from other sources when they do not engage in the activity.

79. Something is boring or tedious because one does not obtain enough stimulation from it to outweigh the hurt one feels from exerting oneself to do the activity. Thus one finds it boring to reread the same material, to continue to eat the same food, or to listen to someone say something one is already familiar with, because these things no longer provide stimulation.

Models and behavior

80. Behavior is structured by mental categories and models.

81. Without models, behavior is random.

82. Each individual uses categories and models in order to act in a non-random fashion.

83. When categories or models are changed, behavior changes.

84. Individuals develop and use their own categories and models.

85. Each individual employs models in order to deal with feelings.

86. Most behavior can be explained in terms of feelings and the models employed to satisfy them.

87. When models are inconsistent with reality, people experience tension.

88. People act in order to rid themselves of this tension. When they act they change reality to be consistent with their models. For example, there is a glass on the left side of the table, and you want the glass to be on the right side of the table. Therefore reality (the glass is on the left side) is inconsistent with your model (you want the glass on the right side). Because of this inconsistency, you experience tension. Therefore, you act to rid yourself of this tension. You change reality (by moving the glass from the left side of the table to the right side) to be consistent with your model (you want the glass on the right side). When reality (the glass is now on the right side) is consistent with your model (you want the glass on the right side), then the tension is released, you no longer experience tension, and you no longer feel pressure to act.

89. People act to remove their greatest sources of tension. The greater the tension, the higher the priority.

90. People select the model and action which produces the least inconsistency with their other models, i.e., the least tension.

91. Humans and other animal species develop models, select models, and act for the same reasons.

92. The mind evolved to a) recognize categories, b) recognize inconsistencies, c) deal with feelings, d) produce models, e) select between models, and f) execute models.

Language

93.   A shared language based on sounds is a means by which individuals coordinate their use of the same sounds with similar categories and models.

94.   In a shared language, specific sounds (or other phenomena) trigger the specific categories and models in the minds of other individuals that the sounds are associated with.

95.   A shared language allows individuals to exchange and pool information about their individual categories and models.

96.   In human language standardized sounds were associated with the individual categories and models that pre-humans were already employing as an animal species.

97.   Human language enables humans to discuss their feelings, behaviors, and mental operations, which they and the other animal species have in common.

98.   Humans are animals who can tell each other what it is like to be an animal. Humans are talking animals.

99.   If we want to know what animals feel and think, all we have to do is listen to humans talk about themselves.

100.   Humans speak because they feel tension to say something. Once they have said what they want to say, the tension, or pressure, is released and is no longer there. When person A finishes saying something, and person B asks person A to repeat or explain what he has just said, person A finds it annoying to do so, because the initial tension is no longer there and person A has to force himself to comply.

101. Certain animals make sounds to other animals or to humans a) when they want something, or b) when they are bothered by something (have something to say). They stop making the sounds when a) they get what they want, or b) they have said what they wanted to say. This indicates that animals feel the same tension to make sounds that humans feel and release it in the same way. This indicates that their minds operate in the same way that human minds operate.

102. Animal species have to form categories in order to recognize phenomena, and have to formulate models and apply them in order to act non-randomly.

103. Human categories and models are primarily sensory images. Consider buying a loaf of bread, eating an ice-cream cone, or having sex with a specific person. You think about these things primarily in visual images, not in words. If I say, "A kangaroo buried a watermelon in my front yard," how do you experience this in your mind? You see your own visual images of a kangaroo, a watermelon, burying something, and a front yard, rather than collections of words in your mind which describe a kangaroo, a watermelon, burying something, and a front yard.

104. Members of a species use means such as sounds in an effort to communicate their feelings, categories, and models to each other. Thus cats use sounds for a variety of purposes, including calling, answering, indicating discomfort or pain, seeking positive reactions, trying to get others to comply with what they want (establishing consistency), criticizing, threatening, and expressing what is on their mind, such as telling about their experiences or complaining.

105. Many species use sounds in an effort to activate feelings, categories, and models in other individuals.

106. Human language enables humans to communicate in generalizations, or words, which individual humans relate to their own personal categories and models.

107. Species differ as to how specific their communications are, i.e., the degree of detail in which they can describe their categories and models. Words communicate categories and models in greater detail than basic sounds. However, human language is severely limited when it comes to communicating the full detail and complexity of categories and models. Consider how difficult it is to use words alone to describe a person's appearance to someone who has never seen the person before, and to do so well enough that he would have no difficulty recognizing the person within a crowd of people. Consider also how difficult it is to use words to describe to another person all of the details and feelings that you experienced when you watched a film, read a novel, listened to a piece of music, or took a trip. Although words enable us to easily distinguish between "a chair" and "a couch" when we talk, it is difficult to use words to accurately describe a specific chair or couch to another person. When we want to communicate something specific to others we have to provide them with a visual image by showing them the item, showing them a photograph or a drawing of it, or using gestures.

108. It is very possible that a species could evolve a language which enabled it to communicate categories and models in much greater detail than human language. Such a species could communicate more accurately and rapidly, could achieve a much finer degree of cooperation among its members, and would be much more successful than a species that relied on human language. In fact, the gap in ability between such a species and humans might be at least as great as the present gap between humans and other animal species on earth.

109. Theoretically a shared language could be just as specific and descriptive as the personal categories and models held by individuals. Other things being equal, the closer the language of a species is to this ideal, the more successful the species.

110. One can view a potential progression taking place from sounds, to words, to increasingly specific words.

Culture

111. Because each individual uses his own categories and models, no two individuals have the identical understanding of a situation.

112. Inconsistency produces tension, and people seek to establish consistency to remove this tension.

113. In order to establish consistency, people try to get others to adopt and comply with their personal models.

114. When we see someone do something, we behave as though we are doing it ourselves. We consider others as an extension of ourselves. If they do, say, or think something we would not, we view it as a mistake on our part and act to correct it by trying to change their behavior.

115. People use a) resources, and b) negative reactions, such as criticism, to get others to adopt and comply with their personal models.

116. People adopt the personal models of those who control resources in order to get a share of their resources.

117. Culture is the net result of individual efforts to establish consistency within a specific group.

118. Many individual and group models produce more negative results than positive results.

119. The ability of humans to communicate in greater detail through words has enabled human individuals to communicate their specific likes and dislikes to each other and to establish a much more elaborate repertoire of correct and incorrect behaviors in their societies than have other species. Although other species are concerned

with avoiding negative reactions, they do not communicate or understand criticism in as fine detail as do humans and therefore do not adjust their behavior to as fine a degree. Therefore other species do not a) wear clothes, b) hide their sexual activity and elimination from others, or c) stand up straight, cover their mouths when they yawn, and use napkins.

120. A species which uses a language which is more specific than human language will have rules for correct and incorrect behavior which are more detailed than the rules used in human cultures. Humans will be unable to understand these rules or act in accordance with them, just as animals do not understand or act in accordance with human rules. Therefore, human behavior will appear as crude and uncouth to such a species as the behavior of animals does to humans.

Categories and models

121. Categories are an efficient means of dealing with sensory phenomena.

122. Phenomena which are not categorized produce tension and attract notice.

123. Categories are formed by recognizing repetition. For example, when humans speak and write, they use synonyms in order to avoid repetition which will produce a second, competing, unwanted, distracting category in the mind of the listener or reader. In poetry and song, on the other hand, humans use repetition to produce additional rhythmic patterns in the mind of the listener. Music consists of repetitive sounds, sequences, and phrases which enable the listener

to establish categories. It is significant that music relies heavily on numerous forms of repetition, and to a much lesser extent on symmetry, to produce categories.

124. The organization of phenomena into a category releases tension and produces pleasure.

125. The quest for stimulation is the search for unfamiliar phenomena to categorize.

126. People use the arts, learning, entertainment, and travel in order to organize unfamiliar phenomena into new categories and thereby experience pleasure. The arts include music, painting, sculpture, literature, poetry, photography, film, architecture, crafts, fashion, and decoration.

127. Successful art is designed a) to be different than existing categories so that it is not already categorized and therefore produces tension and is interesting, and b) to be easily categorized so that the tension is released with little effort and pleasure is easily produced. Orientations are employed by artists to enable phenomena to be easily categorized, and orientations are violated by artists to a limited extent to produce tension and interest.

128. The fewer categories that are needed to categorize phenomena, the less effort is required, and the more attractive the phenomena. For example, lakes and lawns can be categorized with few categories and are peaceful and pleasing, and because younger faces have fewer features than older faces, they can be categorized with fewer categories and are more attractive.

129. Once phenomena are categorized, they are no longer stimulating. No tension remains to be released. No matter how attractive a specific phenomenon is initially, once it has been fully categorized, it is no longer interesting. This is true of art, literature, music, clothing, jewelry, other possessions, and a person's appearance.

130. The play activity of the young provides parents and other adults with stimulation, i.e., pleasure. Members of a species value, maintain, and protect their sources of pleasure.

131. Models relate categories together, and are an efficient means of dealing with categories.

132. Models are also used to explain unknowns. It is important for our survival that we be able to recognize and explain unknowns, because unknowns may constitute threats or opportunities.

133. Learning consists of the placement of phenomena into categories and models.

Orientations

134. Phenomena which are not oriented produce tension.

135. The orientation of phenomena releases tension and produces pleasure.

136. The more oriented phenomena are, the less tension is produced, and the more attractive the phenomena.

137. The less oriented phenomena are, the more tension is produced, and the less attractive the phenomena.

138. Humans employ orientations in order to reduce the effort the brain has to make to organize phenomena into categories.

139. The use of orientations enables humans to easily organize phenomena into categories. Examples of human orientations include

symmetry, repetition, rectangles, circles, lines, horizontal and vertical, parallel and perpendicular, consistency, centering, equidistant placement, simplicity, perfection, thoroughness, grouping on the basis of similarity, and the use of solid colors.

140. An orientation can be approximate; it does not have to be mathematically perfect. Thus the colored designs on the individual members of a species can be approximately symmetrical, centered, or repetitive. An orientation only has to be close enough to perfect for the members of the species to be able to recognize the orientation. Humans use tools to apply their orientations with mathematical precision.

141. The presence of an orientation in the appearance of members of a species indicates that members of that species respond to that orientation. For example, if the facial or bodily designs on members of the species are symmetrical, centered, or repetitive, then members of that species respond to that orientation.

142. The symmetrical, centered, and repetitive designs on the faces and bodies of individuals are aesthetically pleasing to the members of that species.

143. Individual differences in designs on faces and bodies result in individuals appearing more or less attractive than other individuals to members of their species.

144. Specific orientations and violations of orientations are used to draw attention to specific areas of the body.

145. Many other animal species have the same orientations as humans.

146. The orientations that are used in the colored designs on nonhuman species are the same orientations that humans employ in their construction and decoration of clothes, vehicles, everyday objects, architecture, and the arts, and in their behavior.

147. The extensive use of repetition and symmetry in a) the designs on nonhuman species, and b) the designs that humans use for and on their clothes, vehicles, everyday objects, and architecture indicates that nonhumans and humans form categories in the same way and therefore their minds operate the same way.

148. Symmetry is a form of repetition. In symmetry, one half of the design repeats the other half, but from the opposite direction.

149. An individual's body maintains an approximate symmetrical appearance between the right and left halves as the individual develops and ages.

150. Humans apply orientations to their objects and behavior to produce the categories they want to perceive and want others to perceive.

151. Humans violate the orientations in order to produce tension and attract attention. In order to attract attention they use contrasting colors, off-center placement, diagonals, and inconsistency.

The mind

152. The fact that the mind and the body both a) resist effort, b) experience fatigue, and c) are better able to handle difficult tasks after a period of rest indicates that they operate in a similar manner.

153. The mind seeks to a) recognize inconsistency, and b) establish consistency.

154. The human brain gets humans to expend physical effort which enables the brain to reduce mental effort.

155. Humans can only focus on one category or model at a time.

156. When we focus on one category, we do not recognize other categories.

157. When we focus on a category, we have to give up our previous category. Therefore we often forget what our previous category was.

158. Other animal species also have single-focus minds.

159. Pack hunting is so successful because prey focus on one predator, or category, at a time.

160. Our progress in science is so slow because each individual has a single-focus mind. We can only focus on one category at a time. Therefore, when we consider one category, we can not consider others. As a result we only see what we focus on. Our single-focus mind can only perform one mental operation at a time. Thus we can only make one observation, develop one category (or model), or apply one category (or model) to data at a time. Also, we can not a) observe, decide, or act, and b) analyze at the same time. When we observe, decide, or act, we can not analyze; and when we analyze, we can not observe, decide, or act. Because we can not both do something and analyze what we are doing at the same time, we have little conscious awareness of what we are doing and why we are doing it. Because we have a single-focus mind, we have to do science through piecemeal accumulation, and add one bit of information or analysis at a time.

161. A species whose individuals have multiple-focus minds could deal with more than one category (or model) at a time, and could perform more than one mental operation, such as both observation and analysis, at the same time. Such a species could understand situations and behavior, respond appropriately, and develop science and technology at a much faster rate than a single-focus species. In comparison with a multiple-focus species, a single-focus species would be mentally retarded. A multiple-focus species could be produced through a) evolution in certain environments, or b) genetic engineering.

162. A group is a collection of individuals whose single-focus minds are focused in different directions. Therefore a group operates as a multiple-focus mind, which recognizes more opportunities and more threats than an individual would recognize alone.

163. The more individuals there are in a group, the larger the number of threats and opportunities that will be recognized.

Consciousness

164. Physical and mental activities require conscious attention when they must be learned or changed. They must be changed when it becomes clear they are inappropriate and when obstacles are encountered.

165. Conscious attention is required to examine and select alternatives. Examining and selecting alternatives requires much more conscious attention than monitoring routines.

166. Physical and mental activities which are repeated without change become routines. They can be executed very quickly because they require little conscious attention except to monitor their execution and their relevance.

167. Because conscious attention and selection involves more mental operations than does the execution of routines, it is much slower.

168. The more tension produced by a phenomenon, the more likely one is made consciously aware of the phenomenon.

169. One must apply conscious attention when a) one recognizes things, b) one tries to find something, c) one tries to understand what is happening, d) one tries to understand why something is happening,

e) one chooses between alternatives, f) one decides how to deal with a situation, g) one decides how to deal with changes, h) one decides what one ought to be doing, i) one sets objectives, j) one decides how and when to carry out objectives, k) one decides what one needs to have in order to carry out objectives, l) one establishes priorities, m) one decides whether to act, n) one decides what to do next, o) one decides what to do in the future, p) one thinks about what could happen, q) one decides why one should not do things, r) one takes precautions, s) one recognizes obstacles, t) one decides how to act when one encounters obstacles, u) one solves problems, v) one decides how to make improvements, w) one checks on one's progress, x) one recognizes that one needs to find an alternative, y) one realizes that the situation is different than one thought, z) one tries to change one's behavior, aa) one tries to change the behavior of others, bb) one imagines a possible outcome, cc) one imagines a desirable outcome, dd) one dreams, ee) one considers or decides what to do if something happens, ff) one recognizes when something significant happens, gg) one considers past events, hh) one thinks about what one should have done, or ii) one evaluates things and events.

170. Any species which does one or more of the activities mentioned just above has consciousness.

The study of brain and behavior

171. Rather than view each species as having a unique evolutionary past, unique mental operations, and unique behaviors, it is more useful to view different species as sharing a common set of mental operations and behaviors which have been modified for survival in particular niches.

172. We have assumed that the behavior of each species is unique.

173. However, the behavior that is unique to a species is a thin veneer over a common set of feelings, behaviors, and mental operations which are shared with other animal species.

174. By focusing on the differences between species and the differences between cultures we have overlooked the greater significance of the similarities between species. Differences between species and between cultures are inconsistent, produce tension, and attract our attention. Similarities between species and between cultures are consistent, do not produce tension, and do not attract our attention.

175. Feelings, categories, models, consciousness, and communication did not originate with humans. They originated with animals. Humans have them too because humans are animals.

176. Language and technology did not free humans from their animal programming, or feelings, but rather gave humans more power to implement their animal programming on each other and their environment.

177. Perhaps the biggest obstacle to understanding ourselves is our pretentiousness, or the belief humans are unique, special, and important, and more so than other species. This pretentiousness has interfered with and delayed our understanding of a) our location in space, b) our evolution, c) our mind and behavior, and d) the similarity between human nature and animal nature, and our realizing that e) other species have as much right to the environment as we do.

178. Every behavior of humans and other animal species can be understood in a scientific manner.

179. Each and every thing an individual does reflects the structure and operation of the brain.

180. An understanding of human behavior and the human mind will likely precede and produce a greater understanding of the behavior

and minds of other animal species.

181. We will find simple ways to accurately describe and explain behavior, the mind, and the brain.

Humans and other species

182. Human exploitation of other species is based on superior power rather than natural right.

183. Humans act like the Nazis of the animal kingdom, and treat other species worse than Nazis treated Jews.

184. Just as the Nazis envisioned a Thousand-Year Reich for their race, humans envision a long and glorious destiny for their species on earth and in space.

185. Humans do not act any better or any worse than any other animal species would act if it had moved into the dominant position.

186. The argument that "it is acceptable for humans to harm animals provided humans are benefited" is no different than the arguments that "it is acceptable for Europeans to harm Africans provided Europeans are benefited," "it is acceptable for men to harm women provided men are benefited," and "it is acceptable for Nazis to harm Jews provided Nazis are benefited."

187. Other animal species are so similar to us, that when we do something to another species, we might as well be doing it to ourselves.

188. Humans live as though they are the only species on earth that matters. They do not consider the consequences of their actions for the members of other species.

189. Humans consider each individual human precious, but each individual member of other species insignificant.

190. Humans show an almost complete lack of empathy and respect for members of other animal species, who are experiencing many of the same feelings and thoughts that humans would experience if humans were in their situations.

191. The food chain is cannibalism on a large scale. Animal species are so similar to each other, that animal-eating species are effectively eating themselves.

Humans and the environment

192. Humans are in the process of converting the entire earth to human use at the expense of other species.

193. Humans find the appearance of nature chaotic and irritating. Therefore they apply human orientations to nature in order to reduce the effort of looking at it. Thus they produce lawns, gardens, and parks which conform with human orientations. Human orientations include the extensive use of rectangles, circles, lines, parallel and perpendicular, horizontal and vertical, repetition, symmetry, consistency, perfection, and grouping on the basis of similarity.

3. SPECIFIC BEHAVIORS IN RESPONSE TO FEELINGS

Contents

CONSERVING TIME AND ENERGY

Brief contents

Detailed contents

Introduction	40
Economizing activity	40
Exercise 1: Using as many muscles as possible	40
Tactics for conserving time and energy	47
1. Minimizing exertion	49
2. Minimizing time	54
3. Taking risks	58
4. Taking what others have	59
5. Using animals	60
6. Using a tool	60
7. Replacing a defective tool	63
8. Obtaining one's own equipment	64
9. Obtaining multiple copies	65
10. Combining activities	65
11. Performing an activity less often	67
12. Keeping items where they are used	69
13. Keeping items where they can be easily found	70
14. Not repeating one's efforts	70
15. Procrastinating	72
16. Doing an activity which is easier or more fun	74
17. Reducing one's workload	76
18. Not doing an activity	77
19. Getting rid of an activity	80
20. Avoiding requests by others	81
21. Arranging to spend less time and energy in the future	82
22. Acquiring lasting items	85
23. Limiting variety	86
24. Obtaining what can be fixed locally	87
25. Taking what one will need	87

Detailed contents

Introduction

People try to expend a minimum amount of time and energy in their physical and mental activities. The feeling which encourages them to do so is hurt. People employ tension in order to exert themselves (to act), and they experience tension as hurt. Therefore, people feel hurt when they exert themselves, and they try to avoid this feeling by exerting themselves as little as possible. This hurt is intensified by fatigue. People engage in activity because the hurt or pleasure they experience from other feelings overrides the hurt they feel from exertion. When people do exert themselves, they try to spend as little time as possible in an activity, because they feel hurt from exertion and they feel anxious about all the other things they have to do. As a result of hurt and anxiety, people employ numerous tactics to conserve time and energy. People experience hurt and anxiety when they first consider effort. This provides them with the maximum amount of time in which to conserve time and energy.

Economizing activity

People minimize their activity. They keep as much of their bodies immobilized as possible, and normally limit themselves to localized movements.

Exercise 1: Using as many muscles as possible

Stand facing a full-length mirror. For the next minute continue to move as many different muscles as you can at the same time. How does this differ from your usual behavior?

People use great economy of movement. When they are active, the remainder of their body is usually stationary and as relaxed as possible. When people can, they use one hand or arm instead of two. When they move, they usually do only one, and occasionally two, thing(s) at a time. Often this consists of one or two of the following: looking, walking, talking, eating, drinking, changing to a more comfortable or relaxed position, scratching or rubbing themselves, or biting or chewing on something. When they work or play, their movements are often highly localized. When people engage in a repetitive movement, such as drumming their fingers, tapping their foot, or repeatedly thumping one object against another, this is usually of short duration.

When people execute a model, there is little wastage of time and energy and seldom any need to repeat a movement. Movement is monitored and adjusted and the placement of fingers, hands, arms, legs, and feet is normally exact. When items are picked up, carried, or manipulated, they are properly balanced. Almost all movements are accurate the first time. As a result, there is little unnecessary or excess movement, and the expenditure of time and energy is minimized.

People use and coordinate their hand and arm movements in ways which conserve time and energy. When they only need to use one hand they do so. Thus they use a single hand to pick up, hold, carry, and put down a light object; turn on a switch or faucet; open a lightweight door or drawer; throw something that is not heavy; or scratch or rub themselves. They use the hand that is closer to what they are dealing with, rather than their distant hand. When people are already holding an object in a hand, they frequently use the empty hand to do a task. However, they also frequently move an object to the other hand in order to be able to use the hand they customarily use for a specific task or to use the hand that is closest to the task. It takes less effort to move an object from one hand to the other than it does to put the object down and have to pick it up again. People also have a preferred hand when they need strength or precision for a task, such as writing, putting away dishes, or unlocking a door. They transfer objects to and from a preferred hand when they perform tasks. People frequently use their distant hand for a task when they are leaning or lying in a position which would require more effort for them to move in order to use the nearer hand to do the task. In addition, given the structure of the body, there are tasks which are easier to do using the hand and arm from the other side of the body, for example, washing under one's arms or scratching or rubbing a shoulder. People also use both hands to do many things. They lift, hold, and maneuver an object with one hand in order to place the object in positions so that it takes less time and energy for the other hand to deal with it. The other hand may be used to open the object, unzip it, twist it, cut it, pull or tear part of it off, empty it, scrape it, fill it, stir it, fasten it, measure it, write on it, clean it, or close it.

It is not easy to tear off toilet paper using only one hand. If you jerk the paper in order to separate the piece you want, you usually cause the roll to turn and you end up with much more paper than you wanted. If you want to control how much paper you get, you usually have to hold the roll steady with one hand to tear off a section with the other. [#1156]

Normally it is easier to raise an object to a level where it can be easily dealt with by the other hand than it is to lower one's torso to the level of the object. People also use both hands together to carry or open something heavy or unwieldy, to pull or push something apart, or to squeeze both sides of larger objects. People often use a single hand to do a task that they would normally use two hands for, if they are already holding something with the other hand, or if they are sitting, leaning, or lying in a position where it would take more effort to move into a position which would allow them to easily use two hands.

I am lying on the bed on my left side with my head propped up by my left hand, forearm, and elbow. From time to time I write something with my right hand, and I use my right hand to push the top off the ballpoint pen and push it back on when I've finished with it. I grip the pen with the three smallest fingers of my right hand and push the top off with the forefinger and thumb of the right hand. I don't want to roll over on my back or to sit up in order to take the top off the pen with both hands. (However, when I am sitting at a table or desk, I hold the top of the pen firmly with my left hand and pull the pen out with my right hand.) Later I lie down fully on my left side with the side of my head flat on the bed and keep only one eye, the right one, open while I write. The second eye isn't needed, because it is too low to see what I am writing. [#1157]

The use of other body parts is coordinated with the hands in order to minimize effort.

I am carrying a glass of water in my left hand and use my right hand to get my keys out of my right pocket so I can unlock my office door. After

I unlock the door with my right hand, I still need to extract my key from the lock. I balance on my left foot and push the door open with my right foot while holding the key firmly in my right hand. This separates the door from the key. This takes less time and effort than putting the glass of water down first and then using both hands to unlock the door and extract the key. [#1158]

I am sitting on the bed with the bottom of my right foot flat on the bed and my right knee up to provide support for the clipboard I am writing on. My left leg is on the bed, but the left knee is bent and the left foot is resting on top of my right foot. This prevents my right foot from sliding forward as I put pressure on my right knee while I write. [#1159]

Because people constantly minimize movement, their willingness to move is a good indicator of the importance of a particular feeling or behavior. Therefore the frequent use of animated facial expressions and gestures by people in their efforts to get positive reactions from others indicates just how significant positive reactions are to people. Similarly the effort people devote to achieving and maintaining socially acceptable appearances and behaviors indicates just how much people want to avoid negative reactions from others. (See the chapters on Seeking Positive Reactions and Avoiding Negative Reactions in Volume One of this series.) In addition, the fact people engage in so much unnecessary movement in order to establish and maintain orientations indicates how important orientations are to humans. (See the chapter on Employing Orientations in a later volume of this series.) Also, the effort people devote to getting stimulation of various kinds reveals how significant stimulation is to them. Such efforts include reading novels, playing sports, dancing, and playing on playground equipment. In addition, people enjoy watching entertainers who are highly active, such as actors in action films, clowns, gymnasts, wrestlers, boxers, figure skaters, and professional dancers, because this is unusual behavior.

When faced with the necessity of exerting themselves, people normally consider alternative approaches, calculate the relative cost of each approach, and commonly select the one which uses the least time and energy. They decide in what order to do things, when to do them, and where to do them in order to conserve time and energy.

Conserving time and energy

I was carrying a heavy bag of books when I got out of my car at the university campus. I had parked near the building where my office is located. However, I had to decide whether or not to lug the books with me across campus to the post office so I could pick up my mail. This meant I would have to carry them back again to my office. The alternative was to first carry the books up to my office on the fourth floor, leave them there, walk back down the stairs, go to the post office, return, and then walk back up the stairs again to my office. When I thought about it I decided the easiest thing would be to carry the books with me across campus to the post office and not take the extra trips up and down the stairs, and this is what I did. [#1160]

I find my ability to concentrate and do mentally demanding work is very limited. Therefore I try to start off each day with demanding work while I am most alert. I put off easier tasks like sewing, reading a novel, and washing dishes until later in the day when I feel too tired to tackle something demanding. [#1161]

People differ in what they personally find easier to do in terms of saving time and energy in specific situations. When my wife wants a parking space she's willing to spend a lot of time searching for one which is very close to her destination. She says it takes little effort to drive around looking for a space, and once she finds one she is just a skip and a jump from where she wants to go. Most of the other people seem to agree with my wife, because the parking area close to the entrance of a building or store is usually packed and you see other cars driving around the same area searching for a space even when there are lots of empty spaces a little further away. I'm different because walking doesn't bother me. I'll take the first parking space I see and walk the extra distance. Sometimes I go directly to a parking space off to the side so I don't have to bother hunting for a space in the crowded parking area close to the entrance. Often I can move into a parking space with a minimum of trouble because there aren't any other cars parked next to me. I find it more frustrating to waste time, and to have to maneuver the car through the lanes of parked cars while searching for a space. I dislike worrying about having to avoid all the cars and pedestrians moving in the area, and having to position the car carefully into a space between two other parked cars. [#1162]

People constantly change and adjust what they do in order to try to save more time and energy.

Economizing activity

I've discovered that it takes a lot less energy if I use my foot instead of my arm to hold a heavy door open. Once you've opened the door you just brace the ball of your foot on the floor with your heel against the door and this acts as a doorstop. I do this to hold the door for myself or for others. #1163

I've finally found a dress shirt which is a minimum of bother. It never has to be ironed. All you do is hang it up while it is still damp when you take it from the washing machine. I bought thirty of them, because the more I have the less often I have to do the laundry. #1164

Originally I boiled my vegetables. Then I bought an electric steamer so that the vegetables would taste better. But the steamer took too much work to clean each time I used it. So I put it away and went back to boiling my vegetables. #1165

After I finished my shower and dried myself, I picked up my discarded clothes from the bathroom floor. Then I remembered to hang up the bathmat to dry. But before I could do this I had to put my clothes back down on the floor so my hands were free. I realized this was pretty inefficient, and that I should hang up the bathmat before I ever picked up the clothes. I resolved to do so in the future. #1166

Many techniques for conserving time and energy are learned from other people.

The problem with keeping a pitcher of orange juice in the fridge is that the juice settles in the container leaving the top portion very watery. It's always a nuisance to get out a spoon, stir it up, and wash the spoon afterwards. Often I don't go to the trouble, but this means the orange juice is sometimes too thin at the top and too thick at the bottom. Then I noticed what a friend of mine does. He pours some back and forth between the pitcher and his glass once or twice and this mixes it properly. I've started doing it too, and it is less trouble than using a spoon. #1167

A friend of mine just started teaching and was putting in many hours preparing lectures. I suggested that one way of saving time was to photocopy the material she wants to talk about, cut out the important parts, and tape them to sheets of paper. That way she doesn't have to take time to copy all the information by hand. She realized immediately this would be a great timesaver. #1168

I stayed at a friend's house and found he keeps lots of blank pads of paper around. Whenever he has a thought he wants to remember or thinks of something he should do, he writes it down. I started doing it too while I stayed at his place, and I plan to continue. It's much easier to remember things this way. [#1169]

When I spent a month in Montreal I had to catch the bus to get to the nearest metro (subway) station. I would get out of the bus at a particular corner, wait for the traffic light so I could cross the busy street, and enter the station. Then one day I noticed that other people on the bus were simply getting out of the bus, turning the corner, and going into another entrance of the same metro station. They didn't have to cross the street at all. I hadn't known this other entrance was there. But once I saw what others were doing, I did the same thing too. [#1170]

There are a number of things that people do which appear to be a waste of time and energy. Often when people are fatigued they turn to something else that they find more stimulating. This might be pleasant tasting food or drink, a novel, music, television, or a computer game. They may also seek positive reactions through talking to other people. These activities appear to be a waste of time because they do not generate tangible resources, such as money. However, these activities do provide pleasure, which is a primary goal of behavior. The reason people want tangible resources, such as money, is to use them to obtain pleasure and avoid hurt. People work so they can obtain resources that they can exchange a) to get pleasurable experiences, and b) to avoid unpleasant experiences. When people interrupt work to obtain pleasant stimulation, they obtain some of the goals they are working for. Many tasks are difficult or take a long time to complete. Therefore one is unable to complete them quickly and release the tension driving one to do the task. As one becomes more fatigued it becomes increasingly difficult to make progress on the task. At such times people welcome activities in which it is easy to release tension and experience pleasure, such as various forms of stimulation including eating, drinking, smoking, watching TV, or playing a game. Also, when people seek stimulation or positive reactions they still do so in ways which conserve time and energy, because they minimize their physical and mental activity during their efforts to obtain stimulation and positive reactions. Another way in which people appear to waste time and energy is when they change activities. When they change the model they are using, they may change what they are doing. As a result much of what they have already done to satisfy their previous model may appear to be wasted effort. For example, they may decide to stop collecting stamps and to collect coins instead, or to stop investing in real estate and to invest in stocks instead. The effort they had previously dedicated to collecting stamps or investing in real estate now appears to have been wasted. People may also change their mind and decide to go in the opposite direction and have to retrace their steps, which is a waste of time and energy. On other occasions people may have to repeat their movements because of their mental limitations.

> When I have lots of errands to do, such as things to buy or places to go, I find it is just too complicated to try to do more than about half a dozen chores in a single trip. Even though I use a list, it's just too much to try to deal with many more chores than this on one excursion. A similar thing happens when I'm straightening up. I'll organize the things I have to put away into lots of separate piles. But when I go to put the piles away I find I can only handle about two or three piles comfortably at a time. I could easily carry a larger number of piles with me. It's just that it's mentally hard to deal with several things at once. When I've finished putting away two or three piles, I return for two or three more. #1171

Tactics for conserving time and energy

People constantly seek to minimize the time and energy they expend physically and mentally. They employ numerous tactics to do this. These include the following:

1. Minimizing exertion
2. Minimizing time
3. Taking risks
4. Taking what others have
5. Using animals

6. Using a tool
7. Replacing a defective tool
8. Obtaining one's own equipment
9. Obtaining multiple copies
10. Combining activities
11. Performing an activity less often
12. Keeping items where they are used
13. Keeping items where they can be easily found
14. Not repeating one's efforts
15. Procrastinating
16. Doing an activity which is easier or more fun
17. Reducing one's workload
18. Not doing an activity
19. Getting rid of an activity
20. Avoiding requests by others
21. Arranging to spend less time and energy in the future
22. Acquiring lasting items
23. Limiting variety
24. Obtaining what can be fixed locally
25. Taking what one will need
26. Doing something properly so it will not have to be done again
27. Finishing a task
28. Coordinating with others
29. Getting others to do things your way
30. Getting help from others
31. Following others
32. Making a copy
33. Selecting and changing a time and place
34. Using routines
35. Using orientations
36. Using categories
37. Simplifying categories
38. Using models
39. Simplifying models
40. Using a simple indicator
41. Breaking up a task into smaller units

Tactics for conserving time and energy

1. Minimizing exertion

People normally seek to minimize their physical exertion. For example, when possible they walk rather than run, sit rather than stand, do not get up from a seat if they can avoid it, walk around large obstacles rather than climb over them, call someone to the telephone rather than go get them, take the elevator or escalator rather than the stairs, lean against something rather than stand upright, and restrict their movement to a hand or arm rather than use their whole body. They often use an electric mixer, rather than a whisk or spoon, to mix ingredients when preparing food; buy precooked meals or eat in restaurants so they do not have to cook for themselves; and throw trash into a wastebasket rather than carry it over to the basket. They use a photocopier rather than write out a copy by hand; bookmark a location on the Internet in their computer so they do not have to write out the address; and push a button on a remote-control device, rather than use a key to open their car door, get out of their car to open the garage door, or get up to change the station and volume on a television set. People are also willing to let others do as much as possible for them. Often they will let the bank teller fill out their deposit or withdrawal slips and they will let the cashier bag their groceries, rather than do so themselves. People are frequently willing to endure discomfort in order to avoid effort. Thus in winter they will often remove snow and ice from their car windows without bothering to put on their gloves, take out the garbage without putting on their coat, and walk from their car to their destination without zipping up their jacket. Also, people usually say as little as necessary except when they are trying to satisfy their feelings, such as seeking positive reactions or establishing consistency. People normally use words rather than gestures to explain things, because gestures require more effort. However, when it is easier to point than to explain where something is or who someone is, people are more likely to use a gesture.

When people walk from one place to another they usually try to take the most direct route. For example, when you have an open area between buildings, people have many different points they start from and head for, and everyone wants to take the shortest route. It's just impossible to put sidewalks between all the places that people walk. No matter how many sidewalks you put in, people are always making new paths across the lawn. If you tried to pave all the paths, there'd be practically no lawn left. #1172

I overheard a teenager ask her mom as they left the public library, "Do we have to walk?" "C'mon dear, it's only a block," her mom replied. The girl wanted to ride in the car, rather than walk. But I suspect her mother didn't want to get the car and drive around searching for a new parking place. #1173

Donald, a good friend of mine, has a stereo and over fifty albums. I asked him if he would like to go to the record store in town with me, and he agreed. Then Donald found out we would have to walk instead of drive and he said he had a previous engagement. Donald is nineteen years old and sort of plump. He could use the exercise but didn't want to have to walk all the way downtown and back. I asked what his previous engagement was and Donald started to stammer out ohs and ahs and finally managed to say, "Something else." #1174

This morning when I fed the cat I used a regular-sized fork that was standing in the dish drain. This fork was right at hand and it was easier to get it than it was to walk over to the utensil drawer, pull the drawer open, get out a smaller-sized fork that I regularly use, push the drawer closed, and walk back to the sink and the can of cat food. I normally use the smaller fork because it is slightly less trouble to wash. #1175

I try to buy clothes for my family that don't need to be ironed. We just throw them in the washing machine, put them in the dryer, and wear them. #1176

I often remain squatting in front of the clothes dryer as I unload it. It's a lot easier than repeatedly getting up and down. #1177

I bought a new refrigerator with an ice-making machine. This model pours ice water, shaved ice, or ice cubes directly into a glass that you hold outside the refrigerator door. So you don't have to open the door, unload ice trays, refill the ice trays, or pour cold water from a container in the refrigerator and refill the container. #1178

When I tried to pull one garbage bag out of the box of garbage bags, all the bags came out, because they were folded together. This was a nuisance because I only wanted one. I had to refold each bag individually to make sure I'd only get one at a time. So now I spend a little more money and buy a box of bags which are folded separately. #1179

When people engage in sports they frequently find ways that minimize exertion. For example, people take the ski lift up the mountain and then let gravity pull them downhill on their skis. They don't climb the mountain. They ride the rapids down river, they don't paddle up river against the current. When they take a bike trip to visit a volcano in Hawaii, they and their bikes are first transported up the road to the top of the volcano in vans, and then they coast their bikes downhill. #1180

Many people do all kinds of "anti-social" things to avoid effort. When they want to get rid of their chewing gum they stick it under their desktop or theater seat rather than carry it to a trash can. When they clean their nose they flick the material away from them rather than get a tissue to put it in. When men pee in the toilet they often don't make the effort to lift the surrounding seat first. If they pee on the seat, they don't bother cleaning up afterwards. Then there are students who underline and dog-ear the pages of library books because they don't want to take the trouble of photocopying or writing out information. #1181

In sum, people normally adopt courses of action which require the least effort on their part.

People also attempt to minimize their mental activity. For example, they often make a list or write a note for themselves rather than try to remember something; use an index or directory, rather than search for information; ask questions rather than find out for themselves; telephone other people rather than write them; avoid reading directions on the products they use; and use a concept or model developed by someone else, rather than develop their own.

When people want to use a device, they try to get out of reading instructions if they can. Sometimes they ask others what to do, and sometimes they decide to go ahead and try to operate the device anyway. The other day my wife was driving a car we've just leased and she decided she would try out the cruise-control buttons. She pushed a couple of buttons and said, "It's not working now." Later she stated, "Now it's working again." I know she doesn't have a clue what cruise control is or what the buttons are for. I suggested that she read the car manual in the glove compartment which explains how to use cruise control, but she wasn't interested. #1182

It's a lot more work to follow a recipe when you cook something than it is to wing it. You have to try to understand and follow the instructions, get the required ingredients, and measure everything. It's a huge chore. If I'm cooking something new, let's say moussaka, I'll look at a recipe the first time I do it. But from then on, whenever I fix it, I know approximately what to put in and I just do things to taste. It's a lot easier and more convenient this way. Often I don't have all the required ingredients anyway. I can alter things the way I like them, and use less meat and more vegetables. As a result the dish is never identical from one time to the next. I think if you cook a lot you develop self-confidence that you can make substitutions and alter quantities, and as long as it tastes good it will turn out well. #1183

I use e-mail every day. You are usually seated at your computer anyway, so you just type a line or two and push a key to send it. It takes so much less effort than it takes to compose a letter, address an envelope, get a stamp, and mail it. Often when you try to phone someone they aren't there, but if you send an e-mail they eventually get your message. If I haven't heard from my kids or relatives I start to wonder how they are. It just takes a minute to send them an e-mail and ask if they're OK. They e-mail me back and I don't waste any more energy worrying about them. #1184

Many students prefer courses in the arts and social sciences rather than natural science courses. Courses in the arts and social sciences usually contain familiar material and they require less mental work than science courses. You often have to read material in science textbooks several times before it makes sense. However, students want to avoid reading and rereading because this involves mental effort. Even though there are more jobs for graduates with degrees in the sciences, students want to study something that is easy for them. #1185

Students have all kinds of techniques they use to avoid work. No one wants a heavy workload in their courses. If students can find an easy elective, they can get an easy mark, bring up their average, skip classes, and get more sleep. Therefore, they like courses without a final exam. When they do have an exam they try to borrow a set of lecture notes from another student who takes good notes. Also, if they have to do a group project in a class some students try to do it with the smarter students, rather than with their own friends. As one student explained, "If you pick people who are really brainy, they want to do the whole project themselves. Even if they don't, they always finish the project faster than your friends would." #1186

A student in a course I teach came up to me after class and asked, "Could you tell me when I've got a 50?" I didn't know what he meant, and he explained, "I don't have time to do more. I just need one more credit to get in the education program, and all I need is a 50 to pass this course." In other words, as soon as he had put in the minimum, or just enough to earn a 50 in the course, he was going to stop doing anything and probably stop coming to class. #1187

Numerous facilities are constructed in such a way as to limit the expenditure of energy. For example, many kinds of furniture are designed to minimize exertion. Thus couches, chairs, and toilets are at knee height and allow one to save the energy it takes to move all the way down to floor level and back up again. At the same time, because the furniture is at knee level and low enough to support the backs of people's legs in addition to their buttocks and backs, it provides a very secure resting place for the body and little energy is needed to maintain the upper body in a vertical position. Many chairs and vehicles have arms and armrests which allow one to use one's forearm alone rather than one's entire arm in carrying out activities. Most tables, desks, and counters are at a height which allows one to perform activities using only one or both arm(s), forearm(s), and/or hand(s). Therefore people do not have to move their torso or whole body to perform activities.

When people have a choice of facilities at different locations they normally opt for the one that is closest. For example, they go to the nearest mailbox to mail a letter, store to make a purchase, public phone to make a call, video center to rent a film, or library branch to get a book. When they use a more distant facility, they usually have a reason, such as the fact that the more distant facility is cheaper, cleaner, more attractive, faster, easier to use, provides more choice, or has personnel who are friendlier or more attractive.

2. Minimizing time

People normally choose the option which takes the least amount of time. Thus many people drive rather than walk; fly rather than take a train, bus, or ship when traveling a long distance; use the telephone rather than go in person; take a shower rather than a bath; use priority post, special delivery, or a facsimile machine rather than the regular mail service; use an electronic calculator rather than perform calculations by hand; replace a slower computer with a faster one; use a word processor rather than a typewriter; heat up TV dinners rather than prepare a meal from scratch; and use a microwave oven rather than a conventional one. People often try to move close to the places they must travel back and forth to, in order to minimize the time they spend traveling. These include their place of work, the schools that their children attend, shopping centers where they shop, and locations where they can get fast public transportation.

> The ATMs, or automatic teller machines, at the banks let people withdraw cash, make deposits, pay bills, and transfer funds. It only takes me a few minutes to use a machine even if others are waiting ahead of me to use one, but inside the bank I often have to wait for fifteen or twenty minutes in a line to reach a teller. #1188

> The breadmaking machines work almost on their own. You used to have to spend most of Saturday morning baking bread, but now all you do is add the ingredients, push a button, and presto you have bread. #1189

> You can use an electric hair blower to dry your hair in about three to five minutes. Otherwise you can leave your hair alone and let it dry in the air, but this takes fifteen or twenty minutes. Most women use a blower because it takes them less time to get ready for work or school. Another advantage of a blower is you can use it to style your hair, and your style stays in place. #1190

> When you go to pay at a store, there's a real art to getting waited on as quickly as possible. When there is a choice of lines, such as at the various checkout counters at the supermarket, I usually consider them all before I select one. Then I normally choose the shortest line. However, there are other factors to take into account, such as how many items each person in a line is buying. Obviously you'd rather stand behind four people

who are only buying one item each, than behind two people who are each buying a shopping cart full of items. Nevertheless, sometimes it's better to stand in a short line of people with lots of items in their carts than to get at the back of a long line of people who are buying just one or two items each. This is because it takes lots of time for each person to get their money out and for the clerk to make change and bag the items. I also pay attention whether the clerk behind the cash register looks experienced or like a new employee or trainee. A new employee is usually unsure of herself and frequently makes everyone wait while she gets help finding out the price of an item or dealing with alternative means of payment. I avoid a line with a new employee or trainee like the plague. In some stores no one lines up and one or two clerks wait on a large number of people gathered around the counter. In this case I find if I stand in front of the cash register I usually have to wait less time than other people. After a clerk serves a person and gives them their change from the register, she frequently waits on the next customer she looks at, and that's the person who is closest to the cash register. There's another strategy I sometimes use when I'm waiting with a friend. We stand at two different spots along a counter or in two different lines. The first one who gets waited on places the orders for both of us. #1191

People often conduct their activities in a particular sequence in order to minimize the time involved.

My silverware always stains if I let it dry on the dish rack. The only way to prevent the stains is to dry the silverware with a dish towel while it is still wet. Therefore I always wash my silverware last so it will still be wet when I've finished washing up and get out the dish towel to dry everything. If I wash it before this, it dries in the air while I'm washing other things, and I have to rinse it again to get rid of the stains. #1192

When you do your yearly income tax, you have to fill out the main form as well as separate detailed "schedules" of expenses and deductions. The calculations in the schedules have to be entered on the main form. I've learned by experience not to bother trying to fill out the main form until I've completed the schedules. Otherwise I have to keep changing all the figures on the main form as I make various changes in the schedules. #1193

Conserving time and energy

People also adopt strategies which enable them to save time. For example, students often put on their coats and gather their books together before the end of the lecture in order to get out of the classroom as quickly as possible. People frequently leave a sporting event before the end of the game in order to get their car out of the parking lot and avoid the delays when everyone else tries to leave at the same time. Also, people are told to remain seated while an airplane that has just landed is taxiing to the terminal, because they are eager to collect their carry-on luggage and stand in the aisle to get off the plane as quickly as possible.

While I'm walking to the vending machine to get some candy and pop, I fish the coins out of my pocket and get the right amount of change together. This way I don't have to waste any time when I get to the machines. #1194

When I'm using my computer and am waiting for a familiar page to appear on my screen, I usually move my cursor to the next position where I'll have to click, so I don't waste any time. When the outline boxes appear for the options, and I'm still waiting for words to appear within the boxes, if I know which one I want, I go ahead and click. This lets me save time, because the computer will immediately jump ahead to the option I want. #1195

People frequently expend extra energy in an effort to save time. For example, they will rush to get an elevator, catch a bus, or cross a street before the traffic light changes, rather than wait calmly for the next elevator, bus, or light.

Often before a train or commuter train arrives at its destination, many people stand up and wait in the aisles so they can get off sooner. Because they have to stand and maintain their balance in a moving car, they expend much more energy than if they remained seated. #1196

Sometimes when I wash dishes I just push my sleeves up, rather than take the time to roll them up properly. But as I wash the dishes my sleeves keep sliding down and I try to push them up with my chin because I don't want to use my wet hands and get the sleeves wet. Often my sleeves get wet anyway, because water splashes on them as they slide down. For some reason I never stop what I am doing, dry my hands, and roll my sleeves up properly. #1197

At the bank one usually has to fill out a deposit or withdrawal slip when one conducts a transaction. These slips are located at various tables. However, I usually don't bother to fill out a slip at a table. Instead I pick up a slip and try to fill it out while standing in line waiting for an available teller. It is much more difficult filling out a slip and writing out a check while standing in line. One has to juggle the things one is carrying while extracting and using a pen, checkbook, or savings-account book. It is difficult writing because one doesn't have a firm surface to write on, and because the line one is standing in keeps moving. It's clear it takes a lot more effort to fill out these things while in line. The only reason I do it is because if I stopped beforehand to fill out the slip at a table, someone else might get ahead of me in the line and I'd have to spend more time in the bank. #1198

People expend a considerable amount of resources in order to save time. Many of the tools and appliances they buy and rent are designed to use less time.

When I looked for a new VCR (video cassette recorder) today, I wanted a model that had a lot of convenient features, like rewinding a video tape very fast, skipping over commercials when you play back a program you've recorded, and avoiding the advertisements at the beginning of a movie you've rented to see. #1199

My computer is getting too slow. I got it several years ago and it doesn't have the power of the new models. It takes forever to load programs, find things on the Internet, and print pictures. I've started pricing new models and I hope to get one soon. #1200

I get into arguments with my husband when I need to wash clothes. We have a spinner washer that we keep in our closet. It can only wash a small load of clothes at a time, but my husband wants me to use it because it saves money. We just fasten it to the faucet in our sink and it doesn't cost us anything to use. However, I prefer to use the Laundromat, where the machines wash a large quantity of clothes in the same amount of time. Even though it costs money to use the Laundromat, I tell him that the time it saves makes it worth it. Washing clothes in bulk saves time. #1201

3. Taking risks

Many people take risks in order to save time and energy. For example, they will jaywalk across busy streets, continue wearing their dark clothes rather than change to clothes which can be easily seen when walking on streets at night, ride a bicycle at night without lights, cheat on tests, eat fruit without washing it first, drink water that has been left standing in a glass for a day or more, and not bother to read directions before operating a new tool or appliance. When they drive, many people drive faster than the speed limit; drive when sleepy or drunk; drive in fog and storms; drive without cleaning the ice from their windows or the snow from their lights; pass a slower car when they are not sure if anything is coming toward them; drive up an empty lane in traffic and try to cut ahead into the busy lane they want to be in; and cut across a corner gas station lot, rather than wait in line for the traffic light to change so they can turn right. When taking a risk involves breaking the law, there is the additional risk of being caught and punished.

Occasionally you have students try to give an oral book report on a book they haven't taken the time to read. Sometimes they just talk in platitudes, or bullshit, about what they think the book is about. Other times they may base their entire report on just a few pages in the book. When you ask them specific questions about the book it becomes painfully obvious they haven't read it. #1202

Many people don't make the effort to fasten their seat belt when they ride in a car. They say things like "I hate them," "I can't be bothered putting one on," "I think seat belts are a pain," and "It's too much trouble to fasten it when I'm wearing my winter coat." #1203

I watched a man in his car who was waiting at the red light. As soon as he saw that the traffic at right angles to him was stopping, which meant that the light was changing, he drove straight ahead. So he drove right through the red light before it had changed to green. He did this at each red light he came to along the street. #1204

People leave their cars in all kinds of places they aren't supposed to in order to avoid having to walk a block or two to get to their destination. Some park in spaces for the disabled, in loading zones right in front of store entrances, and in front of fire hydrants. Others park in driveways between buildings which are needed by other drivers to get to and from parking areas behind buildings. Some double-park in the street, put on their signal light, and run into a store. Other drivers are forced to swing into the oncoming lane in order to get around them or are blocked and can't get out of their parking space. #1205

When one takes risks one is more likely to fail, which can cause one to spend more time and energy than if one had not taken the risks.

Reggie was having a hard time finding a parking space near the store we were going to. He remarked, "Look at those two vacant spots," and drove into a space clearly marked for the handicapped. I pointed out he was in a handicapped parking space, and Reggie said, "I don't care." When we came out of the store an hour later I was quite amused to see that Reggie's car had been towed away. #1206

After we cleaned the basement, Dad tried to carry all five bags of trash at the same time outside to the garbage cans. He wanted to make one trip only. But a bag slipped out of his hand, fell, and split open. He had to spend several minutes cleaning up the mess. #1207

Our house is surrounded by trees, so we have a lot of leaves to rake in the fall. It is too much trouble to bag all the leaves and take them to the dump. So we rake the leaves into the woods next to our yard. But if a wind comes up, it blows the leaves back into our yard and we have to rake them all over again. #1208

My daughter knew that the brakes weren't working properly in her car. The brakes wouldn't engage until she pushed the pedal much further down than usual. However, because the brakes still worked she didn't take the time to get them fixed. So one day they didn't work at all. She pushed the brake pedal all the way down to the floor and drove into the rear end of the car just ahead of her. #1209

4. Taking what others have

People also conserve time and energy by taking resources away from others. They may steal or persuade others to give them their possessions, money, relationships, ideas, and so on. It is much less trouble to take what another person has purchased, earned, saved, established, made, or invented, than it is to expend the effort to obtain these resources on one's own. (See the chapter, Trying To Get What Others Have, in this volume.)

5. Using animals

People use various animals for a variety of tasks in order to save themselves time and energy. This includes using horses and cattle for plowing; and horses, donkeys, camels, and elephants for transportation and moving heavy objects. Dogs are used to detect drugs and explosives at airports, customs facilities, and border stations, which is more efficient for security personnel than having to conduct thorough searches themselves. Guide dogs enable blind humans to move about without requiring the aid of another human.

6. Using a tool

People employ a phenomenal variety of tools which allow them to perform tasks with less energy and in less time than they could without them.

Many people consider an electric dishwasher a necessity rather than a luxury. It holds three to four times as many dishes as your sink does. It washes and dries the dishes for you, and all you have to do is load it. Then you don't have to put the dishes away, because you can leave the clean dishes in the dishwasher until the next time you need to use them. #1210

A computer is a wonderful timesaver. When you write a report on a typewriter, you have to retype the entire report every time you make any substantial changes. But with a computer all you have to do is make the changes and let the computer run a revised copy off the printer. The computer even tells you when you've misspelled a word. It's also a great file cabinet, because you can store everything you are working on or have finished, and keep it organized and handy. E-mail lets you send notes to anyone and get notes from them in a few seconds. And the Internet lets you get information on anything you want to know, from a list of features on the latest cars to descriptions of the stores and clubs in a city you plan to visit. #1211

Often tools are very specialized. For example, in the kitchen people use a multitude of devices to store, prepare, and serve food. These include items as diverse as a toaster, egg separator, cheese knife, ice-cream scoop, sugar spoon, mortar and pestle, cake-decoration kit, vegetable grater, aluminum foil, and dish-drying rack. Many kitchen tools are designed to deal with a single food item.

> I just bought two knives at a kitchen store. One is for removing the peel from oranges, and the other is for shelling and deveining shrimp. I tried the one for oranges and wasn't impressed. It didn't do the job any better than I could with a regular knife. I'm going to try the other knife the next time I fix shrimp gumbo. [#1212]

A comparable variety of tools are employed in practically every area of human activity.

In addition to tools which conserve physical effort, there are tools which are designed to conserve mental effort. Thus an alarm clock or timer frees a person from having to pay attention to the time, a calculator makes it unnecessary to recall and employ mathematical operations, a pencil and pad of paper enable one to make notes rather than try to remember information, and a dictionary, encyclopedia, or other reference book enables a person to quickly locate specific information.

Tools are normally designed with the intention of minimizing the expenditure of time and energy. Thus a redial button on a telephone makes it unnecessary to remember a telephone number and punch it in again, a hand-held device which starts your car from a distance allows you to avoid waiting in the car for the engine to warm up, and special function keys in computer software put complicated sequences into action. Generally speaking, any feature on a tool that enables the user to save additional time and energy is considered desirable. However, when a tool requires considerable time or energy to learn to use, operate, maintain, or clean, the tool becomes less attractive.

> A blender is great for mixing the drinks I like, such as piña coladas and mango shakes. But afterwards it takes several minutes to take the blender apart and clean it properly. So I rarely use it. [#1213]

Often tools are redesigned to save even more time and energy. Thus certain glue or paint is designed to dry very quickly, so one does not have to wait as long, and certain paper towels and diapers will absorb more liquid, so one uses less energy cleaning up. Substances are sometimes combined so that one does not have to perform two separate operations. Thus shampoo and hair conditioner are mixed and sold in a single bottle, so that a person only has to handle one bottle and apply one substance, not two, when she washes her hair.

People frequently upgrade and replace tools with "better" tools which require even less time and energy to use. For example, rather than use a dial telephone provided by the telephone company, people will buy a more expensive programmable telephone which enables them to dial an entire number by touching a single button. Rather than get a television set with manually-operated controls, people will spend much more money for a television set which can be controlled by a remote hand-held device that they can operate while seated in a chair.

> The microwave lets us cook and reheat food faster than we can in our regular oven. It takes much more effort to clean the pans and dishes you use in an oven, and immensely more effort to clean the inside of an oven than a microwave. With a microwave you can cook your food, eat it, and have everything cleaned up in the same amount of time it takes you just to cook something in a conventional oven. [1214]

People frequently spend considerable amounts of money for devices which allow them to do things faster and/or with less effort. Often the amount of time and energy that is saved is small relative to the expense of the equipment.

> When I buy a portable cassette player I'm going to get one with auto reverse. This plays first one side of the tape then the other automatically. As a result you don't have to turn the cassette tape around by hand. This feature costs considerably more, but it is more convenient. [1215]

> My microwave was quite old and heated things very slowly, so I decided to get a new one. The new one I bought was much lighter in weight and heated food very quickly. However, it lacked certain features that my original microwave had. For one thing the light wasn't as bright and the window on the door had a screen over it, so it was much harder to see

what was happening to your food as it heated. Also, the buttons on the new machine were smaller and you had to pay more attention to pushing the right one. Another thing, instead of having dedicated buttons, such as one just for defrosting your food, the new machine made you push a button up to ten times to get the right setting. I decided I had had enough of this new model and I took it back to the store to exchange it. I wanted an up-to-date machine that was faster but also had all the convenient features I was used to on the old machine. #1216

When I get an extra $1000, I'm going to buy my own photocopier to have at home. I know I'll only use it once every week or two, but it will save me the time and nuisance of going to a local copy shop. It takes about fifteen or twenty minutes to go to the shop and get the copies made, and making copies at home would take a minute or two. Of course if I want to wait I can always make my copies for free where I work. But I'd rather make them when I want them and not have to wait at all. #1217

This suggests that the important factor is the fact that time or energy is saved, not how much the equipment costs. Normally the only thing that limits the number and variety of tools that people have is their ability to get money to acquire them. People are often willing to go into considerable debt to obtain additional tools, and they frequently gain attention and are the object of envy when they have a tool that others do not have or when they have a "better" tool than others have.

7. Replacing a defective tool

People frequently replace a tool which is not working properly. A tool that works properly requires less time and energy to use.

I have lots of identical ballpoint pens, and whenever the one I'm using doesn't work as well as it should, I throw it away. Otherwise, I'll repeatedly forget which one it is, pick it up again, find it doesn't work as well as it should, and have to go search for a better one. The only way to break this cycle is to get rid of the faulty pen. #1218

As your car gets older, more and more things go wrong with it. If it isn't working or is at the garage it's hard to do all the other things you need to do. It doesn't take long before you start to think about replacing it with a newer model. #1219

I had an older VCR (video cassette recorder) that developed so many problems that I knew it wasn't worth getting it fixed. It had difficulty playing the video tapes I recorded, and it couldn't play certain movies I rented. Then it quit recording TV programs altogether. Several months later I bought a new one. #1220

8. Obtaining one's own equipment

A major way in which people conserve time and energy is by obtaining their own personal equipment, devices, appliances, vehicles, tools, and facilities. As a result they do not have to try to borrow or steal these items from others or to share them with others, and the items are always available for their own use. Moreover, because people do not have to share these items with others, they can use them for as long as they want and precisely in the ways they want to.

Whenever I wanted to get into my office building on the weekends, I had to go to the security office. They would phone a security officer and arrange for him to meet me at the front door of the building. Not only did I have to go out of my way to walk to and from the security office, but I often had to waste ten or fifteen minutes waiting for the officer to arrive to unlock the front door. After doing this a few times I realized it made a lot more sense to get my own key to the building. So I went through the proper channels and was assigned my own key. This is much more convenient, because I can get into the building whenever I want and I don't have to wait for anyone. #1221

When you don't own your own car, you are dependent on others for rides. You can not go anywhere you want whenever you want, because you have to wait for others to offer to take you and you are limited to where they want to go. When you have your own car you can stop and see whatever interests you as often as you like. If you are riding in someone else's car, you don't have this option. Also, if you go somewhere in your own car, such as to the beach or to a party, you can leave whenever you want. You don't have to leave early or wait around because you depend on the person with the car deciding when they're ready to go. #1222

9. Obtaining multiple copies

People frequently obtain multiple copies of a particular item. Examples include pens, paper, scissors, bottles of aspirin, tape dispensers, corkscrews, nutcrackers, glasses, plates, and knives, forks, and spoons. This allows them to save time and energy in various ways. If an item is misplaced or does not work right, one has other copies of the identical item that one can use. One is not prevented from doing what one wants to do because one does not have the necessary item. It takes a considerable amount of time and energy to try to buy an item every time it is misplaced. Also, it takes less effort to use multiple copies of clean dishes and utensils and then wash them all at once, than it does to have one copy of each item and to wash it every time one wants to use it.

> After I got involved in the stock market I could never find my handheld calculator when I needed it. Either I didn't know where I'd left it, or else I remembered I'd left it at home or in my office. So I bought three more cheap calculators and I just leave them around. If this turns out not to be enough, so that there isn't one always nearby when I need it, I'll get even more. [#1223]

10. Combining activities

People also seek to conserve time and energy by combining activities. They may arrange to do several things in a single location, do similar things in an interval of time, do a second activity when they have to wait during an activity, or do two or more things at the same time.

People often organize their activities so they can do more than one thing while they are in a particular location. For example, they usually plan to buy a number of different items when they go to the grocery store, or to do a number of different errands while they are downtown or in a shopping mall. People frequently make a list so they will remember to buy everything they need or remember to do all of the errands they have to do at a particular location.

People also combine activities by doing similar things in a single interval of time. Thus they will collect the trash in all the wastebaskets in the house at once.

I feed the outside cat at the same time that I feed our house cats. I have the cat food out anyway, so it's easy to pour some in the dish outside the back door. #1224

When I unload the dish-washing machine, I pick up as many similar items at the same time as I can. I'll take all the cereal bowls or dinner plates I can gather at once. They go in the same location in the cabinets, where they are usually stacked on top of each other. This way I can unload the dishwasher a lot faster than if I picked up things one at a time. #1225

Often when one is engaged in an activity, one participates in additional activities at the same time. As a result one uses one's time and presence in a specific location more fully. Sometimes one does this during slack periods while doing a specific activity. For example, one might wash dishes or make a telephone call while waiting for something to cook, write out notes while waiting to talk to a party on the telephone, or read a newspaper or magazine while riding to work or waiting for another family member to finish shopping.

People often wait until they can do more than one thing at the same time. They may decide it is not worthwhile going to the grocery store to buy a single item, and wait until they need additional items. Similarly, they may put off going to see the doctor about a problem, until they have an additional problem to ask him about. At that time they can bring both problems to his attention. When people are stationary they frequently decide they will wait to do something until they have an additional reason to move.

I often eat breakfast at my desk. But when I finish eating I don't get up right away and go wash out my coffee cup and throw the trash away. Instead I put these things to the side and leave them there until I have to get up later for some other reason, such as go get the mail. It's easier just to stay seated where I am. When I do get up for another reason, I deal with the breakfast stuff. Similarly, when I want to adjust the heat or turn on the fan, I also usually wait until I get up for something else. This way I don't have to get up a second time. #1226

In other cases one does two or more tasks at the very same time. For example, people will shave or brush their teeth while they are in the shower, listen to the radio or a recording while driving, or talk on a cordless telephone while washing dishes, folding laundry, walking, or driving.

I often do more than one thing while I'm getting ready in the morning. As I brush my teeth I usually walk around the apartment and do a little straightening up. While I shave I listen to a cassette tape to help me learn conversational French. At night I sometimes floss my teeth while I watch TV. [#1227]

I know a number of women who put on their makeup while they drive to work. As they drive they look in the rearview mirror to put on their cover-up, lipstick, and blush. And when they stop for a red light they put on their eye shadow and mascara. Today I saw both a passenger in a car and a man driving a truck busy brushing their teeth. [#1228]

People commonly eat, drink, smoke, or chew gum while they are doing other things, such as walking, talking, working, watching television, and reading.

11. Performing an activity less often

People make various arrangements so that they do not have to perform a specific action as often. For example, one can turn something on and then leave it on while one is not using it, so that one does not have to make the effort to turn it off and on again. For example, people often do not turn the lights, radio, television, computer, or music player off when they leave a room and plan to return soon; and they leave the water running while brushing their teeth, taking a shower, or washing dishes when they do not need it instead of repeatedly turning it off and on. They may leave a car engine running or a door open for the same reason. Thus people frequently waste resources rather than repeatedly exert the effort necessary to conserve them. People may also make sure that it is possible to do something before they attempt it, in order that they will not have to return to do it a second time. Thus they may telephone ahead to find out if a business or facility is open or if a certain item they want to buy or rent is in stock.

When I pick up a music cassette to put in my cassette player, it's rarely at the beginning of the tape. I look to see which side will play the most tape before I'll have to turn it over again, and I listen to that side first. [#1229]

After my family bought a dishwasher, we stopped washing dishes and putting them away as often. After breakfast and lunch the dirty dishes were placed out of sight in the machine, and were not washed until after supper. We frequently did not bother putting the clean dishes in the cupboards. Instead we took them directly from the machine when we needed to use them. #1230

Often one obtains a larger quantity of supplies than one needs at the time, so that one does not have to return as frequently to obtain new ones. For example, when one buys gasoline at the service station, one can have the entire tank filled; when one buys toothpaste, one can buy several tubes; when one obtains postage stamps at the post office, one can buy extra stamps to use in the future; and when one buys groceries at the supermarket, one can get enough items to last the next two weeks.

My soft contact lenses wear out in about a year. Although they cost several hundred dollars locally, I can order a pair by mail for about $50. But it's always a bother to get around to placing the order, and besides the company usually wants me to send them a record of a recent eye examination. So when I placed an order this past summer, I decided I would save myself a great deal of future time and bother, and I ordered four pairs all at once. #1231

People also obtain sufficient quantities of an item so that they do not have to perform tasks involving the item as often. Thus the more shirts, socks, pants, and underwear one has, the less often one has to do laundry. Similarly, the more plates, dishes, and silverware one has, the less often one has to wash dishes.

Another arrangement people make is to prepare more than they need at the time so that they will have the item ready for use in the future.

When you have to take a prescription drug, it's a bother to pry open the childproof top and dig a pill out of the bottle each day. So I place the pills in a pillbox with a separate compartment for each day of the week. The plastic lids are easy to open and you only have to fill the box from your regular bottle once a week. Actually I put two pills in each compartment and only fill the box once every two weeks. #1232

It takes a lot of work to prepare a meal. Therefore, when I fix something like spaghetti, I try to make more than I need. This way I can get another meal out of it in the future. I just store the excess in the refrigerator. Lots of people prepare more food than they need on the weekends and then freeze the rest to eat during the week. There are other things I do too. For example, I take the skin off chicken to reduce cholesterol. However, it takes a lot of time to remove the skin and excess fat and it's a messy job. Therefore, when I buy chicken I get a large package. I skin all the pieces at once and freeze all the pieces that I don't need for dinner that night so I can use them for future meals. I put each piece in a separate bag so I don't have to try to separate several pieces that are frozen together when I want a single piece. It's a lot easier to do it this way than it is to go to all the trouble to skin a piece of chicken each time I need one. #1233

12. Keeping items where they are used

People normally keep things where they use them. As a result it takes less time and energy to get things when they are needed. For example, toilet paper is kept next to the toilet; toothbrushes and toothpaste by the bathroom sink; soap, shampoo, and hair conditioner by the side of the bathtub; music recordings next to the tape or disk player; food in the kitchen; automotive tools in the trunk of the car or in the garage; the telephone directory next to the phone; the wastebasket next to the desk; the letter opener and stapler on the desk; credit cards in one's wallet; coats and umbrellas in the closet nearest the outside door; and the TV Guide and the remote control next to the chair or couch one uses when watching television. Normally items are kept as close to the area where they are used as possible, so that they are usually within arm's length and it is not necessary to move one's entire body to obtain them.

Often people require a specific item in more than one location. As a result they obtain more than one copy of the item, and place a copy in each location where it is needed. This includes such things as lamps, electric sockets, bars of soap, boxes of facial tissue, pens, paper, wastebaskets, and radios. As a result people do not have to carry an item back and forth between locations and do not have to try to remember to do so. Also, when the item is not easily portable, but is available in various locations, they do not have to travel back and forth between a single source of the item and the various locations where it is required. Thus by installing separate water supplies at a kitchen sink, a bathroom sink, a bathtub, a toilet, a washing machine, and an outside lawn, people can reduce the amount of energy they would expend carrying water from a single source to all the places where it is used.

13. Keeping items where they can be easily found

By storing items in specific locations, one is usually able to remember where they are and can expend less time and energy locating them. Thus many people use specific drawers and shelves for storing such items as silverware, pots and pans, dishes, food, stationery and envelopes, sweaters, underwear, music recordings, tools, books, playing cards, cosmetics, towels, and sheets. For example, they may place the records and receipts they will need to calculate their income tax in a specific file as they receive them.

People also group items together on the basis of similarity. As a result it is easier to find them when they are needed. They may organize the same kind of items together, for example, all their books on bookshelves, or all their files in a file cabinet. They may also group different kinds of items together on the basis of function. For example, they may place the various materials they use to write to other people, such as an address book, pens, paper, envelopes, and stamps, in a specific drawer.

14. Not repeating one's efforts

People use a variety of means to avoid repeating their efforts, and this prevents them from expending extra time and energy. Thus people often minimize future labor in regard to an item by dealing completely with the item the first time they handle it. A person uses various approaches to do this. One is to ensure that one does not waste time having to familiarize oneself with the item again at a later date simply because one has forgotten one's original decision concerning the item. For example, as soon as one ascertains that an item is not significant, one can throw it away. One can also do what is required as soon as one becomes familiar with the item, while one's course of action is still fresh in one's mind.

> Once a month I get a brochure from my book club announcing new selections. I open the envelope and look at the literature on the new

books. I usually fill out the request form then and there. Otherwise, I'll have to look through their literature all over again later. #1234

One can also mark the item in such a way that one will remember what kind of decision one has already made concerning it.

We get a number of weekly magazines at home, and after I've finished looking at an issue, I tear the upper-right-hand corner off the magazine cover. I can't throw the issue away because my wife hasn't looked at it yet. But this tells me I've already looked at it so I won't bother picking it up again. #1235

When I've finished going through a page of notes, I put an X on the top of the page to tell me I've finished with it. This way I know not to look over it again, and I can store it with the other notes I'm finished with. I don't like to throw notes away before I've finished my current project, because if I lost my report or couldn't find a particular piece of information, I'd have to go back to my original notes. #1236

Other approaches are also used. One often saves items that one is likely to use again that one has spent time obtaining or preparing. This makes it unnecessary to invest time obtaining or preparing the same thing over again. Thus one may keep Christmas decorations or a list of the people one sends Christmas cards to for use in subsequent years. Or one may file away lecture notes and tests to use again the next time one teaches a particular course. One may store such items out of the way so that one does not have to deal with them again until one wants to. Thus one may put an item in a separate container for items of that kind, such as in a specific closet, box, or file folder, where one can find it when one wants it again. One may also write out instructions so one will remember how to handle a particular situation the next time it occurs, and not have to go through an expensive learning process again. Thus one might add notes to a recipe, write out instructions on how to fix an appliance if a problem occurs again, make a list of steps to follow to do a specific operation in a computer program, keep notes on the outcomes of specific investment decisions, or write down the advice one receives from another person so one can reread it in the future. One may also make a copy of one's work and put it elsewhere for insurance in case the original is lost or destroyed.

15. Procrastinating

Another tactic is to put things off until one has to do them. This allows one to avoid expending time and energy at the present time.

> I bought several pairs of jeans at a sale two years ago. I never bothered to get the legs hemmed, and because I didn't need them, they've been hanging in my closet all this time. But my older jeans were wearing out. So I finally took the ones in my closet to the tailor and got them hemmed. Now I wear them all the time. [#1237]

> When I went and got my travel shots, the nurse kept reminding me to be sure to come back and get the booster six months later, so I wouldn't have to go through the whole series of shots again the next time I traveled. After six months I called up to make an appointment to get the booster and the nurse said they were understaffed and really busy and I actually didn't need the booster for another six months or even longer. I think she was just trying to put off dealing with me until a later date. [#1238]

> It is such a chore to do all the paperwork to get your income tax return ready, I seem to do it later each year. Even though it is due in April, last year I didn't get it done until September, and this year I didn't get it done until October. Maybe if I delay long enough I'll be able to do returns for two years at the same time. I don't have to pay a penalty for being late because so much money has already been deducted from my pay slips that the government owes me a refund. On the other hand it would be good to get the refund as soon as possible. I think lots of people pay an accountant to do their return for them so they don't have to go through the hassle themselves. [#1239]

> Students commonly put off doing their schoolwork. They say, "I'll do it later," "I'll study after this TV show," "This is my favorite show. I never miss it," "I can't say no to my friends when they want to go out and have a good time," "I'll do it tomorrow," and "I'll get up early and study in the morning." Many really don't want to do the work, and even dread it. Also, many wait until the last possible minute to do it. One girl said, "I leave my French labs until the last minute, because they are never fun and I hate doing them." Another said, "I don't get around to an assignment until the little voice in my head goes from 'You've still got lots of time,' to 'You have to do it NOW!'" Even when there is a major exam, many students do little to prepare until just beforehand.

"I knew the whole week I had to study for the exam. But it's funny how it's harder to manage time when you have a lot of it, than when you only have a little. Since I had so much time I figured I'd get around to it later." Sometimes students start working on their assignment so late they have to turn it in after the due date and often get a lower grade. When they ask for an extension, most are honest and say they just need more time, but others make up any excuse that they think will work. [#1240]

There is a novelty item which you can get. This is a circular pin with "ROUND TUIT" printed on it. This is because procrastinators are always saying, "I'll do it when I get around to it." [#1241]

Normally one does not intend to procrastinate, but does so because other tasks have a higher priority. However, one may also procrastinate by design. One may intentionally delay doing something one intends to do, and use this delay as a means of conserving time and energy.

I don't start on a project or a paper until I have just enough time left to do it. If I start it early I end up spending a lot more time on it making changes and trying to improve it. But if I wait until the last minute, I say exactly what I want and don't have to make any changes. [#1242]

Sometimes when I have something important to do, I will do several less important things first. I know I will do the important thing, and be sure to get it done on time. However, if I start working immediately on the important thing, I will continue to put off the less important things and I don't know when I will get to them. But by doing the less important things first, I get both the less important things and the more important thing done. It's a way to get more done in the same amount of time. [#1243]

Sometimes one is too busy doing other things or just too tired to do them at present, and as a result of procrastinating one can wait to do things when one is not as busy or as tired.

I have another assignment to finish, but I'm too tired to concentrate on it. So I think I'll go to bed and do it tomorrow. [#1244]

People procrastinate in regard to both major and minor activities, including completing work and school assignments, paying bills, washing dishes, and taking out the garbage.

In some cases one expends less time and energy over the long run as a result of procrastinating. For example, the longer one delays certain activities, the less often they have to be done. Thus the longer one delays cleaning the bathroom, changing the kitty litter, mowing the lawn, or washing the car, the less often one has to do so. If one plans to vacuum the rug once a week, but only does so once every two weeks, then one uses half the time and energy. Letting tasks accumulate as a result of pro-crastinating can also allow one to reduce one's expenditure of energy. This reduction occurs when one does similar tasks at the same time.

> I don't collect my mail every day; I get it once a week. This saves me trips to and from the post office and allows me to handle the mail all at once. Often there are several items of mail that I can deal with in an identical way, such as throwing them away, filing them, or answering them. It takes less time and energy to process them all at once in the same way. Similarly, I also wait until I have several items that need to be sewn or to be taken to the dry cleaner so I can deal with them to-gether. #1245

If one procrastinates, some tasks may never have to be done at all. Either someone else may do a task, so that one does not have to do it oneself, or the situation may change and no one may need to do the task. Pro-crastinating can also allow one to put off a task until a time when the task will require less energy to do. Thus if it is raining or snowing outside, one expends less energy by waiting to do one's shopping when the weather is better. Similarly, one comes out ahead if one waits to do a chore in town when one can get a ride there with one's neighbor and does not have to walk.

16. Doing an activity which is easier or more fun

People frequently avoid effort by doing something that is easier or more fun than what they are supposed to do. People often daydream, get something to eat or drink, socialize, smoke, check their e-mail, play a game, read a novel, or watch television. This is a way of temporarily avoiding the physical or mental exertion that is required by a more difficult task. As one person explained, "My problem is that I choose to do work that is interesting and enjoyable before I tackle the most important or harder tasks."

Students do all kinds of things to put off doing their schoolwork. Some play a video game or surf the Internet. Students tell me, "I would much rather play basketball than do my physics lab," "Doing *anything* is more fun than studying. I would rather clean the bathroom that I share with three other guys, and believe me, that is not fun," and "I never like studying, especially when it's something that doesn't interest me. My mind wanders onto hockey, work, parties, women, weekends, and anything else that has nothing to do with schoolwork. I sit there and hope that the phone will ring or someone will knock on the door so I'll have a valid excuse to stop studying." [1246]

One evening I was going to a movie and asked my friend, Ralph, if he'd like to come too. Just then I remembered that Ralph hadn't finished his essay which was due the next morning. But this didn't stop Ralph from coming with me. When I asked about the essay, Ralph said, "I'll do it when we get back." After the movie Ralph suggested we go to a local bar for a few beer. I asked about the essay and he said, "I have two hours in the morning before class. I'll do it then." The next morning Ralph wasn't in class, so I figured he was sleeping, doing his essay, or just cutting class. When I got back to the residence Ralph was watching TV. I asked about the essay and he said, "It's only worth five percent of the grade anyway. I'll make a hundred on the next one." [1247]

I have a hierarchy of things I regularly turn to to avoid doing what I am supposed to do. These range from things I don't mind doing to things I hate doing. For example, I prefer to clean the kitchen than do my homework. I prefer to do my homework than clean my room. I prefer to clean my room than go to the gym. I prefer to go to the gym than do my laundry. And I prefer to do my laundry than write a paper. [1248]

When I'm really tired and should go to bed I often watch TV, and when I'm too tired to watch TV or read, I just eat. I think that going to bed is such a big job that I put it off as long as possible and do anything else that is more fun, or that is easier. Going to bed is work. Before I go to bed I have to double-lock the doors, turn off the apartment lights, change to my pajamas, floss and brush my teeth, wash my face, put some water in the humidifier, make sure there is some dry food in the cat's dish, put a glass of fresh water by my bed, clear the bed, turn back the covers, and turn off the bedroom lights. It's a big job, and I put it off and find other things that are pleasant to do instead, and as a result I get even more tired. #1249

When one works at a task which takes some time or effort to complete, one is unable to get rid of the tension that drives one to work on it. This is because the tension will not go away until one makes headway or completes the task. As one becomes fatigued working at the task, it is harder to concentrate on it and more difficult to make progress and thereby release tension. Therefore one feels more resistance to working at the task, but the tension to do so remains. It is frustrating when one can not get rid of tension. Therefore, people turn to alternative activities in which they can easily release tension, such as various forms of stimulation, including talking, drinking coffee, smoking, or playing a computer game. The release of tension is experienced as pleasure.

17. Reducing one's workload

People also conserve time and energy by deciding or arranging to do less. They may decide they do not need to do a particular task, or they may reduce the amount they had planned to do. Thus they may take fewer educational courses, spend less time at a task, gather less information, write a shorter manuscript, or reuse something they have already done. They may avoid their regular tasks or work by taking sick leave, getting others to do their work, using an excuse, or goldbricking.

> Sometimes I ask my boss for a couple of extra days to get a job done. I can usually use one of these days to relax. Also, my boss is unlikely to give me something new to do during this time. #1250

> I have a technique I use to get out of my longer work shifts at a department store. Occasionally one of the other employees has an urgent need to take a day off. I'll offer to trade my longer shift for their shorter shift. They usually agree because they have no real choice. #1251

> I work just enough shifts as a waitress to make ends meet, which add up to twenty hours a week. I could work more shifts or get a second job, but what's the sense of it? This way I have more time for myself. #1252

When I want some time off, I get one of my family to call in to say I am sick and can't come to work that day. Because I get someone else to call in, my boss can't yell at me. And by the time I go back to work she's usually not as mad because she's had a couple of days to forget about it. #1253

I work at a car rental company in Moncton. After I started work the other employees taught me many ways to do less than I was supposed to. Cleaning cars between rentals is an important task, and customers complain if we neglect to do so. Ideally, we clean everything, and this includes doing a thorough job on the doorjambs and windows, pushing the seats all the way back to clean and vacuum the front, and pulling the seats all the way forward to vacuum the back. But I learned you can make a car look clean in a short time by just cleaning the seats, floor mats, and doorjambs, and maybe giving the dash a quick wipe down. There is no need to focus on every inch of the car. It looks just as clean. Another thing is we don't have to be where we are supposed to be. Initially we would wait in the office to answer phones and book rentals, wash cars, or wait for flights to arrive at the airport. Then we learned that all we have to do is forward all the phone calls to the company cell phone, so no matter where someone calls all we have to do is answer the cell phone. This means we do not have to sit at work bored out of our minds waiting for calls and for flights, and all we have to do is appear at the airport twice a night when a flight arrives. We just have to have the cell phone with us. Now we can take a car and go for a ride, or else we can stay home and watch TV. If we are worried that we are running up too much mileage on a car when we drive around, so that someone might notice, we drive a little in each of several different cars. We take advantage of this to the fullest. Sometimes if no one has already made a reservation we don't bother leaving home and going to the airport to meet the flights. And if we are expected to clean a car between flights, we resent it and do as fast a job as possible so we can return home. #1254

18. Not doing an activity

One of the most effective ways of conserving time and energy is simply not to do a particular activity. One can leave things the way they are and ignore many of the things that one might do. For example, one can leave one's bed unmade; leave one's clothes where one takes them off; not replace a roll of toilet paper, box of facial tissue, or bar of soap which has been used up; leave milk, bread, butter, cheese, jam, or peanut butter on the counter and not put them back in the refrigerator or the cupboard; decide not to bother washing the fruit one is about to eat; go ahead and eat a piece of food or candy one has dropped on the floor without bothering to wash it; not scrape the remaining food off a plate or out of a pan into the garbage can, but wash it down the drain when one washes dishes; not wash one's hands after using the toilet or before eating; not write those one owes a letter to; not volunteer to take on tasks or write the minutes at a meeting; not replace a missing button on a shirt; not complain about rude or incompetent service; and not bother explaining to another person what has happened to oneself and one's family members.

My wife handed me a cup of coffee and I carried it upstairs. She called up to me and asked if it was sweet enough. I sipped it and told her, "Not quite. But it's OK." I decided to drink it the way it was, because I didn't want to take the trouble to carry it back downstairs to put more sugar in it. #1255

It's been over ten years since I reprogrammed the numbers on my automatic dialing phone. I don't use at least half these numbers anymore, and there are other numbers I use all the time that I've never programmed into it. I just haven't gotten around to changing them. Even though I use the phone every day, other things always seem to be a higher priority. #1256

I always let stacks of letters and papers accumulate. I intend to deal with them, but I never seem to get around to it. What happens is that I leave them where they are until I clean up, and then I put them in a box or out of sight in a closet. #1257

I've quit spending the time necessary to balance my checkbook each month. It was always off by a few cents anyway, and it could take an hour or more trying to find out why. So now I just assume everything is balanced. I know that if there is a real discrepancy I'll learn about it soon enough anyway. #1258

After you move into a new apartment, every once in a while you get some mail in your mailbox for the person who used to live there. It is really hard to find the time to write on the envelope that the person has moved and then return it to the post office. I usually put this off for so long that I don't bother doing it. What's the sense of returning mail after six months or a year has passed? I've also learned that when I actually do write a message on the envelope and take it to the post office about half the time they deliver the same mail back to me again. #1259

I was waiting to try on a dress in a clothing shop when a woman shuffled out of a dressing booth and over to a mirror so she could see how a sweater and skirt looked on her. The pants she was wearing when she entered the store were pulled down around her ankles. "I didn't want to take off my shoes," she explained as she passed me. #1260

I find when I order something through the mails and am not satisfied with it, I practically never mail it back. It's a lot of trouble, and I just never seem to get around to it. This isn't limited to Christmas gifts or new books I buy from a catalogue. I recently subscribed to a magazine that sounded great on paper but it wasn't what I wanted at all. I could have cancelled and gotten the unused portion of my money back, but I never did and eventually the subscription expired. I bet that's true with most money back guarantees. The companies know that their dissatisfied customers won't get around to mailing the product back and so they won't have to make good on the guarantee.

I also think this is how most of the book clubs and record clubs make their money. Once you accept their very attractive bribe of free books or records and join the club, they send you a notice each month of the selection they are going to mail you if you don't notify them in time that you don't want it. And because you often do not get around to sending in the notice stating that you don't want the selection, their selection arrives in the mail and they bill you for it. Although you can return it if you want, you rarely do so. Even when you know you want to return the selection, you have too many other things that are more pressing that you have to do, and you don't get around to it. So you end up paying them for a selection you don't want. #1261

Lots of the conflict in my family deals with items that someone has used and not bothered putting back. This includes many different things, such as an eyebrow pencil, lipstick, tape, scissors, wrapping paper, or a cassette player. People are always trying to pin the blame on someone or threatening to do something that will prevent the person from taking the item in the future. I frequently hear, "Who had it last?" "You know it doesn't belong to you," "Why didn't you put it back?" "You have your own. Why did you take mine?" "Where did you last use it?" "Go and look for it," "Don't take it again," and "I'm going to have to put a lock on my door." #1262

A variation on not doing an activity is to do only what one has to do and ignore everything else. For example, one can only visit stores which sell what one needs at the time, limit one's reading to the things that pertain directly to oneself, and spend time only with those people who are important to oneself.

The woman just ahead of me in the line at the post office was holding a postage meter. When she reached the counter the clerk told her, "We have cases that make it easier to carry the meter." The woman replied, "We already have one. It's buried beneath other stuff in the office. I'm just too lazy to dig it out." #1263

19. Getting rid of an activity

People also conserve time and energy by ridding themselves of activities. There are several means by which this is accomplished. One is simply to throw something away so one does not have to deal with it in the future.

My wife left a jar full of spoiled jam for me to clean out and wash, because "the jar is worth forty-five cents." When she wasn't looking I threw it away. I didn't want to spend several minutes cleaning out this yucky jar to save a mere forty-five cents. #1264

When you clean up an area you run into all sorts of things you've been saving just in case you might use them again. But if one thing is clear after so many years, it's that you're not going to use them again. Also, they take up space, and if you keep them around you'll just have to keep dealing with them in the future. I usually put them in a bag for the Salvation Army Thrift Store. But if I don't have a lot of things to send to the thrift store, it's not worth the trouble of taking the bag to them, and I dump it in the garbage. #1265

Many items are recognized as disposable in order to conserve time and energy. As a consequence one does not expect to clean, store, or reuse them. Examples of disposable goods include facial tissues, paper napkins and towels, ballpoint pens, wrapping paper, tin cans, paper and cardboard packages, plastic wrap, and plastic and glass containers.

> When we had a party this weekend we used paper plates and plastic cups, knives, and forks. It was a great deal cheaper than buying actual plates and cutlery, and we just threw them away at the end of the party. Otherwise we'd have had to spend an hour or two washing dishes. #1266

People also quit informal and formal activities in order to free up their time for other pursuits. They quit hobbies; sports; jobs; training programs and educational courses; and various duties, committees, and offices in organizations; as well as the organizations themselves. Sometimes when people are given a task they complain about having to do it or they do a poor job, so they will not be asked to do it again.

> When Mom asked me to unload the dishwasher, I always put the dishes away in the wrong places. I knew this drove her crazy, and that she'd rather do it herself than waste time looking for things in the kitchen. Finally she stopped getting me to unload the dishwasher, so my plan worked. #1267

20. Avoiding requests by others

People also save time and energy when they do not respond to requests from others. They may avoid people who will ask them to do things, ignore requests, pretend to be busy, use an excuse, or fail to show up or deliver what they have promised.

> I am so busy at work that when I go home to visit my parents I want to relax. However, my father doesn't understand this, because he expects me to do farm work or cut wood. Therefore, I visit them as seldom as possible. #1268

> If Mom starts bugging me about watching my little sister, I tell her I have too much homework to do, or that I'm worried about a big test that's coming up I need to study for. Then she usually leaves me alone. #1269

> When people call and ask me to join a committee or take on an additional chore at work, my first reaction is to try to think of a good excuse

not to. Often I suspect ahead of time that someone is going to call me, and I plan a good excuse. One great excuse is that I have to be out of town. But often this is not the case, so I fall back on the idea that I have already taken on so much that I can't take on another chore or committee. I do have to play it safe, however. So I make sure I have one committee I've already agreed to serve on so it won't look like I'm shirking my responsibilities. #1270

21. Arranging to spend less time and energy in the future

There are a variety of ways in which people arrange to expend less time and energy in the future. They leave things ready to be used in the future, and they remove objects that will be in their way. They also go to the trouble of preparing things so it will take less time and energy to deal with these things in the future. In addition, they do things at the present time in order to avoid the tension they will feel to do them in the future.

One approach is to leave things ready to use again later. Thus one may keep a hair blower or other appliance plugged into a wall socket so one does not have to plug it in again the next time one uses it. One can also take actions so that an item takes less time to process in the future. For example, one can soak dirty dishes so they will be easier to wash later, leave the clothes one will be wearing again the next day near the bed instead of putting them away, or place a piece of dirty clothing in the appropriate laundry bag so that one does not have to sort the laundry before a wash. When one has an item already in hand, it often takes less effort to go ahead and put it where it will be dealt with next, than it does to put it down and have to find it again at a later date. Thus one can place a letter one has just written by the door so that one can pick it up on one's way out and mail it. People also frequently remove items which are physically in their way. As a result they can more easily pursue their activities. For example, they may put away everything that is on a countertop before using the counter to prepare a meal, clear a space on a table in order to do schoolwork, or throw the wrapper from a package into the wastebasket rather than leave it on the floor because it would be in the way when they walked across the floor.

People often expend time and energy in order to avoid having to expend even more time and/or energy in the future. Thus they may write down the numbers they frequently call, so they do not have to look them up repeatedly in the telephone directory; order printed stationary, so they will not have to write out their own address each time they write someone; put objects back where they got them, so they can find them easily the next time they need them; have a garage built, so they do not have to clean their car after each snowfall; organize and file memos, reports, and letters, so they can easily find them again; save their coins, so they will not have to try to get more from a bank or store when they use a Laundromat or vending machine; design multiple-choice questions to replace essay questions, so they will not have to spend as much time grading exams; double knot their shoelaces, so they will not repeatedly become undone and have to be retied; and dog-ear a page or use a bookmark where they stop reading a book, so they do not have to spend time searching for their place when they return to the book.

> When there are several parking spaces to choose from, I don't always take the first one I see. I'd rather drive a little more to find a space that is easier to get out of when I want to leave. In a parking lot I take a space where nothing is in front of me, so I won't have to back out when I leave. When I parallel park on the street, I prefer a space which is just before an entrance to a driveway or alley, because no one can park in front of me and it is easier to drive away. I avoid a diagonal space which is right next to a large van or truck, because it is more difficult to see around the other vehicle when I have to leave and back out. [1271]

> After I bought a video cassette recorder, I recorded lots of TV programs. I must have had forty tapes with six hours of programs on each one. Afterwards, I found it took a lot of time going through them all every time I wanted to locate a particular program I'd already recorded, and it was very frustrating when I failed to find what I wanted. So one afternoon I spent a few hours categorizing tapes by subject matter, numbering each tape, and making an index of everything I'd recorded. This has made a big difference in saving time looking for programs. [1272]

People often deal with a problem that appears likely to increase in size over time. For example, they will repair a sweater before it unravels further, fix a leak in a pipe before the floor or walls are damaged, and take an aspirin as soon as they get a headache to prevent it from getting worse.

Conserving time and energy

Efforts to expend less time and energy in the future frequently involve other people. For example, one can try to get others to change their behavior so one will have less work to do.

> I keep reminding the kids to put their garbage in the garbage can. When they put banana peels and other food in the wastebaskets, I have to wash the wastebaskets more often. [#1273]

Also, carrying out successful coverups can avoid destruction of one's reputation and social relationships and thereby prevent considerable expenditure of time and energy attempting to rebuild them.

People also expend time and energy in the present to avoid having to expend the same amount of time and energy in the future. They do the activity now so they do not have to do it later. Thus in an airport they will take more steps in order to get a seat close to the boarding gate so they will not have to walk as far later when they are told they can board the plane.

> Many people run errands during their break periods at work. They will do things like pick up something for the evening meal, shop for a clothing item, go to the dentist, or get a present for their child to take to a birthday party. This way they don't have to do these things after work when they are tired or busy doing something else. [#1274]

Often people do things at the present time because they know they will be more rushed and feel more tension if they wait to do the same things at a future time. For example, if they prepare their own lunch or lunches for their children for the next day before they go to bed, they will feel less pressure than they will if they have to make the lunches the next morning when everyone is rushing to get to work or school on time.

> At night I choose and lay out the clothes that my kids and I will wear the next day. This takes about twenty minutes. It is better to do this the night before when time is not of the essence. [#1275]

People also do things at the present time simply to avoid the pressure (tension) they know they will feel to do them in the future.

I always try to wash all the dishes before I go to bed, because I don't want to deal with them the next morning. I want to start the day with a clean slate without having things left over from the day before that I still have to do. This way I can keep my mind clear and focus on what I need to do during the new day. #1276

22. Acquiring lasting items

People frequently attempt to obtain quality goods which are highly durable and require a minimum of repair. As a result they do not have to spend as much time and energy repairing and replacing items.

When I bought my personal computer I bought one with the reputation of being a real workhorse. I plan to make heavy use of it and don't want to have to deal with any repairs. I did the same thing when I selected my printer. The one I bought has about the lowest repair rate in the industry, because it averages 5000 hours of operation before it needs servicing. #1277

I always buy a particular brand of facial tissue because it is quite strong. When I've bought cheaper brands they easily shred and fall apart when I carry them with me. #1278

Often people go to considerable trouble to make sure they obtain the item which will require the least time and energy in the future.

When I decide to buy something, I try to get the best one I can afford. This way I can go for years without any trouble with it. You should have seen me when I planned to buy a TV and a video cassette recorder. I went to all the shops in town, talked at length to sales clerks, and called up stores in Toronto and talked to them too. #1279

People are often willing to spend more money in order to obtain higher quality goods which are less likely to break down in the future.

Many people are willing to spend more money buying Japanese cars, like Hondas and Toyotas, because they have much better repair records than North American cars. #1280

People frequently find out from others about the relative quality of different brands, and use this information to decide what to buy.

There are several branches of an electronics retail store here in the province. I bought both a computer and a telephone answering machine from them and I've had mechanical problems with both of them. I mentioned this to one of their employees, and he dismissed it with the comment, "That equipment was made with outdated components. But we're using much more advanced technology today." I reported this to a friend of mine who's in the market for a computer. He said that based on my experiences, he certainly won't buy a computer from them. #1281

I like to look through *Consumer Reports* before I make an expensive purchase, because the magazine does a thorough comparison of brands. I was glancing through an issue the other day and saw an article which compared different brands of video cassette tape. I have always bought a particular brand of tape because it was recommended to me by several clerks in a local store. The store sells a variety of brands at the same price, so I didn't think they would have a vested interest in recommending one brand over the others. However, the article in *Consumer Reports* gave the brand I've been buying a low rating. Because of their article I now buy a different brand. #1282

23. Limiting variety

People also save time and energy by limiting variety. Similar objects can be treated in a similar fashion. Not only can one employ the same motor patterns in dealing with them, but they require less mental attention than dissimilar objects.

When I buy socks, I always get the same kind. I only buy one brand, style, color, and size. This way I don't have to spend lots of time matching socks together after I wash them, I never have to worry whether I am wearing matching socks, and when the washing machine swallows one I don't have to throw its mate away. I know the machine is sure to gobble up another one sooner or later anyway. #1283

Multiple copies of an item can all be processed the same way. Thus one can wash identical clothing items at the same machine setting, and one can stack identical dishes more easily than one can stack dishes of different sizes. Also, when one buys all of one's clothes in only a few colors, it is much easier to coordinate one's clothes together.

24. Obtaining what can be fixed locally

Another tactic is to attempt to buy only what one can get fixed locally. Not only does this save one the trouble and delay involved in shipping the item to be fixed elsewhere, but in some cases a local firm will pick up and return the item that needs to be repaired.

> When our university department decided to buy several electric typewriters for students to use, the foremost consideration in my mind was to make sure that the typewriters could be serviced by people right here in town. Therefore I bought the brand carried by a local firm which services the machines they sell. The second consideration was to minimize the repairs that would have to be made. Therefore I ordered machines without an automatic carriage return, because that is the feature which has to be repaired most often. [1284]

> I am never going to buy another European car. When I bought my last one, there was a garage here in town which specialized in European cars. However, it has since gone out of business. Now you have to go to another province to get a car like mine properly serviced. Also, it always costs a great deal more to get parts for a foreign car. [1285]

25. Taking what one will need

In order to save time and energy, people generally take items they may need with them. Often they regularly carry items on their person, such as money, credit cards, a checkbook, authorization cards, keys, medications, and cosmetics. There are other objects they keep inside containers they have with them. Thus a person may have pens and blank paper in their briefcase and a spare tire and a snow shovel in the trunk of their car.

> When I go to the laundry room in my apartment house, I carry a number of things in addition to my dirty clothes. I have a roll of quarters in my pocket that I've gotten from the bank for the washing machines. I also

carry a plastic bag which contains soap powder, a measuring cup, and a fabric softener. It's a lot easier to keep these things in the plastic bag and to carry the bag with me than it is to try to remember what I need and to get it all together each time I do laundry. #1286

When I go to watch TV, I try to make sure I have everything I'm going to want to eat and drink before I sit down. Otherwise I'll have to keep getting up to get things. #1287

Sometimes people carry items that they do not know they will need, "just in case" they do need them. For example, most people carry extra money in case they have an unexpected expense, and some people carry an umbrella in case it rains.

I try to take everything I'm going to need when I travel, ranging from mosquito repellent to extra glasses. The problem is you don't always know what you are going to need, and I always take more items than I use. When I went to South America I took a good pair of hiking boots along and never used them. But if you don't take an item you need, or if you run out of something, you can waste part of your vacation and get pretty frustrated looking for a good replacement. #1288

I was on a hiking trip in the Galapagos last summer in which our party became split up. The guide was quite incompetent and had us looking for wild donkeys in this thick thorn brush which covered several hills. Before long we were separated into two groups and could no longer see or hear each other. Fortunately, I carry a whistle in my day pack for use in an emergency and I gave it to the guide to blow to make contact with the other group. #1289

As a result of taking things with them, people do not have to spend time and energy a) returning to get them, b) trying to obtain adequate substitutes, or c) trying to find ways to do without them.

26. Doing something properly so it will not have to be done again

By executing a task properly one is unlikely to have to do it again. This can produce a considerable saving in time and energy. For example, if one is careful when doing a mathematical calculation or typing a page, one is less likely to make mistakes and will not need to do it over. Similarly, if one hires someone who does a task properly, one is unlikely to have to go to the expense and trouble of correcting mistakes and rehiring and training someone else who will do the task properly.

The man who built my house really did an outstanding job. When I moved in, the neighbors told me I was really lucky to get one of his houses because he has such a good reputation. And they were right, because the man uses good materials and thicker insulation than most of the other builders. I certainly recommend him if you decide to buy a house. #1290

My wife inherited a very poor set of teeth and needed root canals and caps for most of them. We spent several thousand dollars having this work done locally, and my wife had to go through a great deal of discomfort and stress while the work was being done. However, the dentist she used made the caps too short and didn't seal them properly. As a result she had all sorts of problems with them afterwards, and we had to spend several thousands more having the job done correctly by a second dentist. #1291

I began having serious engine problems with my car and decided to sell it and get a new one. However, before I could sell my car, I had to get it fixed up. I took it to a garage which charged me much more than I had expected and failed to get rid of the problems. So I took it to another garage and after I got the car back it still didn't run properly. In order to keep my expenses for repairs down, I next took it to a school for mechanics which agreed not to charge me for labor. However, they took forever to get to it, and I had to keep after them. After the school finally got around to "fixing" it, I tried to drive it home but it conked out on me and I had to have a tow truck take it back to the school. This time the school decided to install another used engine and this cost a lot more money. Afterwards the car still didn't run properly. So I went to all this trouble and expense and still had to sell it for next to nothing. Moreover, leaving the car to be repaired was very inconvenient for me, because I needed the car to travel to work and to do my errands. It was an extremely frustrating experience. #1292

27. Finishing a task

People constantly strive to finish what they are doing. When one finishes a task one does not have to work on it again and is free to think about and work on other tasks. When one does not finish, however, one has to use a lot of time and energy each time one returns to work on the task. Not only does one have to prepare oneself mentally to work on the task again, but one has to refresh one's mind as to just where one is in the middle of the task, and one has to make sure that the materials one needs are all still at hand and have not been moved elsewhere.

28. Coordinating with others

When people coordinate their activities with the activities of others, they greatly reduce their expenditure of time and energy. Thus by speaking the same language as others, eating the same food that others do, wearing the same kind of clothes that others wear, and working at an activity that others recognize as a job, one is able to communicate with others, does not have to grow one's own food or make one's own clothes, and is able to obtain money to buy things.

Another way that people coordinate with others is through scheduling specific times to meet together and to complete tasks. Individuals reach agreements on times and places to meet and on objectives to be accomplished.

> At home this morning my wife and I arranged to meet at the grocery store at six thirty this evening. This way my wife doesn't have to try to find a phone and catch me in my office to tell me what time she will be there. #1293

Organizations schedule times and places when they provide services, hold meetings, deal with requests, and handle problems. One can imagine how difficult it would be to teach a university course without designating a specific classroom, a specific teacher, specific hours for meeting together, and specific assignments.

In every area of human endeavor, there are both big and small advantages from coordinating one's activities with others.

When the company where I work decided to purchase a particular brand of personal computer for the staff, I bought the same brand for myself to use at home. The brand is average to low in quality. It isn't very fast and they don't use the best components. So I would have preferred to buy a better brand. However, I could see more advantages to getting the same brand everyone else had. I figured I'd be able to get the secretary to type something on a diskette at the office for me and then be able to edit it on my computer at home. I found other advantages too. For example, I was able to use the company printer to run off my work. Also, company staff were able to help me straighten out difficulties I had understanding the software, and the company obtained a program to correct spelling that I was able to use too. When my keyboard quit working, personnel at the company's computer center made suggestions as to how to correct the problem and eventually replaced a broken part for me for free. #1294

One encounters numerous difficulties when one does not coordinate one's behavior with the behavior of others.

People in Canada walk on the right side of the sidewalk. If you try to walk on the left the going is much more difficult. You have to keep slowing down to get out of the way of the people walking toward you. #1295

I bought five prerecorded videos when I was in England last summer. They were nature films and very reasonably priced at ten pounds, or about twenty dollars each. But then when I got home I learned I couldn't play them on a Canadian video cassette recorder because the two countries use different formats. If I want to use them I'll have to send each video to Toronto and pay another $200 to have it converted to the Canadian format. That was a year ago and so far I haven't been able to put the money aside to have it done. So I haven't been able to use the videos at all. #1296

The greater the degree of coordination, the more time and energy saved.

29. Getting others to do things your way

An important way in which people try to conserve time and energy is to get others to do things their way. When one can get others to coordinate their behavior with one's own, one does not have to waste time and energy trying to comply with the models and behavior of others and trying to get what one wants when others want something else.

> I used to yell at my son because it took him almost an hour to go to bed. He would keep climbing out of bed and wandering out of his room. Also, because he never put away his toys, I would have to do so for him after he went to bed. Then I changed my approach. Now an hour before bedtime I tell him to start putting away his toys and to put on his pajamas. This way he gets used to the idea, doesn't feel as rushed, and goes to bed without incident. This is a lot less stressful for me and I no longer get as upset with him. #1297

> Some people tailgate, or drive very close, if they think the car just ahead of them is going too slow. Not many drivers like someone "up their ass." They get irritated because if they suddenly put on their brakes the car behind them wouldn't have time to stop and would crash into them. Therefore they have to continue to take the driver who is tailgating them into account as they drive, which is a nuisance. Usually the traffic or the road doesn't allow the driver who is tailgating to pass. Those who tailgate want to force the driver just ahead to drive faster or pull over so they can pass, and sometimes this works. "Tailgating really bugs me. The last thing I want is to have an accident, because I'm worrying about the driver who is right behind me so that I can't pay attention to the cars in front of me. What if I have to make a fast stop and can't because this driver is right behind me?" "It makes me terribly nervous. I don't appreciate someone following me so close it would be hard to fit a toothpick between our two bumpers. They make me so angry I start yelling obscenities." "I'd like to step on the brake so fast I get rear-ended. Then the idiot behind me would be at fault and would have to pay for damages and his insurance rates would go up. Hopefully it would teach the numskull a lesson on driving etiquette. Unfortunately no one has the time and patience to deal with all the hassle after an accident." Occasionally a driver will touch his brakes to warn the driver who is tailgating to back off, will slow down to a snail's pace to irritate him, or will pull over to let him get ahead and then tailgate him in order to give him a taste of his own medicine. #1298

People frequently instruct, correct, criticize, and reward others in order to get others to adopt their models and behavior. This is discussed in detail in the chapter on Establishing Consistency in a later volume.

30. Getting help from others

A common way of conserving time and energy is to get someone else to perform a task for you or to give you information you need to do a task. People hire others to work for them, assign them specific tasks, and monitor their performance to ensure that they do things the way they want them done. A person may ask or tell another to help him, or make his need for help clear so the other person will "volunteer" to help him.

> I was exhausted when I got home from work and I asked my daughter to make a cup of tea for me. #1299

> The other night Alan had a sore ankle from playing hockey. We were watching the hockey game on TV and Alan called out, "Debbie, can you bring me another beer? My foot hurts like hell." To me he said, "It doesn't hurt that much. But hey, why not take advantage of it while you can?" #1300

> A colleague of mine started griping about how punishing the new changes in the federal budget will be. I asked him just what the changes are, and he explained each one to me. Now I know what to expect and how it's likely to affect me, and I don't have to go to the trouble of reading up on it. #1301

> Whenever I don't know how to do something on the computer, I call up the company that made the software and get them to explain what I have to do. This takes a lot less time than trying to figure things out for myself or trying to understand the manual. #1302

However, people often do not provide the help that others want from them.

> My daughter was complaining this morning that there are no clean towels in the bathroom. It was clear she expected me to go get them for her. But I told her instead of complaining she could get them from the linen closet herself. #1303

Getting others to do things for you is also a very common means of establishing consistency with your models. (See the chapter on Establishing Consistency in a later volume.)

Conserving time and energy

People expend less energy when they take turns performing a task for each other. Thus if person A fixes a meal both for himself and person B on one day, and person B fixes a meal both for himself and person A on the second day, both gain. Each person expends less energy than if he had to fix the meal for himself alone on both days. This is because it takes less effort to add a larger quantity of ingredients for the other person when one cooks on a single occasion, than it does to have to cook on two separate occasions with a smaller quantity of ingredients. Frequently, however, people specialize, and repeatedly do a specific task for themselves and others, while others perform a different task for them.

> When I spend the weekend at my girlfriend's house, she cooks the meals and I wash all the dishes. She prefers to cook, and I prefer to wash, so we are both happy with this arrangement. #1304

> My parents both have to rush off to work early every morning well before school starts. So my sister and I walk over to a friend's house and get a ride to school with his mother. Then after work my mother reciprocates by picking up my sister, me, and the friend at school and driving us home. My friend's mother works at the hospital and has irregular hours so it would be difficult for her to pick us up when school lets out. #1305

People usually purchase specific goods and services from a specialist who regularly provides them. As a result they save a great deal of time and energy because they do not have to start from scratch and attempt to produce the good or service by themselves. One needs only to consider the amount of time and energy one would expend trying to do one's own dental work, manufacture a television set, or travel to another continent without any help from other people. If one tries to do things on one's own, one has to determine what to do, amass the necessary equipment and materials, learn how to use them, and then actually carry out the task. In contrast, a specialist has had considerable training and experience, has the equipment and materials on hand, knows where to get additional equipment and materials, has ties with support personnel, and has developed efficient routines. There are numerous goods and services which a person could not hope to provide for himself within a single lifetime if he had to do everything on his own.

Tactics for conserving time and energy

People tend to resent expending their own time and energy helping another person when they feel they are not receiving fair value in return.

It is courteous to hold a door open for someone who is entering or leaving the same door you are, and most people thank you when you do this. But there are people who walk right through and don't acknowledge the fact you are holding the door for them. I take a real dislike to them and wish I had another opportunity in which I could do nothing for them. #1306

When I'm walking down the street and see a car which has become stuck in the snow, I keep my eyes straight ahead. I never look at the occupants of the car because I know they'll expect me to help them push it out. The main reason I do this is that I don't want to go to all the effort of helping them. There's likely another reason too. No one ever helps me get a car unstuck, because I don't own a car. #1307

My girlfriend has terrible math block and never got beyond multiplication and division. However, she needed to get an A in a university course in statistics to make it easier for her to get into graduate school. She wanted me to help her, but I asked her to hire a tutor instead. She had a regular job and could afford to pay for one. I even volunteered to pay for the tutor myself. I know next to nothing about statistics, and I knew that to be able to help her I would have to study and understand each chapter in the text. Well that's what I ended up having to do. She never tried to get a tutor, and every weekend she was a psychological wreck over the course. Not only did I have to nurse her through each chapter, but I had to teach her basic math at the same time. The only way I am able to teach is to explain what is taking place so the other person can apply it on their own. However, my girlfriend was so freaked out that she fought every inch of the way against my attempts to help her understand what was happening. All she wanted to know was what she should memorize to get through the tests. We had many highly emotional struggles over this. At the same time, I had a lot of my own work to do, but I did very little of it because of all the hours that had to go into helping her in that course. It was a hellish experience for both of us. My girlfriend really needed my help, but I really resented all the time it took. I felt she was asking too much and I really wished she had gotten a tutor. She did get an A in the course, but it half killed me. #1308

People frequently help each other in my community. However, the way people feel about this depends on the situation. If there is a death or illness in a family people like to do something to help out. The common response is to cook a meal and take it over to the family, or make some gesture, such as light their fire, so their home will be warm when they return from the hospital. Occasionally someone goes beyond this and feeds and milks a person's animals or cooks for a family while a member is incapacitated. Most families have received this kind of help at one time or another from community members, so people feel it is proper to give it to others in return, and when they do so they feel good about themselves. Often a number of people contribute at the same time, and this lessens the load on each individual. For example, one tobacco farmer had had bad luck with his crops for three or four years and was in danger of going under. So without his asking, everyone in the neighborhood got together one weekend and went and helped him bring his crop in. You also get mutually helpful arrangements. For example, a friend of my father doesn't grow enough hay to feed his animals over the winter. So when my father has to get his own hay in, this friend brings his truck over and works with him a couple of days. In return, my father gives him a few loads of hay.

However, if people feel they have to do too much for a neighbor, they resent it. Sometimes people go on vacations for a week or two and ask a neighbor to look after things for them. This can be quite an imposition. For example, one man was looking after a house last winter and the power went out and the pipes froze and burst. As a result there was water on the floor of their house which was starting to freeze and had to be removed. Another case involves some neighbors of mine who go to Florida for a week in the winter and expect me or another neighbor to go get their mail every day. It's not that far away, it's just that I don't remember to stop at their mailbox when I drive home. Then when I'm all settled at home, I suddenly remember, "Oh, my god. Got to get their mail." I have to get properly dressed and go out again. They also have a cat that needs to be fed, and this cat has a mean outlook on life. Not only does she claw people, but she likes to hide. Their house isn't that far away, but it's still a pain, and last winter their neighbor had to trudge through a snowstorm to get there. I think there's also the idea that these people are off enjoying themselves while you have to stay home and do their chores. They didn't leave because of an emergency. Therefore they should be home to look after things themselves. #1309

When you are in a relationship and are much more giving than the other person, you grow to resent the fact. As for myself, doing things for the other person is a way of expressing love. Often these are small things, such as going to the trouble to get the other person a small gift they would really like, voluntarily giving them a back rub or foot rub when they've had a hard day, or cheerfully going to a party or movie they want to go to that doesn't particularly interest me. But when they never respond in kind I really notice the fact and feel I am being used. When they don't do these things for me, I feel unloved. #1310

After people do something for someone else they frequently make sure the other person knows. Often they drop it into their conversation, and sometimes they bring it up repeatedly.

My two daughters had been watching TV in my bedroom and left some dolls and other things behind in the room. I told my younger daughter to take them back to their room, and she objected that they all belonged to her older sister. However, my older daughter was downstairs doing the laundry so I told my younger daughter to take them out anyway. Later I overheard my younger daughter ardently complaining to her sister that she didn't appreciate having to carry a whole box of her sister's things across the hall to their room. #1311

People usually feel they are getting fair value in return for their services, when a) they are paid for their expenditure of time and energy, b) they remember that the other person performs a similar service for them, or c) they receive ample recognition and signs of appreciation for their service. Because of this, other people commonly thank them for expenditures of energy on their behalf, and feel it would be rude or inconsiderate if they neglected to thank them.

31. Following others

People conserve mental energy when they follow the lead of others. Those leading have to expend the energy planning what to do, remembering the correct sequence of events, and deciding when to carry them out, while those following can coast mentally.

When you go to church it is infinitely easier to follow what the rest of the congregation are doing than it is to try to remember when to stand, sit, kneel, sing, and reply to what the priest says. People keep looking at each other to try to get it right, because it is always embarrassing when you get it wrong. I went to a baptism the other day and a soloist sang a number of hymns during the service. After she sang several verses of one hymn the priest stood up and began to talk, but was interrupted when the woman sang the elaborate amen. It was entertaining to see the priest screw up for a change. #1312

Normally in ballet class no one wants to be at the head of the line at the barre. The person in front has to pay strict attention when the teacher shows the class what they will have to do. If the person doesn't pay strict attention, she won't remember the correct movements or get the timing right and will make mistakes, which is embarrassing. The students standing behind her don't have to pay attention as carefully because they can just follow what the person in front of them is doing. Before class people try to find an empty space at the barre so they can stretch and warm up. But as the time for the beginning of class approaches people near the head and tail of the barre frequently start shifting positions, because most students don't want to be stuck at the head or end of the line. If you are in the second position and the person ahead of you suddenly leaves and moves to another location at the barre just before class starts, then you are stuck at the front unless you have time to move and there is space elsewhere at the barre to move to. The person at the very back of the line faces the same problem, because when everyone turns 180 degrees to repeat the exercise in the opposite direction, the person at the end is suddenly at the head of the line and has no one to follow and must try to remember what to do. #1313

If you've traveled a specific route for years, but others have always driven you in their car, you are often at a loss if you suddenly have to drive the route yourself. You haven't made a point of remembering which turns to take. #1314

32. Making a copy

In order to avoid the mental effort of deciding what to do, people often copy what they have already done or what someone else has done.

Sometimes you have to fill out lots of copies of a form in the identical way or with slight changes. It is a lot easier to just copy the parts that are the same from one form to the next, than it is to try to remember again and again what you are supposed to write down. For example, I have to fill out twelve rent checks for my apartment for my landlord at the beginning of each year. After I fill out the first one, I just copy the same information on the other eleven checks except for the month. I also have to fill out a form every time I want to get something photo-copied at the printing center. When I have a lot of separate jobs for the printing center to do, I get the right number of forms and copy the same information from one form to the next. Then I make the few additions on each form that are unique for each job. This takes less time and effort than filling in each form from beginning to end, because this way I don't have to think about it. #1315

33. Selecting and changing a time and place

People frequently select and change the time and place they do things in order to conserve time and energy. For example, they may leave early in order to avoid rush-hour traffic, and they may decide to go to the bank at a time when there will not be many other customers waiting in line to see a teller. They may move to a location which is close to their place of work, a shopping area, a school for their children, or a park where they can walk their dog. Also, people usually travel to facilities which are closest to them, and to facilities which they can use with the least effort and in the least amount of time.

Businesses with a drive-through window for service, such as many fast-food restaurants, are quite popular, because you can place your order, pick up your food, and pay, all through your car window, and you don't have to wait very long. This is better than going to a regular restaurant, where you have to spend time and energy finding a parking place, walk-ing to the restaurant, waiting for a table, waiting for a waitress to take your order and serve you, waiting for your bill, waiting to pay the cashier, and walking back to your car. #1316

The bank I decided to use is only half a block from my place of work. It also has more branches than any other bank in the country. That means when I travel to another city I can always find a branch of the bank nearby where I can get cash from my account. #1317

Conserving time and energy

When you go to the movies, it's important where you choose to sit. You want to get a clear full view of the screen, so you don't want someone's head in your way. Otherwise you have to try to see around them, so it's harder to watch the film and get involved in it. I always try to pick a seat where no one is directly in front of me or the people I am with, and I try to pick a seat where no one is likely to sit down directly in front of me. This might be an empty seat in the row ahead which is next to another person, because when the theater isn't crowded most people do not want to sit right next to a stranger. If I do have to sit behind someone, I try to make sure that the person is short so I can easily see over them. Out of courtesy, I also try to pick a seat that is not directly in front of people in the row behind me. [#1318]

In addition, people frequently change the business they deal with, the person they deal with at a place of business, or the time or location when they use facilities, in order to conserve time and energy.

There is a health-food store in town where the owner likes to talk at length with each customer at the checkout counter. So even if you are next in line you often have to wait five minutes to pay for your goods. I quit shopping there and go elsewhere, because I find it too annoying waiting to get out of there. [#1319]

I work at McDonald's, which is right next door to KFC, or Kentucky Fried Chicken. Both of these are fast-food restaurants. When KFC has a promotional sale, our business picks up. Customers get tired waiting in line at KFC and come over and eat at McDonald's. [#1320]

There is a bank I use where one of the three tellers doesn't have a clue. She's been there for years, but she doesn't know where to begin when you give her anything but the simplest transaction to do. She either can't do it, or she makes mistakes. Then she ends up getting one of the other clerks to straighten it out for her. So you waste tons of time when you have to deal with her. It is very annoying. I finally decided I wasn't going to deal with her again. So when I reach the head of the line and she's the next teller available, I let the next person behind me go ahead of me to her window. [#1321]

One of the video-rental stores in town has an excellent selection, but when you go to pay for the film you have to stand there for ages while they grill you for personal information to make sure you'll return the film. It's like a police interrogation. I didn't want to go back to this place, but they had a film I couldn't find anywhere else in town. So when I handed them the film I wanted to rent, they told me their computer no longer had the information about me they had collected before, because it automatically erases information if you haven't rented a film during the past month. Therefore I was faced with going through the interrogation again. I told them, "I just hate dealing with this place." I left the film on the counter and walked out. [1322]

I try to go to the gym at times when there aren't a lot of people, such as early in the morning or late at night. Otherwise other people are using all the lanes in the pool to swim laps, or I have to wait to get a turn at the exercise equipment I want to use. [1323]

There is a great deal of difference in ease of use when you trade stocks through various Internet brokers. When you do a trade some firms require you to fill in lots of information, which slows down your trade and requires a lot of work. Others firms use trading forms which remember past information and require you to fill in very little new information. In addition all the firms provide you with real-time, or current, quotes. The best ones give you streaming quotes on all the stocks you follow, and the worst ones make you fill in lots of information in order to get a single real-time quote and then disconnect the service if you haven't used it for a few minutes. As a result you end up placing lots of trades with the firms which provide you with free streaming quotes and have trading forms which are easy to use, and you eventually cancel your accounts with the other firms. [1324]

34. Using routines

A primary way in which people conserve time and energy is through the use of routines. Routines are specific sequences of action which have been performed often enough that they are carried out automatically with little conscious attention. These are patterns of behavior which have become second nature to most people. People employ countless routines during a day, including such common ones as walking, brushing their teeth, using the toilet, shaving, dressing, feeding a pet, making their bed, fixing breakfast, eating, washing dishes, driving, talking, performing familiar tasks at work, and exercising. When people are in ambiguous situations and have to decide between alternative courses of action, they usually have to give their full conscious attention to what they are doing and have little attention available for other things. This is often mentally fatiguing. Routines, in contrast, free people to direct their consciousness onto other subjects. Because patterns of behavior which are repeated are quickly converted into routines, they enable people to conserve considerable amounts of time and energy. Routines are much less fatiguing than learning to do something new or trying to do something in a new way. Initially people resist learning something new, because it takes so much effort, but once they learn it and it becomes routine, they no longer resist it. Often routines seem to require almost no effort to carry out and one hardly notices them.

> I'll never forget when I first started to learn a one-footed spin in figure skating. The first time I tried it all of my muscles were struggling with each other to keep me upright as I turned and I was wet with sweat. But it didn't take many attempts before my body knew what to do. Although my spins were poor, it was as though my muscles knew what they were doing, and didn't have to exert themselves very much. [#1325]

An important advantage of routines is that one knows just how much effort to exert in order to accomplish a specific task. If one exerts more force than necessary, one wastes energy; and if one exerts less force than necessary, one also wastes energy because one has to use force a second time in order to accomplish the task. Also, when one uses too much or too little force, one may produce damage, perhaps by crushing or dropping an object.

> When I made the bed this morning I started pulling the pillows off the bed one by one. My arm suddenly jerked, because I was unable to lift one of the pillows. This pillow is much heavier than the other pillows, because it is filled with water. I forgot my wife is trying out a new type of pillow to see if it is more comfortable to sleep on. I had tried to lift it with the same amount of force I was using to lift the other pillows, but couldn't. [#1326]

Routines are so comfortable that they can become counterproductive. Thus one may continue an old routine even when it becomes obvious that if one learned a new routine one would save much more time and energy. People resist trying new things because it takes much less effort to repeat their old routine than it does to learn something new.

> I have a colleague who is writing several books. He uses a typewriter and I keep telling him to switch to a computer so he can cut his writing time in half. It's not a question of expense, because our company would issue him a computer. It's just a question of inertia. He's like the people who keep typing with two fingers, or the musicians who never learn to read music. But who am I to criticize? I've had an update on my word-processing software for several years which would save me time, but I've never taken it off my shelf and installed it. Because I don't make the effort to install it, I continue working with the old inferior software. Also, even though everyone else uses e-mail, and swears by it, I've never learned how to send it. I just continue phoning and mailing letters. #1327

35. Using orientations

Humans have specific orientations which enable them to conserve effort. These orientations involve the use of symmetry, repetition, circles, rectangles, lines, horizontal and vertical, parallel and perpendicular, consistency, centering, equidistant placement, simplicity, perfection, thoroughness, grouping on the basis of similarity, and the use of solid colors. People apply these orientations in their construction and decoration of clothing, vehicles, architecture, gardens, furniture, crafts, household items, and other objects. The use of these orientations enables humans to recognize phenomena with less mental effort, and to apply fewer categories in dealing with their environment. Phenomena which are not oriented require much more effort to recognize and categorize. Orientations are considered in a later volume in this series.

36. Using categories

People use categories in order to provide order to data. Categories enable people to organize sensory data, recognize phenomena, and construct and use models. The more effort it takes for humans to categorize phenomena, the less attractive they find the phenomena. For example, older faces have more features than younger faces, such as wrinkles; require more effort to categorize; and are less attractive to observers. Natural ecological areas are more chaotic than landscaped parks, lawns, and golf courses; require more effort to categorize; and are less attractive to observers. When orientations are used in the design and organization of phenomena, observers find it easier to categorize the phenomena and they find the phenomena more pleasing.

37. Simplifying categories

By simplifying categories, people need less effort both to use the categories and to communicate them to others. People simplify categories by labeling phenomena, using generalizations, using shorter labels or words, employing nicknames and abbreviations, and by adopting acronyms, such as IQ, TV, VCR, CD, EBITDA, UK, USA, USSR, PC, BS, IBM, AT&T, J&J, and 3M. (These acronyms stand for intelligence quotient; television; video cassette recorder; compact disk; earnings before interest, taxes, depreciation, and amortization; United Kingdom; United States of America; Union of Soviet Socialist Republics; personal computer; bullshit; International Business Machines; American Telephone and Telegraph Corporation; Johnson and Johnson, Incorporated; and Minnesota Mining and Manufacturing Company.)

> People use an enormous number of acronyms when talking about technology. For example, people discussing telecommunications talk about IP, or Internet protocol; HTML, or hypertext markup language; DSL, or digital subscriber lines; and WAP, or wireless application protocol. People who talk about semiconductors say ICs, or integrated circuits; DSP, or digital signal processor (chips); MOS, or metal-oxide-semiconductors; and LED, or light-emitting diodes. In regard to computers, people say RAM, or random-access memory; PROM, or programmable read-only memory; BCD, or binary-coded decimal; and ASCII, or American Standard Code for Information Interchange. [1328]

> Most nicknames are shorter versions of a person's name. Tom is shorter than Thomas, Joe than Joseph, Beth than Elizabeth, and Bea than Beatrice. [1329]

When people simplify categories, they reduce mental and vocal effort.

38. Using models

Models are highly efficient means of summarizing relationships between phenomena. People use models to describe and explain phenomena, to make predictions, and to set objectives and carry them out. Models frequently explain phenomena and predict how phenomena will act. Examples of models include the following:

Bees and wasps sting.
On average women live longer than men.
Water damages paper.
Rent is paid at the first of each month.
It is more likely to rain on a cloudy day.
Don't cross the street without looking both ways because you could be
     struck by a vehicle.
If I need milk I can buy it at a grocery store.
I am going to get something to eat.
I need a job to be able to support myself.
I need to find out what the weather will be like today.

39. Simplifying models

People try to find the simplest workable models, or the easiest way to understand things. People seek to keep their models simple, use categories which are most inclusive, and use the fewest variables possible. Simple explanations are easier to remember and use than complicated explanations. Science can be characterized as the search for simpler models to describe and explain reality. Science seeks to identify causal factors and to discard irrelevant factors.

40. Using a simple indicator

People frequently use a simple indicator to reduce the chance of wasting time and energy. Thus people assume it is not worth going to visit someone if their house is dark, assume it is raining if the ground is wet, assume they will not need to carry an umbrella if the sky is clear, assume someone is not there if they do not answer their telephone, assume it is

105

not worth checking that a business is open if no cars are parked outside, assume something is worth seeing if a crowd is gathered, and assume a movie is worth viewing if it is recommended by people who like the same kind of movies they do.

My bedspread has a complicated scene with flowers, butterflies, and birds printed on it. The design has a top and bottom, but this is difficult to see until the bedspread is fully opened. In the past when I made my bed in the morning, I didn't know where the top of the bedspread was until I had spread it over the whole bed. It bothered me when I had it the wrong way, with the top of the design at the bottom of the bed, and I often felt compelled to turn the bedspread around. Then I noticed that there was a small bird at the bottom edge of the design with his head in the same direction as the top of the bedspread. Thereafter I just looked for the edge with the small bird on it before I spread the bedspread on the bed. Still later I noticed that all the birds in the design had their heads toward the top of the bedspread. This made it even easier because now any bird I found indicated where the top was. As a result, I never made a mistake again, and never had to reverse the direction of the bedspread again. [1330]

There are several parking lots where I work, but only one is close to my office building. When I approach this lot in the morning, I look to see if the parking places which are most distant from the office buildings are already full. If they are I don't bother driving into the lot and searching for an empty parking place, because I know others have already done so and I am highly unlikely to find one. It would be wasted effort. So if the most distant parking places are already full, I drive past this lot to a lot which is further away where there are always empty places. [1331]

41. Breaking up a task into smaller units

Many tasks require doing a large number of different activities over a prolonged period of time. In many cases it would be very difficult or impossible both physically and mentally to carry out and complete all aspects of a task at the same time. People make tasks manageable by breaking them up into smaller tasks and working on the smaller tasks one at a time.

Sometimes I have a large number of items, such as file folders, which I need to arrange alphabetically. I could take each item and locate the proper place to insert it in the growing stack of items I've already arranged alphabetically. But I find it much faster to separate the items into three or four shorter piles, organize each short pile alphabetically, and then finish by arranging the shorter piles into a single pile. I think this is because you can find the right location for each item a lot faster in a shorter pile. #1332

When I look at the big picture and all the things I have to do to get something finished, I feel completely overwhelmed and demoralized. Sometimes my anxiety level shoots sky high. The only way I can calm down is think specifically about the small thing I have to do next in order that the project will eventually get done. I've learned, never think about everything you have to do, just think about what's next. #1333

Feelings

People resist making the transition from an inactive state to an active one. This is true both for physical activity and for mental activity. Thus people resist a) changing from a relaxed state to a tense state; b) thinking about, planning, and directing activity; and c) recognizing and formulating categories and models. Activity involves an increase in tension, and tension is experienced as hurt. There are degrees of hurt, just as there are degrees of pleasure. We are often not consciously aware of the hurt we feel, just as we are often not consciously aware of the pleasure we feel. However, we frequently respond to hurt and pleasure even when we are not consciously aware of them. For example, we take each breath in response to the increasing discomfort that we feel when we do not take a breath, but we are not normally conscious of this discomfort. However, the longer we go without taking a breath, the greater this discomfort becomes and the more it intrudes on our consciousness. Then when we take a breath the discomfort disappears. As a result of the tension and hurt we feel from activity, we constantly try to minimize our physical and mental exertion.

This resistance to activity increases with fatigue. Fatigue increases the hurt we feel when we exert ourselves. As hurt increases we are more likely to become consciously aware of it. When we are made consciously aware of hurt we are notified that we need to change our model and behavior.

Nevertheless, despite our resistance to effort, we frequently do engage in activity. We exert ourselves in response to our other feelings, because the hurt or pleasure from our other feelings often outweighs the hurt from exertion. For example, our anxieties are often sufficiently strong to overcome our resistance to act. When this is the case we become active to try to remove the source of our anxieties.

> I find myself growing increasingly anxious as a deadline approaches. As the point nears where just enough time remains to meet the deadline, I become so anxious I can hardly deal with other things. Everything else becomes unimportant and I just want to get this done so I can get it off my back and out of my mind. Another person I know finds that when he puts off something he needs to do he suffers from headaches and gets very warm as his blood pressure rises from worry. #1334

In contrast, when people stop exerting themselves and relax their muscles and their mind, they release tension and feel pleasure. They experience the release of tension as pleasure. When people stop activities they feel much better. It feels good to relax. People seek the most relaxing positions they can find, and frequently change positions in order to relax a greater number of muscles. People also find a hot shower or bath or a massage relaxing and therefore a source of pleasure. When people consider exerting themselves, they are faced with making a transition from a relaxed state associated with pleasure to an active state in which they will feel tension and hurt. Therefore they resist exerting themselves.

Tension, hurt, and effort

In order to carry out an activity people have to employ mental and physical tension. People experience tension as hurt. The less active people are, the less tension and hurt they feel. People avoid activity in order to avoid hurt. Therefore hurt encourages people to conserve energy. This hurt is frequently described as annoyance, irritation, frustration, a bother, a nuisance, a hassle, or "a pain." Both effort and thinking about the need to make an effort involve tension. Knowing that one has to, or may have to, exert oneself produces tension. One can feel a lot of resistance to simply getting up from a relaxed, or comfortable, position. Often we do not feel like undertaking a task or continuing one. The sooner we can stop being active, the better we like it, and if we could instantly complete a task satisfactorily we would gladly do so. People often adopt the first idea that looks as though it would solve a problem and do not continue searching for better ideas. People would experience the least tension and hurt if they did not have to act, or exert themselves, at all. As one person states, "I put off things because it bothers me to do them." It is unlikely this resistance to physical and mental effort would occur if activity were a pleasurable or neutral experience.

People also experience an increase in tension and hurt when they have to repeat a task or are saddled with an unexpected chore.

> When you have something on your mind you want to say to others or tell them about, you feel a strong desire to do so. But if they don't understand what you're saying, they'll want you to repeat what you said or explain to them what you meant. This is a chore that you'd rather not go through. You're no longer primed to say it, and it takes work to recall and repeat or explain what you previously said. Often you wish you'd never said anything in the first place. [#1335]

> When we have empty plastic shopping bags at home, we fold them up and put them in a pail. Then we take one out when we need a bag for the garbage can in the kitchen or for something else. The problem is that at least a third of the bags in the pail are too small for our garbage can. It is very frustrating to go get a bag from the pail, unfold it, see that it is too small for the garbage can, have to fold it up again, replace it in the pail, and then have to take out another bag which may or may not be big enough. I get so annoyed and angry, I just want to throw the small ones away. [#1336]

> There are times when something happens that makes you just feel like crying. Sometimes it's a big piece of bother like a tax audit. Or it's a move by the opposite political faction at work that you'll have to deal with. Occasionally it's an appliance you depend on that goes on the blink.

Or maybe it's something you finally got done that has to be done all over again for one reason or another. Often my initial response is to just feel sick. With everything else I have to do, who needs it. [#1337]

There are degrees of tension and hurt. Thus one feels more resistance to certain tasks than to others. Normally the more effort a task involves, the more resistance one feels to doing it. Thus people would rather sweep their floor than dig a ditch, shine their shoes than paint a house, and wash their hands than wash their dog.

I have certain pet peeves as a housewife. One are the boxes of laundry detergent which say, "Push here to open." All they provide are a few perforations in the side of the box, and you have to have the thumb of Superman to push it open. Another thing I hate is trying to open a packet of cheese in a packaged dinner. It is practically impossible to tear open because of the glue in the packet. [#1338]

People also resist mental tasks, and prefer easier mental tasks to harder ones. Thus people do not like to read instruction manuals, even when operating unfamiliar equipment, and would prefer to read a novel than learn mathematics. One student stated, "It's just so much work to understand the stuff (calculus). I didn't sit down to study for my exam because I knew I'd be there for hours trying to figure it out. And the thought of that freaks me out."

Feelings, such as pleasure, anxiety, discomfort, and anger, often override the feeling of resistance to activity and encourage people to exert themselves. For example, people try to get positive reactions by cracking jokes, or to get stimulation by going to a movie, and do so in order to satisfy their personal feelings, despite the effort these activities involve. The stronger the personal feeling, the more likely it will override the resistance people feel to engaging in activity. When one needs to go use the toilet, the longer one waits, the stronger the feeling of discomfort becomes, and the more likely one will actually make the effort and go. When people do not respond to feelings, there is no incentive for them to engage in mental or physical activity.

Many situations produce either tension or the release of tension, and this is experienced either as hurt or pleasure. People frequently act in response to this hurt or pleasure. This hurt or pleasure is often sufficiently strong to outweigh the hurt, or resistance, people feel that discourages them from acting, or exerting themselves. Thus people can feel so much tension when they see an orientation violated, such as a picture frame which is hanging "crooked," or not perfectly horizontal and vertical, that they exert the effort to "straighten" it. Similarly, people can feel sufficiently bothered by inconsistencies between their own models and the models of others, that they make the effort to criticize other people's models and to argue against them. In these cases, the tension people feel from the violation of an orientation, or from the inconsistency between other people's models and their own, is stronger than the tension, or resistance, they feel which discourages them from acting, or expending energy. Another outside source of tension, which usually overrides the tension required by effort, is produced by authority figures, such as parents, teachers, and employers, who control a person's resources. People frequently act in order to avoid the displeasure of those who control their resources. See Model 1, which begins on the next page.

> When parents are paying their tuition and living expenses, university students do not want to disappoint them. They want to do well in their courses and graduate. One student explained, "My parents pay for my school. They would be so mad at me if I ever failed a course." Another said, "Once I failed a class, but I didn't tell my parents. I knew they'd be disappointed in me. I don't know what I am going to do, because I have to take the course over again, and I know my parents will notice." #1339

People do not act when the feeling of pleasure from an activity fails to outweigh the tension and hurt required to carry out the activity. They also do not act when the hurt they receive from other sources for not doing an activity fails to outweigh the tension and hurt required to carry out the activity. Boring, or tedious, activities are those in which the tension and hurt from exertion exceeds the pleasure obtained from the activity. Therefore people do not want to make the effort to listen to things they already know, because the things they already know do not produce tension, and therefore people obtain no release of tension and no stimulation and pleasure from the communication. Similarly, people do not want to make the effort to reread novels or see the same films over again, because they know what happens in the books and films already, and there is no

Model 1: Whether or not one engages in an activity

E = **Effort** (tension and hurt) required to engage in an activity
P = **Pleasure** obtained or expected from the activity
O = Tension and hurt that is experienced from **other sources** if one does not engage in the activity
F = Additional effort (tension and hurt) required to engage in an activity when **fatigued**
A = **Activity**
→ = produces
↑ = the greater the
↓ = the less the
> = is greater than
< = is less than

1. Tension is experienced as hurt. When tension increases, hurt increases.

2. The release of tension is experienced as pleasure. When more tension is released, more pleasure is experienced.

A. People avoid activity because the effort hurts

E → no A

As a result of the effort required (E), people do not engage in activity (no A). Activity produces tension and hurt. Therefore people do not engage in activity unless there are other reasons to do so. Thus people avoid activity altogether when possible. They prefer to have others do chores for them rather than do the chores themselves, and they avoid exercise. When people are active they try to minimize their activity. They use as few muscles as possible when they move, try to take the most direct path when they go somewhere, and prefer to use a hand-held remote control to operate equipment.

B. The greater the effort required, the less likely people will do the activity

$$\uparrow E \rightarrow \downarrow A$$

The more effort required to perform an activity, the less likely people will perform the activity. Effort requires tension which is experienced as hurt. The more effort required to perform an activity, the more tension and hurt people experience if they do the activity.

C. People engage in activity when the pleasure from the activity outweighs the hurt produced by doing the activity

$$P > E \rightarrow A$$

When the pleasure obtained or expected from an activity (P) exceeds the effort required to do the activity (E), people engage in the activity (A). In other words, when the tension released from an activity (pleasure) is greater than the tension required to engage in the activity (effort), people engage in the activity. For example, when the pleasant stimulation produced by movies exceeds the effort it takes to watch the movies and arrange to see them, then people will continue to want to see movies. This is also true of reading a novel, watching a television program, playing a game, eating a snack, or talking to a friend over the telephone.

D. People do not do an activity, when the hurt produced by doing the activity exceeds the pleasure gained from the activity

$$P < E \rightarrow no\ A$$

When the pleasure obtained or expected (P) is less than the effort required (E), people do not engage in the activity (no A). In other words, when the tension released from an activity (pleasure) is less than the tension required to engage in an activity (effort), people do not engage in the activity. People do not want to make the effort to read a novel again that they have just read, or see a film again that they have just seen. Because they are familiar with the novel or film, there are no unknowns, they experience little tension, they have little tension to release, and as a result they experience little stimulation and pleasure. Therefore the effort required to reread the novel or to pay attention to the film a second time outweighs the stimulation and pleasure that is gained.

E. The more pleasure received from the activity, the more likely people will do the activity

$\uparrow P \rightarrow \uparrow A$

The more pleasure people receive or expect from an activity (P), the more likely they are to engage in the activity (A).

F. People engage in an activity when the hurt from other sources for not doing the activity is greater than the hurt required to do the activity

$O > E \rightarrow A$

When the tension (hurt) experienced from other sources for not do-ing an activity (O) is greater than the tension (hurt) required to do the activity (E), people do the activity (A). Thus in order to get rid of the anxiety produced by a strange noise in their home, people investigate to find out what caused the noise. In order to avoid the hurt produced by criticism from others, people make the effort to behave in socially acceptable ways and to dress appropriately. In order to avoid the hurt produced by guilt, people try to be nice to others and to take care of those who depend on them.

G. The greater the hurt from other sources if one does not do an activity, the more likely one is to do the activity

$$\uparrow O \rightarrow \uparrow A$$

The greater the tension and hurt one experiences from other sources if one does not do an activity (O), the more likely one will do the activity (A). Thus the more likely one will be criticized, be spanked, or lose one's job if one does not do an activity, the more likely one will do the activity.

H. People do not do an activity, when the hurt produced by doing the activity exceeds the hurt from other sources for not doing the activity

$$O < E \rightarrow no\ A$$

When the tension experienced from other sources for not doing an activity (O) is less than the tension required to engage in an activity (E), people do not do the activity (no A). When people know they will not be criticized or punished for failing to do an activity, they are unlikely to do that activity.

I. Fatigue reduces the willingness of people to engage in activity

$$(E + F) \rightarrow no\ A$$

Because of the tension and hurt produced by effort (E) and by fatigue (F), people do not engage in activity (no A).

$$\uparrow F \rightarrow \downarrow A$$

An increase in fatigue (F) produces a decrease in activity (A). When one is fatigued one is less likely to engage in activity. Thus one is less likely to engage in activities and strenuous activities at the end of the workday when one is physically and mentally tired.

$$P > (E + F) \rightarrow A$$
$$O > (E + F) \rightarrow A$$

In order for one to act (A), the pleasure from the activity (P) must be greater than both the normal effort to conduct the activity (E) and the additional effort to do so when fatigued (F). In other words, when the tension released from the activity (P, or pleasure) is greater than both the tension normally required to engage in the activity (E, or effort) and the additional tension caused by fatigue (F), then one engages in the activity.

Also, when the tension from other sources (O) is greater than both the tension normally required to engage in the activity (E) plus the additional tension caused by fatigue (F), then one engages in an activity (A).

tension produced, no tension to be released, and therefore no pleasure, or stimulation, to be gained. It is simply not worth the effort. Also, people do not want to keep eating the same food, because they know what it tastes like and obtain little pleasure and stimulation from it. When other people try to get a person to do something that the person finds boring or tedious, the person resists. Effort is punishing, and what is gained from effort must exceed this punishment for a person to be willing to act. See Model 1. (See also the chapter on Seeking Stimulation in a later volume.)

It might seem that it is logically impossible to release more tension from engaging in an activity than is required to engage in the activity. However, it is necessary to distinguish between the effort required to engage in an activity, and the pleasure received from the activity. It does not take much effort to turn on the radio and listen to it, or to turn on the television and watch it. The amount of stimulation received is based on the nature of the program one hears or watches, i.e., the amount of tension produced and released by the program. It takes as much effort to go to see a movie which is boring as it takes to see one which is stimulating, just as it takes as much effort to read a book which is boring as it takes to read one which is stimulating. If the movie is boring, then it is not worth the effort expended going to see it and watching it. And if the book is boring, then it is not worth the effort expended reading it. On the other hand, if the movie is stimulating, then it is worth the effort expended going to see it and watching it. And if the book is stimulating, then it is worth the effort expended reading it. The pleasure, or stimulation, from the movie or the book is generated by successfully providing the viewer or reader with tension and release experiences. This tension is usually produced by threats and unknowns, and is released when the threats are successfully avoided or removed and when the unknowns become known. The more tension that is produced and released, the more pleasure the viewer or reader experiences. Similarly it does not take much effort to buy a lottery ticket, open an envelope, or answer a telephone call. The amount of tension released and pleasure experienced depends on whether or not it is a winning lottery ticket and how much the ticket wins, what the contents of the envelope are, and who is on the phone and what the caller says. Many lottery tickets are not worth purchasing, many envelopes are not worth opening, and many telephone calls are not worth answering; but some really are.

Conserving time and energy

A person performs many more activities for himself than for others. This is because a person experiences his own feelings, but does not experience other people's feelings. A person performs activities because his own feelings outweigh and override his resistance to performing activity. In contrast, a person does not experience the personal feelings of other people. Therefore the personal feelings of others are often unable to override a person's resistance to engaging in activity. As a result, a person is not inclined to engage in activities for others. Thus people feel more resistance to effort when someone else asks them to do something, than when they decide on their own to do the same thing for themselves.

> When I'm lying on the bed and my wife asks me to get her a glass of water or something else, it's the last thing I feel like doing. But I go ahead because she always does so much for me. Sometimes I feel guilty because I have so little desire to do what she asks me to do. [#1340]

Even though feelings provide a necessary push which overrides the resistance to act, people still attempt to minimize their effort when they engage in activities. They try to find the easiest way to do whatever they feel motivated to do. Therefore tension and hurt, or resistance, are still present and this encourages people to economize their efforts. When people decide to go see a movie, they do not lose their desire to conserve time and energy. They do not drive back and forth between all the theaters in town to pick a film to see. Instead they look at a listing of movies in the newspaper or call the theaters on the telephone, choose one movie to see, and travel directly to it. In addition, people often avoid tasks and aspects of tasks that involve the most effort, and people frequently put them off until they feel forced to do them.

> Even when I do something I enjoy, there are always things about it that I don't feel like doing. Usually these take more mental effort to figure out. I usually resist them as long as possible until I just have to do them to get the job finished. [#1341]

People do not conserve time and energy simply for the sake of conserving time and energy, but rather they do so in order to avoid the underlying tension and hurt. As a result people also act in ways which enable them to avoid tension and hurt yet which do not conserve time and energy. Thus people often perform tasks before they need to in order to remove the tension which is hanging over their head reminding them that they must eventually do the tasks. Therefore someone will go ahead and perform a task so he does not have to think about it and bother with it later. For example, a person will wash dishes the night before, rather than wait until the next day. Or he will buy Christmas presents early so he does not have to buy them later. People will also do things before they have to in order to avoid the additional tension they will feel if they have to rush to meet a deadline later. Thus they may get out of bed early, or they may leave early for an appointment, to attend a concert, or to catch a plane or bus. If they wait until later they will feel more tension to rush. Such actions often do not conserve time and energy, because people must use the same amount of effort to do the task whether they do it now or later, but by carrying out these actions early people do reduce the amount of tension they feel in the future.

> If the kids make their lunches the night before, we don't have to rush around as much the next morning trying to get ready. It's less stressful. #1342

People also take other measures to reduce their present tension. One way is by asking for an extension so they have longer to accomplish a task. Another way is to avoid tasks with deadlines, so that they can take as much time as they wish to complete their tasks.

> When you are asked by a journal to do a book review you are often given a year to complete it. Of course, with everything that you have to do that needs to be done right away, the year quickly passes and you still haven't done the book review. During this time you have the book review hanging over your head, nagging at you. Finally you fear you won't meet the deadline and you rush to get it done. After going through this once, I decided I didn't want all the stress and I wasn't going to write any more book reviews. I only want to do things that I can take my own sweet time to finish. #1343

Because people seek to avoid physical and mental activity, their daily exertions reflect this. People are reticent to get out of bed in the morning unless they have a compelling reason to do so, such as to go to work, school, or the toilet. During the day people spend most of their time sitting instead of standing, or standing instead of walking or running. Sitting or standing uses less effort. When people do engage in activities, they use as few muscles as possible. As a result most activities involve localized movement, usually of a single hand, forearm, or arm, rather than one's entire body. When possible people communicate through speech, rather than through gestures and actions, because speech requires less effort. People normally try to keep their physical exertions short, and frequently rest between exertions. When people do engage in activity, they frequently shift from one combination of movements to another to avoid fatigue.

> People find it hard to exercise regularly and easy to find reasons to stop. In most sports, people spend more time standing around than they do actually running, jumping, or whatever. Even at the exercise centers people spend more time relaxing than exercising. When they use weights to exercise certain muscles, they sit or lie down to relax the rest of their body. Then between sets of exercises they rest the muscles they were exercising. Afterwards they relax by taking a shower, and they may use the whirlpool or sauna for extra relaxation. [1344]

People frequently feel tired and sleepy during the day. Later in the day people become increasingly tired and less willing to take on demanding physical and mental tasks, and they find it difficult to switch from one physical or mental activity to another.

> It was late at night and I was putting away the last things in the kitchen before going to bed. Then my daughter dropped something on the kitchen table. The noise was so grating, I winced. I was just too mentally exhausted to handle it. [1345]

> When I'm really tired at night I get impatient and irritable. I worry I'm acting short with my family. [1346]

At the end of the day people's primary desire is to go to sleep.

Fatigue

There is also the factor of fatigue, and this increases the desire of people to avoid effort and to conserve time and energy. People seek to minimize the effort that is involved in an activity because activities are quite weary-ing. People get tired very easily when they engage in physical or mental activity. Physical tasks often take a lot of effort and are physically ex-hausting. Even a simple activity like standing can be quite fatiguing after a while.

I often get too tired to do something I've planned to do. For example, I may plan to go out to a club on a Saturday night and then when nine or ten o'clock rolls around, I'm just not up for it and stay home. At other times there's a late show on television I think I'd like to watch, but I find I'm falling asleep when it's time for the program to begin. I usually just go to bed early. #1347

When people move to music they repeat certain movements until they get tired, then they change to a different set of movements. You see this with social dancers, musicians playing music, musicians moving on stage in time with the music, and listeners tapping their foot or swinging their hand. #1348

A common reason why university students skip classes is they are too tired to go. Sometimes they have been up late studying or preparing an assignment, and sometimes they have been out partying or barhopping. "If I go out drinking the night before, I'm not fit to go to my classes the next morning. But if there's a class I must go to, because of a test or presentation, then I stay home the previous night." Many students find early morning classes at eight or eight thirty too hard to get up for. Others say that at the end of a long day they are just too tired to go to their late afternoon class. #1349

Last night my husband and I made plans to go to a Halloween party. We had our costumes ready to put on and the beer we were taking sitting on the table. Because we were tired we decided to take a nap before we left. We didn't wake up until two thirty the next morning, after the party was over. #1350

Last spring break a couple of friends and I went to Florida. After Christmas it was all we could talk about. It was the only thing on our minds, and we couldn't wait to go. Finally, when spring break arrived, we were off. But because of our limited time, we had to drive straight down without making any stops, except for gas. This took its toll on us, and when we got down to Florida we were dead. We needed a couple of days to recover before we could go out and have a good time. But then we had to drive all the way back nonstop. Looking back, it was fun, but it wasn't close to what we had hoped for. #1351

Mental tasks, such as concentrating, remembering, organizing, developing useful categories, solving problems, planning ahead, reading, and writing, can all be mentally fatiguing.

After I concentrate on something for about an hour, I get tired and sleepy. This can be a research problem I'm trying to solve or a report I'm writing. #1352

After two or three hours playing chess or a computer game in which I have to make decisions and pick the best strategy, I'm just wiped out mentally. My mind feels numb and I'm not good for much for the rest of the day. Other people even comment that I seem really out of it. #1353

I sell insurance and today lots of people came to my office and wanted to make changes in their policies. So many people came that I didn't have time to write down what they said. Instead I just made a note or two. Now I am so tired, because I had to remember afterwards what they all wanted and I had to write this out. #1354

One of my tasks is ordering books for a bookstore. This involves looking through catalogues from publishers, and deciding which books are likely to sell and how many copies to order. It is a mental killer, because you have to make one decision after another. When someone interrupts you or you finish going through a catalogue, you suddenly realize how mentally exhausted you are. It always takes me a while to get reoriented to deal with other things. It is so tiring that I don't like to go through more than one or two catalogues during a day. #1355

I worked all day Saturday on my income tax. That morning I got several boxes of loose papers together, sorted them, and located my receipts. I spent much of the afternoon organizing receipts and adding them together. By evening my mind felt dazed. The next morning I continued adding the receipts together. By noon my mind felt dazed again, just as it had the evening before. My mind was still fatigued and hadn't had time to recuperate. #1356

> Late in the afternoon I'm usually tired working on my current project and know I don't want to continue. So I start casting around for something different to do so I don't waste my time. When I find something that uses my brain in a different way, I can put in a couple of productive hours working on it before it's time to go home. #1357

Working while fatigued is a punishing feeling, and the more time and energy one devotes to a task the more fatigue one experiences. When one is tired, experiences which are normally pleasurable, such as obtaining stimulation, positive reactions, and sex, become less appealing. When one is tired there is an increase in the hurt one experiences from effort. Therefore one is less responsive to pleasant feelings. See Model 1 above.

When muscles are used they quickly tire. Effort causes people to feel tired, stiff, sore, weak, faint, and out of breath. Frequently when one engages in a task, one finds that one lacks energy and does not have much strength, or that the task takes a lot of effort and is physically hard to do. When one first engages in an arduous task, one tires quickly. When one makes movements that one is not used to, one soon becomes tired and sore. If one repeats the task frequently, such as once a day, one develops additional strength to deal with it and feels less tired by it. However, if one stops doing the task for a number of days, when one starts doing it again, one feels tired. Even if one is "in shape" in regard to certain types of activity and exercise that one does regularly, if one repeats these same movements many times without resting, one's muscles become sore.

The more arduous a task, the more fatiguing it is. Thus activities such as doing pushups, weight lifting, wrestling, wading through a snow bank, and giving someone a strenuous massage are quite tiring. Activities such as eating and talking are much less fatiguing. Similarly, mental activities such as solving problems, dealing with inconsistencies, and reading unfamiliar technical materials are more fatiguing than reading novels, seeing a film, watching television, listening to music, or fantasizing. The harder one has to concentrate on a mental task, the more fatiguing it is.

> We had a European chess master visit our computer class in high school. He put on a blindfold and played a student in the class and won easily. He told us he had made money when he was younger doing this in the

Middle East. We all wanted him to play our teacher, who is a chess enthusiast. When he agreed, we asked him to play blindfolded again. But he said he didn't want to because it is very tiring. #1358

Often when one starts to move, one activates muscles which are already tired, stiff, or sore from previous activities.

When I got up out of bed this morning my back felt kind of sore, and as I moved I realized my neck and head ached also. When I moved, my head throbbed. But I no longer noticed this as I fed the cats and took out the trash and garbage. Then I started to make the bed, and for some reason I felt weak. So I lay down on the bed. After a few minutes I got up and finished making it. I felt tired and muggy headed, so I lay back down for a while. My wife brought us our morning coffee and suggested we take a walk. I just didn't have the energy. But later I felt more like it. So I got up, shaved, and had a shower. By the time I finished getting my breakfast, my wife had finished dressing and we left for a walk. #1359

Using tired or sore muscles is an unpleasant experience, because it hurts. The same thing is true when one is tired from performing mental activity. As a result, people resist effort in order to avoid the hurt associated with fatigue. People frequently put off arduous physical and mental tasks when they are tired, and wait to do them when they are rested.

I have a heavy computer in my office that I have to take home. At the end of the day I'm always tired and don't feel like carrying it to my car. So I've decided to wait and tackle the job first thing in the morning when I'm rested. #1360

When I encounter a difficult problem in the afternoon, I often don't have the energy to try to solve it. So I decide to deal with it the next day after I've had a good night's sleep. #1361

Although people can focus on how their muscles feel when they move, and can notice when they feel tired or sore, people are usually busy focusing on other things and do not notice how their muscles feel. When people do not focus their attention on their muscles and how they feel, their body can still experience tired and sore muscles. Regardless of where a person's attention is focused, their body continues to receive information on itself and to react to this information. When people stop concentrating on other things, they often become consciously aware of how tired they are. Once they are consciously aware of their fatigue they are able to alter their models and stop exerting themselves in the same way.

Anxiety

Another feeling which is involved with the conservation of time and energy is anxiety. Whereas people seek to conserve energy because they dislike the tension and hurt produced by effort, people seek to conserve time because they dislike anxiety. Often there are deadlines that must be met, and other people who are dependent on their being met. People frequently feel anxiety over the amount of time a task is taking, worry whether they will get it done in time or will finish it at all, and fear the negative consequences if they fail to do so.

> I get very anxious when I'm supposed to do something or get somewhere by a specific time and it's not certain I'll be ready on time. As the deadline draws closer, I get quite hyper. It's really stressful. I've learned to start early enough and to get things done in advance so I can stay calm and don't have to go through this anxiety. #1362

> I hate waiting in lines. There is so much else I need to be doing. And lines always take longer than you think they will. Sometimes I get so impatient and fed up I decide I'll come back later and I just leave the line. Another thing that upsets me is the modern labyrinth, or the telephone-information service provided by many businesses and organizations. When you call you are told which buttons to push to get certain options, and each button leads to further options. Often the option you want is not provided, or else you are asked to leave a message and someone will supposedly call you back. Sometimes the option you choose is busy and you have to wait fifteen minutes or more on the phone to get through. It is the most frustrating thing to deal with. I just

hate it. It takes forever, and often doesn't get you the information or result you want. I try to do anything I can to speak to an actual person, which is the only way out of the labyrinth. #1363

A major source of anxiety is the pressure of the other things that must be done after one has finished what one is currently doing. Often the subsequent tasks must be dealt with by a specific time, and again other people are frequently dependent on their being done on time. People always have more tasks to do than they have time for. The more time one spends on one's current task, the more pressing the subsequent tasks become, and the greater one's anxiety and sense of frustration. This encourages one to try to hurry up and finish one's current activity and to minimize spending more time and energy on it. When one encounters unexpected obstacles or must repeat tasks, one can become quite upset because one has other tasks waiting to be done.

I try to finish what I am working on as quickly as possible, because everything else I have to do is shouting at me that it needs to get done. #1364

Today I went to the bank to get a cash advance on my credit card. It took forever because I was dealing with a new teller who didn't know me, and she wanted to see lots of identification cards and then didn't think my signature matched the signatures on the cards. There were many other errands I had to do afterwards, and I couldn't believe the amount of time this was taking. The teller kept saying, "You'll be glad to know your money is secure, and no one else is going to take it." And I kept saying, "I don't care about that. What I care about is all this hassle and the amount of time it's taking." #1365

The other day I spent over an hour traveling to this furniture store and then another couple of hours looking through their catalogue and their showroom. There were several items that were exactly what I needed for my apartment, but unfortunately none of them were in stock. I really got pissed off. Here I had gone to all this trouble and couldn't get what I wanted. I felt so frustrated I gave the staff a piece of my mind. #1366

Learning that one must do an unexpected task can also heighten one's anxiety, because one knows how many other tasks one has waiting to be done.

Functions

When one conserves energy, one requires less food. Also, one has more energy available to obtain additional resources. When one conserves time, one has more time available to obtain additional resources.

Excess behavior

Excess behavior is behavior in response to feelings which results in one acting contrary to the purposes the feelings are designed for. As a result, one loses resources rather than gains or protects them. For example, effort produces hurt and this feeling of hurt causes people to avoid effort. As a result people do not waste their time and energy. However, there are situations in which people avoid effort and the hurt associated with it to such an extent that they lose resources.

The attempt to avoid hurt may cause one to conserve time and energy to such an extent that one does not obtain necessary resources. One may shun efforts that would improve one's own chances of survival or those of one's offspring. Thus one may seek to avoid work, try to find the easy way to do things, and attempt to get resources by the least effort. When this is the case, one is likely to choose the activity that is easiest, even if it provides fewer resources. One is also more likely to be uncooperative, provide a sloppy performance, and quit before finishing.

> Most of the young adults I know just want to work as little as possible and have as much fun as they can. They aren't interested in having a career or working hard to get somewhere. My brother works as a waiter, but only enough shifts to make ends meet. He spends the rest of his time partying with his friends, playing video games, and sleeping. #1367

> My son dropped out of university in the middle of his first year "to get a job and train to be a kung-fu master." He has a history of dropping out

of martial-arts courses, so I don't think he'll stick with this one. The real reason he dropped out was he didn't want to do his coursework in university and used kung fu as an excuse. He said if kung fu doesn't work out, he'll become a professional billiards player. He knows even less about billiards than he does about kung fu. [#1368]

Many people lose opportunities because they never get around to doing something. One guy was an outstanding athlete and was planning to apply for an athletic scholarship, and I think he would have been certain to get it. But he kept putting it off and putting it off, until when he finally got to it, he had missed the deadline. Another person told me, "I planned to go on a ski trip, and needed to find someone who would do my shift at work. But I kept putting off calling up to arrange a replacement, and when I finally called, the person could no longer substitute for me. Because I was so lazy, I missed out going on the ski trip."

Others are penalized because they do things late. "I left off writing a paper and had to turn it in late. The teacher deducted marks because it wasn't on time." "Numerous times when I have put off doing my homework and had to rush to get it done, I've left out things or made simple mistakes that I would have caught if I hadn't rushed. Often I don't have time left to proofread a paper, or check whether my math answers are accurate, or make sure I understand a concept when I'm studying for a test." "I didn't start to study until right before my exam. When I wrote the exam, I was so sure I was going to fail that I screwed up on the stuff I knew, which wasn't very much anyway." [#1369]

During the Vietnam war I knew young men in the United States who were opposed to the war and to fighting and considered themselves conscientious objectors. They wanted to apply for official conscientious-objector status, but never made the effort of submitting an application. I suspect some of them were drafted, sent to fight, and killed. [#1370]

One may also alienate others through one's efforts to get them to do things for oneself. As a result one may gain a reputation for being lazy and exploitative, be avoided by others, and obtain fewer resources from them.

A friend of mine has a terrible history of taking jobs on government-funded research projects, and then quitting before the project is finished. Often she is active in designing the project and conducting interviews, but then leaves in the middle of analyzing the data. She quits as soon as she has worked enough months to qualify for unemployment benefits for the rest of the year. She leaves them high and dry, and they have to scramble to find and train someone else to complete the work. I would never hire her for anything or recommend that anyone else hires her. #1371

Often socially unacceptable or illegal occupations, such as prostitution, selling drugs, and confidence games, are more appealing than legitimate jobs, because they provide more money for less effort.

Similar forms of excess behavior occur in terms of mental effort. People normally try to avoid mental effort. Therefore they are happy to adopt the concepts and models of others, because this is much less taxing than developing their own concepts and models. Numerous concepts and models that people learn from others do not accurately reflect reality, and therefore have limited usefulness. In fact, some of these concepts and models are so inaccurate that they do more harm than good, and cost more resources than they provide. When people do engage in mental effort, they frequently adopt the first idea or solution that occurs to them which appears to satisfy their requirements, rather than continue to look for a better idea or solution. As a result they often do not gain as many resources as they would gain with a better idea or solution.

Society and conserving time and energy

Society helps its population conserve time and energy in a variety of ways. These include a) using established, predictable practices, b) providing standardized objects and procedures, c) providing objects and procedures which conserve effort, d) distributing facilities geographically, e) providing duplication, f) matching the provision of facilities and services to demand, and g) providing individuals with their own equipment to use.

Societies provide established, predictable practices. Established practices save people time and energy because people know what to do and what kinds of results to expect. They do not have to try to understand each situation anew, nor do they have to take the time and energy to invent their own practices. Because there are recognized locations, times, and means within the society for obtaining specific goods and services, it takes less effort to obtain them. For example, because one knows that food is obtained at the grocery store, and that the grocery store is open from eight o'clock in the morning until nine o'clock at night and is closed on Sunday, one goes to the grocery store at the right time to get food. One does not waste time looking for food in the wrong place or at the wrong time. Similarly, knowing a telephone number to use to get emergency help, such as 911, lets one obtain outside help without wasting time asking others who to turn to, and one does not have to locate a telephone book to look up a specific number. Practices such as wearing wedding rings, having job titles, and wearing uniforms notify others what they can and can not expect from individuals, and enable them to waste less time in inappropriate behavior. Established behaviors, such as obeying traffic signs and traffic police, or pulling one's vehicle to the side when an emergency vehicle needs to pass, provide efficient cooperation between people.

In order to conserve time and energy, societies provide many standardized objects and procedures. This permits a more efficient exchange of information and goods. For example, language, units of measurement, money, and rates of transmission of electric current and communications are standardized. Sizes are also standardized in the case of most clothing, electrical connections, railway tracks, paper products, books, computer disks, music recordings, and video cassettes. Standardization and duplication encourage the production of interchangeable parts, which reduce the time and energy involved in assembly and repair. Standardization also permits the development of equipment which can be easily connected and used together. For example, standard electrical connections make it possible to join various components together in a computer system, and standard paper sizes make it possible to use the same paper in different photocopiers and printers. Communities and societies often coordinate their activities with other communities and societies on a regional, national, and international basis. This permits considerable savings in time and energy in regard to the activities which are coordinated, such as communication, transportation, and the control of crime.

Society and conserving time and energy

Societies provide their members with objects and procedures which have been designed to conserve effort. Thus the times during which facilities and services are open and available are posted. Individuals are assigned identification numbers which speed the processing of their communications and transactions. Furniture is placed in public areas to enable people to sit down. In addition, new equipment, information, and methods of organization are constantly being designed and altered to enable people to perform their work in less time. Vehicles, computers, office and business machines, appliances, instruments, and communication devices are produced and improved which work faster and incorporate new labor-saving features. This includes photocopiers, laser printers, instant-development photography, automatic bank-teller machines, and videoconferencing facilities. Equipment and machinery are frequently designed to be operated by a single finger, hand, arm, or foot. Sources of information are developed to permit faster and more effective decisions. Examples include computer databases, voting by telephone, seismic sensing, and location systems using satellites. New methods of organization are instituted to enable people to save time and energy. Examples include computer networks, credit and debit cards, ordering goods by facsimile machine and the Internet, and paying bills by telephone and computer. The society also provides specialized tools and facilities which are too expensive for individuals to own, but which enable individuals to save time and energy. Examples include electrical power plants, sewage systems, roads and road-construction equipment, public-transportation systems, snowplows, firefighting equipment, and hospitals.

Facilities and services are located and organized to enable people to save time and energy. Often facilities are distributed geographically to shorten the time it takes people to travel to and from them. Examples include schools, fire and police stations, parks, churches, and hospitals. Businesses compete with each other in their ability to save individuals time and energy, and know that people usually go to the closest facility. Shopping malls and franchises are placed in numerous locations in order to reduce the time it takes people to travel to them. Fast-food restaurants are designed to provide easy access and speedy service. Convenience stores, or small neighborhood groceries, survive despite the fact they provide less selection and often charge higher prices, because they are closer to people's homes. Many facilities and services are made available at times when most people want to use them, and in some cases are accessible on a twenty-four-hour basis. Services are set up which save users time and energy. For example, letters and parcels are picked up and quickly delivered between homes and businesses over short and long distances.

Organizations and businesses that deal with the public normally provide considerable duplication of equipment and personnel in order that people need less time and energy to obtain goods and services. The faster that organizations and businesses can deal with clients and customers, the greater their appeal to the public. Therefore gas stations provide multiple gasoline pumps; banks provide a number of service windows and automatic tellers; barber shops and hairdressing salons provide multiple chairs; grocery stores provide numerous checkout counters; casinos provide many slot machines and blackjack tables; libraries provide multiple desks, computer terminals, microfilm viewers, and copiers, as well as multiple copies of popular books; and airports and bus stations provide many entrances, ticket desks, docking and loading stations, waiting areas, telephones, lockers, and toilets. Often facilities are placed in various locations so that people have less distance to go to get to them. Thus office buildings, large stores, shopping malls, and sports stadiums often have multiple entrances, stairwells, escalators, elevators, telephones, food stands, restaurants, water fountains, trash cans, and toilets. These may be placed on different floors and at different locations on the same floor. Commercial and public organizations normally hire duplicate personnel to be able to provide faster service to the public. These include clerks, waitresses, agents, officials, stewards and stewardesses, cashiers, and guards. Often duplicate items are made available in order that personnel do not have to replace them frequently. Thus stores put multiple copies of most goods on their shelves; vending machines stock numerous duplicates of specific kinds of soft drinks, candy bars, and cigarettes; public toilets are supplied with multiple rolls of toilet paper; and tourist offices provide duplicate copies of brochures.

The provision of services and facilities within a society is adjusted to deal with demand. Thus when more people want a service, additional equipment and personnel are used to provide it. As a result the society reduces the amount of time and energy individuals spend obtaining a service or access to a facility. For example, additional clerks and cashiers are provided when lines of customers become longer, and more public transportation vehicles are provided at times when most people travel to and from work, school, sporting events, parades, and vacation areas, or to visit relatives during holidays.

Within organizations each individual is provided with most of his own equipment to use so that there are no delays in sharing the equipment with others. Thus in an office everyone has their own desk, chair, computer, telephone, telephone book, stapler, dictionary, filing cabinet, and wastebasket. Separate divisions within the organization are assigned their own specialized equipment in order that they can operate more efficiently. For example, each division may have its own photocopier and color printer. Not only do they keep this equipment on their premises, but they do not have to share it with other divisions. Therefore it is more accessible to division personnel and more likely to be available when they want to use it.

Environmental impact produced by conserving time and energy

Human efforts to conserve time and energy markedly increase human impact on the environment. People discard items which require more effort to maintain, restore, or fix than they do to replace. Thus people use disposable napkins, facial tissues, towels, diapers, and menstrual pads rather than cloth ones that need to be washed. Inexpensive items which need repair are normally discarded and replaced with new items.

When you handle paper you discard a great deal of it which is unused. When you write or type something on a piece of paper, often much of the sheet of paper is blank. But when you are finished using the sheet of paper, you find it easier to discard the entire sheet than to cut away the unused portions and use them later. You always have a stack of fresh paper available so it is easier to get a fresh sheet when you want to write or type something else. Normally too, you use one side of a sheet of paper instead of both sides. And you rarely use any of the paper that is sent to you from inside and outside your organization. You don't save it to write on in the future; you throw it away. Fresh paper is cheap and easy to get, so you don't put any effort into using it carefully, protecting it, and reusing it. It's the opposite when we deal with sophisticated appliances and automobiles. Because they are expensive and it takes considerable effort to get them, we use them carefully, protect them, and reuse them. #1372

Expensive items are often repaired until a number of repairs are needed or until the cost of repairs reaches a sizable percentage of the cost of a new replacement.

People are inclined to adopt anything that saves them time and energy, regardless of the cost to the environment. Each individual wants any and every device which will save him time and energy, because each one he uses reduces his tension, or hurt. People want to replace devices which are slower and require more movement and mental effort with devices which are faster and require less movement and mental effort. Moreover, each individual wants to own his own utensils, appliances, equipment, vehicles, and tools so that they are readily available for his personal use. Attempts to share these items with others are costly in terms of time and energy.

I have a personal computer at home, and in order to print my files I initially used a printer at the computer center where I work. But this was quite time consuming. I would carry my data diskette into the center and have to wait until their printer wasn't being used. Then when it was my turn, I would have to put my own ribbon, print head, and paper into the machine. Next I would have to stand there and feed my paper in the printer a sheet at a time. Afterwards I would have to rearrange the equipment back the way it was before I used it. As a result it took several hours to obtain a copy of a report. After a week or two of this I broke down and ordered my own printer to use at home. At home I can leave my printer set up the way I want it and don't have to change anything. Also I bought a printer with an automatic sheet feeder so I don't have to stand around and feed in paper as the printer prints my files. It wasn't cheap, but it's a great timesaver. #1373

This effort to supply every human individual with a full array of items, and multiple copies of many of these items, produces enormous impact on the environment. In addition, multiple copies of facilities, such as schools and hospitals, must be provided so that they are conveniently located for local use. As a result humans do not have to waste time and energy traveling to distant facilities. Again, these multiple copies must be constructed and supplied at the expense of natural areas.

At the same time there is a steadily escalating effort to supply and support each human with an ever larger technological infrastructure. New items and improved items are constantly being invented and adopted which enable humans to accomplish specific tasks with less effort. This equipment is increasingly complicated, and therefore increasingly costly in resources to produce and maintain. As a result each individual human has more and more impact on the environment as the individual is supplied with increasingly elaborate and sophisticated means of conserving time and energy. There is every reason to expect this process to continue.

One reason people adopt expedient measures in dealing with other species is because such measures require less time and energy than ethical alternatives. It takes much less effort to clear-cut or burn a natural area that one wants to convert into a farm or house lot, than it does to remove the individual members of plant and animal species and place them safely in another location. Normally it takes less effort to injure and kill members of other species than it does to avoid harming them.

PROTECTING SELF AND RESOURCES

Brief contents

Detailed contents

Detailed contents

Introduction

People normally go to considerable effort to protect themselves and their resources when they are actually threatened. They seek to protect themselves from attack and mistreatment, and they attempt to protect their resources from being taken by others. The resources they try to protect include food and water, time and energy, property, possessions, jobs, money, reputation, sex, positive reactions, relationships, stimulation, and self-image. People view their resources as an extension of themselves. Therefore, when people protect their resources, they protect themselves. The feeling which encourages people to protect themselves and their resources is anger. Anger enables people to act aggressively. It helps them challenge and drive away others. As a result anger often enables people to protect themselves and maintain access to their resources. People feel anger as soon as they realize others are trying to attack them or take their resources. This often allows them to respond quickly enough to protect themselves and their resources. Signs of anger enable a person to communicate the message, "Don't mess with me, because I can get violent," to others. Anger is an activator. Anger frequently produces fear in those it is directed against that they may be hurt, and it often causes them to retreat.

Another feeling, anxiety, also helps people protect themselves and their resources. People feel anxiety when they think they might be harmed or lose resources, whereas they feel anger when they are in the process of being harmed or losing resources or just after it has happened. Anxiety helps people avoid future threats, whereas anger helps people protect themselves and their resources from present threats. (Anxiety is considered in the chapter on Taking Precautions in this volume.)

Situations frequently occur in which both parties, the individual who is initially threatened and the person who initiates the threat, are engaged in defending themselves and their own resources from each other. When one is attacked or one's resources are attacked, in order to defend oneself, one frequently attacks the other party, who in turn usually seeks to protect himself by attacking back. Thus if A damages B's property, and B files a lawsuit against A, then A may use every means at his disposal to protect his money, reputation, and other resources from the threat of B's lawsuit.

How people threaten others and their resources

People threaten other people in a variety of ways. These include the following:

1. Causing them physical injury
2. Causing them discomfort and pain
3. Causing them hurt
4. Taking their time, energy, and mental focus
5. Doing or saying things inconsistent with their models
6. Making them do things inconsistent with their models
7. Preventing them from executing their models
8. Using their resources without asking
9. Taking their resources
10. Cheating them out of their resources
11. Damaging or destroying their resources
12. Taking resources which they expect to obtain or receive
13. Causing them to lose their resources
14. Failing to provide resources which they expect to receive
15. Keeping resources which are loaned
16. Not reciprocating
17. Combining threats

1. Causing them physical injury

People threaten the ability of others to function when they do something which can cause them physical injury. They may do so by accident or intent. People injure others through practical jokes, play, sports, car accidents, punishments, hazing, trying to get others to do what they want, assault, rape, war, torture, poisoning, pollution, and medical practice.

> The majority of drivers don't give pedestrians the right of way. I can't tell you how many times I've almost been mowed down by some jerk when I was crossing at an intersection. The same thing happens when I'm walking through the parking lot at a shopping mall. You'd think

with all that space drivers would go around you. But no, they drive right for you. It's like they can't see you, even though they are staring right at you. You have to move out of their way if you don't want to be run over. This problem is not limited to town. Every year several people are hit by cars and killed on the local highways. Often they are kids walking along the side of the road or riding their bicycles. #1374

A friend of ours, Glen, was dancing with a girl, Olive, in a club when a guy approached them. This guy had been staring at Glen all night and Glen thought the guy must be gay. Then the guy punched Glen in the face. When we asked the guy why he hit Glen, he said Olive was his ex-girlfriend and Olive was using Glen to make him jealous. Glen felt exploited by Olive and is still looking for a perfect way to embarrass her and get revenge. #1375

During the baseball season one of our best players, Andrew, was very successful when batting against a pitcher named Todd on an opposing team. After Andrew got four hits in four trips to the plate, Todd threw a pitch at Andrew's head, sending him sprawling to the ground. This made Andrew and our whole team very angry. The next time Andrew was at bat he pretended the bat slipped out of his hand and it went flying and just grazed Todd's head. The result was a brawl between the teams. #1376

Four male friends of mine were walking back to their apartment when a group of more than fifteen guys jumped them. The four were beaten up pretty bad, and their injuries consisted of broken ribs, a broken arm, and a broken nose. I asked them why they didn't run. One told me, "I didn't want people to think I was a pussy. I'd rather lose a fight than run away." Another told me, "I thought about running, but none of the others did. If I ran and they stayed, everyone would say I was a wimp." #1377

Vincent and Judy were very capable students and took many of the same courses. Both were asked to present student research papers at a convention in Montreal. While they were at the convention they went to a dance and had too much to drink. Vincent asked Judy if he could walk her back to her room and she agreed. Their rooms were right across the hall from each other. Vincent invited Judy into his room to talk and have another drink. Judy felt it was safe enough, but after a drink Vincent got fresh. Judy was very upset and left his room. Vincent didn't like being rejected and followed her into her room and beat her badly. Another student who was in the hall managed to get Vincent away from Judy and took Judy to the hospital. She was cut and bruised and had a concussion. Vincent was very lucky that she didn't press charges. #1378

In addition, people may threaten to injure others.

A good friend of mine often gives me a ride home from work. Unfortunately he likes to show off by racing around curves and by speeding up very fast in a highway entrance lane to get ahead of cars traveling in the regular lane. This bothers me because he is taking unnecessary risks, but I appreciate the rides and don't want to say anything. #1379

When we were kids we would sneak around the neighborhood at night, hide behind bushes, and see what different families were doing in their houses. We would pretend we were commandos or Indians. We quit after this man came out his back door and threatened to shoot us if we did it again. #1380

After my girlfriend got pregnant, her father kept threatening to kill me. I thought he would too. Once he got drunk and rammed his car into mine when I was in it. #1381

2. Causing them discomfort and pain

People cause others discomfort when they make them stand or kneel for a long time; when they cause them to be cold, hot, wet, itchy, thirsty, or hungry; when they prevent them from breathing; and when they keep them immobilized.

It's no fun when you have to go to bed without dinner, because your mom wants to punish you or she doesn't get around to fixing it. #1382

People cause others pain by hitting, slapping, pinching, poking, biting, kicking, spanking, squeezing, or twisting them, and by stepping on them or causing them to fall.

One time when I was a kid, several of us were standing in a doorway waiting for the rain to let up so we could get to the next building. One

143

boy decided to run for it, and as he took off I tripped him. I know now it was a mean thing to do. But he fell, then he turned and shook his fist at me. Naturally, I claimed I hadn't done it. #1383

People may also threaten to cause others discomfort and pain.

Sometimes all three of my young children try to get attention at the same time by making as much noise as possible. Then I bang my fist on the kitchen table, which scares them, and I send them upstairs to their rooms. My husband takes a wooden spoon and advances upstairs. The spoon is just to scare them, but it works, and we finally have some peace and quiet again. #1384

3. Causing them hurt

People frequently feel hurt by others. They may feel hurt as a result of criticism, rejection, or embarrassment. Others may interrupt, ignore, disagree with, criticize, insult, ridicule, accuse, humiliate, argue with, yell at, or swear at them, or treat them rudely or with disrespect in some other way.

I get really provoked when someone speaks to me only when we are alone, say when we pass each other in the hall. But when they are with a group of their friends they won't even acknowledge me. It's like they don't think I am worth speaking to unless they have to. #1385

I babysat for a couple, and everything went fine while I was there. The kids went to bed on time, I picked up their toys, and then I watched TV until their parents returned. They paid me and I went home. About an hour later their father showed up at my house. He was really mad and insisted I return the money I had stolen. I told him I didn't take anything, but he didn't believe me. He gave me a warning and went home. The next morning he phoned and apologized. He said the envelope with the money was in the kids' room and they were playing "store" with the money. #1386

My family traveled out west to Alberta for my cousin's wedding and we stayed with my uncle. At the same time some close friends of ours at home took a bus tour through the western provinces. These friends had several free days at the end of their bus tour and phoned us up at my uncle's house. They expected us to invite them over and they hoped to be able to stay with us. We hadn't known they would have any free time, we had no means of providing them with transportation to get there, and we couldn't ask my uncle to put them up because he had been in a rotten frame of mind since we arrived. One thing that had upset him was that we were unable to get there in time for his birthday party. We explained to these friends that we were already dealing with an impossible situation and didn't dare irritate the uncle further. However, the friends reprimanded us for not inviting them over. At the end of our trip, when everyone had returned to Prince Edward Island, it was still clear that the friends were unhappy that we hadn't invited them to stay at my uncle's place. Another thing, when they called us in Alberta, Mom was taking a nap because she was trying to recover from my uncle's busy schedule. But as she rushed to answer the phone, she fell down the stairs and hurt her knee. Mom had to spend the rest of her stay with her leg up taking pain killers, and her knee still continues to bother her. Mom has told these friends how she got the knee injury and that it ruined her holiday, but the friends just gloss over this because they consider the fact they were "slighted" more significant. [1387]

When people feel hurt they may become angry and they may react aggressively.

My wife and I were talking to our daughter on the telephone. When I started to criticize our daughter, my wife told me to get off the phone. I felt humiliated and angry. [1388]

Groups of young males in cars commonly yell at and sass pedestrians. They'll yell sexual things at women or comments about a male's physical appearance. It gets you quite angry and you wish you had a good means of revenge. Once a sports car drove close to me and the guy in the passenger's seat spit on me. I wrote down the license-plate number and reported them to the police. [1389]

Some guy called my girlfriend at work and asked what color panties she was wearing. When she didn't respond he started begging her to tell him. She was quite upset and called the phone company to report him. But of course she didn't know who he was. [1390]

I was standing waiting for a trolley in Toronto, when I saw this girl and guy half a block away walking quickly in my direction. The girl was barefoot and had a thin piece of cloth around her which barely covered her large breasts which flopped up and down as she walked. I didn't realize it was so obvious I was staring, but when the couple passed me the guy glared at me and said something in an angry voice I didn't understand. #1391

I had an awkward time when I walked into a group of guys who were talking about me. They were saying that all I'm good for is a piece of tail. I was really insulted and gave those bastards a good blasting out. #1392

My sister is nineteen years old and my brother is eighteen. Each becomes irate if the other dares to set foot in their bedroom without being invited to do so. This weekend my sister was home from university, and my brother went in her room and sat on her bed to chat and catch up on her news. My sister began to scream at him. She pulled him off her bed, shoved him out of her room, and slammed and locked her door. My brother was hurt and angry. He shouted loud insults through the closed door and stomped downstairs. #1393

Last weekend my father was driving my brother and my brother's friend home from town. My brother was talking to his friend about surveying, and said "thingamajig" to refer to a piece of equipment. Dad interrupted their conversation to provide the correct word, which was theodolite. My brother replied, "Yeah, whatever," and continued talking to his friend. Dad drove the rest of the way home in silence, but when they got home he began to yell angrily at my brother. My brother yelled back at Dad, because he didn't see anything wrong with what he'd done. Then he marched upstairs to his room and slammed the door. #1394

My mother mentioned that someone she knew was suffering from kidney stones. My brother explained to my mother what kidney stones were, what caused them, and the various treatments doctors use. I felt sure Mom already knew this, but she let my brother continue without interrupting him. Dad, however, became irate and suggested that my brother should skip the rest of his education and go straight into practicing medicine. He accused my brother of being a know-it-all, and wondered aloud if there was anything under the sun that my brother did not know. My brother became angry at his remarks. He was about to shout something at my father, but stopped himself and stomped off to his room. Dad accused him of running away, and spent the next hour muttering to himself and everyone around about his know-it-all son. [#1395]

4. Taking their time, energy, and mental focus

People may cause a person to lose time and energy. Thus they may cause him to do unnecessary work.

> When you regularly wash dishes, some of the practices of your family members produce a lot of extra work for you. "When my brother eats his dinner, he has to have his vegetables on a different plate than his meat and potatoes. I can't understand why. It all goes down the same way. And he can't use the same glass twice when he wants a second glass of milk. It drives me crazy, because I end up with extra dishes to wash." "It really bugs me when people don't rinse out their glasses after they've had milk. I hate trying to wash out the ring of dried milk at the bottom of the glass." "I can't stand people who leave their dishes on the table or in the sink and don't rinse them. It's gross to see the food dry and harden on a plate. Then you have to scrub and scrub to get it off." [#1396]

> People frequently get upset with others in their household when they do things which inconvenience them. "I get upset when someone gets out of the shower and doesn't wipe their feet. This leaves the floor all wet. Of course I don't know this when I go in the bathroom wearing my socks. They get wet and I have to change them." "The thing that bugs me most is when someone leaves a layer of dirt in the bathtub when they finish their bath. So when you want a bath you have to clean the tub first. Otherwise you scratch your ass on the bottom of the tub. It's not funny." [#1397]

People also disturb, annoy, or hassle a person, and thereby prevent him from focusing on and doing the things he wants to do.

> There are all kinds of things that annoy others and make it impossible for them to concentrate on what they are trying to do. "I can't bear to be in the same room with Dad when he drinks his tea, because he slurps so loudly." "My boyfriend crunches potato chips like they are going out of style. 'CRUNCH, CRUNCH, CRUNCH.' It's disgusting and really annoys me." "My aunt has the irritating habit of grinding her teeth,

which she does when she plays cards or watches TV. You can barely hear it, but it is just enough noise to really bother you. The funny thing is that no one in the family will tell her she does it. We just sit there and endure the torture." "I hate people who snap their chewing gum. I was in a hospital waiting room and the person next to me kept snapping her gum so loudly I couldn't hear myself think." "My sister was sitting in the corner reading, and Mom was filing her nails. All of a sudden my sister jumped up, ran across the room, and ripped the file out of Mom's hands. The sound annoyed her that much." "I was sitting in class and the girl behind me kept blowing bubbles with her gum and then slurping the gum back in her mouth. I couldn't concentrate on what the professor was saying because I was so busy thinking of ways to kill her. And to make matters worse, it was a three-hour-long class." "What I hate most are the people who sit behind me and kick or push my chair repeatedly with their foot or knee. Sometimes this happens when I'm in a movie or on a trip. It makes it impossible to watch the movie, read, listen to others, or rest. They must be the most inconsiderate people on earth." Others are annoyed by sounds such as someone humming, a TV set blaring away, a woodpecker banging on a tree, or tinfoil being folded. "Things that happen first thing in the morning can irritate me the most. Recently it has been my landlady singing. It's so bad, she sounds like a cow in labor." [1398]

I go to the library to avoid distractions when I need to study. But sometimes there are distractions in the library too. Recently a guy near me started to cough. I was so deep in thought that it startled me and I jumped. But he kept coughing as though he had a scratch in his throat. It was very distracting. I kept thinking, "When is he ever going to stop?" He had no respect for the rest of us, because he never got up to get a drink of water. Another time there was a sharp click, click, click noise. I finally figured out that someone was clipping their fingernails. [1399]

Whenever my daughter starts to sing or whistle, my son yells, "QUIET!" as angrily as possible. He claims he can't concentrate on his homework when she makes noise. On the other hand, he has no problem leaving the TV on while he does his homework. [1400]

In high school the guy who sat behind me in French class used to run his fingers through my hair. It gave me the willies every time. No matter how many times I told him to stop, he never would. It's what bugged me most about school. [1401]

Our choir director can't stand someone seated in the front row swinging their foot while he plays the piano. He says it disturbs his concentration because he watches the foot going back and forth. The other day I decided to put this to the test. I sat in the front row and halfway through the practice I started swinging my foot. Within a few minutes he played a wrong note, and of course he blamed it on my foot. #1402

Anyone with a fourteen-year-old brother knows what irritating means. My brother is a sports nut. Every evening he gets his faithful hockey stick and ball out and heads for the porch. All you hear is that ball hitting anything and everything. You don't dare walk in front of him because you enter a combat zone. His specialty is hitting everyone on the rear with the ball. I got a bruise that lasted a week, which taught me never to turn my back on him. When hockey season is over, out comes the baseball glove. He pounds the ball into the glove as hard as he can for hours on end. Talk about annoying. #1403

People take resources from a person when they interrupt him and prevent him from concentrating on and doing what he would rather do. For example, they may try to get his attention, make a sales pitch, or assign him something to do.

If you want to cause true unhappiness in the world, ask one of your children to help you do something, like set the table, cut some vegetables, feed the cat, or shovel snow off the steps. My children try to ignore the request, complain angrily, or tell their sibling I said the sibling has to do it. It's clear they hate to do anything which interferes with what they are doing, such as watching TV, playing a video game, reading, or talking on the phone. #1404

Dad would come home in the afternoon and find the simplest things not done around the house. Things like bringing in the milk or the mail. Dad told us, "Shut that TV off right now. It's hypnotizing you, and you aren't dealing with reality." #1405

I was watching TV when Dad walked into the room. The TV show was half over, and Dad wanted to understand what was happening in the show and began asking me questions. But I couldn't answer the questions and follow what was happening in the show at the same time. So I said,

"Dad, will you be quiet? I'll tell you in a minute." Other times Mom and Dad will get to talking about something and they won't stop. I'll tell them, "I'm trying to listen to this program. Go out in the kitchen if you want to talk." #1406

Sometimes when Dad takes his afternoon nap, someone phones him. Even if we tell the person that Dad is sleeping and doesn't want to be disturbed, the person may insist on speaking to him. I'll go in and wake Dad, who gets very mad. "What is it?" he'll say. "Someone wants you on the phone." Dad will ask, "Is it five o'clock yet?" "Well, almost," I'll reply. #1407

It seems that every time I take a bus over to Fredericton to see my boyfriend, I get stuck sitting next to some lonely, elderly lady. Don't get me wrong. They are nice and everything, but they seem to talk constantly about their family, friends, grandchildren, and problems. I've spent an entire trip looking at family pictures. Sometimes I am tired and just don't feel like talking to anyone. I become very irritated and touchy, but I still haven't found a way to politely say, "Shut up!" #1408

I hate it when someone calls me in the evening at home who is selling something or collecting for a charity. I feel I have to answer the phone because it might be an important call. I hate these interruptions and feel it is a major invasion of privacy. So I tell them to send me anything they want to say in the mail and I'll look at it when it is convenient for me to do so. Lots of times they can't be bothered sending me anything. #1409

Nothing is worse than going into your office to get a lot of work done and having a colleague drop in with an hour or more to kill who wants to chew the fat. The longer they stay the more my frustration level climbs, but I don't want to be rude and ask them to leave. The best I can do is say I have to go somewhere else. This means I have to leave my work area and come back later. The bad thing is that I lose my opportunity to really get a lot done. #1410

When I decided to return home early from my vacation, I switched my ticket to another airline and had to change planes in Los Angeles. But when I went to change planes this eager beaver working behind the ticket counter decided my ticket must be bogus and did everything she could to prove it. I guess she was trying to establish what a diligent employee she was. Even though she wasted half an hour of my time trying, my ticket was completely legitimate and she eventually gave it up. Needless to say, I did not appreciate this. #1411

5. Doing or saying things inconsistent with their models

A person's models are an important resource for the person, because they enable him to survive, satisfy his feelings, and maintain a positive self-image. When others say or do things which are inconsistent with a person's models, they create tension for the person. The greater this inconsistency, the more the person considers his resources to be under attack. (See the chapter on Establishing Consistency in a later volume.)

My older brother irks me tremendously. I can't stand it when he stands in front of the mirror in the mornings and brags about himself. He always says the same things. He talks about how nice his hair is, how good looking he is, and how all the women go crazy over him. It bugs me so much it almost turns my stomach. Every time I tell him to shut up, he just brags some more. #1412

One of my roommates has a habit that gets under my skin. She constantly talks about her boyfriend. You can come up with any topic and Jerry has done it, plans to do it, or is thinking about it. All of us, especially me, tease her about this. #1413

I think it is really disgusting when people leave used condoms lying around, such as in parks and on campuses. Others agree with me. "People leave them wherever. They are really tacky." "I told my roommate, 'I don't care if you have sex in our bedroom, but you can damn well flush the rubbers down the toilet.'" #1414

Most people do not appreciate being called the wrong name. "My name is Anna, and I hate being called Annie. When people call me Annie I refuse to respond." "I see red when anyone calls me Jeannie. My name is Jeannine. When someone calls me Jeannie, I correct them. I really don't like Jeannine, but I hate Jeannie even more." #1415

I gave a male friend a ride in my fiancé's car, and someone called my fiancé to tell him before I even got back home. The person who tattled was incensed that I used my fiancé's car for this purpose. #1416

I contracted with a publishing house to publish an architectural book for me and paid them with a publishing grant I had received from the government. The quality of the photographs was a very important issue for me and the publisher led me to believe I would be very satisfied with their work. But when the book was published the color in the photographs wasn't true. I was very upset and refused to let the book be released. I'm going to hire a lawyer to try to get the money back from the publisher. #1417

My father came home drunk from a Christmas office party. My mother was so angry he was drunk that she broke her favorite dish over his head. My father objected to her using her favorite dish and went outside and sat in the backyard. #1418

A man in our neighborhood had a number of pets, which he claimed he loved very much. His neighbors liked his pets because the pets frequently visited and were fed at the neighbors' houses. However, whenever the man decided that one of his pets didn't like him or caused him inconvenience, or whenever he found a new pet whose color better fit his color scheme, his original pet would disappear. He told one neighbor that he had gotten rid of one pet by hanging it. So when more of his pets disappeared, his neighbors feared he had strangled them, and were very upset. The neighbors asked him about the missing pets, and he told them he had taken them to the humane society to find them a good home. But when neighbors called the humane society, they were told this was completely untrue, and that the man had never contacted the humane society. Thereafter when the neighbors asked the man about the pets, he repeatedly changed his story as to what he had done with them. On the insistence of the neighbors, the humane society investigated, but they said without proof he was strangling his pets, they could do nothing. Basically, the position of the humane society was that they can intervene if a person starves or beats his animal, but if all the person does is kill the animal, that is his prerogative. #1419

I grew up in a rural area on a small farm. Therefore there were always a lot of animals around. I love animals. They can become good friends and help pass many boring hours. Nothing upsets me to greater extremes than seeing someone being cruel to an animal. I have seen a lot of animals, especially dogs, kicked, slapped, or hit unnecessarily. This drives me nuts and makes me very angry. My whole family agrees with me on this issue. We try to help the situation by taking in many little animals who need a place to stay, much to Mom's dismay. #1420

6. Making them do things inconsistent with their models

People sometimes coerce a person to do things that he does not want to do, because it is contrary to his personal models. This may be something that the person considers wrong, gross, meaningless, inefficient, or stupid. The person may feel under pressure to comply in order to please others, because he wants something from others, because others control his resources, or because others have power over him.

One summer I worked for the forestry service on a team surveying logging and recreation roads. The head of my team was very destructive. He delighted in chopping off any plants and branches which might be in his way. Whenever he encountered wildlife he would shoot it with his pistol or chase it and try to catch it. I found I could clear a view for the surveying instruments just as fast by simply bending a few limbs out of the way and intertwining them into the other limbs. However, the head of my team didn't like the fact I wasn't chopping everything down and kept pressuring me to do so. #1421

When I was in graduate school we had to take a required course with a senior professor, and all he wanted us to do was to write papers and do research designs based on his personal theory. Unfortunately this professor had a really cockamamie theory which did not fit reality, so the course was a total waste of time. However, in order to pass the course we had to act like proper disciples and show the greatest respect for his theory. Each week one of us had to give a presentation of work we were doing glorifying this theory. Well the day came when I had to make my presentation. That day the professor brought a visiting professor from Harvard to our class and after I gave my presentation the man from Harvard ripped it to shreds. I agreed with everything he said because I considered the professor's theory a pile of crap. However, I had to stand there and defend his theory to the death in order to pass the course. #1422

7. Preventing them from executing their models

People are frequently prevented or hindered from executing their models. This occurs when someone tells them that they can not do what they want to do; when others refuse or fail to cooperate with them; when they are rejected for a job, educational program, or a relationship that they want; when others provide them with inadequate goods, services, support, or cooperation; or when authorities take their passport, driving license, fishing license, or credit cards away from them.

> I get angry when the purchasing department at my company won't let me buy the equipment I need to do my job. [#1423]

> My younger sister is underage and used my old driving license as an ID (identification card) to get into clubs. When the police caught her they also took my current driving license away. I told the police I didn't know my sister was doing this, but they refused to believe me. Losing my license was very inconvenient, because I had to find another way to get to and from work and to take my kids to their babysitter. I was more than a little pissed off with my sister. After a week, the police decided I really didn't know my sister was doing this and returned my license. I was quite relieved to get it back. [#1424]

> When sporting teams compete against each other, players, coaches, fans, and family members all have specific objectives, and anything which interferes with these objectives makes them irritated and angry. For one thing, they want their team to win and the opposing team to lose. If the other team scores, if the other team is winning, if a player on their own team is injured, if a referee calls a foul against a player on their own team, or if a referee fails to call a foul against the other team, people are likely to feel annoyed and upset. Fans express their irritation by criticizing and insulting players, coaches, and referees; by yelling and throwing things; and by fighting with fans of the opposing team. Players and coaches express their irritation by criticizing and insulting players and referees, and players physically attack players on the other team. Family members are also upset if their relative does not get sufficient playing time or is injured. Family members criticize coaches, players, and family members of the other players. [#1425]

How people threaten others and their resources

People may also prevent a person from doing what he wants when he wants to do it. For example, they may get in his way or slow him down.

Many drivers experience considerable anger over delays, near accidents, and the inability to do what they want to do. Their anger is directed at traffic, other drivers, pedestrians, road conditions, the weather, and traffic lights and signs.

Drivers get upset and mad when someone prevents them from doing what they want to do or nearly involves them in an accident. "I entered a taxi and as the taxi tried to pull away from the curb, the driver yelled at another driver, 'You wouldn't let me out if your life depended on it. God damn it!' Later when others wanted to pull into his lane he wouldn't let them enter. He also got annoyed at pedestrians crossing the street in front of him, and muttered, 'They think they own the road,' and 'You do that again fellow, and you won't have to worry about walking.'" "I was in a car with Edward, a friend of mine. He almost went nuts because none of the cars would stop so he could get out of his driveway. He stated, 'Come on, let me out! Look at that ignorant (inconsiderate) old lady who won't let me out.' Later we passed a car that was trying to enter the street from a parking lot and Edward commented, 'No one gave me a break, so I'm not giving you one.' But he did stop to let a driver out of a restaurant lot. The other driver wasn't sure what Edward was doing and Edward became quite impatient with him and began waving and saying, 'Go! Go! Jesus, man, go! I don't have all day.'" "A friend of mine was driving when a half-ton truck pulled out in front of him. My friend roared out, 'The crazy country folks are in town today.' He pulled up beside the truck and yelled, 'Watch where you're going, you hick! You're not in the country now.'" "When I was driving with my sixty-year-old mother she was almost cut off by a taxi. She said, 'Jesus, those taxi drivers think they own the streets,' and she yelled at the driver, 'You stupid fool!' Later a young man walked right in front of her and she roared, 'Do you want your tail? You keep doing this and you won't be able to walk across the street.'" "Jane and I were driving on the highway one Sunday afternoon. When we were approaching a town a small boy ran in front of us. Jane slammed on the brakes and yelled, 'You idiot! Are you trying to get run over? Didn't anybody ever tell you to look both ways before you cross the street? Dumb kid!' As we drove through town a car pulled out ahead of us and drove only thirty kilometers an hour. Jane passed him and said, 'Go a little slower, Gramps.

You might get there by Christmas.' When another driver failed to signal a turn, Jane said, 'Stupid fool. Don't you ever use your signals?' Then when a truck pulled in front of us she blew her horn and yelled, 'Goddamn truck drivers. They have no consideration for others.' When another truck passed us, Jane stated, 'Jesus Christ! Why don't you take the whole goddamn road?'"

People can get upset over any delay. "When you are stopped by a red light, it's legal to turn right, provided it is safe to do so. But sometimes the driver ahead of you just sits there and fails to turn right until the light turns green. I can get pretty mad because I've got better things to do than wait around." "Roger and I were circling various blocks looking for a space, when we saw a car in a space ahead with its back-up lights on. We went flying up to the space and sat there and waited for the car to vacate the space. There were six cars behind us and two of them blew their horns. Roger yelled at the driver, 'Jesus, man, are you going to back up or are you going to wait for Christmas?' The car finally pulled out and we drove into the space." "The taxi I was riding in was just behind a woman driver who was carefully negotiating her car between piles of snow that had been dumped on the sides and in the middle of the street. The taxi driver muttered, 'C'mon lady, don't bother stopping. You've got enough room to drive a tractor-trailer through there.'"

A common cause of ire is the difficulty in finding a parking space. "I was riding with Gary, a friend of mine, and we were circling the block looking for a parking space. Suddenly we saw a car pull out of a space half a block ahead. Gary sped up so he could get there first, but someone else drove into the spot. Gary went crazy, blew his horn, yelled, 'You goddamn bastard! You took my spot,' and floored the accelerator." "This summer Mom drove us downtown to buy a birthday present. We looked for a parking space and she finally found one and pulled into it. I told her she was in a space reserved for unloading trucks. She pulled back out, cursing up a storm. 'Jesus! How many of these spaces do they need for loading anyway?' We continued to look for a space and finally gave up and decided to go to a shopping mall. When we got to the mall there were no spaces even close to the entrance. Mom stated, 'I can't wait until winter when all these goddamn tourists go back home.' Mom finally located a place some distance away. She flew into the space and just about hit the car in front of us. The old man sitting in the car facing us just about had a heart attack." "I was riding with Tim, who was determined he was going to get a parking space at the shopping mall right by the

156

front door. When we saw a parking space with a motorcycle in it, Tim stated, 'Look at that damn bike taking up a whole space.' When we saw a truck occupying two spaces, Tim remarked, 'I hate those farmers who don't know how to park. They think they are the only people around.'" "It's very frustrating when a driver parks his car across two parking spaces so there isn't enough room for you to park there too. The other driver probably wants to leave plenty of room so he can get out of the space easily. Some people get so pissed off when this happens that they've made up cards to put on the other car which say, 'Thanks For Taking Two Parking Spaces. I Had To Park Two Blocks Away You Stupid Inconsiderate Bastard.'" "Many people from the country hate to shop in Charlottetown because they have to deal with 'city' traffic. You can drive around and around searching for a parking space. When I'm in the car with Mom I keep telling her to calm down and we will eventually find one. She tries to keep from saying the F-word, so she makes remarks like 'You old Jeezers,' 'The son of a bitch,' and 'You old quiffer.' I continually tell her to park in the parking garage, but she won't do it. She has to find a place within fifty feet of her destination. If she has to walk any distance, all you hear when you get home is 'Well, I had to walk two goddamn miles to the store.' Looking for a parking space with my aunt is a laugh because she won't swear. Instead she grits her teeth and places curses upon the other drivers, such as 'I hope you get a flat tire,' and 'I hope both your wheels fall off, buddy.'" "It's quite funny to drive around when you have time to kill and watch people look for a parking space. You can tell they are infuriated, because you see them pull out recklessly in front of other drivers, use obscene gestures, and carelessly cut back and forth between lanes without signaling."

Another problem is right of way. "I was walking through the large parking lot of a shopping mall and saw an elderly gentleman drive around the south end of a row of cars. At the same time another elderly gentleman drove around the north end of the same row of cars. There was only room for one car in the lane, and both cars met face to face halfway down the lane. Both drivers sat in their cars and blew their horn at each other. This continued for some time with neither gentleman budging. Finally one man reluctantly backed his car up far enough for the other to pass. The other driver sped away at an incredible speed."

People can also feel pressured to hurry up and comply with the wishes of other drivers. "When you return to your car you are likely to have one or more cars waiting for your space. They watch you approach the car, unlock it, put your parcels in the back, buckle up your seat belt, start the car, and try to back out. It both intimidates me and infuriates me at the same time. I shouldn't have to hurry just because some bozo wants my parking space! What I want to do is turn on my radio and sit in my car and sing until all the other drivers who are waiting give up and leave. Maybe that sounds spiteful, but that's how I feel. I'm not alone either. Other people I talk to feel the same way." #1426

One has limited time and energy, and interference prevents one from accomplishing one's goals, or makes it more difficult to do so. Also, the more difficult it is to accomplish one's current goal, the less time and energy one has available to pursue one's other goals and models, and the more frustration one feels. (See the chapter on Conserving Time and Energy in this volume.)

8. Using their resources without asking

There are many ways in which people attempt to use a person's resources without asking. People frequently do not request permission to walk across a person's yard, park in their driveway, pick their flowers, take fruit from their trees, hunt or fish on their land, use their wharf, or have sex with their mate. Family members and roommates sometimes take each other's clothes, use their cosmetics, consume their food or drinks, and use their favorite cup or glass. In addition, when one is temporarily absent others may take over. They may sit in one's chair; change the channel one is watching on the television set; use one's desk; look at the magazine, newspaper, or book one is in the middle of reading; or park in one's parking space.

It's quite annoying to arrive at work and find someone else parked in my space. I'm not allowed to take another space in the assigned lot, and have to search for room in the public lot some distance away. This costs me an extra ten minutes or more. Every time it happens I get quite peeved and go report the other car to the authorities. #1427

One problem I find as a secretary is having staff use my office in the evenings and over weekends. Not only do they see the letters I am typing for others, but they move things around my desk so I can't find them. They also change the settings on my computer and printer and don't take the trouble to change them back. #1428

This first of July there was a fireworks display at the local park. On the shore facing the park, hundreds of people put their chairs and blankets on other people's private lawns to get a better view. I'm certain they never asked permission from the homeowners. If it had been my lawn, I'd be out putting up a barbed-wire fence the very next day. [#1429]

9. Taking their resources

Some people take and keep another person's resources for themselves. They may shoplift; rob a house or apartment; steal a car; put a fence inside someone else's property line; take a person's job; take credit for their work and ideas; sue them; kidnap their children; persuade their mate to leave and join them; and steal radios, cameras, umbrellas, clothing, luggage, or other possessions that are left unattended in public places.

At some garage sales and flea markets doors are not opened before a specific time. Therefore there is usually a line of people waiting to get in. One woman, who is a dealer in used goods, arrives at every sale just before it opens and walks up to the front of the line ostensibly to talk to people there. But she remains in front with her back to the door so when the door finally opens she is the first inside. She does this at every sale and it is very obvious to everyone what she is doing. I think she is strongly disliked for doing this. I know I resent it. Not only does she cause others who have been waiting in line to get in later than they would if she weren't there, but she gets first choice of goods. [#1430]

Last Friday night it was really stormy outside, and someone stole our barbecue unit from our backyard. They must have seen it there beforehand and then waited for a good opportunity to take it. The wind was so noisy outside, there's no way we could have heard them. [#1431]

At a party recently I heard a man tell a friend of his how he had stolen a neighbor's cow. He was celebrating openly, and said he had his meat for the winter. His friend is inclined to do the same kind of thing. [#1432]

When I'm traveling and need some work, I go in a bar and convince the manager I can do a better job playing the piano and getting customers than the person he already has working there. I'm usually successful. I get the job, and the other guy's out of luck. [#1433]

I hired a student with my research grant to take photographs for me. I taught the student how to take the kind of photographs I wanted and told him what subjects I was interested in. I picked him to do the job because he was capable and could do the work without constant supervision. He did a good job, and I continued to hire him, and over a number of years I paid him several thousand dollars for his work. At the end of this time the student stated that he wanted to publish the photographs himself that he had taken. If he published them, he would hold the copyright and I would not have the right to use them for my research. I felt very threatened and upset with him, and I felt wronged. The photographs were an integral part of my research. If I had known he planned to use the photographs himself, I would have hired someone else. However, my research grant had been spent on him, and I didn't have money or time to hire someone else. Moreover, the student would never have taken any photographs if I hadn't hired him to do so. I felt betrayed and that I could no longer trust him. #1434

My husband and I hired a babysitter who looked fine, had lots of experience, and had raised several children of her own. She came to our home from Monday through Friday and was there from early in the morning until my husband returned from work about five o'clock. Occasionally she would take our child, Anita, out during the day. Two months after we hired her we began to notice that some things were missing around the house, but we didn't suspect the babysitter. Then one day I came home early from work with a bad cold. The babysitter was on her way out with a bag full of stuff which she said was for Anita. She said she'd be back in an hour. I had a feeling something was wrong so I insisted she take the rest of the day off and said I would take care of Anita. She objected strenuously that I needed my rest. But I finally won and took the bag away from her. There were lots of our things in the bag, including two of my husband's new white shirts which had never been opened. I fired her and never heard from her again. #1435

I hired a very capable employee for my store named Allison. Allison had a master's degree, was very pleasant, worked hard, and always took the initiative to help others and find things to do in the store. For example, she studied the electronic-cash-register manual in order to learn how to do everything with the machine. I could not have been more pleased and I gave her more and more responsibility and she was in charge whenever

I was out of the store. Then I noticed that when she put aside items in the store to buy later, there were no records of purchases when she took the items home. When I asked Allison about this she said she had bought them when another store employee was working the cash register. But when I talked to the other employee she said Allison had never bought anything from her. Allison had taken a large number of items from the store without paying for them. I watched her and checked the records. I discovered she was reporting that she was working more hours than she was actually there. Also she was faking returns of merchandise. She would write out false returns from hypothetical customers in order to take money from the cash register for herself. I went to the police and Allison was charged with theft. She was the most capable employee I had ever hired. I think her interest in the cash-register manual was to discover how to remove cash from the machine. #1436

I heard a report on TV that a quarter of a company's employees engage in serious theft from their company. This isn't small stuff like using office supplies for personal use. Instead this includes things like writing fake invoices and charging fake expenses in order to steal money. #1437

People sometimes mistakenly think a person has taken their resources.

I went into the bathroom to brush my teeth and looked at the hook where my toothbrush was supposed to be. The brand new toothbrush I had bought was missing. I reassured myself that I had put the new toothbrush there, and then I saw red. I stormed out of the bathroom and called, "Where is my new toothbrush?" Nobody answered. "I put it in the bathroom," I called louder. "Did you look on the bathroom counter?" Mom asked. I stomped back in the bathroom and moved things around roughly. "No, there is nothing here." "Then I don't know where it is," said Mom. I stomped out of the bathroom to get my old toothbrush. I continued to sulk while I brushed my teeth. Then I realized I was being stupid and childish, and this wasn't the way someone who is twenty-two should act. I told myself, "Oh well, it won't matter in a hundred years." I picked up the towel on the counter to dry my hands and the new toothbrush was underneath. #1438

People can also feel a need to protect their resources when others show signs that they might be interested in taking them.

I hate going to parties with my girlfriend. It really stresses me out to see other guys looking at her. I know I shouldn't be jealous, but I am. #1439

When one of those sleazy women comes around my boyfriend, I see red. She'll not add him to her list if I can help it. #1440

Alcohol is important to young adults and an integral part of their social life. At many house parties a guest will arrive with either a case of beer or a pint of hard liquor under their arm. Usually the host will greet the person with a comment about the liquor. "Great! You've got Alpine (a brand of beer). There's cold beer in the fridge and lots of room." "Hope you brought some mix. We're a little low." The liquor acts as a pass key. If the person arriving has no liquor and is unknown to the host, a cool response is usually given. "Sorry, private party." Such a person is suspected of gatecrashing, or coming only "to drink our beer." Once the last of the alcohol is consumed the party begins to thin out at a fast pace. #1441

10. Cheating them out of their resources

There are also instances in which people cheat a person out of his resources. The person may be overcharged or swindled; goods or services may not be delivered after they are paid for; the person may be promised one price, but charged a higher one; there may be hidden charges; goods may be poorly constructed; and those selling faulty goods may be unwilling to replace them.

When I was traveling in Europe I was conned twice. Once I was staying in a youth hostel and asked someone about going to a performance at the national opera house. He said he was going to the same performance and would get tickets for both of us. I gave him the money for my ticket and never saw him again. Another time in a youth hostel, I met someone on a Friday evening with really weepy eyes who told me he had been to an eye clinic and gotten a prescription. He explained that because the bank was closed he couldn't get money to have the prescription filled. I loaned him some money, but then he came back later and said the prescription cost more than he had realized. So I loaned him some more. I never saw him again either. #1442

I used to live on the second floor of a two-story apartment house. I lived at one end of the floor next to the main stairway. At the other end of the floor there was a door which opened on the back stairway. The door to the back stairway looked just like the doors for the apartments. Drug dealers would bring their clients up the front stairway, take their money for buying drugs, leave their clients at the front stairway, and walk down the hall through the door to the back stairway. Their clients thought the drug dealers were entering a door to an apartment and going to pick up their drugs, but what the dealers did was go down the back stairway and run away with their money. [#1443]

I took a one-caret diamond ring to a jeweler in order to get the ring resized. I'd dealt with this jeweler for years and didn't bother getting a receipt for the ring. Later, after I picked up the ring and returned home, I looked at it carefully and realized the jeweler had switched an inferior diamond for the one I owned. I was very upset, but I didn't have any proof as to the quality of the original diamond, and I didn't have the time to get involved in a legal case. [#1444]

There is so much misleading advertising, you have to be really careful and always read between the lines. One of the leading toothpaste brands states in large letters on their package that their 150 milliliter tube provides "50 percent more." It makes you think you are getting 50 percent more for your money. But in small letters just below they state "than the 100 milliliter size." Then there are the cereal packages which claim that you will get many of your daily nutritional needs from a bowl of their cereal with milk. They neglect to tell you that the nutritional needs come from the milk, not from their cereal. When you take a loan from a bank they call you repeatedly at home and badger you to take an insurance policy on making your payments. They tell you the insurance costs only half a percent of what you've borrowed. They don't tell you that they charge you the half percent every month and that over a year it equals six percent, or almost as much as the cost of your loan. So if you take the insurance you effectively double your interest payments. Then there are car-rental firms which advertise a very competitive base price, but add all kinds of extra charges. For example, one firm charges you an air-conditioner tax, a license-plate tax, and an eleven percent tax because their office is at the airport. But they don't mention specific taxes when you ask them about rates or rent the car. When you go to pay your bill you have to get them to explain if you want to know what the taxes are for. However, most people assume the rental firm is charging standard taxes, and they don't ask the firm for an explanation. There are also the advertising letters from magazine-subscription companies which announce you have won several million dollars. But when you open the envelope you discover that you are a winner only if your name is selected in subsequent draws. #1445

I'm convinced that when stock traders for brokerage houses receive a market buy order they frequently assign it the highest price that occurs in a certain interval of time, and when they receive a market sell order they assign it the lowest price which occurs in an interval of time. They constantly buy and sell for their own account anyway. However, the longer they can wait to fill your order the greater the spread they can achieve between the price they assign you and the price they pay or receive for their own supply. Several times now I have been assigned the worst price of the day, and a price that did not occur until hours after I placed my order. One time I sold shares and was assigned a price that was lower than any that occurred in that stock during the entire day. When I complained, the price was "corrected" to the lowest price during the day in which I placed my order. I believe this practice is so endemic in the brokerage industry that none of the so-called watchdog committees will tackle it. They are interested only in riding herd on the occasional broker or firm which deviates from standard industry practice and gives the industry a bad name. #1446

It really pisses me off when I put money in a candy or drink machine and it won't give me anything back. Sometimes you get the item you want but don't get any change back. I often kick or whack the machine to get my coins returned, but this never works. I feel really cheated and just want to trash the machine. One machine where I work has candy bars placed between coils, and when you put in your coin and choose a bar, a coil turns and the bar is dropped into the chute. However, sometimes the coil turns but the candy bar sticks to the coil and just hangs there instead of falling. No matter how much you shake the damned machine you can't get it loose. After this happened to me a couple of times, I figured out what to do. I decided to put in a second coin so the coil would turn a second time, the first bar would come unstuck, and both the first and second candy bars would fall into the chute. When I tried this the first bar did come unstuck. However, the second one just hung there stuck to the coil.

I read a news item about a student who was killed when a drink machine fell on him. The item said they thought the student was rocking the machine to try to get a free drink. I don't think so. I think the machine cheated him out of his money and he was trying to get the drink he'd paid for.

I think the best thing to do whenever a machine cheats you is to put an "OUT OF ORDER" sign on it. If they won't put in machines that work properly, then they don't deserve to have people buy from them. #1447

11. Damaging or destroying their resources

People also damage or destroy a person's resources, or threaten to do so. This may occur intentionally or unintentionally. For example, someone may drive into a person's car, set fire to their home or business, throw a rock through their window, ruin a tool that they have borrowed from the person, run over their pet, injure or hurt one of their relatives or friends, cause the person to lose their job, say something which damages their reputation, or end a relationship with them.

My brother and I live next to each other. One day my son was playing in my brother's yard and broke a limb off a tree. My brother's wife came over to see my wife and said, "Tell your son to stay out of our yard. He broke a tree." I asked my boy about this. He was crying and said he'd only broken off a limb. He couldn't understand why she accused him of breaking the tree. My wife yelled at my brother's wife, "Get out of my house and don't come back again!" #1448

A female friend told me, "You have to look out for your brothers and sisters and make sure they don't do something stupid and get hurt. Once my younger brother got into a fight and I went to his rescue. Blood is thicker than water, you know." #1449

My roommates and I want to be good natured about loaning each other clothes. But it bugs me when I wash a shirt and a roommate borrows it, then later I find it dropped on the floor where people step on it. #1450

Dry cleaners can be a real problem. Once they ripped a large chunk out of my new wool sweater, and then claimed I must have a mouse at home that had eaten it. Another time they put bleach in a load of my designer shirts. They repeatedly lose buttons and then replace them with a different colored button and thread. #1451

People often park too close when they park alongside other cars. As a result someone may open their door and hit the next car. My grandfather returned to a parking lot to find the paint on his door badly chipped, and he had had his car repainted just the week before. When people hit an empty car and damage it, they usually drive away without reporting the accident. #1452

Our youngest brother borrows one of our cars and cruises around town. Sometimes he shows off by peeling the tires or racing with his buddies. Several times he has damaged one of our cars. When this happens, we shove him around and make him pay to have it fixed. All of us, including our parents and our sisters, lecture him about how irresponsible he is. He admits he made a mistake, but that's all. #1453

12. Taking resources which they expect to obtain or receive

People may try to take resources that a person expects to get. This may be one's positive reactions and relationships, one's customers, one's supply of goods, the job one is in line for, or an inheritance.

It was hot and muggy and I had had a hard day at work. On the way home I kept reminding myself that I had a tall glass of ice-cold apple juice waiting for me. My mouth watered at the thought of the cool, golden liquid trickling down my throat. When I got home I opened the fridge and my fantasy was shattered. There was no juice, and I exploded. My sister, her face red with guilt, said, "I drank it by mistake. It looked so lonely all by itself." I stormed out of the house and headed for the beach to cool off my temper. It was not one of my better days. #1454

When I went to high school in Charlottetown, everyone would drink at the hockey games and then head for McDonald's Restaurant afterwards. McDonald's was the major hangout, and occasionally fights broke out between kids. The only major fights were between the guys from town and the guys from Montague. When a guy from town took out a girl from Montague, the next weekend two or three carloads of guys from Montague would come into McDonald's all riled up, looking for the guy, or for anyone else from town for that matter. #1455

I went shopping for clothes with several of my friends. Noreen tried on a top, and we told her it looked really good on her, which it did, and

Noreen decided to buy it. It looked so good that Ann wanted to try the same top on. So Ann took one from the rack that was the same color, and when she came out of the dressing room it looked good, but not as good as it looked on Noreen. Ann decided she would buy the top too. Now any woman knows that you do not buy the same top as your friend, especially not in the same color! People want to look and feel special and unique, and have others recognize this, so they do not want to wear the identical thing as someone else. Ann asked Noreen if it was OK if she bought the same top, and Noreen reluctantly said, "Sure." But as soon as Ann returned to the dressing room Noreen turned to us in disbelief. She could not believe Ann would have the nerve to do this. Noreen said it made her think twice about buying the top, but since it looked so much better on her than it did on Ann, she would wear it with pride. Noreen added that she would love to have Ann wear the top at the same time that she did, because Ann would look like a cow. When Ann returned from the dressing room she asked again if Noreen minded if she bought the same top. Noreen's response was the same as before. The two went to the cashier together and while both tops were being rung up, Noreen chatted with Ann as though nothing had happened. Since then Noreen continues to be mad at Ann for buying the same top and she mentions it to the rest of us at least once a week, but she does not let it interfere with her friendship with Ann. #1456

One of the most competitive things going is the scramble for goods at garage sales on Saturdays, particularly by dealers who need the goods to sell on their tables at the flea markets on Sundays. Dealers try to be the first at a garage sale by going earlier than anyone else or by dropping by the house the night before. Dealers buy the local newspaper and carefully plan out their itinerary beforehand. On Saturdays they dash around in their cars to get to as many sales as possible before other dealers get all the choice items. It's a high-pressure situation and no one wants to waste a moment. One dealer I know drove into another dealer's car when both were rushing around one Saturday morning. Neither wanted to waste any time filing an accident report with the police. So the one who wasn't responsible said he would take $50 to get his car fixed, even though it would probably cost much more. They settled up then and there and drove off to the sales. When dealers are at a sale they occasionally yell, swear, or struggle with each other when both want the same item. Sometimes a dealer will cry out, "That's mine," before he gets anywhere near an item, even though another dealer is busy examining it. Dealers and their wives sometimes employ subtle blocking actions to keep other dealers away from areas where sellers are displaying goods. For example, one will purposely stand in another dealer's way at a table or try to engage him in a conversation while their partner is inspecting and buying goods. Needless to say, dealers develop a great deal of resentment and even hatred toward those who are conniving and "cheat" them out of the goods they feel they have equal right to. #1457

People spend considerable time and trouble searching for a parking space near their destination. Therefore they are pleased when they find one. However, they become very upset when someone steals the space from them. "I get so angry at jerks who know you are about to pull into a space, because your signal light is on, and pull across from the opposite lane into your space." "We drove around downtown for what seemed to be an eternity looking for a space. Cars were parked in every little nook and cranny. Mom just kept driving and was reasonably calm. She rarely curses, and never anything strong. We were driving down a one-way street in the right-hand lane and saw a car pulling out of a space just ahead on our right. In a matter of seconds a car in the left-hand lane pulled ahead of us and zipped into our space. Mom let loose, 'You fucking old bastard!' I was deeply shocked by her response, but I was saying almost the same words to myself about the driver who stole our space." "I was in the car with Mark and he couldn't find a parking place near the store he was going to. So he decided he'd shop downtown if we could find a parking space there. We were lucky and found a place and Mark pulled up ahead of it so he could back into it and parallel park. But before he could drive backwards a compact car scooted into the place. Mark just about went nuts. He roared, 'Where did you get your license, you idiot? You knew I was going into that spot, you bastard!'" "A friend and I were driving around a parking lot looking for somewhere to park. We finally saw a truck backing out of a space close to where we were going and put on our signal light. The driver of another car, coming in the opposite direction, saw the parking space as well. The other driver tried to get into the space before we did and ran into the back of the truck. While the two drivers discussed the damage we eased into the space." #1458

I held a teaching position at a university for three years, and it was a position which would have led to tenure. They very much liked me, my research, publications, and teaching, and they wanted me to stay. However, the chairman told me they couldn't renew my contract because the administration insisted they hire a woman for the position. The woman they hired was a real lightweight who was still working on her Ph.D. #1459

My grandmother made the mistake of giving my brother power of attorney over her affairs. Over the next year he stripped her of all her savings and kept her a pauper. Then he tried to put her in a nursing home so he could take her home away from her. All the stress actually killed her. By taking as much as he could for himself, he sizably reduced the amount of inheritance that I and the other grandchildren received. We were not pleased. #1460

A person may be forced to pay various taxes or pressured to make "voluntary" contributions, which reduces the money he has available for other things. This occurs with income taxes, provincial and federal sales taxes, liquor and cigarette taxes, church offerings, and contributions to charities.

The post office has started charging people five dollars for assessing customs duty on each package from outside the country. People get angry and argumentative when they have to shell out five dollars to get a package without even knowing what's in it or for something which may only be worth a few dollars. I've been told that postal employees no longer want to deliver packages because of the animosity they encounter. Personally, I think the government is being penny wise, but pound foolish. If people feel the government is cheating them, they'll find ways to cheat the government back. #1461

Businesses take resources from a person when they charge the person for goods and services. In cases when a monopoly is involved, when charges are increased, or when the charges seem unusually high, the person may feel exploited. This can occur in connection with bills for medicine, medical care, electricity, telephone service, and cable television. In addition, a business may raise prices or rents, which causes a person to have less resources for other needs.

13. Causing them to lose their resources

People may do various things which cause others to lose resources. For example, people may damage the reputations of others by blaming them or gossiping about them. As a result others may find it more difficult to get jobs, and people may be less willing to associate with them and be less willing to allow their own family members to associate with their family members. Also, people frequently cause others to lose resources when they try to save themselves time and energy. Thus family members make work for each other when they leave the top off the toothpaste, fail to replace an empty roll of toilet paper, drop clothes on the floor, do not put an item back in the refrigerator, or leave a small amount of water, juice, or milk in a container so they do not have to wash or refill the container. Other instances occur when colleagues fail to erase a blackboard or refill the copier paper tray, when neighbors do not pick up after their dog when it defecates or scatters garbage around one's street or yard, or when people break ahead of a person in line or at a service counter and cause that person to be waited on later than he would have been. People may become angry when they think others cause them to lose their resources.

> When my girlfriend comes over to my apartment, she wants me to spend all my time paying attention to her. She doesn't want me to do any reading, or do work I take home from the office, or do any exercises if she's there. Also, my favorite TV program is on only once a week, and if she's at the apartment at that time, she doesn't want me to watch it. It makes me angry. #1462

> I get quite upset when my wife henpecks me in front of others. It makes me look bad, and I feel humiliated and angry. #1463

> When you play at the blackjack tables in Las Vegas, occasionally a player will make a bad move. For example, let's say the dealer has two cards with a six showing. As a result the dealer will draw another card and there is a good chance the card she draws will count ten. This is likely to cause her cards to total more than twenty-one, and she will go bust. The proper move for a player is to sit pat and allow the odds to work against the dealer. But sometimes there is an inept player at your table who will not sit pat, but will ask for another card for his hand. As a result this player gets the card that the dealer would have drawn.

If the player draws a card which would have caused the dealer to lose, and the dealer draws the next card and it is a card which enables her to win, everyone gets mad at the inept player. People will say things out loud in an angry tone of voice, such as "You don't hit when the dealer's got a sixteen!" Experienced players will even stand up, say, "I can't play at a table like this," and go find another table. If the cards have been going well for the players at the table, they believe something like this can cause the cards and their luck to change. A bad move gets you worried, throws your psyche off, and the mood at the table changes. #1464

People often cause someone to lose resources when they tattle on him, such as report him to authorities for improper behavior. As a result the person has to dedicate time, energy, and other resources to dealing with authorities and protecting himself and his resources from them. People who are reported for improper behavior usually feel considerable anger toward those who report them.

One man parked in a no-parking space behind a building. He thought no one would notice his car, but when he returned forty-five minutes later his car had been towed away. Needless to say, he was quite upset. He smashed the hockey stick he was carrying against the pavement and then ran into the building and angrily told off the person who had called the tow truck. Weeks later, he still can't understand why it happened. He argues that his car was only there for forty-five minutes, and no one else needed the space, so there was no reason for his car to be towed away. #1465

People also violate a person's privacy. They may look into their windows, enter a person's home or room, look through their papers or drawers, read something they have written that they do not want others to read, open their mail, or question them about their personal life.

A senior colleague where I work wanted a key to my office. When I didn't want to give him one, he insisted and said I could have one to his office. But of course I didn't want one for his office. He has since come into my office and removed files without telling me. The other day I handed a letter to a senior administrator and while the administrator was reading it this same colleague leaned over and tried to read it too. I protested in a joking manner, "Don't read my private stuff. Don't be so intrusive. It isn't for you." "Oh, I'm not reading it," he said. But of course he was. He is very controlling and has no respect for my privacy. #1466

Also, governments may cause a person to lose resources. For example, governments may jeopardize resources by cutting off subsidies, subsidizing competitors, or creating free-trade agreements. They may confiscate a person's property or force a person to sell their property so the government can use it.

14. Failing to provide resources which they expect to receive

People and organizations also fail to provide resources which a person expects to receive. This may include various goods and services; child support; birthday and anniversary presents; help with housework and other chores; a specific amount of pay or employment; and disability, health, unemployment, and retirement benefits.

> Mom asks me if I'll be home for dinner. I always tell her what time I'll get back so she'll know when to have dinner ready. Because I expect her to have dinner ready, I can't stand it when I get home from a long day and there's no dinner made. Sometimes I have to make dinner for myself, and this really ticks me off. But after I growl for a while and eat something, I feel better. #1467

> When we were hired to pick strawberries we were told we would be working for three weeks and would be paid $2.30 for each crate we picked. They said they would pay us for our work at the end of the picking season. We picked from seven o'clock in the morning until noon, six days a week, and we picked between fifteen and twenty crates a day. Because you are on your hands and knees, your back and knees get very sore, and it is very hot working in the sun. In the middle of the third week of picking, we were told that we were expected to pick a fourth week. Because there were few strawberries left in the field this meant it would take much more time to fill a crate. It didn't matter to the owner how long it took us to pick a crate because she only paid us by the crate. We didn't want to continue picking. However, the owner told us that if we decided to quit after three weeks we would only be paid $1.80 a crate for our previous work, but if we wanted to be paid $2.30 a crate as originally promised, we would have to pick

for the fourth week. During the fourth week, because there were fewer strawberries remaining in the field, we were only able to pick five to seven crates a day. (Amounts in year 2001 dollars.) #1468

A sailor I know was injured while serving with the merchant marine in World War II. That was over forty years ago. He has been trying to get veteran's benefits ever since, but they keep reviewing his case and still haven't made a favorable decision on it. They probably hope he'll die first and they won't have to pay him anything. #1469

It's very upsetting when you don't get paid on time or your unemployment check or tax refund fails to arrive. You can get really annoyed with the government, the post office, or whoever is responsible. Usually your cash has run out and you have already planned just how to spend your check. Often there are others waiting for you to pay them, such as your landlord, or friends who've loaned you money to get by. #1470

Other people may fail to provide a person with proper information, service, goods, equipment, facilities, or repairs.

I'll never forget the time Kimberly and I were deep in the act. When we finished I removed the rubber and found a hole. It was a fucking big hole. I almost shit myself, and so did she. This rubber was our means of protection. The scare is over now. False alarm. But it could have been worse. #1471

It cost us a great deal when we moved into a new apartment. We had to hire movers and get a carpenter to fix the apartment up to make it more livable. But then the landlord didn't do the things he had promised to do. We couldn't take baths or showers because there was the tiniest trickle of water in the bathtub. We had to heat water on the stove when we wanted to take a bath. We couldn't use our major appliances because the electrical sockets weren't grounded. We complained repeatedly, but the landlord did nothing about it. So we found another apartment and moved out. We lost a lot of money but we didn't want to keep putting up with all the aggravation. #1472

I organized a picnic for about fifty people at the beach and rented a car so I could get there early and get things set up. The day of the picnic I picked up the rental car, but when I drove it away from the lot the brakes acted very strange. When I used the brakes, the brake pedal and the entire car jerked and shook. I felt that the car wasn't safe to drive to the beach and back, so I took the car back to the rental lot. The owner already knew about the brakes and told me it was caused by two parts not matching. He argued that the car had recently passed inspection so there was nothing to be concerned about. He refused to give me another car even though he had three others on the lot. He said that all three were reserved and if he gave the car he had given me to one of the other customers they would be likely to complain about the brakes too. I got really mad about this. He was totally uncooperative. I cancelled the car rental and I also cancelled another car reservation I had made with him for the future. I was able to borrow a friend's car, but as a result I was very late getting to the beach. The next day I called the highway safety division and gave them the full particulars about my problems with the rental car. Then I went to their office and took them a copy of my rental agreement, because I wanted to make sure they dealt with this. They said they would check out the car. #1473

I like to play the stock market, but it's never easy to find the kind of stock I really want to speculate on. I'm paying about $500 a year to subscribe to a newsletter on new issues, or initial public offerings (IPOs). The newsletter lets me know about promising issues I might be interested in. Last Wednesday I received the latest issue of the newsletter which had a report on just the kind of stock I like. So I called the underwriter to find out when the stock was being issued, but they informed me it had already been issued two days before on Monday morning. Between Monday morning and Wednesday, when I received the newsletter, the stock had run up from $7.50 to $12.00 a share and was already too expensive to buy. Boy was I pissed off. The latest copy of the newsletter had been mailed out the previous Friday and the stock was issued first thing on Monday morning, so I suspect no one learned about it in time to act on it. I called the staff of the newsletter long distance to tell them I didn't appreciate being told too late about the stock. The fact the stock rose to $18 over the next week didn't improve my mood at all. The editor of the newsletter loves to brag about how well the stocks he recommends do after they are issued. I bet he's really going to crow about this one, and if he does I'm sure going to give him another call and tell him what I think of his lack of professionalism. #1474

15. Keeping resources which are loaned

People also take a person's resources when they keep things they have been loaned. As a result what has been loaned is no longer available for the original owner to use.

> It's a major hassle trying to get things back that you've loaned to others. Often you forget who has it, and you seldom see it again. Most people will never get around to returning things unless you make a concerted effort to get them back. If you remember who has it you don't want to look petty by asking for it back. You certainly don't want to look like you're being critical of the person for not returning the item, or that you don't trust them to return it, because you don't want to make an enemy. There's a real art to trying to get something back gracefully. Sometimes you say that someone else has asked to borrow it, so you need to get it back to loan it to the other person. Or you can say you will be in the neighborhood and can save them a trip so they won't have to bring the item to you. If you've given them something to eat on a nice plate, you can give them something else to eat in a disposable container and ask if they still have your plate. One thing you definitely decide is not to loan them anything else in the future. #1475

16. Not reciprocating

People who provide others with time, energy, money, and goods often expect to have others reciprocate or would like to have them do so. When others fail to do things in return, people often feel they have been taken, used, or exploited.

> When I take a girl on a date, I always offer to pay. But it makes me angry when a girl expects me to pay every time. Girls are constantly crying out for equal rights, so why don't they make everything equal and learn to pay their fair share? Sometimes I'd really like to ask a girl out, but I know I can't afford to pay for both of us. #1476

> When you keep inviting people to parties or to dinner and they don't invite you back, you notice and talk about it, especially when you hear that they have parties and dinners of their own and invite other people,

but not you. If people want to find ways to do things for you they can, but usually they can't be bothered. After we had several parties and this happened, we quit having parties. Now we only invite people for dinner who actually do things for us. #1477

17. Combining threats

A person may be threatened in a variety of different ways at the same time. Such threats may come from one individual, several individuals, or a group or organization.

My ex-girlfriend went psycho on me. She phoned me all the time, drove past my house, got people to hassle me, and even used a key to scratch the paint on my newly painted truck. #1478

Multiple threats can also occur in a serial fashion, one after another.

Donald loaned his friend, Greg, a television set, and Greg paid to have the set fixed so that it would work properly. Just after Greg got it fixed, Donald demanded it back. Greg returned the set and insisted that Donald repay him the money he had spent getting it fixed. However, Donald refused and claimed this expense was rent for using the set. Greg wanted revenge, and he stole Donald's jacket to use for ransom so he could get his money back. After some time the money was returned, and Greg returned the jacket. Several other people became involved in this conflict on one side or the other, and a number of friendships were destroyed. #1479

Losing resources as a result of nonhuman agents

There are other threats to oneself and one's resources which are not initiated by people. Natural threats may be produced by rain, cold, snow, storms, lightning, earthquakes, floods, fire, insects, rodents, jelly-fish, sharks, and allergens. Occasionally a person blames human agents for damages caused by natural agents. Thus the person may blame his reaction to pollen on chemical fertilizers, or attribute storm damages to his home to inadequate building codes or a failure of the weather bureau to provide sufficient warning.

How people protect themselves and their resources

People adopt a variety of measures to protect themselves and their resources. These include the following:

1. Direct opposition
2. Indirect opposition
3. Thinking about and carrying out retaliation
4. Asking others to cease their threats
5. Getting help from others
6. Making one's resources or oneself less desirable
7. Not responding
8. Evading responsibility
9. Taking precautions

People may respond on their own or together with other people.

1. Direct opposition

Direct opposition normally involves a face-to-face response to the person making the threat. People respond verbally by objecting, complaining, arguing, threatening, yelling, swearing, or making rude or sarcastic remarks. Direct opposition also includes confrontations over the telephone and through the mail.

> When people share what they have with others, they frequently restrict how much they allow the other person to have. Thus they say, "Would you like a little," or "Would you like a bite?" instead of "Here, take half." The other day I asked my daughter if I could have a drink of her coke. But when I took a drink, she protested, "It moved!" She felt I was taking too much, because she could see the level in the glass drop. #1480

> My business is downtown and from time to time I have to go out and tell people not to park in the entrance to the alley that leads to the back

of the building. The employees of the building all park in back and we can't get our cars in and out if someone is parked in the way. #1481

Mom doesn't let up questioning my brothers, sisters, and me about where we were, our schoolwork, our personal lives, our friends, and so on. We are adults and she goes overboard. We ask her politely not to dig so deep, and if this doesn't work we growl at her. Mom is more cautious with my youngest sister, who has told Mom several times that she is going to move out because she can't stand to be questioned about every little thing she does. #1482

One day Mom and Dad went to the mall and left the door unlocked and the lights off in the house. My aunt came by, entered the house, and washed the dirty dishes in the kitchen. When we got home we noticed the dishes were done and thought it weird. Then the phone rang. It was my aunt, who told my mother that she had washed the dishes. Mom was furious. She told my aunt never to do it again, and said she didn't want to talk to her anymore. Mom doesn't know what my aunt could have taken from the house, and for the last four months Mom hasn't spoken to her. #1483

It was the first Friday after exams. Four of us girls went to a house party to get drunk and celebrate. Amy had a fake ID, and got our supplies from the liquor store. Once we got to the party we settled back to do some serious drinking. Amy got very drunk and Laura took her upstairs to lie down. But Amy kept coming downstairs and wandering around. Laura tried to take her upstairs again and this time both girls fell all the way downstairs. Laura finally got Amy upstairs again and Amy passed out next to another girl on the bed. Later Amy woke up, the other girl was gone, and a strange guy was in the room asking her for sex and oral sex. Amy told him to fuck off and leave her alone because she had a boyfriend and the boyfriend would beat him up. Then the third girl, Dale, walked in and saw the strange guy hovering over Amy. Dale got Amy up and took her downstairs. Later Dale told the guy, "You must be pretty sick and perverted to try to take advantage of a drunk girl. Her boyfriend will beat you up when he gets hold of you." The party was drawing to a close. Another girl drove us home and we put Amy safely into her own bed. The next day Amy told her boyfriend what had happened. He wasn't impressed that Amy had gotten drunk, and he tried to find out who the strange guy was. #1484

Muriel broke up with her boyfriend, Craig, about three weeks ago. Now whenever Craig sees Muriel with another guy, even if she is just talking to him, he flips out. Craig has even started screaming at her and throwing things around the room. Craig tells Muriel she isn't supposed to be with other guys because it makes him feel jealous. Craig acts like they are still going out or will be again soon, but Muriel tells him they are never going to get back together again. When several of us were traveling by car, we stopped at a gas station for gas and cigarettes. The attendant started flirting with Muriel and later asked us for her name. Craig yelled at him, "You better back off man! That's my fucking girlfriend." Craig didn't want the attendant to ask Muriel out. When Muriel asked Craig what had been said, Craig told her the attendant was making lewd comments and that Craig defended her by saying, "She's a good friend of mine and I would appreciate if you wouldn't speak of her in that manner." But if you knew Craig, you'd know he is never calm about anything and he overreacts over the smallest things, especially if it deals with Muriel. #1485

Whenever I go shopping for clothes with Janice, one of my girlfriends, she never likes anything I try on. Last month we went to a nice store and I tried on a blue blouse I really liked. Janice said the color didn't suit me, and because I valued her opinion, I didn't buy it. Two weeks later we went to a movie together and she was wearing that very blouse. Do you believe the nerve of the girl? I became very angry. But I wish now that I hadn't, because we haven't talked since. The truth is I don't know who was in the wrong. She for buying the blouse, or me for listening to her? #1486

One night three guys left a local club together and walked through the parking lot toward their car. Then another group of five guys left the same club and headed for their car. One of the five shouted at the three guys to keep their hands off his car. There was shouting back and forth and a fight almost started. At this point one of the five stepped forward and said his buddy had had a little too much to drink. He said this buddy had put a lot of money into his car and was very protective of it. The three said they never touched the car and told the five to go to hell. Then they left. #1487

One day I was driving along the highway and exceeding the speed limit just to keep up with the other traffic. The next thing I knew I was pulled over by a traffic cop. I asked why he stopped me and not the others. He replied, "You were stopped, and they'll be caught some other time." He fined me $50 and I was furious. #1488

I was outside and our neighbor was in our yard. My young son was playing with him when he slapped my son across the face. I was stunned, and demanded, "What are you doing?" He explained, "Your son spit in my face." I was angry and told him, "I can not imagine a child three feet high spitting in the face of a man six feet high. Do not set foot in our yard again." From then on my son has been afraid of him. Whenever my son is playing outside and sees the neighbor, he goes and stands on our doorstep until the neighbor is gone. #1489

The Dean of Arts at my university organized a charity night to raise money for the local association to help the mentally retarded. The chairman of our department wanted to please the dean and tried to hustle the department into participating and setting up a booth so that students could pay to throw pies at us or dunk us in a pool of water. This didn't fit my idea of a fun evening, so I suggested that we should organize something appropriate to the occasion, such as raffle off a retarded adult, or set up a large playpen, fill it with retarded individuals, and let people try to guess their collective IQs. The chairman couldn't decide whether I was serious or not. #1490

In addition, people may use obscene gestures and dirty looks to indicate their anger.

I dislike with a passion the irritable way some people chew gum. Some chewers are dreadfully inconsiderate of others. There is one girl in my philosophy class who, I swear, puts at least four pieces of Hubba Bubba bubble gum in her mouth just before class. She chomps and cracks so loudly that my ears ring after I leave class. I don't know her well enough to say, "Do you mind?" So I give her dirty, disgusted looks instead. But she still chomps and cracks. If you want to hear the sound of a cow chewing its cud, come to my philosophy class. #1491

When you deal with rude and difficult customers, it's pretty hard to get even. You can't tell them where to go or punch them out. You just have to learn to take it. But I do have one way of letting them know how I feel. The good old dirty look. I just give them a quick, icy glare. That way I don't get fired, but I'm not likely to get a tip either. [#1492]

People may respond to threats in a physical way by shoving, hitting, fighting, or kicking.

My sister's nineteen-month-old boy, Gilbert, has just come to stay with me and my twenty-month-old girl, Sandy. Sandy and Gilbert frequently fight over toys. They'll take a toy that belongs to the other and try to escape with it. This never works when Sandy tries it, because Gilbert is much bigger than she is. Sandy then screams loudly and beats the toy, some other object, her fist, or occasionally even her head against the wall or floor to try to scare Gilbert away. This display makes no impression on Gilbert, so Sandy attacks him. Recently she bit him on the arm, and when my sister and I came to the rescue, Gilbert was on top of Sandy punching her in the mouth. [#1493]

I was walking down the sidewalk when this car pulled out of a drive right in front of me and just sat there across the sidewalk while the driver waited for a break in the traffic. The driver didn't even care that he had blocked my way. So I kicked his car. This upset the driver and he drove off. Drivers are so inconsiderate of pedestrians. This has happened before, and I've considered opening the back door of the car and walking right through it. [#1494]

When I was in high school there were one or two bullies on each of the school busses who picked on the passive kids, and I was one of their victims. The bullies usually sat at the back of the bus. One day they repeatedly threw a softball and a book at me and hit me several times. I got angrier and angrier, and rushed to the back of the bus and demanded to know who had done it. But the two responsible refused to admit it. When I raised my fist to threaten one of them, he punched me in the mouth. We wrestled together until the bus driver made us stop. I got a bloody nose and the other guy got a black eye. The next day the principal told me the bully's mother planned to lay charges against me for attempted assault. [#1495]

Kenny is his baseball team's best player and it was his turn to bat at a critical moment in a game. The opposing pitcher threw the first two pitches very close to his head, and the third hit him on the shoulder. Kenny felt the pitcher was deliberately trying to hit him and became very angry. He charged the mound and began throwing punches at the pitcher. #1496

My wife and I were playing bridge with another couple. I played a card and my wife kicked me sharply in the shin under the table. She must have thought I did something stupid. But without thinking, I stood up, kicked her in the stomach, sat back down again, and resumed play. When we talked about it afterwards my wife said she didn't say anything when I kicked her because she figured she deserved it. The other couple never saw her kick me under the table and must have really wondered about me. #1497

People also suggest violence by brandishing, throwing, striking, and breaking objects.

Last night when Mom was eating at the dinner table, I disagreed with what she was saying. She got so mad she picked up the platter in front of her and smashed it on the table. Glass flew everywhere. We were lucky none of us were hit. Mom left the table and went upstairs to her room. #1498

Herb is a member of a curling team. The team is very active, but one teammate, Alex, frequently loses his concentration and makes bad shots. When the team played in the championship final of a tournament, everyone played well except for Alex, who missed several crucial shots. Herb was so frustrated and angry that he smashed his broom on the ice, told Alex to get his game back together, and made other rude remarks. #1499

2. Indirect opposition

There are indirect ways to challenge threatening people, so that one does not deal with them face to face. This includes contacting the other person's family, complaining to the police and filing charges, pursuing a lawsuit, writing or phoning the news media, seeking help from a government agency or an elected official, or complaining to a grievance committee or a senior official at the person's place of work.

How people protect themselves and their resources

The landlord announced he was going to raise everyone's rent by ten percent and start charging us for the parking spaces we were using. So we held various tenants meetings. One of the tenants is a lawyer and she helped us file a complaint with the rental-control agency. There was an official hearing and the landlord was forced to limit his increase to six percent and to allow existing tenants to continue using the parking facilities. #1500

I drove through the university parking lot the other day looking for an empty space and finally spotted one. I was just two spaces away when this asshole in a sports car scooted across the grass island separating the parking lot from the street. He whizzed into the space, jumped out of his car, and strode off about his business. There is no way he didn't see me, or know I was getting ready to pull into the space. I had to back up and find a parking space elsewhere. I was mad as hell. I wrote down his license number, went to the campus police station, reported what he had done, drew a map for them so they could find his car, and told them they could see his car tracks across the grass. I think they wrote him a ticket. I was still so pissed off, I told several people during the day just what had happened. #1501

We don't own a car and over the past few years my family and I have spent several thousand dollars on cab fares. We have used one local taxi company, know most of the drivers, and have had many warm, friendly conversations with them. Recently I was driving a car and when I stopped at a red light I saw that a cab from this company was right behind me. I assumed I must know the driver and I waved to be friendly. I was astonished when he gave me the finger. Every time I looked in the rear-view mirror he gave me the finger again. Then when the light changed and I turned right I looked back to see what direction he was taking. I wondered if I had prevented him from turning right because I was waiting for the light to turn. But, no, he drove straight ahead, and when he saw me look back, he gave me the finger again. I didn't recognize this particular driver and couldn't imagine what produced this response. But I was really upset. I swore I would never ride with this company again, and I haven't. I wrote a lengthy letter of complaint to the mayor of the city, consumer services, and the director of the tourist-industry association detailing what had happened. I pointed out, "This would be a nicer place to live if the drivers of this company kept their true feelings to themselves and refrained from giving the finger to their customers when their customers wave hello at them." When I wrote the mayor I pointed out that this taxi company takes a prominent part in the yearly Santa Claus parade. I wrote, "I believe your office could perform a public service if it notifies parents to tell their children not to wave during the parade. The drivers may think the children are waving at them (instead of Santa) and give them the finger in response." I sent copies of all these letters to the manager of the taxi company. My family rides with a different company now. [#1502]

When the staff of the record store saw me shoplift, they called the security guards, who took me to their office in the shopping mall. They had me sign a statement and then the police took me to the police station and charged me. I had to appear in court and pay a fine. They also told me I couldn't enter the mall for a year. Several weeks later I went into the mall to have a coffee with a friend and a security guard came up and said I'd have to leave. It was all very humiliating. [#1503]

One Saturday I was working upstairs in the storeroom of my store when I heard a noise at a window. This young guy was standing on the roof using tools to remove my window frame. Fortunately he didn't notice me, and I ran downstairs and called the police so they could catch him in the act. Then I went outside to see how he had gotten up on the roof and encountered the landlord who told me he was having the outside of the building repaired. Boy, did I feel stupid. I had to call the police back and explain. It didn't matter anyway, because the police hadn't left the station. [#1504]

There are also forms of revenge against those who threaten a person or his resources which do not involve face to face contact.

These new people have moved into our apartment house and play their hard rock music as loud as possible at all hours of the night. We complained to the landlord, but it didn't do any good. Now they just try to get back at us for complaining by playing their music even louder when they are home. They've also started doing nasty things like cutting our mail into tiny pieces and piling leaves and garbage on our car. [#1505]

People often tell other people about the threats they receive from a person. This can hurt the person's reputation, and may encourage others to take precautions so the person does not threaten them or their resources.

3. Thinking about and carrying out retaliation

People think about retaliating when someone attacks them or tries to take their resources, and sometimes they actually do retaliate. Although people normally become angry when someone threatens them or their resources, often they do not decide how they should respond until later.

> This asshole in town started hassling me. Once he yelled things at me from his apartment window when he saw me outside, and another time he sassed me when I passed him at the food center on the second floor of the mall. I'd never met the guy before and it caught me entirely by surprise. When I thought about it, what I really wanted to do was toss him over the second-floor rail of the mall. This would have either seriously injured or killed him and caused me to have all kinds of problems with the police, so it's just as well I didn't. I guess he moved away, because I don't see him anymore. #1506

> I went over to see this girl I was interested in and took a bottle of wine. When I had poured us some wine, her ex-boyfriend came in and helped himself to my wine without asking. It really pissed me off. I just sat there and acted civil to him. But later, I wished I had snapped the head off a wine glass and rammed the stem through his hand. I've detested him ever since. #1507

Often people know the other person well enough to think of something to do that would upset him.

> I like to indulge in a fantasy revenge against my old boyfriend. In my fantasy I'd like to get pregnant by him because he is so uptight about sex and morals. Then I'd like to have an abortion because his family is so Catholic. This would make him less pious. #1508

> Wars between factions at work can be quite upsetting, and sometimes colleagues try to get each other fired. When there is a war on there are all kinds of things you think of doing to the people who are causing you so much grief. In one of our wars I considered sending a key opponent, who abhors homosexuals, a subscription to a homosexual magazine. He lives in a small community and everyone, including the mailman, diligently searches for any dirt they can discover about each other. I also considered putting an insect-mating pheromone on another opponent's

telephone. This would have gotten on his hands, and caused him a lot of unwelcome attention. It's satisfying to think about doing something like this to get back at people who cause you so much trouble, even when you don't do it. [#1509]

People's imagined responses are usually much more violent than their actual responses are likely to be.

Mom was in her car stopped in front of a red light at an intersection. She was in the lane for driving straight ahead. The next lane, on her left side, was for turning left and the traffic light for that lane was flashing yellow. The car right behind Mom started honking for her to go ahead. But if she had done so it would have been both dangerous and illegal. Mom got extremely ticked off at the driver honking at her. She says, "If it ever happens again, I will go back and smack his mouth off." [#1510]

It doesn't surprise me that my boyfriend cheated on me. It's just like him. I just never suspected it would be with my best friend. How could she do this to me? I'm going to punch her goddamn head in the next time I see her! [#1511]

People also imagine how they would like to respond to those who might threaten them.

If anyone tries to hurt my daughter, they'd better run because I will kill them. If anyone gets my little girl pregnant, they're dead. No one, and I mean no one, is going to hurt my daughter in any way. [#1512]

After they are threatened people frequently tell others how they wish they had responded or how they plan to respond if the threat reoccurs.

However, people normally do not retaliate, and there are several reasons why they do not. Retaliation involves an expenditure of time and energy. Also, there is the risk that one's efforts to retaliate will be publicly exposed, and that one will look bad and be criticized or punished. Moreover, there is the risk of a direct confrontation with the other person. In addition, acts of retaliation may be inconsistent with one's self-image, and produce subsequent self-criticism, or guilt. Also, with time one becomes focused on other issues and the desire for retaliation becomes less important.

I couldn't think of something suitable to do before I got over my anger. #1513

I don't believe in revenge, because it can hurt more people than just the person you intend it for. #1514

I spent a lot of time plotting revenge, but nothing ever came of it. #1515

They hurt me, so I want to get back at them. But I almost never do. I just forget about doing something to them. It's good just to fantasize. #1516

It's impossible to drive without getting angry at other drivers for the stupid, inconsiderate things they do. I often wish I could just ram some idiot who pulls out right in front of me without looking. But this is just wishful thinking, because I know I'd lose a lot of time and money afterwards dealing with police, courts, mechanics, and insurance agents. #1517

Nevertheless, occasionally people actually do retaliate and do something to the other person. They may hope to get satisfaction or to teach the other person a lesson. Appropriate expressions are "Give him a taste of his own medicine," "Don't get mad, get even," "An eye for an eye, a tooth for a tooth," and "Revenge is sweet."

I was living on the third floor of a rooming house. When I was two hours late giving my landlord the rent for the month, he gave me an eviction notice. Of course, this upset me. After he evicted me I decided to call the fire marshal to tell him there was no fire escape for the third floor of the building. I felt a lot better after I did so. #1518

During a Christmas party two guys on the hockey team set fire to their teammate's favorite hat. The teammate, Danny, promised them, "I'll get even." After a couple of weeks had passed they figured Danny had forgotten about the incident. But then during hockey practice both of the guys had to stop playing because their crotches itched so badly. Danny had put itching powder into their "cups." He remarked, "Revenge is ever so sweet. Isn't it, boys?" #1519

I went in my sister's room to get my earrings back, but I could only find one of them. I got mad and started flinging things around the room while

I searched for the other earring. By the time I gave up, her room was a mess. When she asked about her room I told her I was responsible. Then I told her off for losing my earring. #1520

Every week we have to pass in an assignment in my math class. A friend of mine always wants to copy my assignment, because he doesn't "have enough time to do it." And because he is my friend, I let him. But after a while I got tired of this and deliberately did the assignment wrong. This time when he copied me, he failed the assignment. I don't want him to know I made him fail, because I don't want him mad at me. However, I do want him to stop copying me. #1521

My roommate was quite inconsiderate and broke my hairdryer. I wanted to get back at her, so I broke an ornament of hers that had sentimental value. It was the only way to make her wake up and smell the coffee. #1522

I was having a rough time with a friend of mine. She kept running down my clothes and my hairstyles. I wanted to let her see how it feels to be hurt. She had been dating a guy named Alex for a long time. So I nonchalantly asked her, "When did you and Alex break up? It didn't take him long to find another girlfriend." I made this up, but I knew she'd feel hurt if she thought Alex was cheating on her. #1523

The only person I've deliberately tried to hurt was my girlfriend. She was always flirting with other guys. So one night I went out to a club that I knew she'd be at. When I got there I avoided my girlfriend and asked a lot of girls to dance. Needless to say I got my message across loud and clear. I didn't really want to hurt her, but nothing else seemed to sink in. #1524

After I found out my boyfriend cheated on me, I felt the only fair thing to do was to cheat on him. When he found out he was hurt and angry. Neither of us felt we could trust the other and eventually we broke up. #1525

The coach of our skating club stole over $500 from the club. She quit coaching and the police had to get our money back. The following summer I got a job in a department store and discovered our ex-coach was working there too. I told the manager what she had done and she was fired a week later. I hated her and wanted her to know she lost her job because of what she'd done to the club. #1526

A bunch of teenage boys were playing street hockey in front of my house and I chased them away. Soon afterwards, someone began driving their car over my lawn and throwing eggs at my house in the middle of the night. #1527

I fired an incompetent employee. That night someone threw a brick through my front window. I definitely think it was the man I fired. #1528

Often when people do retaliate they employ a sense of fairness. When they think they have not exacted enough punishment, they exact more; and when they think they have exacted enough punishment, they stop.

I was living with three female roommates and they introduced me to a male friend of theirs and he and I started to date. Then I found out my three roommates told him I wasn't suitable for him. I think they were quite jealous that he was interested in me. I was very angry when I heard this, and I wanted revenge. After I moved into another apartment, I cut out some nude male pictures and taped them to their door. But this didn't satisfy me. So I used a penny to jam their door so they couldn't get out and I poured a bag of water under it. After I did this, I felt I had gotten my revenge. #1529

After my boyfriend broke up with me, I wanted revenge. First I told him I thought I was pregnant, even though I knew I wasn't. Next I thought about getting money from him for an abortion. I planned to tell him I'd spent the money on the abortion, and then use it to buy something nice for myself. However, because he was quite worried that I was pregnant, I was satisfied with my revenge. I didn't ask him for any money, and I finally told him the doctor said I wasn't pregnant. #1530

People also change their minds when they attempt revenge.

I'd been going out with my girlfriend for a year. Then one night, out of the blue, she said she wanted to date other guys. When I got back home I grabbed a steak knife and went over to her place to slash her tires. My first jab at the tire ruined the knife. It bent all to hell, and I sat there in the dark. One minute I was shaking with rage and the next I was laughing my head off at how ridiculous this was. #1531

189

My husband and I were having serious problems in our marriage. One day I was so angry about what he'd done that I threw his glasses on the floor and stamped on them. Then I thought about what I'd just done, and I didn't like myself for doing it. I didn't want to be this kind of person and do things like this, so I realized it was time to get a divorce. #1532

Sometimes people do not carry out an active program of revenge, but use an opportunity which presents itself. Thus they may fail to do something that the other person would like to have done, or they may see an easy way to do the person a disservice.

We had problems with our roommate and fortunately she moved out at the end of the first semester. When we got back after Christmas she had left her carpet rolled up in the middle of our living room. We felt it was in the way, so we threw it in the storage room. The storage room was full of garbage that she'd left behind when she moved. When she finally came to get her carpet she gave us some dirty looks. But we had a good laugh. We felt very good about our revenge. #1533

One of the least costly and least risky things to do is simply to tell others what the individual has done.

There's a man living in my apartment house who murders his pets whenever they inconvenience him and then lies like crazy to avoid getting in trouble. Whenever anyone mentions his name, I tell them the things he does. The other day an attractive woman came by to drop off a box of things for him. When I showed her where to put the box I made sure I mentioned the things this creep does. #1534

People may continue to carry a grudge for a long time, whether or not they act on it.

Ten years ago when I was in school, there was this scumbucket of a kid who kept beating me up every chance he got. He seemed to tower over me and I never fought back. I grew to hate him very much, and I swore that one day I would get even with him. Then recently I was face to face with him in the gym when I was lifting weights. I felt a fit of desire for revenge. He was a short, little dumpy person and I went over and called him down to the lowest. I was about three seconds away from beating him to a pulp. But he backed down, so I saw no reason to start the fight.

My desire for revenge has stayed with me for ten years and has not diminished in the least. I still want to beat him badly and get my revenge. #1535

Acts of retaliation may produce reciprocal retaliation against oneself from the other party. In other words, if A attacks B or his resources, and B retaliates against A, then A may retaliate for what B has done to him.

My brother was supposed to pick me up after basketball practice, and I was in a rush because I had to get to my job. However, I waited and waited and my brother never arrived. I ended up having to take a taxi and I was late for work. So the next time my brother needed a drive somewhere I was purposely late picking him up. My brother was very angry with me for being late. I thought this would teach him a lesson. But from then on I could never trust him because he was always late when I needed a drive. So my plan backfired. #1536

There was a girl in high school that I particularly disliked. She was a real snob, but actually she was no better than the rest of us. I let it go around that she sold herself to the boys at the harbor. Well not long after that a girlfriend of mine asked me if I was pregnant, because she said that was going around. I've always felt the other girl was paying me back for what I'd said about her. #1537

I have two teenage sons, Blair and Calvin. Calvin is the younger boy and he loaned Blair's baseball glove to a friend of his. The friend left it out in the rain and the glove was ruined. When Blair confronted Calvin about this, Calvin told him to shut up and leave him the hell alone. When Blair persisted, Calvin hit him and loosened two of his teeth. To get revenge, Blair locked Calvin outside one Saturday and Calvin had to spend the night in the barn. Calvin was furious and his father had to stop him from hitting Blair with a plate. #1538

During a hockey game a player for the Summerside team was "butt ended" by a Charlottetown player. When you butt end a person you jab him with the end of the handle of your hockey stick. This is a dirty move. You can jab a person anywhere, and in this case it knocked out several of the Summerside player's teeth. Therefore, before the next game the Summerside team had decided they wanted revenge against the Charlottetown team and the player who did this. In the first period of this

191

game, two of the Summerside players charged the Charlottetown player who had injured their player and all three received penalties. When the penalties expired one of the Summerside players went after the same Charlottetown player and both were expelled from the game for fighting. The Summerside team felt frustrated because they were unable to hurt the Charlottetown player. During the second period the Summerside team was still out for blood but this time they went after the Charlottetown player's brother. One of the Summerside players started a fight with the brother and both were expelled from the game. In the third period the Charlottetown team was angry over what the Summerside team was doing and they wanted to fight. During this period additional players were expelled for fighting and the penalty box was never empty. [#1539]

4. Asking others to cease their threats

A person may ask others to stop attacking him or to stop causing him to lose resources. The person may request that others stop annoying him, not destroy or take his possessions, not fire him, or not leave him in the case of a relationship. Sometimes others may not even be aware that what they are doing is hurting the person or causing him to lose resources.

> One of my roommates taps her fingers when we are all sitting around the table in our apartment trying to study. This breaks my concentration and annoys me immensely, but she doesn't even realize she's doing it. However, when you point it out she usually stops. [#1540]

> I was hosting a dance demonstration, and in the middle of the demonstration an employee of the theater turned the lights down so that the audience could hardly see the performers. I didn't know how to operate the lights, so I ran and got the employee, told him we needed the lights on high, pulled him by the hand back to the light switches, and had him turn the lights back up. The employee thought that people would be more in the mood for dancing if the lights were turned low. [#1541]

> I have been working for a company for over ten years and the company decided to close the local office and fire us all. I contacted the company to see if they were interested in hiring me to operate by myself as an authorized dealer in the area in order to continue servicing accounts. They agreed and this is what I am doing now. They let me use their equipment as well as their offices until the lease expires. [#1542]

192

A publisher notified me they had decided not to reprint a book I had written. I wrote them a letter in which I explained how interest in the book was growing and why I expected sales to increase. The publisher decided to reprint the book. #1543

5. Getting help from others

People frequently seek help from others when they try to protect themselves and their resources from attack. Those they turn to may be family members, neighbors, or colleagues who also stand to lose resources or suffer injury; friends that they are mutually dependent on for positive reactions and other resources; those whose models are violated and are morally outraged by the attack; or specialists who are paid for their services. People are normally in a much stronger position to fend off an attack when they have the support of others. When attackers have to deal with a number of defenders, instead of simply one, they are more likely to be injured and lose resources themselves.

6. Making one's resources or oneself less desirable

People also try to deal with threats to themselves and their resources by making themselves and their resources less desirable.

My kids don't like to eat anything that someone else has had their mouth on. The other day we bought a box full of miniature doughnuts. They were different flavors and we each took turns choosing one from the box. Every time my older daughter picked one she took a bite out of it before she put it on her plate. She was making sure her sister wouldn't ask for a piece of the ones she'd chosen. Today I bought everyone an ice-cream cone. When I passed out the cones, my older daughter asked if she could have mine instead. This is because it had more ice cream on it. I asked her why she wanted it and she said, "Because kids love ice cream." I didn't feel like giving it to her, so I said, "I've already licked it," which I hadn't. #1544

When I'm in a club with my girlfriends and I see a guy looking at me that I'm not interested in, sometimes I pretend to pick my nose and to wipe my finger on the back of the person sitting next to me. The person next to me is busy talking or watching others and doesn't notice what

I'm doing. But the guy looking at me does a double take and can't wait to tell his friends what I've done. #1545

Similarly, a business may try to protect itself from a hostile takeover by borrowing heavily to buy another business, thereby making its financial position much less attractive.

People may try to protect themselves by pretending they do not know how to do something that others want them to do, or by pretending that they are not available for a task or a relationship. For example, they may state they already have a girlfriend or boyfriend, when they do not.

7. Not responding

Frequently, however, people do not respond at all to attacks on their person and resources. Failing to respond occurs for a variety of reasons, including the fact one has too much to lose by making a response, one has little chance of winning, one would rather concentrate on things which have a higher priority, or one is caught by surprise and does not have time to think of the best way to respond at the time. Often when one does not respond, one believes one would lose more by responding than one would gain.

> Nobody likes to see the government raise taxes or do away with tax exemptions. But what can you do? Nothing that I could ever say or do would make one whit of difference. #1546

> I have worked at a grocery store for the past five years. Certain customers are constant complainers. Week after week the same individuals voice the same complaints. They say things like "How come butter isn't on special again this week?" "This meat isn't packaged properly, because the juice is running out," and "The bread isn't fresh. But be careful not to squish it." I get so agitated by their complaints that I feel like throwing the nearest jar at them. Instead, I've learned to bite my tongue and curse under my breath. #1547

> I work at a combination gasoline station and convenience store. The store offers free coffee to anyone who wants it. Normally a regular customer will get $20 worth of gas, have a free coffee, and perhaps stay for a few minutes to gab with the boss. The boss believes that the free coffee is an important draw for his business. The coffee regulars all

know the boss on a first-name basis. They know they can always get a free coffee and a few minutes of conversation. The regulars also know they can get credit, pay with a check, or cash a check. The problem is that some people abuse the system. They come in for the free coffee but spend little or no money. For example, one man drives a large vehicle but only buys $5 worth of gas. Then he hangs around and drinks as many as three cups of coffee. There is an unspoken minimum purchase of $10 for a coffee drinker. The fact he only gets $5 of gas for a large vehicle is bad enough, but to have the audacity to drink more than one coffee is unbelievable. Another man lives nearby and comes in several times a day for a coffee but rarely spends any money. We have nicknamed the man, "Mr. Coffee." The other day Mr. Coffee complained to us that the owner's wife was charging him for coffee. The boss has commented, "That bastard gets coffee all the time, but never buys anything." The boss doesn't say anything to the man. He doesn't want to start any trouble, so he just leaves well enough alone. #1548

8. Evading responsibility

People also try to protect themselves and their resources when they attempt to deflect an attack from themselves on to others. They may be blamed for doing something or for neglecting to do something, and they may tell the person attacking them that someone or something else is responsible.

When Jim breaks something, like a glass, he says his younger brother, Tommy, did it. This is smart, because Tommy is too young to talk and defend himself. #1549

My brother was sick one day and stayed home from school. He asked me to bring him his homework assignment from school, and I did so. But then he didn't do his homework that night, and the next day he told his teacher that I hadn't brought him the assignment. My brother hoped to avoid a scolding from the teacher by putting the blame on me. As a result his teacher got angry with me. I was furious that he lied about me. At lunchtime I found him in a classroom with our usual group of friends. I yelled at him and called him names. He was furious that I made public the fact he'd lied, and he began screaming at me. When we'd exhausted our verbal insults, we both felt so frustrated that we began to throttle each other at the same time. Finally, with bulging eyes and red faces, we retreated to opposite corners of the room. By the end of the lunch hour, we had both calmed down and apologized to each other. [#1550]

My best friend had been going out with Tom for over a year when she discovered she was pregnant. I've known Tom all my life and he comes from a very religious family. Tom's parents refused to admit that Tom was the father, and forced him to deny it. But it was quite obvious to everyone that he was. His parents wanted to protect their reputation as a proper church-going family and to protect their son from the obligation of raising a child. [#1551]

9. Taking precautions

People frequently respond to threats to themselves and their resources by taking precautions. This is dealt with in the chapter on Taking Precautions in this volume.

Protecting others

Individuals sometimes try to protect more than a) themselves, b) their own personal resources, c) those they are associated with, and d) the resources of their associates. They may also seek to protect both those they are not associated with, such as strangers, and their resources. Often this is in response to their own ideas of right and wrong, i.e., their personal models. Thus individuals may donate money or work to help protect people who are starving, a group that is discriminated against, a nation attacked by another, or a species or ecosystem threatened with extinction. They are more likely to respond to a situation that they encounter personally.

I was walking across the parking lot of a shopping mall and saw a young man sideswipe and dent the next car as he pulled into a parking space. Afterwards, he just sat in his car. I didn't trust the situation, so I wrote down his license-plate number. Later I watched an older woman walk out of the mall and put packages in his car. Then he drove off. It was clear he wasn't going to take any responsibility for hitting the other car. So I wrote a note to the owner of the damaged car, included the young man's license-plate number and my name and address, and stuck it through the car window. Eventually the owner of the damaged car got in touch with me and the police asked me to come in and sign a statement concerning what I had seen. They had questioned the owner of the car that caused the damage and the young man's father claimed he was responsible for the accident. I don't know what they were trying to pull. Maybe they wanted to avoid having the young man's insurance rates raised, or maybe he already had prior offenses. In any case, I certainly told the police that the son, not the father, was driving the car. #1552

In addition, some people are hired to protect strangers and their resources. These include police, firefighters, and public health workers.

Feelings underlying protection

People feel angry when others attempt to attack them or take their resources. Anger dominates their consciousness and reappears whenever they think about the situation.

Doug and I have been together for five years now. I found out he danced with Alice for one straight hour when I went to visit my parents. I was so mad I could have spit. It doesn't matter if nothing else happened. I don't go looking for other men. It's just as bad as doing something because you don't know if he was thinking about it or not. #1553

I found out my boyfriend cheated on me with every girl in town during the four years we've gone together. I trusted that dirty bastard all these years, and now I finally learn that our damn relationship meant nothing to him. Do you know how this makes me feel? I hate that fucker! You know what? He has been doing his regular routine with this one girl since we started going out. He would meet her at the pool hall every night at eleven o'clock. Now I know why he didn't stay with me later at night. The fucking liar has just taken me for a fool. He'll die for this! #1554

These two young men came into my store yesterday and shoplifted about fifty dollars worth of goods. This makes me so angry, and a lot angrier than losing fifty dollars should. And I'm mad at myself for being so stupid and not realizing what they were doing. I handle new and used goods in my store. They called up first and asked me what kind of goods I wanted to buy. That should have tipped me off to start with, because people usually have something specific they hope to sell, and don't try to find out what I want so they can supply it. Then when they came in, one of the two sold me a few goods while the other, who was wearing a knapsack, wandered around the store. When they left, some of my best stock was missing. I'm a small woman, but I wanted to go look for them and punch them in the face. Later that day I ordered some overhead mirrors which will make it easier for me to spot shoplifters, and I went to the police. I was so angry I had trouble working the rest of the day and trouble sleeping that night. #1555

Anger appears to be a more pronounced form of feeling annoyed or irritated. When people become angry, they become upset and agitated. Anger enables them to respond more aggressively.

Most of the conflicts I have at home are with my brother. He tries to push me around, but I resist. Sometimes I'll even push back if he makes me mad enough. #1556

I don't get really mad that often. It's good when I do though. I can play a lot meaner football. #1557

Feelings of anger and aggression can be quite pronounced. People speak of "hating" another person and "wanting to kill him."

I found out a buddy of mine had deceived me, and I pounded the shit out of him. When his sister came out of the house to break us up, I took after her with a rake. I was so close to killing her. #1558

We don't have a lock on our bathroom door at home. As a practical joke my wife opened the door while our twelve-year-old daughter was sitting on the toilet and left the door open. None of us saw her sitting there. However, as soon as our daughter could get her clothes back on, she marched into the bedroom and whipped her mother with a towel. I've never seen her so furious before. #1559

Feelings underlying protection

One night after Charlie and his girlfriend broke up he went with his friends to a local club. His friends saw that Charlie's ex-girlfriend was at the club and tried to prevent Charlie from meeting her. But Charlie saw her across the dance floor and headed for her before his friends could stop him. Charlie wanted to smooth things over. He had been drinking and became quite agitated when he didn't like the reception she gave him. He repeatedly tried to get her understanding and reassurance, but was rejected every time. Then Charlie blew up. He screamed in her face, called her names, threw the contents of his drink on her, and then threw his empty glass at the wall. His friends took Charlie out of the club. Afterwards Charlie said, "I was so angry with her after the breakup. She never wanted to hear my side of the story. When I saw her that night I wanted to say everything that I'd kept bottled up for so long. When she wouldn't let me, I was hurt. I guess the alcohol and my anger made me act that way." #1560

There are as many as ten to thirty fights a night on the weekends in Charlottetown, and most of these are between teenagers who have been drinking. What I've observed is that before a fight the opponents shake with rage, have a killerlike expression on their faces, and don't talk much. When I fight I go through changes. My blood starts pumping, my head pounds, my movements become quick and nervous, and my stomach churns with fear. Before the fight all I want to do is kill the other guy. During the fight I just want to end it so I won't get injured. And afterwards I try to figure out why I fought. #1561

When people are attacked or when someone takes their resources they become quite upset. So much tension is generated that a person is frequently willing to dedicate considerable time and energy to dealing with this in order to get rid of the tension. This tension is usually greater than the tension produced by other things the person has to do. Therefore it is given a higher priority and a person is more likely to actually act and deal with it. In order to get rid of the tension, the person can attack back, recapture the resources, retaliate, fantasize about what he would like to do to those responsible, or tell others what has happened.

When people are angry they may not respond aggressively. For example, they may look upset, they may cry, or they may not show how they feel. "A girl who sits near me in a university course always saves a

seat for a particular guy in the class. She tries hard not to appear obvious about this, but he knows what she is doing and always sits next to her when he arrives. Then one day another girl came and sat on the other side of the guy. The guy spent most of the class talking to the new girl. The first girl was visibly annoyed. She sat facing directly forward with her arms crossed and did not smile. She purposely did not look in his direction for the remainder of the class. At the end of class the guy tried to ask her something, but she pretended she didn't hear him and walked away."
"When I was in junior high my boyfriend was crowned Junior Prince at the Valentine's Day dance. Then he had to dance with the girl who was crowned princess. I was so jealous I wouldn't speak to him for days, and I finally broke up with him because of this. I can laugh about it now. I don't know what I expected him to do. Refuse to dance with her in front of the whole school, I guess."

> Many women cry when they become angry. The following statements were made by women. "When I get very angry, I cry. Even if I don't want to cry, I can't help it." "If I get really angry, I usually end up crying. I can't figure out why, but that's what usually happens." "When I get very angry, I sometimes lose control of my emotions. Often I erupt in tears." "When I get mad I'll throw anything in sight. Afterwards, when I'm by myself, I usually start bawling." #1562

People also experience anger in conjunction with other feelings. People may become upset and angry when they feel hurt because they are criticized, rejected, or embarrassed. When someone hurts them, whether physically or emotionally, they often become angry. They may also become angry when they envy others, or when something meaningful to them is violated. For example, they may react strongly to seeing an animal whipped, or when they learn of police brutality or an abortion.

A second feeling which helps people protect themselves and their resources is anxiety. Anxiety is considered in the chapter on Taking Precautions in this volume. People tend to feel anxiety when they think that they might lose resources, and to feel anger when they actually do lose them.

Functions of protection and anger

People frequently have to act to protect themselves and their resources from others. When people are no longer willing or able to protect their resources, others frequently take their resources away from them. Those who take their resources may be mates, relatives, colleagues, friends, acquaintances, or strangers. For example, other people may try to get one to do things for them; siblings may try to capture the attention one receives from one's parents; peers may try to win one's boyfriend, girlfriend, or spouse; colleagues may seek to take one's tasks or positions at work; a business partner may cheat one out of profits; neighbors may take liberties with one's property; an ex-mate may seek to take one's money, possessions, or children in a divorce settlement; children may attempt to take one's property when one becomes elderly; and relatives may try to take one's inheritance. People constantly test each other's willingness and ability to protect themselves and their resources. As a consequence people learn who they can and cannot take resources from, and which resources they can take from others.

Time and again people must struggle to hold on to their resources, and anger motivates them to do so. When people are angry they are more likely to stand up for themselves and their resources and do something to stop others. Because they are angry they are more willing to confront others directly and to attack them. Therefore anger and aggression enable people to better protect themselves and their resources.

People experience anger as soon as they realize that they or their resources are threatened. This immediate reaction provides them with the maximum amount of time in which to deal with threats. Because they feel angry immediately, they are able to respond aggressively while they are being attacked and while their resources are being taken. As a result they are more likely to stop the attack, prevent the loss of resources, and regain the resources which are being taken.

Anger as an activator

When people show anger and aggression they appear more threatening to others. Feelings of anger are often revealed by a person's facial expressions, body postures, and voice inflection. Such signs let others know that the person is likely to act aggressively. As a result others treat what the person says and wants more seriously. A person's anger causes others to feel fear that they may be attacked and hurt. Consequently, they are more likely to back away and are less likely to continue in their attempts to mistreat the person or take his resources.

Cheating, or using anger to obtain resources

Some people also intentionally use displays of anger to get others to cooperate with them and to give them what they want.

> A man I'm dating throws temper tantrums to intimidate others so he can get what he wants. The other day he went to buy a set of sheets that was advertised, but when he got to the department store, they were sold out. Then he tried to get them to sell him a more expensive set of sheets at the same price as the sales item. When they wouldn't do it, he insisted on speaking to the manager. He was very loud and an embarrassment to the store. He threatened the manager, "I'll sue you until your ears bleed." He was so obnoxious that the manager finally agreed to sell him the better set at the sales price. #1563

> I was working in a gas station when a driver pulled up to the full-service pumps. He gruffly told me to fill his car up with gas and to check the oil and transmission fluid. Then he got out of the car and asked if he would get a free car wash with the fill-up. I responded politely that no, on the Island it is illegal to offer incentives like a free car wash or free dishes to sell gas. The man went into a rage. "What kind of fucking outfit are you running here?" he demanded. "I want to talk to the goddamn owner!" Fortunately I was called up front to do a car wash at this time, and a fellow employee received the full brunt of the man's rage. To make things worse, the station was out of transmission fluid. This gave the man more to react to. "What kind of fucking outfit are you running here? I'm going to straighten your fucking owner out!" When the man confronted him, the boss was full of apologies and gave him a free car wash. Unfortunate-

ly this meant I had to deal with this jerk again. When he spoke to me I could see there was blood in his eyes. I asked for his car-wash ticket, but he refused to give it to me until I washed the whitewalls of his tires. When I finished washing the whitewalls he gave me the ticket and laughed. It was obvious he wanted to irritate me as much as possible. He ordered me, "Do a better fucking job than you did on the transmission fluid." I was glad when I was finished with him. #1564

Excess behavior

Excess behavior is behavior in response to feelings which results in one acting contrary to the purposes the feelings are designed for. As a result, one loses resources rather than gains or protects them. For example, the feeling of anger causes people to act aggressively when others threaten them and their resources. As a result people protect themselves and their resources. However, there are situations in which people become angry and aggressive and as a result actually lose resources.

The expression of anger can be dysfunctional. Instead of enabling a person to better protect himself and his resources, an angry response may put the person and his resources at greater risk. For example, a person may argue back when he is criticized by his boss and thereby hurt his position at work. Similarly, a parent who is opposed or treated with disrespect may strike and injure his child.

> The newspaper had an article about a man in the United States who shot and killed this kid for messing around his apartment building. He told the police that some kids were causing damage and he recognized this kid as one of them. The man was arrested, and I assume punished. #1565

Feeling and expressing anger after one has already lost resources does not help one protect them. In the following case, a girlfriend responds with anger after she learns that her boyfriend has done something which she decides has destroyed their relationship.

I went with this guy for several years. Then one night when I was babysitting, he called up and asked if he could come over because he had something important to tell me. As stupid as I was, I was all excited because he was coming over, and I made a pizza. But when he arrived, I could tell by the look on his face that his news was not going to be good. He took both of my hands and told me that he had met a girl a couple of months before when he was drinking in a club, had slept with her, and now she was pregnant. He explained that she didn't matter to him and he didn't want anything to do with her or the baby.

I started kicking and punching him. I threw him out of the house, but dragged him back in so I could hit him some more. He ran over to his car. But I wasn't satisfied so I went after him. He rolled down the car window and said, "I know how much you wanted to go to the concert this weekend. So here's your ticket." I ripped up the ticket and threw it at him. Then I started kicking his car and put a couple of dents in it and busted his headlight.

Six months later he tried to get together with me again, but I told him to forget it. I was hurt really bad, and I won't forget that incident for the rest of my life. #1566

After one has lost resources, it is usually too late to protect them, and expressing anger is a waste of energy. Often the best one can hope for is that others will see or hear about one's anger and will be warned not to do this again. Nevertheless, when a person continues to feel angry toward someone who has attacked him or his resources, he may mount a more determined defense in the future and he may take better precautions so that it does not happen again. Also, when a person continues to feel angry about something that happened, the anger may encourage him to try to recapture a resource which was taken from him if the opportunity arises.

A person may also act inappropriately by redirecting his anger and aggression at individuals and objects which are not responsible for threatening him and his resources.

After my brother wrecked the family car, he attacked the car. The accident was entirely his fault, but he kicked in the rear window, and broke off a windshield wiper. #1567

In addition, a person may express his anger when those who threaten him are absent and do not witness his anger. Thus an angry person may slug a wall or break objects when he is alone. Such actions are a waste of time and energy, and a person may even injure himself in the process.

When a person thinks about situations that are happening or have already happened and does not reveal the anger he is feeling, he wastes time and energy, because those he is angry with do not witness his anger.

> I went early to a movie theater to see a foreign film I'd heard a lot about. It was the last night the film was showing and when I got there a long line of people were already standing outside the theater. It looked like a small theater but I figured I was likely to get a seat. However, as the time approached for the theater to open, more and more people arrived and joined their friends in the line ahead of me. I got so angry at them for breaking into the line, I felt like hitting them. But I just stood there and didn't say anything. #1568

At best, such mental activity can serve as a private rehearsal for the actual expression of anger in the future.

Protection by groups and societies

Individuals cooperate together to protect themselves and their resources. Many people work in groups to obtain resources. Therefore, it is to be expected they would continue to work in the same group to protect themselves and their resources. Members of families cooperate to protect each other from physical attacks and attacks on their resources, including their reputations, possessions, and jobs, by outsiders. Organization members cooperate to protect themselves from opponents and competing organizations. Company employees cooperate to protect themselves from competition, government constraints, and disruptive employees. Political-party members cooperate to win political positions and keep them, and use many means to attack, remove, and defeat their political opponents. Sporting teams cooperate together and compete against other teams to obtain, keep, and protect status. They also fight together when members of the team are physically attacked. Groups, organizations, and societies normally oppose changes which would reduce or remove their resources.

Societies, communities, and organizations often hire and train specialists to protect individuals and property. Societies have soldiers and national police, communities have local police, and organizations have lawyers, security guards, bouncers, and enforcers.

Fighting plays an important role in hockey, and fighters are a necessary part of each team. Unfortunately the public has little understanding of the significance of fighting in the game. Instead the public tends to focus on the excitement or the violence connected with fighting.

Let's look at why there are fighters present on each team. One fighter, Eddie, states that he was injured more often playing university hockey, where there is practically no fighting at all, than he is now playing in the fight-riddled Junior B League. The reason for this is simple. During a game players try to prevent opposing players from scoring in any way that is within the rules. When an opposition player becomes a scoring threat players can use their sticks to slash and hack the player until he loses the puck. In a game such as a university match where there is no fighting, they can slash and hack with reckless abandon because there is no threat of being beaten up by an opposing player. However, when fighting is allowed the players keep their sticks down, because they know if they slash and hack they will most likely be forced to fight. Because ninety percent of the players do not want to fight, only the tough guys can slash and hack and often they are penalized for doing so. Eddie states, "In varsity games even the little pussies will hack you all night long. But if these little fellas played Junior hockey they would get the tar beat out of them for doing that shit." In theory, if there were a team with no tough guys, then when a team with tough guys played against them, the team with the tough guys would win because they could hack and slash all night long without any threat of a fight.

Some teams have few or no gifted players. When they play against a team with gifted players, one of the most effective ways to improve their chance of winning is to remove the outstanding opposing players by injuring them. In every hockey league the stars are targeted on the ice. The only reason stars are still playing is because of their "bodyguard," or enforcer. While the enforcer plays the game he keeps an eye out for the star and protects him. Because we do allow fighting in hockey, a player is going to think twice about giving an opposing star a good hack to the wrist or ankle when he is going to have to answer to a six-foot-four, two-hundred-forty-pound goon. It is unsafe for a star to play on a team without a recognized enforcer. One star on a team which lacked a well-known enforcer was blindsided by a cross-check to the head which knocked him unconscious and caused a major concussion. Many thought he would never play again, and it was almost two years before he returned to the ice.

Fighters on the team are called policemen or enforcers. They control the behavior of the players on the ice. No one wants to fight a tough guy. Therefore you do not see players misbehave on the ice. A player recounted, "Once this past season an opposing player ran our goalie. Our tough guy fought him and the rest of the season that player never went near our goalie." James, who is the policeman on his team, said, "I serve and protect. I protect the scorers on my team by fighting anyone who even tries to hurt them. I guess as far as serving goes, I serve the penalty that I get for pounding on a fella." Fighting serves an important purpose in hockey. It protects the players from getting hurt by opposing players, and it does, believe it or not, make for a cleaner game. Without fighting hockey would be rougher than it already is. Fighting decreases violent actions during the game. There are less injuries within the hockey leagues because of fighting. If the prominent players in a league are injured, the league suffers from a lack of talent and the quality of play is reduced. According to one fighter, "Our job is to protect the skilled players so they can have room to move around." Fighting protects the players who are less willing and able to protect themselves.

You do not have to be big and strong to be a fighter in hockey. What you have to have is a lot of heart, the ability to take quite a bit of pain, and most of all little fear of the guy you are fighting. Players who fight are referred to as tough guys. There are usually one or two guys on every pro or semi-pro team who are strictly there to fight the other tough guys on the other teams in the league. These fighters are usually not given much playing time and are used only when needed. Some fighters are also skillful players as well and are more highly valued than those who only fight. A player who is both a fighter and a skillful player will not be seen fighting until his team is on the losing end of the game. This is because as long as his team is winning or tied, the team wants him playing on the ice instead of sitting in the penalty box. He can not score if he is sitting in the penalty box for fighting. Hockey players who fight can become very successful at what they do. If they become tough enough and are still able to put the puck in the net, they can move up in the ranks of hockey. The National Hockey League, or NHL, is the most prestigious level of hockey. To be a fighter in the NHL, you must be the toughest of the tough guys while at the same time be able to compete with the most skillful players in the world. In the NHL referees normally let two players fight it out. As soon as one fighter seems to have the upper hand the team forwards pull the fighters apart.

Most fighters have an aggressive nature and have fought on every team they have played with during their careers. Malcolm, Sandy, James, and Eddie have been used as fighters on every team they have played on. Malcolm became a fighter because he began playing hockey at an older age than his peers. He was less skilled than they were, and he needed to find a way to compensate. His decision to be a tough guy landed him spots on many teams during his career and he continues to fight in almost every game he plays in his league. Sandy became a fighter because he was bigger than everyone else when he was a boy and his coaches expected him to fight. He enjoys fighting in his Junior B league. Sandy says, "I know my role and I have really begun to enjoy it to the extent that I look forward to fighting every night." Sandy can also score goals, but he is used more often to fight the opposing team's players. James has been "fighting my whole life." He is a born fighter. His father and uncles fought when they played, so it is in his blood. He enjoys fighting and finds respect in being an intimidating presence on the ice. He has been penalized for fighting more often than anyone else in his league. Eddie is the opposite of James. He only fights when he feels it is necessary. He is what some would call "a smart fighter." Eddie is not an intimidating force on the ice, but he gets the job done and is rewarded with lots of playing time. He plays in the same league as Sandy. Their league is known for rough play and being a hotbed for fighters.

Fans enjoy fights. If you ask fans what they go to see at a hockey game, their first response is to see their team win, and their second is to see a good toe-to-toe scrap. People are more likely to attend games with fights than games without them. Fans get the wrong idea when they see a fight during a game. They think the fighters want to hurt each other for no apparent reason. The most popular games in the NHL are those that involve two of the premiere fighters on opposite teams. Fighters in the NHL and other leagues are among the most popular players. When they are always on the ice with a star they guard they can quickly make a name for themselves. Although fighters are some of the lowest-paid players in their league, the respect they get on and off the ice can be said to compensate for less money. At the same time fighting on the ice can produce a hostile mood which spreads through the crowd resulting in fights in the stands. James says, "I have seen some awful things happen in the stands, that we, the players, never intend to happen." Hockey is an intense game and fighting escalates the tension. Fans are involved in the game and a small argument can turn into an all-out brawl among the fans and between fans and players. Fighting also produces injuries. A little blood and a broken nose are common. Blows to the head and landing on the hard ice can sometimes produce concussions and in rare cases even death. There are also a handful of players who fight simply because they like to fight. These players never make it very far in the ranks of hockey and end up doing most of their fighting outside a downtown nightclub. They give hockey a bad name and can be seen as the bad boys of hockey. Sandy states, "Those guys are scary. There is no place for them in the game." #1569

A system of laws, police, courts, and punishments is provided by society to protect its members from those who try to injure them or take their resources. These agencies are set up in order that individuals can avoid the risks involved in direct confrontations with those threatening them. Individuals are expected to let these agencies protect them and their resources and individuals are subject to punishment "if they take the law into their own hands." As a result, people who wish to attack others and take their resources have the foreknowledge that if they do so, the society is likely to become involved on behalf of the victims. In most cases the means which the society uses to protect individuals are superior to the means that individuals have available to protect themselves.

Societies also try to protect themselves from internal and external attacks. Demonstrators, revolutionaries, terrorists, gangs, and vandals are dispersed, arrested, punished, locked up, and/or killed. Societies seek to protect their resources, including their members, from threats by other societies. Thus they react to threats of territorial expansion, military attacks, terrorism, trade tariffs, economic competition, and mistreatment of their citizens on the part of other societies. In order to protect themselves, societies also use military threats, military actions, terrorism and assassinations, sabotage, trade embargoes and tariffs, suspension of diplomatic relations, confiscation of assets, and persecution of citizens and immigrants from the other society. Societies also aid opposition and dissident groups in other societies in order to change the leadership of those societies. Societies frequently use their own mass media to generate public anger in response to threats from other societies.

REMOVING PHYSICAL DISCOMFORT

Contents

Introduction

People experience a variety of types of physical discomforts. They feel bothered by physical discomforts and seek to remove them as they experience them. By removing physical discomforts, people prevent damage to their bodies.

Physical discomforts

People experience a wide variety of discomforts at different times. These include hunger, thirst, hot, cold, itching, soreness, aches, pain, and fatigue. They feel irritation as a result of a clogged nostril or ear, a particle between their teeth, something in their eye, or an object which abrades or pushes into their skin. They also feel discomfort when they need to breathe, urinate, or defecate.

When people experience discomfort they usually seek to remove the sensation. They adopt various measures, depending on the nature of the discomfort. Thus if they are hungry they eat, and if thirsty they drink. If they feel too hot they may remove clothing; move less; drink something cool; move to a cooler area, such as the shade; or make their environment cooler, perhaps by opening a window or turning on a fan or air conditioner. If they feel too cold they may put on more clothing or warmer clothing; move more; drink something hot; move to a warmer area; make their environment warmer, such as by starting a fire or turning on an electric heater; press against another person; or press their hands, arms, or legs together and against other parts of their body. When they itch, they scratch themselves. If they are sore they seek to remove the feeling by changing positions or rubbing the area. If soreness increases when they move, they try not to move at all. In the case of aches and pains people usually examine the area to see if anything can be done to alleviate the feeling. When they experience fatigue, they normally reduce their tempo, decrease their interaction with others, and seek to rest. When they feel an irritation, they seek to remove the source. For example, they may try to clear a clogged nostril or ear, extract an object that is between their teeth or in their eye, and remove or get away from an object which rubs against them or presses into their skin. When they feel discomfort in their throat, mouth, nose, and chest, they breathe. When they feel discomfort because they need to urinate or defecate, they normally take measures to do so. If the discomfort is strong, they act with greater speed. Physical discomforts are usually experienced at specific locations of the body, which makes it easier for people to identify the cause and deal with it.

In addition, people take various preventive measures to deal with discomforts before they occur. For example, they eat regular meals to avoid feeling hungry, and they use the toilet before going somewhere where a toilet will be less accessible. They frequently take extra clothing and carry medications with them in case they need them.

> I never go on a hike on a nature trail without carrying a bottle of water with me. It's no fun to get thirsty and have to worry about hurrying back to get a drink of water. It can ruin your hike. #1570

> I usually get seasick when I go out on a boat. So I take a ginger pill an hour ahead of time, and it works really well. #1571

> I buy a pack of chewing gum before I take an airplane flight. Then I start chewing before we start to land. Changes in air pressure bother my ears and chewing gum helps a little. #1572

> Nothing is worse than having to go to the toilet when you're watching a film in a movie theater. Not only do you have to climb over other people, but by the time you get back to your seat, you've missed something important. If you decide to wait until the movie is over, the fact you have to go can bother you and prevent you from enjoying the film. I always go during the previews just before the film starts, to reduce the chance I'll have to go later. #1573

Feelings which encourage people to remove discomforts

Exercise 2: Removing discomfort

Stop breathing. What feeling encourages you to resume breathing? How strong is this feeling? What happens to this feeling after you take a breath?

The feeling that causes people to remove sources of discomfort is discomfort. Discomfort intrudes on people's consciousness, is unpleasant, and has a strong nuisance value.

> It's very irritating when you have something in your eye, or a splinter in your skin. I can't concentrate on my work until I get it out. The other day I was walking outside and got an object in my eye. It was probably a piece of rock salt. I thought it would go away, but it stayed. I was supposed to give a talk, and I realized I would do a better job if I got rid of whatever was in my eye first. So I sent word ahead I might be a few minutes late for the talk and went to the medical clinic to see what they could do. Fortunately they weren't busy. They checked me out, gave me some eye drops, and I got to the talk on time. [1574]

A second feeling is the feeling of pleasure when one removes a source of discomfort. For example, one feels pleasure when one scratches an itch, or no longer feels too hot or too cold.

> I was in the men's bathroom of a bar and overheard one man say to his friend, "If anybody tells you getting laid is the best feeling in the world, call them a liar. When you're crackin' for a piss, nothing beats taking it." [1575]

The release of tension is experienced as pleasure. For example, people like warmth because warmth relaxes muscles, releases tension, and produces pleasure. Therefore people enjoy lying in the sun, hot showers and baths, hot tubs, whirlpools, saunas, hot drinks, smoking, heat lamps, hot-water bottles, and electric heating pads. People also enjoy massage because massage relaxes muscular tension, and thereby produces pleasure.

Functions of removing discomfort

When people act to remove physical discomfort they protect the welfare of their bodies. By eating they supply their body with nutrition and energy; by drinking they obtain necessary water; by avoiding heat or cold they reduce the chance of tissue destruction; by scratching they remove insects and dead skin; by altering positions they decrease the chance of pressure sores; by examining aches and pains they consider and discover ways to remove the cause; by ceasing to move when movement causes them greater discomfort, they reduce the chance of causing further stress and increasing the injury; and by reducing their tempo, withdrawing from others, and resting, they restore their strength. When they seek to clear a clogged nostril or ear, or to extract an object that is in their eye or between their teeth, they effectively clean the area and remove sources of infection. When they stop an object from rubbing against them or pressing into their skin, they remove a source of tissue destruction. When they breathe they obtain the air their body needs. By urinating and defecating they rid themselves of wastes. As a consequence of these measures people maintain their bodies in a functional state.

Excess behavior

Excess behavior is behavior in response to feelings which results in one acting contrary to the purposes the feelings are designed for. As a result, one loses resources rather than gains or protects them. For example, the feeling of discomfort causes people to remove the sources of discomfort. As a result people protect themselves from damage. However, there are situations in which people remove discomfort, but cause themselves damage.

In attempting to remove discomforts, people sometimes cause themselves bodily damage. For example, people often use medications with harmful side effects in their efforts to remove discomforts. These include medications such as analgesics, cold remedies, corticosteroids, laxatives, and drugs which induce sleep. People also apply treatments to reduce discomfort, in order that they can apply additional stress on their bodies. When an activity causes pain, the body is effectively applying a natural cast which inhibits movement and prevents further stress. However, if one uses a painkiller or muscle relaxant to counteract the pain in order to continue the activity, one is in effect discarding the cast. People do this in regard to muscle pain, eyestrain, and headaches which they sustain through work and sports. As a result they are able to put additional stress on their bodies and are more likely to damage themselves.

Society and removing discomfort

Society uses various approaches to facilitate the removal of discomfort. It provides a variety of facilities, services, personnel, and products to help individuals prevent and cope with discomforts. These include hospitals, doctors, dentists, nurses, drugs, anesthetics, drugstores, pharmacists, physical therapists, books on ailments and health care, massage, heaters, fans, air conditioners, humidifiers, refrigerators, hot-water bottles, heating pads, heat lamps, insulation, muscle supports, ice packs, skin salves, cotton swabs, beds, toothpicks, dental floss, toothbrushes, soft clothing, comfortable shoes, rugs, padded furniture, mattresses, cushions, padded prayer benches, antipain pills, muscle relaxants, suppositories, restaurants and cafés, water fountains, and vending machines with snacks and drinks.

Society and removing discomfort

Seat heaters have been recently introduced into cars. They seem frivolous, but one of the first things you notice when you sit down in a car on a cold day is that your rear is cold. When I turn on a seat heater I get so warm within a few minutes that I have to turn the heater off. #1576

Society also provides numerous practices which reduce discomfort, such as building houses with rooms for sleeping, providing heating and cooling systems in houses and public buildings, using padded seats in public transportation, expecting people to wear clothing designed for specific seasons, and turning patients in hospital beds at regular intervals to prevent bedsores. Society also provides various beliefs for guiding behavior, such as "You need eight hours of sleep every night," "Get three meals a day," and "An apple a day keeps the doctor away."

TAKING PRECAUTIONS

Brief contents

Detailed contents

Detailed contents

continued on next page

Taking precautions

Introduction

People are very much concerned with taking precautions. They take precautions to protect themselves and their resources. People take countless precautions to better ensure that they get food, water, and shelter; conserve time and energy; protect themselves from various dangers; avoid accidents; obtain stimulation; protect possessions; avoid negative reactions from others; and keep their sources of positive reactions. People take precautions by avoiding threats, removing threats, and reducing threats. The feeling that drives people to take precautions is anxiety. Anxiety involves an increase in tension. It is a punishing feeling which often dominates a person's consciousness. People experience numerous anxieties, or worries, about threats to themselves and their resources. People take precautions in order to reduce anxiety and to prevent anxiety from occurring. As a result of anxiety and taking precautions, people better protect their bodies and their resources. A great many precautions are instituted by groups and societies to better protect their members and their interests. People experience anxiety as soon as they become aware of a potential threat. This provides them with a maximum amount of time in which to take precautions. (See also the chapter on Protecting Self and Resources in this volume.)

Identification of threats

People are very interested in identifying potential threats to themselves and their resources. When people consider options and adopt courses of action, they consider the things which could interfere with or interrupt their progress. They remember past threats, watch to see that they do not reoccur, and try to be prepared if they do. They are also alert to the development of new threats, as well as to threats they may encounter in the future.

When I get ready to go outside, I take a look at the weather. If it looks likely to rain I wear my raincoat and rubber overshoes and stick a small umbrella in my briefcase. I don't wear my leather jacket, because water is bad for leather. #1577

When I travel I write the numbers of my credit cards and passport on a piece of paper, and stick it in my suitcase. I would certainly need this information if my wallet were lost or stolen. I also carry an extra pair of glasses, because it would be such a hassle getting my glasses replaced if they were broken. It would ruin my trip, because I couldn't see without them. #1578

People also learn of threats informally through talking to relatives, colleagues, friends, and acquaintances. An important focus of talk is bringing threats to the attention of others, and determining to what extent specific threats will affect the parties who are talking to each other.

People also pay attention to the news media. A large percentage of the news in newspapers and on the radio and television deals with dangers to one's person and resources. Actual and potential deaths and injuries are regularly reported on in relation to automobile, motorcycle, and airplane accidents; fires, storms, floods, tornadoes, volcanoes, and earthquakes; sports; swimming and boats; wars and terrorists; shootings and assaults; criminals; smoking, alcohol, and drugs; disease; pollution; and contact with harmful substances, such as asbestos, mercury, pesticides, and radioactive wastes. Threats to resources are identified through reports concerned with theft, vandalism, and fraud; natural and man-made disasters; and recession, inflation, and unemployment. Reports on changes in government policies mention regulations, penalties, subsidies, and taxes, as well as unemployment, welfare, and pension benefits. Media reports serve to warn people where and how they may undergo bodily harm or a change in the status of their resources. People show considerable interest in the news which could have an impact on them personally, and as a result people are better able to take precautions to protect themselves.

Every spring my sister was the first one out in our backyard. She wanted to be the first person in Charlottetown to get a tan and went to great lengths to do so. She tried to shelter herself from the wind and held up aluminum foil to try to concentrate the sun's rays on herself. She remained outside as long as she could before the cold drove her back inside. My parents would tell her, "You're crazy. The sun's not hot enough to give you any color," and "You'll catch pneumonia." But my sister would feel smug because she could already start to see some results. She was a sun worshipper and every summer she had a golden tan. That was ten years ago. Now her attitude toward the sun has completely changed. She never sunbathes anymore. Instead, her favorite part of the backyard is a shaded area. She buys special lotion which will protect her from the sun's rays, and she is much paler than the rest of us. What made the difference was the public information on the harmful effects of the sun. My sister has always been concerned about harmful substances, such as tobacco and alcohol. Now she has added the sun to her list of things to avoid. [1579]

People also regularly monitor how they are doing, in order to determine whether there are likely to be threats to their well-being. Thus people are concerned with their current status and progress in regard to their marriage, children, friends, work, employers, customers, and neighbors.

I just hate when I argue with my fiancée. It's threatening, because we both really want to get along and stay together. After we argue I want to make up as soon as possible and to see some signs from her that everything is back to normal. [1580]

My girlfriend's teenage son has started coming to me to talk, and wants to show me various things he's accomplished. It's great progress. Six months ago he ignored me and just answered in monosyllables. [1581]

People also monitor how well the people are doing that they rely on for positive reactions and other resources.

Be sure to call me as soon as you arrive, so I'll know you got there safely. [1582]

When I started going to teen dances, my parents had a big idea how to make sure I didn't step out of line. They made my younger brother tag along with me. Then if I danced with a guy, danced weird, or had a drag on a cigarette, my parents were told immediately. It was like being a prisoner. [1583]

As people become aware of threats, they focus on them and decide whether or not to do anything about them.

There is a four-year-old in my neighborhood who constantly plays in the road, and was nearly hit by a car twice this past summer. Neighbors become very nervous when they see him in the road and frequently take him home. #1584

Sometimes when I walk down the sidewalk I see a cat crossing the road or standing on the edge of the street. I usually slow down or stop because I don't want to cause the cat to try to avoid me and be hit by an approaching car. I would just feel awful if this happened. #1585

Concerns about threats tend to change over time.

Right up until the time I was seventeen, I wanted very badly to have a baby. Then I started hearing about all the unpleasant stuff and all the things that could go wrong during pregnancy and childbirth. It made me decide that if I was going to have a child, I would adopt one. But now that I've gotten older and more used to my body, my attitude has changed. Now I think I would like to have one myself. #1586

What people worry about and take precautions against

Worries, or anxieties, are very common.

Rarely do we get through a day without one worry or another. People find thousands of reasons to worry. Everyone worries, even though most do not show it. I worry constantly. #1587

People take precautions to protect themselves and others from the things which they worry about happening. There are a huge number of subjects and events that people worry about and take precautions against. These are so numerous and these change so frequently that it is impossible to mention them all. Nevertheless, as an aid to discussion, one can group some of these worries and precautions into the following categories:

1. Unknowns
2. Meeting objectives
3. Health and physical comfort
4. Physical safety
5. Social acceptance
6. Appearance
7. Relationships
8. The welfare of loved ones
9. Education, work, money, and possessions
10. Sources of stimulation

Practically anything can produce anxiety, depending on the context in which it occurs. Something that seems mundane or trivial in other contexts can generate considerable concern. Consider ordinary things, such as a paper clip, a coin, or an insect. People can become quite anxious if they can not find a paper clip when they need to fasten their overdue report together, if their child has just swallowed a coin, or if an insect crawls inside their clothes.

We must also recognize that a) there are many things that individuals worry about which they do not take precautions against, b) individuals take precautions in response to a specific worry at some times but not at others, and c) some individuals take more precautions in certain situations than do other individuals.

1. Unknowns

People find unknowns a big source of tension and anxiety. They often continue to feel tension until they can convert an unknown into a known. Once they succeed in making this conversion the tension disappears. People try to satisfactorily explain unknowns in order to remove this tension. The biggest unknown is the future and what will happen to oneself and to the people and things one depends on.

Often when people are faced with an unknown they imagine the worst that could occur. They consider that they could lose what they value most. They can imagine being fired, arrested, or killed, or the death of a loved one.

When you get a letter or a phone call you want to know who it is and what they want. When it is a letter from your employers or a long-distance call, you often worry whether your job is threatened or if your relatives are safe and sound. #1588

Whenever I have a health problem I start imagining the worst. If my allergies make it difficult for me to breathe, sometimes I just lie there and resign myself to death. #1589

Before my hockey game starts, I always worry that we'll lose. #1590

When my kids are late getting home, I start worrying whether they are OK or if they've been in a car accident. #1591

When my spouse doesn't get home when she's supposed to, I always imagine the worst. I fear she may have had an automobile accident or may be having an affair. #1592

After my girlfriend and I had an argument, she left our apartment and didn't come home all night. I called all of her friends and relatives to find out if they knew where she was. I drove everywhere looking for her. I also called the police and the hospitals. I was even worried that she might have committed suicide. #1593

When I was in the second grade, one day the gym teacher told me I had to stay after class. I was frightened and worried about what was going to happen. I immediately feared the worst and that my teacher would call my parents and they would punish me by not allowing me to watch TV. Then when my teacher talked to me she said she could see I had a great deal of talent, and she would help me achieve excellence in gymnastics. In other words, I was discovered! I felt so much relief. #1594

A policeman called me on the phone today and asked if he could drop by my office. I asked, "What is it about?" and he said he'd tell me when he arrived. Naturally I kept wondering what he wanted to see me about. After he arrived he explained that I was seen in the area where a bomb exploded. He wondered why I was there and if I had seen anything. I explained why I was there and he was satisfied. It's a lot easier dealing with something when you know what it is, than trying to deal with something unknown. #1595

It would be much less expensive in mental effort if people did not imagine anything at all happening when they are faced with an unknown, but instead would patiently wait to find out what will occur or to learn what has already occurred. Fears about the unknown consume mental energy and interfere with focusing on other things and achieving various goals. However, if people did not imagine what the unknown might be, they would be completely unprepared if the unknown is a real threat. If you hear a noise and do not consider what might have caused it you will be completely unprepared if the cause of the noise is a threat. If the cause is a predator, it is very much to your advantage to grab a weapon, hide, or run before the predator appears and attacks you. This preparation is only possible if you imagine that the cause of the noise might be a predator. Imagining that an unknown is the worst that could occur allows people to prepare for the worst that could occur. If you imagine the worst and plan how to deal with it, then you can deal with the worst if it occurs.

> When I was a child in 1945 a man delivered a telegram for my mother at our home. Before she opened it, she lay down on the bed and asked me to bring her the smelling salts. She suspected my father had been killed fighting in Europe, and she prepared herself in case she fainted. I don't remember what the telegram said, but I know my father was fine and survived the war. [#1596]

By imagining the worst beforehand people can also cushion the shock in case the worst occurs. When you think you know what is going to happen, you can be much better prepared than if you are caught by surprise. If a doctor is going to give you a shot or a dentist is going to pull your tooth, you would like to know this beforehand and prepare yourself mentally for the pain, rather than be surprised. It is much less shocking. Also, when people imagine that the worst could occur, they are more likely to make the effort to take precautions to reduce the chances of it occurring.

2. Meeting objectives

People have considerable fear that they will be unable to meet their objectives. Their objectives include the feelings they are trying to satisfy, the models they are trying to use, the tasks they are trying to complete, and the goals they are trying to reach. People are particularly likely to feel anxious when they encounter obstacles or feel their progress is too slow. A major reason why people conserve time and energy when carrying out tasks is so they can get to the other things they have to do.

> Sometimes I feel like I'm drowning in stuff I have to do. I think this is based on a fear I won't get things done. [1597]

> Some of my most successful working days occur right after a day in which I got absolutely nothing done. I am so annoyed with myself for wasting a day that I can't wait to get back to work and make some headway. [1598]

People are afraid of not meeting objectives, because they know that they will disappoint others and themselves. In addition, most objectives carry deadlines, and there may be serious consequences if one fails to meet them.

People take numerous precautions to ensure they do meet their objectives. They prepare beforehand, start early, put aside distractions, ignore objectives with a lower priority, work overtime, sacrifice sleep, get help from others, devote additional concentration to the objective, and obtain time extensions.

3. Health and physical comfort

People worry about and seek to protect their health and physical comfort, and they attempt to avoid various forms of discomfort and pain. People are concerned with getting enough food, maintaining a healthy weight, obtaining proper nutrition, doing proper exercise, and getting enough rest and sleep. At the same time they seek to avoid unhealthy food and drink, try to avoid additives and medications with bad side effects, attempt to avoid contact with pollutants and background radiation, seek to keep stress under control, and are concerned about developing diseases and other physical problems.

People take numerous precautions to ensure they will be able to maintain their health and physical comfort. They work to obtain suitable shelter, food, water, clothing, and medication. People seek to get the equipment and supplies necessary to keep themselves adequately clean and dry, and at a comfortable temperature. When their supplies are in danger of becoming exhausted and when their equipment is not working properly, people experience anxiety and seek to replace and restore them.

Conserving time and energy

Reducing effort by leaning, sitting, and lying down

1. (*left*) Store owner leaning on a counter. Vietnam. H.H.

2. (*right*) Ice cream vendor leaning against her stand. Montreal, Canada.

Reducing effort by leaning, sitting, and lying down continued

3. Leaning against a concrete wall. Montreal, Canada.

4. Lying and leaning on a couch. Vietnam. H.H.

5. Leaning and sitting on a bed/couch. Vietnam. H.H.

Minimizing movement

6. Sitting on edge of fountain with feet in water. Taj Mahal, India. H.S.

Minimizing movement

7. Sitting on edge of fountain with feet in water. Montreal, Canada.

8. Sitting on concrete bench. Montreal, Canada.

Conserving time and energy

Minimizing movement continued

9. Sitting and leaning on concrete bench. Montreal, Canada.

10. Sitting, standing, and waiting for Old Home Week parade. Charlottetown, Prince Edward Island.

11. Sitting and leaning with pigs and children before the morning work assignment. Ongaia village, Kilenge-Lolo District, West New Britain, Papua New Guinea. M.Z.

12. Sitting and standing before voting. Ongaia Village, Papua New Guinea. M.Z.

Minimizing movement continued

13. Boy sitting in a basket shop. Vietnam. H.H.

14. Patrons at a coffee shop. Vietnam. H.H.

15-17. Tourists sitting, leaning, and lying on a boat en route from Phuket to Phi Phi Island. Thailand. H.S.

15.

16.

Minimizing movement continued

17.

Various species minimizing movement
18-19. Zoo. Singapore. H.S.

18.

Various species minimizing movement

Localized movement

20. Tourists moving as few body parts as possible while eating a snack.
Viet Cong tunnels, Cu Chi, Vietnam. H.H.

21. Choosing an escalator rather than the stairs. Eaton Centre, Toronto, Canada.

Employing a means of reducing effort

Employing a means of reducing effort continued

22. Choosing a conveyor rather than walking. Airport, Toronto, Canada.

Employing a means of reducing effort

23-24. Lines of people waiting to ride the elevator rather than climb the stairs. Eiffel Tower, Paris, France.

Employing a means of reducing effort continued

25. Removing the top layer of a multiple-layered plastic tablecloth for the next customer in a Dim Sum restaurant. Chinatown, Montreal, Canada.

Minimizing distance and effort

26. Providing multiple paved pathways between buildings on a university campus. Charlottetown, Prince Edward Island.

Using slave species for transportation and carrying loads

27-29. Old Home Week Parade.
Charlottetown,
Prince Edward Island.

27.

28.

Using slave species for transportation and carrying loads continued

29.

30. Line of carriages for a tour of Old Montreal. Canada.

Using slave species for transportation and carrying loads

31-32. India. H.S.

Using slave species for transportation and carrying loads continued

33. Afghanistan. H.S.

Resting during the day

34. University students during exam week. Charlottetown, Prince Edward Island.

35. Attendant at a
beach rental service.
Waikiki Beach,
Hawaii, H.S.

36. (*below*)
Travelers en route
from New Zealand
to Australia. H.S.

Resting during the day continued

37. Children taking a nap during an excursion to a public park. Ho Chi Minh
City, Vietnam. H.H.

38. Musicians resting between sets. Caodai Temple, Vietnam. H.H.

39. (*above*)
   Taking a break while
   working on a garden plot.
   Ongaia Village,
   Papua New Guinea. M.Z.

Combining activities

40. (*right*)
   Drinking and walking.
   Singapore. H.S.

Removing physical discomfort

Removing physical discomfort

41-42. Sitting and lying in the shade instead of in the hot sunlight. Santo Domingo, Dominican Republic.

Removing physical discomfort continued

43. Dogs lying in the shade instead of in the hot sunlight. Luxor, Egypt. M.E.

**Taking
precautions**

**Warning
signs to
reduce risks**

44.
Sign on
electrical
power box.
Charlottetown,
Prince Edward
Island.

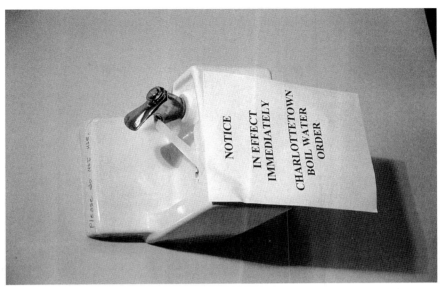

45. (*left*) Sign in a residential area. Charlottetown, Prince Edward Island.

46. (*right*) Sign on a drinking fountain when the city's water is contaminated. Charlottetown, Prince Edward Island.

Warning signs to reduce risks
continued

47. (*left*)
Sign at a public swimming pool. Charlottetown, Prince Edward Island.

48. (*right*)
Sign in Stanley Park. Vancouver, Canada.

WARNING!
Coyotes in the Area

Coyotes are wild animals and can be dangerous. Do not encourage them to approach. They are smart, fast, and will take what they can get.

All pets must be kept under direct control. For your safety and the safety of the animals . . . .

KEEP THEM AT A DISTANCE!

NEVER FEED COYOTES!

VICTORIA PARK POOL
OPEN 11a.m. - 8p.m. DAILY
• PROPER SWIM ATTIRE MUST BE WORN
• NO SPLASHING, PUSHING OR HORSEPLAY
• NO RUNNING ON THE DECK
• BATHERS MUST SHOWER BEFORE ENTERING POOL
• NO BREAKABLE ITEMS IN POOL OR ON THE DECK
• NO SMOKING IN OR AROUND THE POOL
NO DIVING

49. Sign in front of a building with snow on its roof. Charlottetown, Prince Edward Island.

50. Signs on a propane storage tank. Cavendish, Prince Edward Island.

Warning signs to reduce risks continued

51. Sign on the front door of an Atlantic Veterinarian College building. Charlottetown, Prince Edward Island.

52. "Prohibited to enter the water with glass bottles full or empty." Sign at Boca Chica beach, Dominican Republic.

Traffic signs to reduce risks

53. (*left*) Speed limit sign. Santo Domingo, Dominican Republic.

54. (*right*) "No heavy vehicles permitted on Sanchez Street." Santo Domingo, Dominican Republic.

Traffic signs to reduce risks continued

55. Parking spaces reserved for the disabled. Charlottetown, Prince Edward
Island.

56. Bridge out ahead. Notice that the signs are designed at 45 degree angles,
rather than horizontal and vertical, in order to attract more attention.
Prince Edward Island.

Traffic signs to reduce risks

57. No cars permitted on this street. Katmandu, Nepal. H.S.

Safety devices

58. Workers wearing hard hats, or helmets, in a house construction site. Charlottetown, Prince Edward Island.

59. Safety requirements at a construction site. Charlottetown, Prince Edward Island.

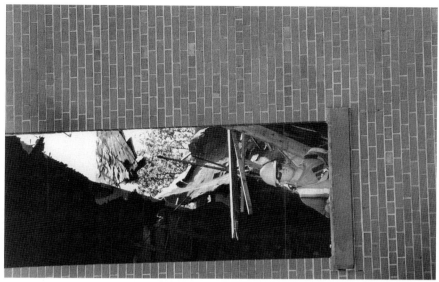

60. (*left*)
Workers wearing hard hats and a safety jacket in a construction site. Charlottetown, Prince Edward Island.

61. (*right*)
Worker wearing a hard hat and safety glasses inside a building which is being gutted. Charlottetown, Prince Edward Island.

Safety devices continued

62. "Dummy tape," or a strip of yellow plastic tape, placed at the edge of the second floor in order to warn workers on the second floor where the edge is so they will not fall off the building under construction. Charlottetown, Prince Edward Island.

63. Sign and fence used to keep the public outside of a construction site. Charlottetown, Prince Edward Island

64. Children wearing life preservers in the water. Boca Chica beach, Dominican Republic.

Safety devices continued

65-66. Life preservers worn by participants in dragon boat races. Charlottetown, Prince Edward Island.

Safety devices

67-68. Skaters wearing elbow, knee, and hand protectors. Palais de Chaillot, Paris, France.

Taking precautions

Safety devices continued

68.

69. Frame surrounding an open manhole. Charlottetown, Prince Edward Island.

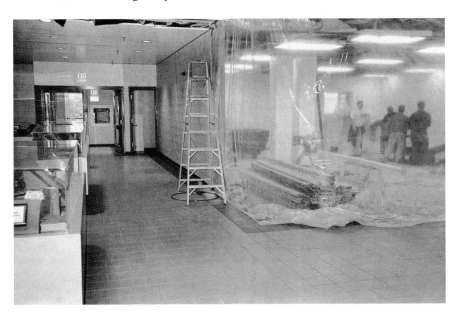

70. Plastic sheeting used to prevent dust from renovations entering the remainder of the building. Charlottetown, Prince Edward Island.

Safety devices continued

71. Fence surrounding an electric power facility to keep the public out. Prince Edward Island.

Safety devices

72-75. People who are about to be slung upward are placed in a safety harness. Amusement park, Jardin de Tuileries, Paris, France.

72.

73.

Taking precautions

Safety devices continued

74.

75.

Using guardrails for greater safety

76. Concrete guardrails on a bridge. New Zealand. H.S.

77. Guardrails on a boat. Turkey. H.S.

Using guardrails for greater safety continued

78. Guardrail to prevent people feeding ducks from falling into the water. Public gardens, Halifax, Canada.

79. Guardrail behind a bell at the edge of a cliff. Navplion, Greece. E.T.

Using guardrails for greater safety continued

80. Guardrails along the walkway, stairs, and ramp to the beach. Stanhope Beach Complex, Prince Edward Island.

81. Guardrails at steps into the whirlpool at an exercise facility. The floor is often wet and slippery. Charlottetown, Prince Edward Island.

82. Country bridge over a river with a single guardrail to hold on to. The one or two trunks of wood that one walks on total about five inches in diameter. Some people remove their shoes so they will have greater control when walking across, and occasionally someone falls into the water. Often both the "platform" and the guardrail can be disconnected to allow a tall boat to pass underneath. Vietnam. H.H.

Taking precautions

Keeping large animals isolated from humans

83. Polar bear in zoo. H.S.

Keeping large animals isolated from humans

84. Rhinoceroses in zoo. H.S.

Holding on for greater safety

85. (*above*)
On a teeter-totter.
Victoria Park,
Charlottetown,
Prince Edward
Island.

86. (*left*)
Holding on to
fence rails for
support.
Vietnam, H.H.

87. Holding on to statues. Singapore. H.S.

88. Holding on to the mast of a yacht with hands and feet. Charlottetown, Prince Edward Island.

Taking precautions

Holding on for greater safety continued

89-90. Holding on versus not holding on to an elephant. Thailand. H.S.

91-92. Children holding on to pole on a merry-go-round, while a parent holds on to them. Toronto, Ontario (*above*), and Charlottetown, Prince Edward Island (*below*).

Holding on for greater safety continued

93. Adult holding on to a child on a giant slide. Charlottetown, Prince Edward Island.

**Supervising
the safety of
children**

94. Children swinging. Victoria Park, Charlottetown, Prince Edward Island.

**Supervising
the safety of
children**
continued

95-96.
Making sure
that a child
does not fall
off of a large
decorated
frog.
Luzerne,
Switzerland.

Supervising the safety of children

**Supervising
the safety of
children**
continued

97-102. A child is stopped from collecting balloons in a city street during a wedding. Salamanca, Spain.

Supervising the safety of children

Taking precautions

Supervising the safety of children

101.

102.

Taking precautions

Security and safety workers

103. Canadian military personnel in an Old Home Week parade. Charlottetown, Prince Edward Island.

104. Royal Canadian Mounted Police officers in an Old Home Week parade. Charlottetown, Prince Edward Island.

Security and safety workers continued

105. Security guard. Notice the extra ammunition attached to the stock of his gun with rubber bands. Manila, the Philippines. H.S.

106. Traffic patrolman at a school crossing, Charlottetown, Prince Edward Island.

Security and safety workers continued

107-108. Lifeguard and notice board. Stanhope Beach Complex, Prince Edward Island.

Security and safety workers

The sign on the beach reads:

Beach / Plage: STANHOPE
Temp. Air / Temp. L'air: 24°c / 78°F
Temp. Water / Temp. L'eau: 18°c / 66°F
Tide High / Marée Haute: 9:45 PM
Tide Low / Marée Basse: 3:15 PM
Surf Condition / Condition de L'océan: Safe no -1 actuabits in frea
Surfguards: Ellen & Aleisha

Security and safety workers continued

109-111. Attendant directing traffic and attaching safety belts at a race track with miniature cars. Cavendish, Prince Edward Island.

110.

Security and safety workers continued

Remaining in
supervised
areas

112-113. Preference for swimming in area surrounded by floats. Stanhope Beach Complex, Prince Edward Island.

Taking precautions

Remaining in supervised areas continued

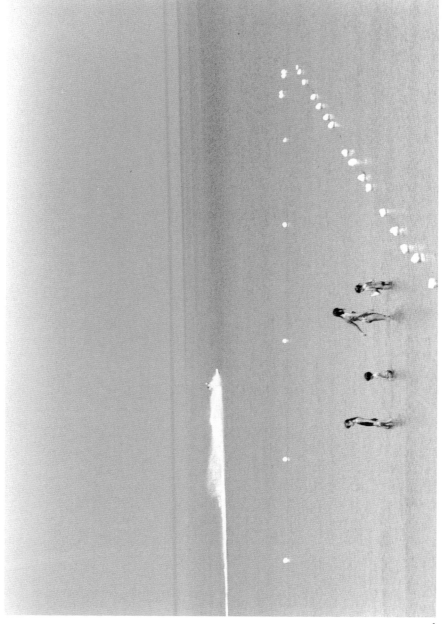

Safety precautions

114. Lowering a large float during a parade to get underneath electrical wires. Charlottetown, Prince Edward Island.

Safety precautions

Protecting self and resources

115-117. Street vendors selling souvenirs. Notice the "handles" on each side of the cloth displaying wares. Street vendor running and carrying sales goods in order to avoid being picked up during a police sweep of vendors. Bridge (Pont d'Iéna) between the Eiffel Tower and the Palais de Chaillot, Paris, France.

Protecting self and resources continued

What people worry about and take precautions against

It is very disorienting when you run out of everyday items like toilet paper, toothpaste, soap, milk, sugar, and clean underwear. Actually you make very sure you don't run out, so you don't go through the stress. Likewise, it is upsetting when there is no electricity, heat, or hot water at home, or your toilet doesn't work, and it becomes a top priority to get them working again. #1599

People are generally quite concerned with getting proper nutrition. They worry about not consuming the correct amounts of vitamins and minerals, eating enough vegetables, and getting enough vitamin C and fiber in their diet. They also worry about being too fat or too thin, and seek to modify their weight through controlling what and how much they eat, and by dieting and taking diet pills, eating food supplements, and exercising.

Another serious concern is with avoiding food and drink which is unhealthy. This includes food and drink which is no longer fresh, including meat, dairy products, vegetables, and water. People also try to protect their food and drink from contaminants by covering them and keeping pets away from them. They also try to avoid eating certain substances in such quantity that they could cause health problems. These include sugar, salt, monosodium glutamate (MSG), and cholesterol.

At first, I didn't even know what cholesterol was. But once I knew, it scared me. I try to cut it out of my diet by buying cholesterol-free foods. #1600

I eat as few eggs as possible because of all the cholesterol they contain. I also try not to go overboard with red meat, and when I do eat meat I cut away pieces of fat and skin and discard them. #1601

People also worry about drinking alcohol, and doing so to excess.

I don't like to drink alcohol because I read it kills brain cells. Every little bit you drink has an affect. Sometimes when I go to a bar with friends, I just order fruit juice. #1602

I think that I have been going out and drinking too much. I don't want to become a lush. #1603

People are also concerned with other substances which they ingest which could produce negative consequences. These include fertilizers, pesticides, animal-feed hormones, food additives, and medications.

When I was a young fellow there was no such thing as chemical spraying from the air. Everything was done by hand and farmers used as few chemicals as possible. But these days you couldn't pay me to eat a potato, they are so full of chemical garbage. I'd rather do without. I call them "cancer things," because that's what they are to me. Everyone I grew up with has either passed on, or is being diagnosed with the damn disease. #1604

I don't like using cortisone, aspirin, and other medications when I can avoid them. I'm sure all their side effects will come back later and haunt me. #1605

I know that drugs are there to help us, not hurt us, but I still don't feel safe. If I have an ache, rather than take an aspirin, I'll apply heat or just put up with it. Also, I have never taken birth-control pills because they increase the risk of having a stroke or heart attack. Some drugs stay in your system for a long time and can cause birth defects in your children. I just don't like to pollute my body with unnecessary things. The only medicine I'd be willing to take would be a prescription from my doctor. #1606

Pollution is another concern. People do not want to come into contact with harmful wastes and byproducts in their air, water, and soil. They also worry about the effects of smoking tobacco and secondhand smoke.

I grew up in a family of smokers, so I guess that's why I smoked too. I had a difficult time quitting, but I did so with the help of my doctor. I had a pretty good cough going there at one time. I never realized that cigarettes could hurt a person so much. Those damn things can kill you. #1607

I want to live as long as possible. Who gives smokers the right to ruin our lives as well as their own? #1608

I don't want to breathe cigarette smoke. When someone is smoking I move away or turn my head in another direction. If I'm riding in a car,

What people worry about and take precautions against

I open the window. Also I don't like to breathe the fumes from car exhausts when I'm walking outside. Sometimes I hold my breath until I get around the back of a car. #1609

People are also concerned with environmental hazards. These include sunlight and electromagnetic waves from microwave ovens, cell phones, television sets, and computer terminals.

When I grew up everyone wanted to get as dark a suntan as possible. There are still people today who don't want to believe sunlight is harmful. That's their problem, because the news media have reported on the dangers often enough. #1610

I have spent every summer of my life baking in the sun. So I know I'll look like a dried-up old prune when I'm older. #1611

In addition, people worry about dangers associated with climate, including frostbite, freezing, dehydration, and sunstroke.

People are concerned about physical and mental stress. They worry about anxiety and its potential to cause them physical damage through loss of sleep, ulcers, and high blood pressure, and they seek to reduce it.

I know that stress is one of the worst things for your health. I try to allow myself plenty of time to do things. Otherwise I can get pretty hyper trying to meet deadlines. #1612

People are also concerned with protecting their health through exercise. Thus they attempt to exercise, try to perform a healthy mixture of exercises, seek to correct physical problems through special exercises, and attempt to avoid exercises which cause physical problems.

I worry constantly about my health. I keep myself in excellent shape, so I don't know why it concerns me so much. #1613

I worry a lot that I'm not getting regular exercise. Now that I'm fifty, it's all the more important if I don't want a heart attack. #1614

I've been doing fifteen minutes of exercise every morning and it's helping my back. Now my back isn't as sore during the day. #1615

233

I quit lifting weights, because they caused my right elbow to hurt all the time. [#1616]

I used to work out every day. I didn't lift a lot of weights. Instead, I jogged quite a distance. But even using the best sneakers, I developed problems with my ankles and one of my knees. At first I thought I must be doing something wrong, like landing on the wrong part of my foot. But my doctor told me my pain was just from jogging too much. I don't do much jogging anymore. [#1617]

People also worry about getting diseases and developing other health problems. They worry about many potential threats, including childbirth, heart attacks, strokes, breast cancer, skin cancer, lung cancer, appendicitis, arthritis, blindness, Alzheimer's disease, herpes, and AIDS.

Although the idea of using a midwife has become more popular, many expectant mothers, especially those with their first pregnancy, prefer to have their baby in the hospital. They feel more secure about the hospital setting, in case anything were to go wrong with the delivery or the baby were to need immediate medical attention. [#1618]

I worry about getting cancer. Both my mother and grandmother died of cancer so it seems to run in my family. [#1619]

People frequently adopt measures to reduce the chance of catching a disease or developing some other health problem.

I usually wash my hands before I eat, because you never know what you have been touching, and you wouldn't want to get it on your food. [#1620]

After I use a public toilet, I wash my hands. Then I use a paper towel to turn off the faucet and open the door. I don't want to put my hands where others have had theirs. [#1621]

I wish I would floss every day so I won't get gum disease. But really, I only get around to it once every week or two. [#1622]

I have high cholesterol and a heart problem. So I've cut back on eating meat and French fries, which I love. I also walk to work and use the treadmill at the gym. [#1623]

You sure want to use a condom when you have sex these days. There's AIDS and everything else they don't know how to cure. #1624

Mom told me not to sit on the toilet seat in a public washroom because I could get AIDS. #1625

People also become concerned when they develop moles, lumps, sores, pains, and other physical problems, and worry about what they portend.

One morning I noticed some blood in my urine. I didn't waste any time. I got out a medical reference and read what they said could cause it. Then I went to see my doctor that same day. #1626

When people develop an illness or physical problem, they worry about it continuing or becoming worse.

I suffer from colitis. One attack caused me to lose twenty-five pounds. I kept vomiting and bleeding and the least amount of exertion left me exhausted. I keep hoping that I won't get sick again and have to quit school. #1627

I've been laid off work for about a year because my back causes me so much pain. I hope it gets better so I'll be able to go back to work and can start traveling again. #1628

I became very sick when I visited Vietnam. It must have been the food and water, and I developed a high fever and intestinal bleeding. I was scared I was going to die and would never see the people I love again. But after a couple of days I got better. #1629

People are also concerned about efforts to correct their health problems. They worry about correct and incorrect diagnoses, as well as complications from medications and surgery.

4. Physical safety

People worry about and take precautions in relation to threats to their physical safety. Their concerns include vehicle accidents, machinery accidents, heights and falls, the dark, certain natural phenomena, other species, the supernatural, certain people, particular impulses, and other physical dangers.

People are concerned about vehicle accidents which may injure or kill them. Drivers worry about drunk drivers, speeding drivers, teenage drivers, bad weather and road conditions, and falling asleep at the wheel. Passengers worry about riding with an unfamiliar or unsafe driver. Pedestrians worry about being hit by a car when they cross a street or walk along a road. Many people worry about an airplane crash when they fly, and in winter people try to be careful in the vicinity of a snowplow.

You never know when there's going to be an accident, so I always wear my seat belt. #1630

I worry about having to drive twenty-five miles from work to home when it's storming outside. #1631

I usually get frightened when someone is driving I've never ridden with before. I feel we are about to be in an accident. The idea of being seriously injured, maybe even paralyzed or killed, keeps going through my mind. #1632

My wife and I took a trip to Spain and found that the taxi drivers in Madrid spread cloth over the seats of their taxis, and the cloth covered up the seat belts. When we told taxi drivers we wanted to use the seat belts they would passionately explain to us that in Spain the law does not require passengers to wear them. It never occurred to the drivers that we actually wanted to put them on. So when we needed a taxi to go from our hotel to the airport, we insisted that the driver remove the cloth so we could use the seat belts. He argued that it wasn't necessary for us to wear them in Spain. But he removed the cloth anyway because we told him we would take another taxi. #1633

Because so many young people are killed in car accidents, we want our children to drive cars that will protect them well if they get into accidents. Our daughter studies in Vancouver and needs a car because their public transportation system is so inadequate. My wife and I thoroughly examined the crash-test results to see which cars provide the best protection, and we found two models with superior safety records. Both models had front and side air bags. However, only one of the models had an additional side air bag to protect the head and we decided to get that one. Then a relative in Vancouver told us that front-wheel drive would be much safer on wet and icy roads. The model we were planning to buy had rear-wheel drive. So we switched to the model we had previously rejected, because it did have front-wheel drive. However, we decided to wait half a year before buying it because they announced plans to install a side head air bag too. #1634

I grew up in Vietnam and immigrated to Canada. When I went back to visit Vietnam I was really frightened when I had to travel on the roads. There are no traffic rules or traffic lights. Drivers take too many risks and have too much ego. They are careless and speed everywhere. The buses race and compete to get ahead of each other. Life is very cheap and you hear of deaths from accidents all the time. Before when I lived in Vietnam I never realized how dangerous it is. #1635

Another source of concern is the occurrence of injuries when operating machinery. People may be cut or crushed when they use chain saws, power tools, factory machines, or tractors and other farm machinery.

I've always been scared of power tools. Even though I'm extra careful, I nearly cut two of my fingers completely off in a snow blower. #1636

Many people are scared of heights, because the injury could be very serious if they fell. As a result they are wary of climbing on ladders, houses, buildings, trees, and ledges.

I have a real fear of heights. I think it's because I'm afraid I might jump off. This is why I won't sit in balconies. Once I was on the roof of a church with my husband. I was so scared I couldn't move and began screaming. I had to close my eyes while my husband carried me on his back and another person supported me from behind. #1637

Lots of people seem apprehensive about elevators. I guess they think of what would happen if the elevator fell all the way to the bottom floor. I find when I step into an elevator I do so gingerly. #1638

Even when heights are not involved, falling is still a concern. People worry about falling when they use stairs, climb on furniture or boxes, use the bathtub, walk on snow and ice, and skate. They fear this might cause a head, hip, back, or ankle injury, or if the person is pregnant, an injury to the fetus.

One of my fears is spraining my ankle when I cross the street in high heels. #1639

Many children and adults are also apprehensive about what may be lurking in the dark that could cause them harm. Consequently, numerous people do not like to go outside at night, or into dark basements and attics, particularly if they are by themselves.

I don't like to walk home alone at night. I'm worried about rape. #1640

I have a great fear of the dark. Even though I'm in my late twenties I have to have a light on while I sleep. If I wake up in the middle of the night and it's pitch dark, I freak. I know it's ridiculous to have to turn on a light so you can close your eyes and sleep. But the fear is so embedded in me, I can't help it. #1641

Main Street is definitely the worst place to walk after dark. You always get honked at or yelled at and this is really scary if you are alone. You never know what kind of people might be there. People stand in door-ways and along the sidewalks or park their cars to watch the action. What an atmosphere! It always manages to scare me. #1642

The females I know are restless at night when they get out of a class or leave the campus library. The campus is not brightly lit and there are so many buildings and trees, you can't see who might be hiding around. Some of my female friends already have their car keys in their hands as they leave a building, so they can get in their cars and drive away as fast as possible. #1643

Many natural phenomena cause people to feel threatened. These include thunder and lightning, storms, droughts, floods, tornadoes, hurricanes, earthquakes, volcanoes, and meteors. People are also concerned about the results of environmental damage by man, such as the destruction of the ozone layer, global warming, and the possibility of nuclear winter.

Numerous people are scared of certain species of animals. These include rats, mice, lizards, snakes, hornets, wasps, bees, flies, roaches, earwigs, caterpillars, worms, ants, scorpions, spiders, sharks, jellyfish, bears, wolves, cats, and dogs. In the case of many of these species, people are worried about being attacked, bitten, clawed, or stung; catching a disease; or having an allergic reaction.

> A friend of mine has a major fear of dogs. If she visits someone who has a dog she sits there paranoid the whole time. [1644]

> I am terribly afraid of stinging insects. I think it would be like having someone stick a needle in you. I've never been stung, but needles hurt, and I think being stung would be worse. The noise they make! You know whenever they are around. Buzz, ew! I can just feel them landing, and crawling, and sticking it in (shudders). Eck!!" [1645]

> I have had a fear of caterpillars most of my life. I can't look at one without recoiling. My most common nightmare is boys throwing caterpillars on me, and whenever I have it I cry out. I probably have this nightmare about once a month. [1646]

> I have an enormous fear of birds. I'm terrified and can't stand to be near one. When I was a child a number of us found a bird. Then one of the girls stepped on it and killed it. Maybe my fear started then. My boyfriend's family has a number of stuffed birds in their house, but when they saw how much they upset me, they moved them to the attic. [1647]

Many people worry about religious teachings and the supernatural.

> I worry Jesus will come back to earth at any time and I won't be ready for him. [1648]

Numerous adults are frightened of ghosts, and many children are scared of monsters or the bogeyman.

> I always have my night light on when I go to bed, because of scary monsters under my bed. They won't come out when the light is on because they know I can see them. [1649]

People also worry when there are rumors of satanic cults active in their area. Horror films help to reinforce these fears.

Satanism is pretty scary to most people. Few people know much about Satanists other than "They run around in black robes with hoods and kill animals." There have been a few incidents on Prince Edward Island. Several years ago people were ripping off tombstones, but only the ones with crosses on them. Some years before that a group of people were seen meeting around Dead Man's Pond in Victoria Park in Charlottetown. They lit candles, chanted, and sacrificed black cats. [#1650]

When I was a kid people told me don't ever go to Dead Man's Pond because there are bad people doing bad things there. [#1651]

There are a variety of categories of people which others find frightening. These include drunks, drug addicts, violent individuals, bullies, enemies, groups of young males, members of gangs and motorcycle gangs, the retarded, the mentally ill, the handicapped, the elderly, rapists, people carrying weapons, terrorists, serial killers, escaped criminals, certain minority groups, and unidentified strangers.

Drunk people make me real uneasy. They are not in their right mind and I'm afraid what they might do. They may play around and give you a gentle slap, or they may really belt you one. [#1652]

Many women don't want to give their name, address, or telephone number to someone they know nothing about. [#1653]

People often avoid the neighborhoods and other locations frequented by the types of people they consider frightening.

People are also afraid of their impulses which could endanger their physical safety.

Sometimes when I'm somewhere high I start wondering what it would be like to jump off and tumble down slowly through the air. I feel this urge to find out what it would be like, and the urge scares me because I fear I might just do it. I don't think I'd actually jump, but the fear I might is scary at times. This is why I don't like to sit in theater balconies or to stand near the edge on top of buildings or cliffs. I avoid them whenever possible. [#1654]

I worry mostly on weekends. I head out to a club on Friday or Saturday night, have some drinks, get mouthy, and get involved in a scrap. I usually end up getting my face beat in. I'm making more enemies every weekend, and it isn't safe to go out anymore. There is no way I can have a good time. #1655

There are numerous other physical dangers which people worry about. These include broken glass, electric power lines, fires, explosions, war, drowning, and suffocating because of food stuck in their throat.

In winter our back door freezes shut and we can't get it open. I worry we won't be able to get out if there's a fire. #1656

I never like to swim in water over my head, because I fear I could drown. Then I learned to snorkel and use a mask and fins. The mask let me see under water and the fins made me a much more powerful swimmer. I became bolder and would venture out in water over my head. But last spring I was in the Dominican Republic and needed to swim across a ten-foot-deep channel to get to a shallow reef. I was terrified, but managed to do it anyway. #1657

Whenever I handle my propane camping stove I think about the possibility it could explode. I store it in a place which doesn't get hot, and I try to keep the fuel tank filled up so this is less likely to happen. #1658

When people consider physical dangers, they often think of injuries which they would personally find difficult to adjust to. Depending on the individual, this might be loss of eyesight, being badly burned, having their face disfigured, breaking their back and being unable to walk, suffering a brain injury, or seriously damaging their knees when playing sports.

5. Social acceptance

People worry about being accepted by others and maintaining this acceptance. They are concerned with what others think and say about them, and whether they will be included in social activities. Many people feel insecure when they are with others they do not know and when they are in groups.

Moving to a new community can be a frightening experience. I had lots of fears about the other kids not liking me and that I wouldn't fit in. #1659

Taking precautions

Like most teenage girls, my sister worries about being popular and if the boys like or dislike her. She also worries whether her friends and other people think she's a bitch. Personally, I think she is. #1660

I know from experience that school kids who want to play on a sports team have lots of worries. They worry whether they will make the team, fit in with the other players, be played in the games, and get a big reputation around school. #1661

I worry whether I'll make the basketball team in junior high this year. I really want to make it, but I was cut last year. I also wish I was more popular, kind of like Lloyd, the big jock stud of my school. All the girls chase him, and everyone looks up to him and listens to what he says. #1662

I worry constantly about what others think about me. When I am really self-conscious I wear baggy clothes. #1663

One of my friends refuses to go to parties because he is afraid of groups of strangers. He doesn't want others to know this because he thinks they will consider him odd or crazy. He is afraid of strangers because he worries about what they think of him. I finally convinced him to go to a small party of people we both know, and he enjoyed himself. But he still won't go to big parties. #1664

People do not want to be criticized by others or lose the resources they receive from them. They worry whether the things they do will hurt their reputations and alienate others. They do not want to damage their relationships with others as a result of their sexual behavior, lack of industriousness, failure to do what others want, problems they cause others, or the behavior of their friends and relatives. They do not want to ruin their reputations by associating with individuals and groups with a bad reputation, because this is likely to cause them to be seen the same way and to lose positive reactions and other resources from other people. Therefore they avoid those who are thought to be criminals, homosexuals, alcoholics, or involved with drugs. Similarly females avoid other females who are thought to be promiscuous or pregnant and unmarried, and adolescents avoid younger siblings and parents because they do not fit the definition of "cool" held by their friends.

When the radio plays a loud song I get up from my chair and turn the volume down. I don't want to disturb my neighbors in the apartment house. If they complained I could get kicked out by the landlord. It would be a lot of bother finding and moving to another place, and besides I like the apartment I am in. #1665

The only time I wear my seat belt is when I'm driving with my parents. They always want me to put it on. #1666

When I was in grade school I got into ice sports. One day I was last in a race and I waved at my mother and older brother when I passed them. They were sitting together in the stands and my brother was so embarrassed he wanted Mom to pretend I wasn't related to them. #1667

You really have to be sure you can trust the man you're having sex with in case anything ever happens, like pregnancy. Also, you have to be sure he'll be discreet about what goes on between the two of you in the bedroom. I'm not a big fan of guys who kiss and tell. #1668

There was a group of girls who did everything together, and talked about whatever was happening in school, at home, and with boys. One of the girls had a boyfriend who insisted on having sex. She felt if she didn't give in she would lose him, and without a boyfriend she would lose her status with her girlfriends. Later, when she discovered she was pregnant, she didn't know what to do and she confided in her girlfriends. Her girlfriends became worried they would get a bad reputation if they continued to associate with her. They thought people would assume that everyone in their circle was the same. So they started to spread stories about how different she was from the rest of them. They stopped talking to her, and moved away when she approached them. One of her friends said, "I didn't really think of her any differently. But if I continued to hang around with her, the guys might think I was that way too. Or even worse, my parents might start to come down on me about it." After the girl gave birth to her child, her girlfriends started to trickle back to her one by one. They didn't feel as threatened anymore. #1669

I've just found out I'm pregnant, and I'm so worried and confused. What are people going to say about me? How am I going to tell my parents? They are going to kill me. I'll probably get kicked out of the house. My life is ruined just because I didn't think it would happen to me and didn't always take precautions. #1670

Taking precautions

Many people go to great lengths to protect their reputations. One well-respected man won't buy liquor at a local liquor store because he does not want people he knows to see him. He doesn't want anyone to think he drinks a lot. So he travels about thirty miles out of his way to another liquor store where he hopes no one will recognize him. [#1671]

People also worry about doing things which will reflect badly on themselves by making them look foolish, stupid, lazy, rude, unclean, different, selfish, stingy, unreliable, bad, inferior, antisocial, or incompetent. Examples include forgetting someone's name, where they put something, or what they were trying to say; failing to speak to others; having body odor or bad breath; getting pieces of food or food stains on their teeth or clothes; putting their clothing on improperly; accidentally exposing private parts of their bodies; falling; not doing their share; acting nervous; making mistakes; and doing a poor job speaking or performing in public.

Most people worry about being late for work or school, because they don't want to make a bad impression. Some prefer to skip class rather than attract everyone's attention when they walk in late. [#1672]

I cannot use public washrooms because I am so nervous that others will hear me. No matter how bad I have to go to the toilet, I will hold on until I can find a private one. Once I went to a hockey game, and from the moment I arrived I desperately needed to use the toilet. However, I painfully sat through two hours of hockey in the cold rink trying hard to avoid thinking about having to go. I got agitated and cranky and certainly didn't enjoy the game. [#1673]

My mom is visiting our relatives in Vietnam and was telling me over the phone that she is going to the wedding of her friend's son. I told her I wanted to give them a present of some money. She said she was giving them $40 U.S. I told her to give them $60 U.S. from me. "No, no," she said, "you can't do that. I would be embarrassed if you gave more than me." I told her, "I'm younger and working. I have more money." But she said, "I'm older. Don't insult me." Mom was worried she would look bad. Because she is older, if she gave less than me she would look less generous and less a person. So we compromised and decided that we would each give the same amount. [#1674]

What people worry about and take precautions against

I went to my first native sweat lodge ceremony with a friend of mine. The ceremony consists of four rounds. During each round every person in the sacred circle inside the sweat lodge has to say a prayer in turn. I was told it is customary for a person to say "Juguoae Niskam," or "Come here, Creator," at the beginning of their prayer, and to say "Welalin Niskam," or "Thank you, Creator," at the end of their prayer. I was worried I wouldn't remember these words, but I nodded my head as though I understood. As the people ahead of me said their prayers, all I could think about was what I was going to say in my prayer. It was a little nerve-wracking. I was going to have to say an oral prayer, and possibly a personal one, in front of complete strangers. I would also be saying it in front of my friend, who would probably laugh in my face about it afterwards. At the same time, I would have to place the prayer in context, similar to what others in the lodge were saying, or else I would look stupid. In addition, I would have to pray to a deity I had never prayed to before. There was no way I could pass and not say a prayer, because I would look lazy to the others. Also, it was getting extremely hot in there. All these factors were piling up on me, along with lots of steam, as it became my turn to say my prayer. I began by screwing up the first line. I said, "Jugalee Numiskam," instead of "Juguoae Niskam." I was corrected, and then I managed to thank the Great Spirit for creating earth and the universe, and I asked him to guide us humans into living in harmony with all other life on earth. It was a fairly undetailed, uninteresting prayer. If there is a scale for grading prayers, mine wouldn't rate very high at all. However, the purpose of the ceremony is not to prove how good you are at making prayers, but to cleanse yourself mentally, physically, and spiritually. I wish my thoughts had focused more on this, instead of trying to think up prayers to say. I wondered if others were having the same difficulty. It wouldn't surprise me if they were, because most of us were strangers. Very likely, if it were a true Mi'kmaq sweat lodge, and everybody were members of the same tribe and knew each other well, they would be able to achieve wonderfully pure thoughts throughout the whole ceremony and could just let their prayers flow out of them. The one thing about a sweat lodge ceremony, however, is even if the others consider my prayers stupid, they are not allowed to tell anyone else what is said during the ceremony. #1675

People take precautions to avoid embarrassment, criticism, and rejection, because they hurt. (See Volume One of this series.)

6. Appearance

Most people worry about their appearance, because of its importance in their getting positive reactions and avoiding negative reactions. People are concerned about the shape and size of their head, face, nose, chin, eyes, lips, teeth, and ears; the color of their eyes; the length, color, and style of their hair; and their complexion and makeup. They worry when they encounter problems with their appearance, such as messy hair or makeup, baldness, blemishes, acne, crooked teeth, wrinkles, and sagging skin. People put considerable effort into trying to get their appearance the way they want.

I often worry about my appearance. I look at all those beautiful girls and I get very jealous. I know I'm not ugly, but I feel I have to make myself up and look my best even if I leave my place for just five minutes. I try to wear my clothes so I'll catch someone's eye. So I may wear a tight, short skirt and a tight, thin blouse. All this trouble is worth it when you get a few second looks. #1676

I worry about how I look to other people and what they say behind my back. I keep wondering what my hair looks like, if my makeup is smeared, and things like that. If something is out of place, people look at you funny and it makes you uneasy. #1677

Washrooms in schools and nightclubs are filled with girls trying to look their best by fixing their hair, clothes, and makeup. #1678

My brother spends a lot of time in the bathroom brushing and styling his hair. Often he puts water on his hair as he brushes it and then lies down on his bed with a pillow pressed against each side of his head. He's trying to flatten the sides and give height to the top. He usually has to lie there for quite a while waiting for his hair to dry. Once he tried to curl his hair but it just stuck out all over. He threw the curlers out the bathroom window and went back to the pillows. #1679

I used to worry about my hair slowly falling out. But I soon realized there was nothing I could do about it. So I don't let it bother me anymore. #1680

I worry a great deal about my appearance and my health, because I'm not getting any younger. #1681

In addition, people worry about the effects of pimples, acne, warts, scars, and tattoos on their appearance.

People are also concerned about parts of their anatomy other than their face and head. Depending on the person, they worry about the shape of their stomach, legs, thighs, arms, and neck. Many males worry about the size of their muscles, and many women worry that their breasts are too small. Members of both sexes worry that they are too fat or too thin.

I'm somewhat concerned about my weight. I'm not fat, but I haven't been exercising lately, and I hope it doesn't catch up with me. #1682

I feel insecure because my body doesn't fit the image of attractive women that you see in popular magazines and on television. #1683

Both sexes are concerned with the effects of aging, and women worry about getting back in shape after childbirth.

Many people are also concerned about how they are dressed. They worry whether the clothes they wear match together, are in fashion, look good on them, fit in with what others are wearing, and project the image they want to project. People take precautions to ensure that they and their clothing are clean and presentable.

7. Relationships

People are concerned about any difficulties that occur in their relationships with their mates, parents, siblings, children, other relatives, and friends.

I'm worried that my grandmother has lost a lot of respect for me. Last weekend my boyfriend was at my apartment. We were lying on the couch and were getting drunk with all our friends. Quite unexpectedly Granny stopped by. She acted normal, but I could tell by the look in her eyes that she was shocked and hurt. #1684

My friend, Amy, is a cause for worry. We've been best friends since grade school and I don't like it when she's mad at me. Last Thursday she arrived at my apartment at two o'clock in the morning with another girl and two guys, none of whom I've seen before. They were all sloshed and wanted to stay at my place for the night. It would have been alright, but I was studying for a test and Amy was being a total bitch. I wouldn't let them in and she got awfully mad and hasn't talked to me since. #1685

People worry frequently about their ability to establish worthwhile relationships when they do not have them. When they do have relationships, they worry about their ability to maintain them, and the possibility they will be left with no one. They also worry about their loss of resources if something happens to those they are involved with.

People have many worries about establishing relationships, including whether they will remain alone, find dates, locate a suitable boyfriend or girlfriend, and marry or remarry.

My cousin, who is nineteen, has no luck whatsoever finding a girlfriend and this worries him constantly. Even though he is a well-liked, good-looking guy, I know he questions his personality and his appearance. Every weekend he is out partying at the local lounge, getting drunk, and attacking any beast that glances in his direction. This just makes matters worse, because he's getting a reputation as a desperate tail-hound octopus. If he were seen there with an attractive girl, his stock would rise considerably, and the babes would be crawling all over him. #1686

Finding a mate is troublesome. I have difficulty thinking that there is someone on this planet who is perfect for me. I worry I will choose the wrong person. #1687

When they are in a relationship, many people have various worries about what is happening and what will happen. They worry whether the other person will want to continue the relationship, learn things about them that will cause them to leave, or find someone they would rather be involved with. They also worry if they are involved with the right person and whether third parties will succeed in destroying their relationship.

I sometimes feel scared that if I do or say something wrong, he'll stop loving me. #1688

My problem is that I'm twenty-two and my girlfriend has only just turned eighteen. I think her parents are conducting a personal vendetta against me, because they think I'm a cradle robber. #1689

My boyfriend worries me. He thinks it is imperative to have sex and is really persistent. I won't do it, even though we've been going out for several months. I find it hard to trust him, because sex is constantly at the forefront of his mind. #1690

It's normal for me to worry about my boyfriend. But now that I've moved away to go to university, I can't keep an eye on him. I hope he is being faithful. #1691

I'm scared every guy I go out with cheats on me. #1692

I'm worried my girlfriend is going to find out I'm cheating on her. I'm also scared I'll get some girl pregnant. #1693

A divorced woman I know started talking to a male friend of mine at a party. My male friend's wife joined them immediately and she kept her arm on his. It was clear she was worried about the divorced woman and she was being very protective. #1694

June and I broke up a couple of weeks ago. We still see each other regularly and I love her dearly, but I'm not one of her foremost priorities. June doesn't put anything into the relationship, and that worries me. Deep down I think she loves me, but that's questionable because of the way she treats me. Last weekend I met a girl out of town, Marie, and she is crazy about me. She wants to come visit me this weekend. Hopefully June will get jealous and show her real feelings toward me. This is another thing that worries me. Marie is a very sweet, caring individual who is very easygoing. Her qualities are the opposite of June's. It worries me that maybe I am meant to get stepped on and be treated like dirt. It sounds stupid, but I think maybe it's true. It may just be fate. #1695

I really don't want to forget my wife's birthday. She would figure she doesn't really matter to me. But she does enormously. #1696

My husband left me for another woman. He came back, but I worry he might leave again. #1697

People also worry about breaking up with friends, and having parents leave the family.

I worry that Dad will leave us when my little sister gets older. He's told me he's going to. #1698

In addition, people worry about relationships ending for other reasons, such as death, and the possibility that they will be left alone, be lonely and unloved, and even die all alone.

People are also concerned about avoiding and ending relationships they do not want to have. They worry about hurting the other person, and what people will say and think if they do.

My cousin is really annoying and weird. She keeps showing up at my door. I don't know how to get rid of her without being rude. But that might be the only solution. #1699

I worry whether I'll be able to dump my boyfriend. We've gone together for a year and I'm bored with him. I guess I'll hang on to him until something better comes along. #1700

8. The welfare of loved ones

People are very much concerned about the welfare of those who provide them with positive reactions and other resources, such as financial help. They worry about the health of their loved ones, and about their various needs.

I just hope my kids are born with nothing wrong with them, and that they grow up OK. #1701

I give my daughter weight-control pills, because I'm worried she'll put on too much weight. #1702

I worry about what will happen to my wife if she keeps taking birth-control pills. I really don't want a vasectomy, so I'm not sure what to do. #1703

I worry about my father's health. He's had a heart attack and his health is not all that good. #1704

I am concerned about my brother. His cancer is not getting any better and he is quickly going downhill. Every time I visit him I wonder if it will be the last time I see him alive. #1705

People also worry about the possibility that a loved one will be injured or killed in a household, automobile, or boating accident, or in a natural disaster.

I worry when my husband drinks and drives. #1706

I worry about my little girl constantly. She's in her terrible twos and you wouldn't believe what she finds around this house. It's a constant concern just wondering how she might injure herself. #1707

People are particularly likely to worry when a loved one is not home on time, is living elsewhere, or is on a trip. They also worry that a loved one may be kidnapped or murdered.

We don't like having our little girl walk home in the dark after her ballet and acting lessons. No one is around and anything could happen. She might be kidnapped or raped. So I walk her to her lessons and go get her when she's finished. #1708

I am studying here in Canada, and I worry how my family in England is doing. If something happened, I wouldn't know for a couple of weeks, because it takes that long for mail to reach me. The only reason they would phone is if someone died. Anything less would be considered minor and too much bother to notify me about. #1709

When our cat is outside I leave the window open so I can hear him if he wants to come inside, and also so I'll hear any dogs who enter the yard and start barking at him. He's an older cat, and when I haven't seen him for two or three hours I often check outside to see if he's OK. When we have a party I try to make sure no one runs over him with their car. At Halloween we won't let him outside at all, because you never know what some kids might do to a cat. #1710

In addition, people worry about the psychological welfare of loved ones. They think about the difficulties their loved ones are having. They are also concerned whether they are dealing with loved ones in the right way, and whether their actions or those of another family member will cause lasting damage.

Taking precautions

My daughter is unhappy and withdrawn. She's also very stubborn when I try to deal with her. I keep wondering whether she'll turn out alright. #1711

I've been late picking up my six-year-old, Monique, at kindergarten three times now. Monique gets quite worried something has happened to me, and has become much more timid. So I try to make sure I'm there in plenty of time. #1712

I worry about my little sister. Mom yells at her and beats her and won't let her have friends. As a result she's very withdrawn. #1713

Mom constantly worries about my sixteen-year-old sister, and for good reason. She's a little troublemaker. #1714

My boyfriend is really losing it. He spends all his money on drugs. He's falling behind on his bills, and occasionally he skips work to get wasted. I try to get him help, but he is too stubborn to take it. I'm ready to give up. #1715

One thing worries me. My sister has marriage troubles and doesn't even know it. She's been married about three years now. Last week I saw her husband leaving a lounge with some woman, and they were draped all over each other. It may have been nothing, but it looked very suspicious. I don't know how to approach her about it. #1716

My husband is a heavy drinker. It's been a tense and unhappy home, and I hope my children will turn out OK. #1717

My wife had a nervous breakdown, and I worry that she'll have another. #1718

I really worry about my mother. Dad is an alcoholic and he becomes a real asshole when he drinks. It wasn't so bad last year when my brother was living at home. But now he's gone off to school. I don't like leaving Mom all alone with Dad. We talk every day on the phone and I hope she will tell me if something is wrong. #1719

My biggest worry is my parents. They have recently split up because Mom is committing adultery. She has a twenty-five-year-old boyfriend who is young enough to be her son. My brother and sister haven't figured it out yet. Mom has them brainwashed into thinking Dad is the guilty party. Dad is much too softhearted. He is renting a small, ratty apartment and still pays all the bills at our house and lets Mom have the car. The bitch doesn't have a job, and the money she has she spends getting polluted at the local lounge. She even has the audacity to bring her boyfriend to the house. The other day I blew up and told her off so badly that she was speechless for the first time in her life. I can't bear to live with her anymore, and we don't speak when we see each other. It worries me that we'll never patch up our differences. If she doesn't come to her senses soon, and stop trying to relive her teenage years, there is no way we can reestablish a mother and son relationship. #1720

People are also concerned whether their friends and relatives will make the right decisions and be successful at their endeavors.

When my friend is unhappy or worried, it upsets me and I worry about her. I fear she'll do something that will be worse for her in the long run. #1721

People worry whether their children will have successful lives, and they try various things to help them do so. They encourage them to work hard, manage money, get jobs, make good friends, make good impressions, be responsible, establish a good reputation, and avoid bad practices. People worry whether their children will do well in school, hang out with the right crowd, get involved with alcohol and drugs, get pregnant, marry well, and lead good Christian lives. In order to help them succeed, people often try to give their children advantages, such as education and property. They also try to improve their appearance, through such means as dental braces and cosmetic surgery. In addition, they may try to develop their children's talents and independence.

I spoke to a mother and her fourteen-year-old daughter. The mother said, "I hear more stories every day about little girls getting pregnant. I don't encourage my daughter to have sex, but I also know I can't stop her. Therefore I put her on birth-control pills. This way at least I know there is no chance of becoming a grandmother anytime soon." Her daughter said, "I don't want to have sex right now. I'm not planning on it for a long time. Mom just worries a lot, and I understand why she's concerned." #1722

My son is doing alright now in his schoolwork, but his mother and I were very worried for a while. He wouldn't settle down long enough to do homework, and we had to force him. #1723

I'm worried my son will decide he's not going to university next year like he's supposed to. #1724

Our grandson married a girl we don't approve of. We worry the marriage won't last. #1725

It really worries me that the world my grandchildren and great-grand-children are growing up in isn't really safe for them. There are so many problems in the world today. It's extremely easy for a kid to get involved with the wrong crowd, and when that happens there isn't very much hope for them. #1726

People are also concerned whether they will be able to take financial care of their loved ones, and how the loved ones will manage if they die.

I thought I used to have worries, but since I got married and had babies I have more worries than ever before. I have to worry about feeding them, clothing them, and providing a home. The pressure is very great, and I never stop thinking about it. #1727

I worry about a terminal illness or a handicap which would prevent me from providing for my family. #1728

When I take a plane trip, I get as large an insurance policy as I can, so my girlfriend and her children can manage fine if something happens to me. #1729

9. Education, work, money, and possessions

People worry about doing schoolwork; taking exams, finishing papers, and giving oral presentations; passing courses; choosing a career; graduating; paying for student loans; getting work; getting a good job; being able to do a job properly; dealing with colleagues and employers; holding on to the job they have; and advancing to a better position. In addition, people are concerned that they may not achieve their career goals, and let themselves and others down.

What people worry about and take precautions against

I'm not doing well in school this year. I'm worried I'll be kept back in grade nine next year. #1730

I really don't have any goals in life, and my choice of a career is extremely foggy. This frustrates me intensely as it is always on my mind. I don't even know what I'm going to major in yet, for God's sake! #1731

I worry most about school. I am on a scholarship and it is hard to keep my marks high enough to hold on to it. With six courses and labs, all my time is spent studying. The workload quickly piles up and is easy to ignore. #1732

I worry about getting a student loan every year. I worry whether I'll get the full loan, whether I'll get it early enough during the year, whether it will last through the year, and what I will do if it doesn't. Then I worry about paying all the money back after I finish college. I also worry about spending so much time worrying about these loans. #1733

Personally, I have many problems. I am on the university hockey team and this takes up most of my time. I worry constantly whether to quit hockey and try to find a job. If I don't I'll be broke all semester. It is nearly impossible to do all three; play hockey, hold a job, and study. My studies always suffer the most. #1734

My life sucks. I don't have a job, and I'm in big-time debt. I owe the university over fifteen hundred dollars, and they've sent a collection agency to get their money. Dad has been saving my ass, but he expects me to get a job soon. He doesn't understand how hard it is to find a job these days. I hope I can get everything under control and go back to university in January. #1735

I worry that my university degree won't get me very far in life. #1736

I worry about my future, because I don't think I'm going to have much of one. #1737

I worry because I'm in a dead-end job at a gym. I want something a hell of a lot better. #1738

There have been so many layoffs in my government department, all I think about is I may be the next to go. #1739

Work is a worry. There is a psycho wench who constantly bosses me around, even though I've worked there two months longer than she has. Also many of the workers think I'm a snob. This worries me because I'm really friendly and caring. But I guess if you don't know me, I could be considered a snob. It's because I'm very shy and just carry on in my way. #1740

I work at a fitness center, and have to do what I can to prevent the children who accompany their parents from being injured. Children are not allowed in the weight room because they could be accidentally struck by people working out, or get their hands caught in the weight machines. However, their parents often tell them they can go in the weight room if they don't touch anything. When this happens I tell the children they aren't allowed inside. Also, the fitness center does not provide a lifeguard at the pool, and parents are required to supervise their children in the swimming area. But some parents leave their children in the pool while they go work out with weights. When this happens I have to find the parents and tell them they have to watch their kids. Sometimes parents encourage their kids to break the rules. Because the pool is very shallow and there is no diving board, no one is allowed to dive or jump into the pool. However parents frequently let their children jump from the sides of the pool. When I see this happen I immediately go tell parents it isn't allowed and explain why. Often parents will watch to make sure I am not looking so the child can continue jumping. One girl who jumped hit her head on the side of the pool, lost consciousness, and began to drown. Fortunately the guy working at the time noticed and saved the girl. It's not easy trying to prevent accidents in my job. #1741

People who own businesses worry about their sales, their costs, and their competition.

I sell stamps and coins at the flea market every week. Business is really slow and I haven't paid for half the stock I bought. If things don't pick up soon I'll have to try another location. #1742

I hope I can sell enough real estate to make a decent living for my family. #1743

I worry whether sales in my store will be good enough during Christmas to pay off my bank loan for the goods I ordered in the fall. I also need a good Christmas to carry me through to the summer. #1744

What people worry about and take precautions against

All of the national chains are setting up local branches and superstores here. People shop at the superstores because they have very competitive prices, much bigger selections than the local stores, and large parking areas next to the store. The local businesses can't compete and are folding. I have a local business and it has been hurt badly. I worry because I find it hard to meet expenses, and may have to close down later this year. #1745

There is a lot of turnover among stock brokers, who are frequently fired or decide to leave to work for another firm. When brokers think this might happen they protect themselves by making copies of their clients' accounts and asking their clients to follow them to another firm. However, firms want to keep their clients and try to protect themselves by insisting that a broker who is being fired leaves immediately, before he has an opportunity to make copies of client records or to contact clients. Often a broker is not permitted to return to his desk. The firm also calls the broker's clients as quickly as possible to ask them to remain with their firm. #1746

Individuals also worry about the careers of those they are involved with and financially dependent on.

My husband has a problem with alcohol. He keeps missing days at work, and I worry he'll lose his job. #1747

My husband is a doctor, and my relatives have him help them get appointments with medical specialists whenever they need one. I worry this will hurt his career. #1748

Many people worry about meeting their expenses with the money they have. They are concerned about earning enough, controlling spending, paying bills on time, paying off loans, maintaining a good credit rating, dealing with unexpected expenses, and coping with inflation.

I'm worried I won't be able to pay off my credit-card debt. #1749

I worry whether my car will break down. I need it to get to work, but it's getting older and the cost of fixing it could be astronomical. #1750

I just lost my job, and I have to make car payments for another year. I know I'll get another job eventually. But what will I do in the meantime?

I have a payment due at the end of this month, one at the same time in November, and another over Christmas. Hopefully I can convince Mom and Dad to spot me some money until I get a job. I wish I still had the money I spent during summer getting drunk in the clubs. #1751

I worry about the cost of food, fuel oil, and everything else going up. I get the same amount of money every month and don't know how I'll do it. #1752

People are also concerned whether their efforts to make money will be successful.

Sales at my business have not been enough to allow me to pay myself a salary. I won't be able to keep my business if things don't improve. #1753

We have a buyer for our store, but we aren't sure how reliable he is and if the deal will go through. #1754

People also worry about suffering an injury or illness at work and if this will prevent them from working.

When you deal with patients, you can't help but think about all the health-care workers who catch AIDS at work. #1755

Because I am a pianist, I worry that something will happen to my hands and I won't be able to play anymore. #1756

People also worry about acquiring possessions, and damage to or loss of what they currently own.

I haven't been able to find a job. It makes me wonder if I'm ever going to be able to afford a car. #1757

Possessions are important to people because they enable them to a) protect their bodies (clothes, a home, smoke detectors, medications, and exercise equipment), b) save time and energy (cars and microwave ovens), c) get stimulation (television sets, cigarettes, books, and music players), d) obtain positive reactions (fashionable clothes, cosmetics, a big house, nice fur-nishings, and sports cars), e) avoid rejection (breath fresheners, deodorants, soap, and washing machines), f) avoid criticism (window curtains and lawn mowers), g) obtain sex (alcohol, contraceptives), h) maintain relationships (telephones, appointment calendars, and stationery), and i) obtain money (professional books, computers, and information on investments). People are concerned with protecting possessions because it takes time, energy, and money to repair or replace them.

> If the weather report says its going to rain, I carry an umbrella so my clothes won't be ruined. I also close the windows in my apartment so my books and computer won't be damaged. #1758

> I'm always careful to put my eyeglasses where they can't be broken. I couldn't do anything without them, and it would be very expensive to get another pair. #1759

> When I visit relatives in town for a night or two during the winter I worry about what could happen to my home in the country. You never know, the furnace might quit and the pipes could freeze. #1760

Efforts are made to protect possessions, such as placing them in special containers or in well-protected locations to keep them from damage. Glassware may be placed in a cabinet, files in a file cabinet, stationery in a box, and stamps for a collection in an album. Often possessions must be protected from environmental stresses. Thus people place tops on containers of liquids, tubes of toothpaste, and felt pens; cover their art prints with glass; keep dust and sunlight off computers and computer diskettes; remove watches when washing dishes or taking a bath; place cars and gardening tools in a garage; cut down dead trees and limbs so they do not fall on their house or car; close house and car windows when it rains or snows; and avoid potholes when they drive.

People will even object to organizational procedures which do not allow them to adequately protect their possessions. For example, they will pass film and cassette tapes directly to personnel at airport security counters rather than let them be X-rayed.

> After I moved, I phoned up my Internet discount-brokerage firm and had them change the address on my account. They did so and didn't ask for any identification or anything. This means anyone else could get access to my account through a simple phone call. I didn't like this at all. So I called the company up again and complained. #1761

People are also concerned about use and misuse of their possessions by others.

> Michael is coming over tomorrow, and he never lets me play with my Ninja figure. It's my favorite toy and I always worry about this. I wish he didn't come over anymore. #1762

Often people do not loan items to individuals who are known to damage them or fail to return them. People may even refuse to loan certain possessions to anyone, often because people consider them irreplaceable.

10. Sources of stimulation

People take precautions to ensure they obtain the stimulation they want. They save their money to buy the necessary equipment and they shop regularly for supplies.

> I like movies, and I recently installed satellite TV which gives me a regular supply of movies to see. I bought some blank video tapes, but I quickly used them up recording movies to see later. I also recorded my favorite weekly series as well as programs on travel to different countries. So every week or two I go buy another ten tapes so I can record more movies and programs. I also need a copy of the regular monthly program which lists what there is to see on satellite TV. This program is like a thick magazine. I arranged for the local newsstand to reserve me a copy every month because I don't want to take the risk that they will sell out and I'll have to try to make do without a copy.
>
> A friend of mine, Jerry, is also into movies and he has the biggest television set I've seen. But it's still not good enough for him, because he can't wait to upgrade to digital TV as soon as the price of digital sets comes down. Jerry also has a satellite system for pirating satellite broadcasts from the United States. This lets him receive all of their movies and programs without having to pay for them. The company that provides these broadcasts keeps trying to alter their signal so that none of the pirates can receive it. Therefore Jerry's system works for a while, then goes down after the company alters their signal, then works again when the pirating service figures out a way to decode the signal again. People say that the last time the company altered the signal many of the company's legitimate subscribers lost their reception, but rather than

take responsibility for this the company said the problem was caused by sunspots. Because Jerry's system is working at the moment he is busy recording all of the latest movies as quickly as possible so he will have something to see the next time his reception is knocked out. #1763

When people know that stores will be closed, they are careful to obtain sufficient supplies of their sources of stimulation beforehand. They take extra care to have an adequate supply when they use these sources on a routine basis, and also when they are addicted to a source of stimulation, such as cigarettes, alcohol, and recreational drugs.

I like to have something sweet after dinner every night. When we go shopping I make sure I get enough ice cream and cookies so I'll have them available through the week. #1764

Concerns during one's life cycle

Each person's worries are normally related to their age and situation. As a result one sees changes in the content of worries at different points in the life cycle.

The worries of young children include being left alone, getting a spanking, scary shows on television, the bogeyman, monsters, strangers, the dark, storms, getting hurt, high playground equipment, drowning, bigger kids, big dogs, dangerous animals, and large vehicles.

I worry when someone comes to our door and I don't know them. #1765

My two-and-a-half-year-old brother has no difficulty interacting with strange children, but strange adults are another matter. He doesn't want to speak to a strange adult and he clings to the person he is with. When he had to have a new daytime babysitter, he acted fine when we took him to visit with her a few times beforehand and to meet her children. But when he was taken there to spend the day without any of his family members with him, he cried so hard he was shaking. We learned afterwards that he didn't settle down for about an hour. Each morning this crying period became shorter. By the end of two weeks he stopped whining for his mother as soon as he entered the babysitter's door. He had finally learned to accept the babysitter. #1766

Children are usually scared of things like the dark, the bogeyman, and so on. When I babysit, I get mad because I'm called upstairs every two minutes to turn on a light or close a closet door. I find that as they get older the boys aren't as afraid of the dark as the girls are. One girl told me that her brothers are just as afraid as she is, just that she's not afraid to admit it. #1767

I used to be afraid of large tractors and snowplows. I still feel jittery around them, but now I know what they are and that they won't hurt me. #1768

Bears scare me the most, because they are big and scary looking. I'm not afraid of the ones in cages, but I'd be scared if I saw one anywhere else. #1769

As children become older there are worries about starting school.

I don't want to go to school because I don't know anybody there. They probably won't like me and I will be teased and beat up. I'll have to play by myself, and I don't like playing by myself. At home I have Brian to play with. He can't go to school with me, because he isn't old enough. #1770

When I start to school, I won't be able to play when I want to. I'll have to do what the teacher says. I have to learn to read and write, and I don't want to. I just want to stay home and play in the sandbox and watch Mr. Dressup on TV. #1771

Children in elementary grades report being worried about going to the doctor or hospital, needles, dentists, bugs, scary faces, being excluded, getting hurt at sports, losing a game, music lessons, war, fire, what others think of them, getting in trouble because of others, making mistakes, not being able to get help from parents and siblings, car accidents, financial problems of their family, the health of their parents, and the death of a person or pet.

I worry about getting hurt playing hockey. #1772

When I go to a gymnastics competition, I worry that I'll forget part of my routine. #1773

What people worry about and take precautions against

I worry that my friends will think I dress funny and make fun of me. #1774

I worry how I'm going to look with braces. #1775

I worry that I'll be left out of games. #1776

Mom leaves for work early. So I worry whether my older sister will help me get dressed and fix my hair and make my lunch. #1777

I worry a lot about getting hurt in a car accident. I'm really scared when I'm with a woman driver. I'm even scared when we pass one on the road. Women are not good drivers. #1778

I worry when Dad can't find work. #1779

I worry when we don't have money that we'll lose our house. #1780

I worry that my parents will get sick. #1781

School children worry about teachers, assignments, getting work done on time, tests, grades, report cards, passing courses and grades, pleasing their parents, how they compare with other students, bullies, getting into the same class with their friends, taking showers with others, being popular, being accepted by the popular crowd, their complexion, dressing correctly, being accepted on sports teams and in band, losing games, the demands in higher levels of school, and attending new schools.

I worry about how I look. #1782

I worry that other students will make fun of me if I can't do the gym exercises right, and that I won't be able to do math exercises as fast as they can. #1783

I'm scared I won't be able to pass the exams in junior high. I've never had to write a big test in my life, and I don't think I can do it. I'm not smart enough to study for such a long time, and I don't want to have to stay in school an extra year. I think I'll end up with the nerdy crowds, who don't have a social life. All they do is sit home and watch TV. I'd hate to be like that. #1784

Taking precautions

When I entered high school, I was so nervous about being liked and being one of the cool guys, that I was willing to do almost anything. Fortunately the only embarrassing thing I had to do was to get my head shaved as part of our hockey-team initiation. It hurt my pride for a while, but the veterans on the squad felt I had suddenly become one of the guys. I was accepted and didn't have to worry anymore. #1785

Teenagers worry about having friends, being accepted by their friends, popularity, being part of the in-crowd, alcohol, smoking, drugs, doing well at sports, dealing with siblings, getting in trouble with their parents, getting in trouble with their teachers, being invited to parties, throwing a successful party, joining clubs, being elected to an office, getting their driving license, getting a car, having a fancy or fast car, wearing the latest styles, getting money, finding a part-time or summer job, getting a job after graduation, whether to go to university, and which university to go to.

I think it is really important to have lots of friends. I know my best friends like me, but I wish I was liked by lots of people. #1786

I've always excelled at sports, and I have a real fear of not playing well. People expect a lot from me, and I'd hate to let them down. I've been like this as long as I can remember. #1787

The idea of high-school parties is starting to scare me. I hear that there are a lot of drugs and alcohol at these parties. I wouldn't know what to do if someone asked me to do drugs or drink. If I took some, I'd be doing something that I know is wrong. But if I didn't, everyone would probably think I was a geek. #1788

I worry how I'm going to get the money to drink myself silly this weekend. #1789

I was nominated once for queen of my school. But instead of being excited and happy about the nomination, I was quite tense worrying if I was popular enough to be elected. #1790

I constantly wonder whether my brother is going to leave home soon, because he drives me crazy. #1791

I worry that Mom and Dad won't let me get my driver's license. #1792

What people worry about and take precautions against

It's really hard when you don't have a part-time job to get money for movies, restaurants, and gas. I hate asking my parents for money all the time. #1793

My biggest worry right now is passing an endurance test in lifesaving. I have to if I'm going to get my job back as a lifeguard this summer. #1794

I'm in a real bind. I don't know whether to go to university or take a year off to work. I'm scared that if I work, I won't ever go back to school. But starting university this year might turn me off school forever, and I'd never go back. #1795

A big source of concern is dating. Teenagers have fears related to dating, kissing, sex, pregnancy, their reputation, and getting a girlfriend or boyfriend.

I'm so ugly, no guy in his right mind will ask me out. I will be the laughing stock of the school. What if all the way through school nobody asks me out? I'll have to make sure I have the right clothes, makeup, and shoes. That way maybe someone will look at me. #1796

I've never asked a girl out in my life. I don't know what to say, and if I do find out, I'm afraid she'll turn me down anyway. I was pretty popular in junior high, but all these new people in high school will probably think I'm weird or something. #1797

Dating is a very scary thing in high school, because kissing and holding hands are not the only things that people do anymore. Guys are always pressuring me to have sex with them. I'm worried that if I don't give in soon none of the boys will ask me out, but giving in may get me into a situation I don't like. #1798

If I slept with a girl who had AIDS, and I got it, then everyone would believe I'm a fag. No one would ever come near me again. My family might even be shunned. #1799

University students worry about getting admitted into the university they want, coping with the workload, living on their own, paying expenses, getting and keeping a scholarship, qualifying for a loan, getting a summer job, selecting courses, doing assignments, exams, oral presentations, professors, passing courses, getting good marks, disappointing their family,

265

dating, sex, getting a bad reputation, finding a boyfriend or girlfriend, finding someone to marry, deciding on a major, getting admitted into the program they want, choosing a career, being able to graduate, what to do after graduation, being able to pay back student loans, getting into a graduate program, and making the right decisions.

I don't know what to take at university. If I take the wrong courses I might end up doing something I don't want to do. I'm very worried that a simple mistake could mess up my future. #1800

I'm petrified that I'll waste away when I don't have Mom to cook for me. She won't have a meal waiting when I get home. I don't know what to do if I run out of food, or if I'll find the time to cook meals. #1801

I'm worried I won't be able to hypnotize my subjects when I do my experiment for psychology. #1802

I worry about money a lot. I earn only enough for half my expenses and my parents have to pay the rest. If I fail out of university, all their money was wasted. #1803

Money is a subject that never leaves my mind. I'm always worried about it, and I have to budget all the time. I work, but I can barely find enough money to pay my bills. #1804

I worry about the price of gasoline going up. I have to drive some distance every day to get to university, and I've really had to tighten up my budget to pay for gas. #1805

I'm worried about my marks. I need a seventy-five percent to keep my scholarship. If I lose it I might not be able to come back to school next year. #1806

It bothers me that I'm not getting enough sex. #1807

My roommate doesn't have a boyfriend at the moment, and she's looking for one. She spends about two hours primping each morning before class. The final product is perfect makeup; expensive, freshly-ironed clothes; and not a hair out of place. She tells me, "I wouldn't dream of going out anywhere without looking my best, because you never know who you might run into. How can a girl who doesn't care about her appearance even hope to get a date, let alone a husband who is worthwhile?" When she doesn't have a date for a local event she gets upset and feels like a failure. #1808

I'm really scared. I'm graduating and I don't know what's going to happen to me. I don't know where I'm going to go, or what I'm going to do. #1809

Finding a job has my stomach in knots. It shouldn't be bothering me, because once I have a job my life will be well under way. But I'm worried I'll be stuck with a job I won't be happy doing and I'll have to do it the rest of my life. #1810

There's only one graduate school which offers the program I want. What am I going to do if I don't get in? My parents think I should apply to more than one place, but I don't want to go anywhere else. #1811

Adults worry about locating work, being destitute, making a good salary, finding a suitable mate, buying a car and home, accumulating possessions, hobbies and interests, being able to afford the things they want, taxes, paying bills, keeping up with colleagues and neighbors, stress, maintaining good health, getting along with their mate, infidelity, pregnancy, raising children, whether or not they are good parents, their children's welfare and safety, and who their children's friends are.

I worry about my future. I want so bad to get a better job. #1812

My biggest worry is about my wedding and how we are going to pay for it. I'm going to strangle my fiancée if she doesn't stop making outlandish plans. She worries that everything will go wrong at the wedding. And she doesn't know whether to invite her mother, because they have very little use for each other. #1813

Our neighbor constantly tries to keep up with us. Every time we mow our lawn, he mows his. If we trim our side of the hedge between our lawns, he sends one of his kids out to trim the other side. He wouldn't want anyone to think he is falling behind. #1814

I'm worried about my golf game, which wasn't very good this last summer. #1815

I am extremely worried that the Montreal Canadiens won't win the Stanley Cup this year. #1816

The thought of pregnancy scares me to death, because I'm young and not ready for it. #1817

I tell my child, "You shouldn't get around with him, dear. He's a bad boy. You can get better friends than that." #1818

Now that my children have left home I would like to go back in the workforce. But I worry I don't have the brains to do anything but housework. #1819

As adults become older, they worry about the behavior of their children, paying for their children's education, decisions made by their children, how their children will turn out, their own health, the best use of their time, accumulating wealth, dealing with aging parents, and retirement.

My wife and I worry whether our son will ever settle down and get a serious job. He's already twenty-five years old. #1820

What am I going to do when I retire? I have only two years to go, and I worry once I stop work I'll find the time long and boring. #1821

I look forward to retiring from my present job. I want to do something else, but I don't have the faintest idea what. If I don't get into another profession, I'm worried I'll end up like my neighbor and start shoveling snow off the lawn just to keep busy. I also worry about money, because it won't be as plentiful. #1822

As people enter old age, they worry about their health, the signs of aging, loss of physical and mental abilities, their children and grandchildren, the health of their spouse, the death of their friends, loneliness, meeting expenses, neglect by their family, entering a nursing home, death, and what will happen to their possessions and pets after they die.

I do worry about my appearance. My face may be wrinkled and my hair gray, but I'm sure not going to dress like an old lady. #1823

Aging is frightening to me, because all too often loneliness is just around the corner. #1824

It wasn't long ago when I would whip anyone when it came to recalling dates. But now I just can't seem to remember them. I miss half of my children's birthdays, and that can be frustrating. I'm really not too keen on the idea of growing old. Aging is for the birds. #1825

I worry about my eighty-year-old husband who sleeps a lot of the time and can't do much for himself. #1826

I am seventy-four and live alone. I have to watch my pennies closely and not spend foolishly, or I won't have enough money for the month. When my pension check arrives late, I get very upset. #1827

I'm all alone now since my wife died. So I've got to take care of myself. I worry that I'll be sitting in some senior citizen's home all by myself. #1828

I'm afraid of dying, but not for myself. Dying won't be so bad, but I don't want my family to go through the pain and sorrow. #1829

The only thing I worry about anymore is my cat. If he is still living when I die, who will feed him and look after him? #1830

My brother and I are both bachelors and we are concerned the government will get our farm when we die. #1831

How people take precautions

People take numerous precautions against the threats they perceive. When people become aware of a threat to themselves or their resources, they normally seek to get more information on the threat.

When I heard on the radio that the ozone layer is becoming thinner over the area where I live, I was concerned and wanted to learn more about it. I asked a friend who reads several newspapers and magazines to save me anything he encountered. The next day he gave me a copy of an article which said the minister of the environment was warning people to keep their kids out of the sun. I made three copies of the article and gave them to my wife and two kids to encourage them to take precautions. #1832

Often people make plans how best to deal with a threat if it becomes an actuality.

If my girlfriend became pregnant, we would both be too scared to tell our parents. So the best thing would be get an abortion. #1833

If I lose my job, I think I'll go back to school and study to be an astronomer. #1834

People facing risks sometimes ask what others would do in their situation.

I loaned a friend of mine a thousand dollars for a couple of weeks. But then he showed no signs of paying it back and kept using excuses to avoid me. I didn't have any proof I had made the loan, and became more and more concerned because I needed the money back. I told another friend about the problem and he suggested I write my delinquent friend a letter about it. I thought this was an excellent idea. In my letter, I outlined the understanding upon which I had made the loan, reported his measures to avoid repaying it, and stated what I was going to do if he didn't pay it back by the end of the week. It worked fine. I got the money back. #1835

My husband dealt with the financial matters of the family before he died. Since then I've had to make the decisions and raise three children by myself. When I'm faced with a decision, I try to think how my husband would handle it if he were still alive. #1836

The precautions that people take are normally geared to deal with specific fears.

I worry that a man might come in my house and attack me while I'm taking a shower. So I always keep the doors locked. #1837

When I want to use a toilet I look first to see if there is any toilet paper. If there isn't and I'm at home, I get another roll from under the bathroom sink. But if I'm in a public washroom, I check another toilet booth to see if there is any toilet paper there. If not, I consider looking for another washroom. #1838

People take action by attempting to avoid threats, trying to remove threats, and seeking to reduce threats.

Avoiding threats

When people recognize threats, one response they make is to try to avoid them. People are able to avoid a great many threats by simply keeping their eyes and ears open and circumventing the threats they notice. For example, when they see a mud puddle in their path they try to go around it, and when they see a long line of people waiting at the bank, they frequently decide to return later. People constantly try to avoid various types of threats. This includes avoiding physical dangers; avoiding dangerous people; avoiding threats to resources, such as possessions, relationships, money, and jobs; avoiding situations which are costly in time and energy, interfere with other needs, or damage reputations; and not acting on urges and impulses which could cause one to be hurt or lose resources.

People frequently try to avoid physical threats. For example, they try to move away from a wild animal, a fire, a fight, a drunk, a motorcycle gang, or a vehicle headed directly at them.

I live in the country and have to drive to work in town every day. But now that winter is here I get really anxious driving on the icy highway. Last Saturday I passed three cars that had gone off the road. This is why I've decided to move to town at the end of this month, and have already rented an apartment there. It's not safe driving on the highway in winter. #1839

When I see a horror movie, I go to bed scared. I'll turn out the light and take a flying leap onto the bed. I won't look under the bed because I'm scared I'll see a man with a knife. I pull the covers tight around me in case he tries to grab my legs. #1840

I won't use tampons because I've heard so much about toxic shock syndrome. It would be just my luck to get it. Everyone keeps telling me that I won't, but I'm just too scared to take the chance. #1841

271

I won't use a public Laundromat. You don't know what kind of diseases you could catch from other people's clothes. #1842

Who would be stupid enough to walk through that park at night? It is really big and you could easily get lost. It's pitch black, creepy, and dangerous. If something were to happen to you, no one would be there to help you. #1843

There have been a couple of food scares in this area recently. One involved salmonella poisoning from cheese produced by a local dairy. After the story hit the news, many people quit buying products from the dairy and some claimed they would never eat cheese again. Another situation occurred when several people died after eating mussels caught here. This was a few years ago, and despite government reports that the problem no longer exists, some people still will not eat mussels in local restaurants. #1844

Similarly, people try to avoid physical and health threats by deciding not to smoke, drink, or take drugs; stand at the edge of a roof or cliff; or engage in dangerous sports.

You won't catch me hang gliding or sport parachuting. No thank you. Life is risky enough without voluntarily upping the odds. #1845

People try to avoid those who might hurt them. In some cases they are afraid they might be hurt. In other cases they have been hurt by them in the past, and do not want to have it happen again.

When I went to see my family doctor there was a child there who was afraid of getting a shot. He was supposed to have his shot along with thirty or so teammates, but he had begged to get it early. He didn't want his teammates to see his fear and tease him about it afterwards. #1846

I don't like to see adults dressed up in costumes on Halloween. It makes me uneasy and I try to stay away from them. I like to know who I'm dealing with. #1847

When I was twelve years old I was babysitting a girl of seven who lived next to me. We decided to walk down the street to a store some distance away. It was a very busy street. Halfway to the store I noticed a truck parked a short distance ahead of us. I didn't think anything of it until we passed the truck and I saw a man inside watching us intently. When we were ahead of the truck it drove slowly ahead of us and parked again. Once again the man watched us as we walked by, and once again he drove ahead of us and parked. By this time we were very scared and we dashed across the street and began to run to the store. As the truck started to move ahead, a car charged out of a driveway and blocked the path of the truck. The man in the car was an off-duty policeman who was watching the situation. The man in the truck had been reported for following children during the previous weeks. But he hadn't done anything yet to cause him to be arrested. A couple of weeks later two friends of mine were out jogging when the same man got out of his truck. He was naked from the waist down and he masturbated as they ran by. After many other incidents were reported, he was arrested. The whole ordeal was disgusting and scary. [#1848]

Once I know a person is a taker, not a giver, I avoid them like the plague. I don't mind giving a lot when I first get to know a person. But then I stop and wait to see if the other person will ever go out of their way for me. Maybe I'll ask them to do a favor and see if they come through. I've learned. I've had "friends" in the past who took and took and then years later when I needed help they weren't willing to do anything for me. I'm not going to be a chump anymore and let takers use me and walk all over me. [#1849]

After I found out my girlfriend had cheated on me, I couldn't even stomach to look at her. I can't imagine getting back together. I know if she did it once, she'd do it again, or at least I'd always be suspicious. [#1850]

There are certain neighborhoods in Charlottetown that people are quite wary of and try to avoid. One such neighborhood has a bad reputation for a number of reasons. For one thing the streets and some of the houses are dirty and run-down. There are also vacant buildings with broken windows. The area contains people on welfare and you see drunks on the streets. There are several bootlegger establishments there, and it is also known as a place where you can buy drugs. A neighborhood gang used to hang out in the area and got in fights and beat up people almost every weekend. Most members of the gang are married now and many of them still live in the neighborhood. Recently, a male was stabbed in this neighborhood by his ex-girlfriend and died.

People from other areas are afraid of this neighborhood. They avoid the area and will not walk or drive through it when it would be more convenient to do so. One of my friends lives in this neighborhood and shares a house with several other people. He tells me he is a little hesitant about leaving the house at night, not only because of the fights, but also because of the crazy people in the neighborhood. A female friend of mine wasn't able to find an apartment elsewhere and moved into this area. She would wake up every night to the sounds of people yelling and tires screeching. She was too scared to go out after dark. Also she didn't feel safe walking into her building at night because of the smell of drugs in the halls. She said the children looked more like beggars than kids, and she would see twelve-year-olds sitting on front steps smoking. She moved out of the area at the end of the first month.

When people learn that someone is from this neighborhood they won't even try to get to know them. People think that if they spoke to them they might get into trouble with an older brother or a jealous boyfriend. If you are repeatedly seen in a bad neighborhood you'll get a bad reputation, and other people will start avoiding you. [1851]

People also seek to avoid threats to their resources. For example, they take various measures to keep possessions out of situations in which they might be damaged or stolen, and avoid handling possessions in ways which can damage them. If they allow others to use their possessions, the possessions may become worn or damaged, others may have the possessions when they want to use them, and others may not return the possessions quickly or even at all.

My younger sister would enter my room, borrow my clothes and other items, and not return them. So I put a lock on my door to keep her out. [1852]

One summer my wife and I housesat for some very close friends. Before we arrived the friends locked their new stereo in a closet, because they didn't want to take a chance we would break it. [1853]

There are all kinds of things at home you have to worry about when you expect guests or repairmen, or when you ask someone to feed your pets while you are out of town. There are always things you don't want them to see or know about. These may be financial statements, private letters, certain photographs, and adult magazines, books, and films. You don't want people talking about you. Then there are the things you think they might steal or break. So before someone comes over I usually go through the house and hide certain things away. #1854

I do a number of things to make sure no one steals things from my apartment. One person I know has a terrible reputation for taking things that belong to others, and I make sure he never comes over. Then when there are maintenance workers doing things outside, I draw my curtains so they won't see what I have inside. Also, when I buy something expensive, I keep the carton in my closet, not in the communal storage area downstairs, so others won't know what I own. #1855

I've learned the hard way that I can not put my better glassware on kitchen-counter tops when they are damp. It must have something to do with tension on the edges of the glass as it dries on the plastic surface. Whatever it is, it cracks the glass. Now I put my wet glasses on the wooden dining table. #1856

I turn down the volume before I turn on my compact-disk player. That way I don't damage the speakers. #1857

There is a fitness center at the local mall. A number of members of the fitness center drive bright, shiny sports cars and they park them at the back row of the parking lot where other drivers are less likely to drive into them. They also park them at an angle, so that other people who park next to them are less likely to chip the paint on their sports cars when they open their car doors. #1858

The maintenance department delivered new desks for our offices on Friday and left them in the halls. They said they would come back on Monday and put them in our offices. However, we pushed them into our offices immediately and locked the doors. We wanted to make sure no one else would walk off with them over the weekend. #1859

People also try to avoid threats to their existing and potential relationships.

Because I'm divorced, some of the friends I had when I was married won't associate with me anymore. They're insecure. They feel I'm a free woman now and I'm a threat to their husbands and their marriages. #1860

When I leave home for the day I put objects against the bedroom and bathroom doors so that the wind through the windows doesn't blow the doors shut. My cat is in the house all day, and when the wind blows a door shut he could be easily cut off from his food, water, and kitty-litter box. #1861

People seek to avoid behavior which would threaten their relationships.

I won't use tampons, because I want to be a virgin when I get married. If you use tampons you lose your virginity, don't you? I mean what guy is going to believe you on your wedding night when you tell him that you really haven't slept with anyone else, you just lost it because of a tampon? #1862

I'm very much involved with my girlfriend, and I don't want anything to mess up our relationship. Therefore, I don't want to see anyone else on the side. I purposely don't go to clubs because I wouldn't want to meet anyone else and be tempted. #1863

People also seek to avoid threats to their money and jobs. For example, individuals put cash in a bank account to avoid the chance of loss by theft or fire, do not tell others how much money they have in order to avoid jealous comments and pressure to share it, avoid stores where they would be tempted to spend their money, and avoid making what they consider to be risky investments.

My younger daughter, Jane, received sixteen dollars on her birthday. Gloria, my older daughter, then persuaded Jane to spend four dollars of it on candy and pop for Gloria and two of Gloria's friends. Afterwards Jane was upset over this and started crying. I suggested she give me the rest of the money to keep for her and she did so. #1864

In the case of work, individuals avoid causing trouble and breaking taboos, try not to let others get them in trouble, try to avoid taking risks, try to avoid criticism and damage to their reputations, and try to avoid letting others take credit for their work.

We had a serious troublemaker working in our department and had to go to considerable trouble to get rid of him. He really didn't want to be here and did everything possible to embarrass us and make us suffer.

How people take precautions

After he left, employers would call us up to find out if we would recommend him for a job in their department. My colleagues were scared to death to say anything negative about the man. They didn't care if he ruined other departments. All they cared about was avoiding any and all risk that they might get in trouble themselves for saying something negative about him, although what damage he could do them is beyond me. So when they were asked over the telephone about the man they would evade the questions, and say things such as "Ask _____ in your department. He knows about him," "If you have any questions, why don't you ask the man himself?" and "He could be suitable in a large department like yours." These communications were verbal. When it comes to written communications, one colleague stated to me, "Never put anything in writing. You don't want to take the chance of a lawsuit." #1865

When I get a good idea in my research, I put a lot of time into developing it. I don't go blab the idea to others. I don't want someone else to mention the idea in something they are writing and get the credit for it before I can get it published myself. #1866

People also avoid situations which are costly in time, energy, and other resources, or which interfere with the pursuit of their feelings and needs.

Some people exploit babysitters. Although babysitters are hired to take care of children for just a couple of dollars an hour, there are families that also want them to do their laundry or wash their floors. One couple called me up at six o'clock in the evening and wanted me there at six thirty. I had been a babysitter for them a few times before. Because they could not find anyone else, I agreed. When I got there, the house was a mess. There was clothing all over the place and the lunch dishes had not been washed. The woman asked me to feed the kids supper and help them clean up the house. She told me that she and her husband were going to dinner at a hotel and would be back about eleven thirty that night. At ten o'clock she phoned me and said she was not coming home that night and that she and her husband would spend the night in the hotel. She ordered me to let the dog out and feed the cat, and then she hung up. I did not have her phone number, so I could not phone back to tell her I had an interview scheduled the next morning. The couple arrived back home at two thirty the afternoon of the next day. They gave me a check for $20 and did not even thank me. I never returned there to babysit again. Neither did any of my friends, after I told them what had happened. #1867

People also try to avoid people and situations which could damage their own reputations or the reputations of those they are associated with or depend on.

A female friend of mine was in a club when a male went up to her and asked her out loud where she was the night before. She was so embarrassed by his question that she has never returned to that club. She felt his question implied she had spent the night with someone and therefore was a slut. Maybe he had heard she was with a guy and wanted to rub her face in it, or maybe he tried to phone her and she wasn't at home. My friend has a straight upbringing and a very proper image. Other people probably didn't notice the male's question, understand the significance of it, or perhaps they have since forgotten about it, but my friend still won't go back to that club. She doesn't want to be reminded of the incident or have others remember it, and if others don't see her in the club they are less likely to remember it and talk about her. #1868

Emily is really sweet, tries to be the best person she can, and attends university. However, her relatives are known locally to be trouble-makers. They drink a great deal, get disorderly, and start fights. They are also known for ganging up on people, and for getting in trouble with the law for breaking and entering. Emily shows no family resemblance as far as her behavior is concerned. But no matter how hard she tries she can't eliminate the impression everyone has of her family. People constantly make remarks to her about her family background. Some people won't associate with her because they expect her to be the same as the rest of her family. #1869

People in my community stay away from those with bad reputations. You need to have a good reputation and you can't keep one if you associate with someone who has a bad one. Those with bad reputations are excluded from community events. For example, one woman is divorced and is reputed to be a prostitute and a drug user. Her presence at community activities is endured, but definitely not encouraged. Once she attended an anniversary party for a well-liked couple. She was not invited, and when she arrived one lady seemed to speak for everyone when she asked, "What is she doing here?" The couple the party was held for didn't really want her there either. During the party everyone watched the woman carefully to see if she would make overtures to the men, and she did speak to some of them. Children of parents with bad reputations are also excluded from events. Last year there was a birthday party for one little boy. The only other boy his age was not invited to the party because his parents have a very bad reputation. They are on welfare, are involved with drugs, and make moonshine to supplement their income. I asked the mother who had organized the party why the second boy was excluded, and she said, "I don't want him hanging around with my little boy. Who knows what he might teach him?" I often see this boy playing alone because other parents don't want their children associating with him either. #1870

When I found out I was pregnant I moved to Montreal to live with my aunt. I told people at home I was going to Montreal to look for work. I had the baby in Montreal and gave it up for adoption. A year later I moved back home to Prince Edward Island. No one except my family knew I was pregnant. #1871

One day I had a conversation with an acquaintance who is a high-school student. As we talked Leo revealed he was increasingly preoccupied with the male physique. He was staring at the other guys in school, and was going to the newsstand to look at muscle-man magazines. He had also started going to known homosexual bars. Some time later I saw Leo in a local nightclub. He was with a girl, and when he looked at me there was murder in his eyes. He did not say anything and in fact turned his back on me. Two days later the same thing happened again. Then about a week after that I saw Leo again in a restaurant when I entered with a friend. He sat with his hand up to his face as though he hoped this would prevent me from seeing him. It's clear he wished he had never told me what he did, and that he wants to avoid me and hopes I will forget all about him. #1872

People also have numerous urges which they subdue and ignore because they do not want to suffer the consequences if they act on them.

I've talked to a number of people about what they would like to do but don't dare. One thing is get money and possessions illegally or immorally. They tell me, "Whenever I see a Brink's security truck, I have a strong desire to rob it," "I'd like to go in a store after it is closed and take whatever I want," "I'd like to run away with the money from my student loan," "I'd like to let someone spend a lot of money on me and not feel guilty about it," and "I'd like to be a hooker just for the money." People also feel urges to do things which would shock people. "I'd like to make a scene in a local bar, like throw a glass through a window," "I'd like to have a baby out of wedlock just to freak people out and destroy my reputation of being a prude," "I'd like to be nude at a public beach," and "I'd like to tell the people I dislike where to go in no uncertain terms." Another desire is to escape. "I'd like to run away from home," and "I'd like to just take off and disappear without telling anyone. I'd leave all my responsibilities behind and go where nobody knows me." People also express a desire for new experiences. "I'd like to hitch-hike across Canada," "I'd like to pretend to be mentally ill so I can see what it is like in a mental hospital," and "I'd like to be blind for a day and then regain my sight, so I can appreciate being able to see." People also reveal urges to do things related to sex. "I'd like to have an affair with an older married man," "I'd like to make love to a man in a public place, such as a public library," "I'd like to be transformed into a man for a day to find out what it feels like," and "I'd like to pose as a urologist so I can embarrass male patients." People also have violent urges. "Sometimes I wonder what it would be like to beat up my girl-friend. But as soon as I think this I dismiss it as an unhealthy thought." "I've been holding a kitchen knife and thought about cutting up some-one nearby. The feeling scares me and I shy away from it." People also want to do things to authority figures they dislike. "I'd like to write hate mail to the leaders of the powerful countries." "I'd like to take the leaders of all the countries and put them on a far away planet so they can blow each other's brains out and leave everyone else alone." One male, who was recently arrested for impaired driving, said, "I'd like to give acid to some cops when they don't know it. I want to watch them get right stoned when they don't know what's happening." The reasons people don't act on most of these urges are because they don't want to get in trouble, go to jail, get a bad reputation, be embarrassed, feel guilty, cause their family to worry, or be physically hurt. [#1873]

Often efforts to avoid a threat do not succeed, and only reduce the likelihood it will occur.

We have to go to lots of trouble to keep our parakeet out of the clutches of our cat. We put the parakeet's cage as high as possible out of reach, but the cat is ingenious in finding ways to get on top of any cabinet or shelf. Once there, the cat knocks the bird cage to the floor and has even managed to break it open. The other day I came home and found the cat on top of the refrigerator, draped around the parakeet's cage. #1874

Removing threats

Another approach used by people in taking precautions is to get rid of threats. Thus they may try to remove those things which have proven to be a threat in the past. As a result, criminals are incarcerated, and animals which are known to be poisonous or attack people are killed. People a) try to remove potential threats before they occur, b) take preventive measures to remove sources of tension, and c) try to act in ways which will remove the likelihood of feeling guilty.

People may try to remove a potential threat before it takes its course. For example, they will fix a leaky roof or pump out a flooding basement before the water causes more damage, or if they are unmarried they may get an abortion before others know they are pregnant.

When I see my shoelaces are untied, I stop what I am doing and retie them. Otherwise I may step on them, trip, and fall. #1875

When I use the bathroom at home, I never lock the door. If I were to have a heart attack, I want to make it as easy as possible for people to get to me. #1876

At night when my eyes were tired or felt irritated I would rub them, sometimes vigorously. Then one morning I woke up and there was a dark cloud, like a nebula, in the middle of the vision of my left eye. Whenever I shifted my eye this cloud would sweep back and forth across my vision. It was very distracting, and I went to see an eye specialist immediately. I think the problem was caused by rubbing my eyes. I had never heard you could injure your eyes by rubbing them. But after this I was careful not to rub them at all. Gradually the cloud started to disappear. #1877

When I put shrimp on the dinner table I put the cat outside. He likes shrimp so much he'll jump on the table to get it. #1878

Chris, one of the guys in our group, had just gotten his driver's license and we went out on the town to celebrate. Everyone but Chris was fairly well tanked and we stopped by Dairy Queen for some ice cream. When we returned to the car, Chris backed up into a police car. That was just great! Chris and the two officers got out to access the damage. The rest of us frantically began stuffing beer bottles wherever we could find a hiding place. You aren't allowed to have open liquor inside a car. Chris kept saying to us, "Holy Jesus, boys, what will I do? What if they arrest me?" There was no damage to either car. Luckily the policemen never saw our beer, and they told us to go on our way and stay out of trouble. #1879

I drive a taxi and routinely lock the doors when any children are in the cab. I also went to City Hall and got permission to disable the buttons for the back windows so no one can open them. I did this because young children would open the windows and start to crawl out, even when their parents were with them. In one case the mother was reading a book while her four-year-old went out the window. I yelled and she just managed to grab his ankles. If a child climbs out and falls in the street the parents are sure to blame me. Some parents don't even put seat belts around their children, but that is not my responsibility. #1880

I watched five teenage males run out of the entrance to the shopping mall while looking back over their shoulders. The oldest and biggest male, who appeared to be the leader, was wearing a black sweatshirt that was ripped at the collar. As they ran across the street he pulled off his sweatshirt and threw it to the ground, which left him half nude. The group continued to look behind them as they ran around the corner and disappeared. A security guard walked out of the entrance and stood looking down the street. I asked what had happened and he said the group had already been banned from the mall for a year because of previous shoplifting offenses. He then left to call the police. I suspect the boys had tried to enter the mall, and the guard had grabbed the oldest male, who struggled and got away, but had his shirt ripped in the process. I think the male threw his shirt away because he was trying to get rid of any evidence that he was the one that the security guard had grabbed. #1881

A man returned to Prince Edward Island and was staying with his brother, a local politician. Then the man went out one night and came home drunk. The politician was embarrassed that people might learn his brother was an alcoholic. Later the politician told people that he had kicked his brother out of the house and told him never to come back. He thought his brother would hurt his reputation and ruin his chances for reelection. #1882

282

No one wants to have a troublemaker working with them. Often he goes outside your department to criticize and embarrass its members. He can hurt your chances of promotion and cause your department to fail to get additional funds. You'd like to fire him, but frequently you can't because he holds a permanent position and continues to do his work. So you do what you can to neutralize him. Often he is very critical of the entire organization and you bring this to the attention of the organization heads. You can also point out that his attacks follow a pattern, and are not just directed at one or two individuals. You mention he isn't really happy in the organization, and suggest where you think he would be happy. Anytime he does something improper or fails to comply with regulations you send him a letter stating this. These letters, together with the cold-shoulder treatment, give him the idea he's no longer welcome. It you are lucky, he leaves. [1883]

A university president was convinced that the best way to balance the campus budget was to cut faculty. He talked of making "tough decisions" and sought to consolidate programs. Normally very few faculty attend faculty meetings, but the meetings at which he discussed his plans were exceptionally well attended. Many faculty saw him as a threat and he was not reappointed to office after his first term. [1884]

When the city finds dangerous bacteria in the water supply they issue an alert and you have to take all kinds of precautions so you don't get sick. Health advisories are released in the newspapers, over radio and television stations, and at work. Warning notices are put on public washrooms and water fountains and distributed to homes. You have to avoid tap water and either drink bottled water or boil your water. Bottled water sells out immediately in all the stores. They advise against taking a shower. When you take a bath or clean your dishes you have to add disinfectant to the tap water. They specify how long you have to boil the water and how long you have to let the water sit with the disinfectant in it before you use it. Chemicals are added to the city's water supply, and when the dangerous bacteria are no longer found in the water supply, the ban is lifted. People are careful about this because there have been deaths in Canada recently from contaminated water. [1885]

Today's newspaper had an article on a large meteor which is approaching earth, and would cause a great deal of destruction if it hits. The article discussed the idea of using nuclear weapons to blow it up before it strikes. [1886]

Other actions to remove potential threats include having tumors removed, decayed teeth cleaned and filled, and gangrenous limbs amputated.

People also take preventive measures to remove certain sources of tension. They often do this before they engage in an activity in which they do not want to be disturbed. Thus they may remove potential discomforts or potential concerns so they will not be bothered by them while they are taking a trip or enjoying entertainment.

> I try to finish all kinds of chores before I go on vacation. Some of these things have been hanging over my head for months. I just know I'll have a much more relaxed time if I don't have to think about doing this garbage when I get back home. Also, when I get chores done that have been annoying me for ages, I feel so good and happy and proud of myself that I'm in the perfect mood for starting my vacation. #1887

> I always go to the toilet before I sit down to a meal, take a walk, or watch a movie. I want to concentrate on what I'm doing. I don't want to have the need to go to the toilet prevent me from enjoying myself. #1888

People also try to remove a threat by trying to do the correct thing in order that they will not be bothered by guilt afterwards.

> My grandmother in California was getting quite old and kept wanting me to come visit her. I'd been putting it off, but then she got sick and I knew I'd feel awful if she died and I hadn't bothered to go see her. So I went, and it's good I did because she died later that year. #1889

> I was standing near the front of a crowd waiting for the doors to be opened at the flea market. A kid had put his arm between the doors to make sure he would be the first in. The doors open toward the crowd, and I leaned over and told him he might want to remove his arm because if the crowd pushed forward his arm could be cut off. He took it out immediately. I'd have felt pretty shitty if I hadn't said anything and he'd lost his arm. #1890

However, despite one's desire to remove a threat, many attempts to do so are not successful and only reduce the threat. For example, a cancer may return after the tumor is removed, or a new administrator may either introduce the same policies which caused the previous administrator to lose his position, or introduce policies which are even more damaging, such as firing employees.

Reducing threats

In most cases people can not avoid threats or remove them. Therefore people commonly use various means to reduce threats. These include the following:

1. Selecting a less risky course of action
2. Conserving resources
3. Preparing and using protection
4. Getting training
5. Exerting extra care, attention, and effort
6. Double-checking
7. Providing a margin of safety
8. Providing backup
9. Controlling others
10. Maintaining resources in good working order
11. Performing acceptably
12. Rectifying a situation

1. Selecting a less risky course of action

People attempt to deal with threats by taking courses of action which are less risky. Thus faced with the possibility of a crash when flying, one may decide to fly with the airline with the best safety record; faced with the danger of losing one's capital when investing in stocks, one may buy shares in a mutual fund or in companies with no long-term debt; faced with the chance of injuring one's back when lifting a heavy object, one may bend one's knees and lift with one's legs; faced with a health problem, one may see a doctor right away; faced with high blood pressure, one may reduce one's weight; faced with a diagnosis of cancer, one may undergo chemotherapy; and faced with the need to drive during the day, one may turn on one's headlights.

> When you are traveling in a car, you're stupid if you don't wear a seat belt. #1891

Taking precautions

I used to ride my bike to work. But I found out that every time I did so, I almost had an accident. Drivers just did not notice people on bikes. So I decided it would be far safer to travel by taxi, and that's what I do now. #1892

When you drive some distance you often get sleepy. I find the best way to try to stay awake is to listen to the radio and to eat. So I turn up the radio and consume lots of junk food along the way. Another way to stay awake is to masturbate without reaching orgasm. #1893

After we moved to a nice home in a better part of town, our best friends would visit and steal jewelry, china, and just about anything they could sneak out with. We learned to invite only two or three friends over at a time, because we could pay attention to them and try to make sure they didn't steal anything. #1894

When I'm traveling in poorer countries, I wear a money belt under my clothes. It makes it harder for someone to steal my money. #1895

People often select a time or place which involves less risk.

I don't see very well at night, so I drive as little as possible after dark. #1896

I enjoy walking by myself in the park during the day, but I would never go there alone at night. Something bad is more likely to happen. #1897

Stores are always getting robbed, so I try to leave as little cash in my store as possible. Whenever cash starts to accumulate I take some to the bank, and I make a night deposit on the way home. I also take the remaining cash out of the cash register at night and hide it. This is the small amount I need when I open the store the next morning. #1898

I'd love to go to Egypt on my next vacation. But given all the political troubles in the Arab world, I think Europe would be safer, so I'm going there. #1899

In addition, people may reduce their participation in a risky activity. For example, they may decide to cut back on smoking or alcohol consumption, consume less high-cholesterol food, or spend less time exposed to sunlight.

The less risky an activity is, the more willing people are to engage in it.

Every Thursday night a party, called a "Pig and Whistle," is held in the student center of the local university. These parties are quite popular and many nonstudents, such as young people from Charlottetown, want to attend. Students are admitted, but must sign for and take responsibility for any nonstudents who want to go. Guys from town (nonstudents) act really friendly and smile a lot in order to get a female student to sign them in. However, female students are scared the guys may get drunk and cause trouble, such as start a fight. Therefore female students will normally only sign a guy in if a friend asks them to. Otherwise they give an excuse why they can't. Male students, on the other hand, have little hesitation about signing in girls from town (nonstudents), because girls rarely cause trouble. #1900

People also try to reduce their risk of getting caught or being punished for an activity.

Janice is a friend of mine and her parents went out of town for the weekend. Janice invited me and another girl over, and later our boyfriends came by. We all hung out at her house and went out to the clubs that night. After we got back to her house we were all tired and slept there that night. Our parents knew that we were there, but they didn't know our boyfriends were sleeping there too. When Janice's parents returned, Janice's little sister told them that Janice and her boyfriend had shared a bed together. Janice called me at my house to let me know that her mother knew. I didn't get much sleep that night worrying about what would happen if Janice's mother called my mom. The next morning I decided it would be better if I told Mom myself before someone else did. I knew she'd be much more upset if she heard it from someone else first. I kept trying to tell Mom, but it just wouldn't come out. Finally, I told her. Mom was not pleased but she did understand and was glad I'd told her. I felt much better after I did so. #1901

2. Conserving resources

Another measure that people take to reduce threats is to conserve their resources so they will have more resources available if they need them. For example, they conserve money by controlling their spending. They adopt various measures to do so, such as not buying things that they feel they can not afford, not buying the things which they assign a lower priority to, carrying only as much cash with them as they want to spend, putting money into a savings account where it is less accessible, and paying off previous large purchases before they make new ones.

> Even though my parents are well off, I have to budget carefully at university because they won't send money at my beck and call. They like to know where every red cent has been spent. #1902

> I was with my girlfriend and her two children in the Toronto airport. It was very hot, and we had to wait a couple of hours between flights. I went upstairs and looked at the restaurant. The restaurant was cooler and was a nice place to sit and wait. But they charged five dollars for a dessert and we didn't have the money. I went back and told my girlfriend why it wouldn't work out. #1903

> Practically all of the men in the bingo hall are there accompanying their wife or girlfriend. Many of the men do not play any bingo during the evening. One man explained, "We can't afford for the two of us to play. She likes to play and I might as well go with her." #1904

> My wife and I wanted to take a trip to Belize. It is tropical and a great place to snorkel. But airplane fares were very high, and when we added together all the expenses, we guessed the trip might cost us several thousand dollars. It was too much money. We needed to pay for university for our kids, so we forgot about going to Belize. #1905

People also limit the amount of debt they take on and they try to make debt payments on time. As a result, less of their money goes to interest payments and they are in a stronger position should they need to borrow additional money in an emergency. People also invest their savings in order to protect their savings from inflation, and seek out the best rate of return for their money. They take numerous precautions to protect their investments, such as diversifying their holdings and maintaining contact with their broker when they are on vacation. People also take precautions so that they do not have to pay out additional money. Thus they put money into parking meters in order to avoid a fine, and they file their income tax forms on time in order to avoid costly penalties.

How people take precautions

The only reason some people wear seat belts in their cars is to avoid punishment for breaking the law. "I'd rather wear my seat belt than pay the fine." "The only time I put my seat belt on is when I see a police car." "I never wore my seat belt until I got a fine. Now I always remember." #1906

People also take precautions so they do not waste their money. Thus they try to purchase specific items as cheaply as possible. They often go to considerable effort to obtain a house, car, or appliance at the best market price. People visit or telephone various stores in order to find the store which sells a particular item at the lowest cost. They frequently buy clothes, appliances, groceries, and other items during sales; place their long distance telephone calls at times when rates are lower; buy stocks through firms which charge lower commissions; buy a larger quantity of an item at a store in order to pay less per unit; and order airline tickets well in advance during seat sales to take advantage of bargain fares. They also ignore or refuse many requests from other people for donations of money.

It you are careful you can save a lot of money on clothes and look as good as those who spend a lot of money. Department stores and discount stores sell some of the same styles as the trendy clothing boutiques. If you shop around you may find the identical item for two-thirds the price or less. You can frequently get two attractive items for the same price that one item would cost in an expensive boutique. Also, basic items, like black, white, or blue pants and tops are sold everywhere, are much cheaper in the less expensive stores, and look the same no matter where you buy them. Often you can wear a lot of inexpensive basics and accessories together with a classy name-brand item, and everyone will think you are a trendy dresser. #1907

I needed to buy a certain compact camera with a powerful zoom lens, and I asked various local businesses what it would cost. They wanted about $600. I also checked the Internet and found a store which charged only $450. So I contacted the store and ordered the camera from them. #1908

When I wanted to buy a music keyboard for composing music, I visited six different stores and called three others long distance. I'm glad I did,

289

because I found a store that sold me exactly what I wanted for several hundred dollars less than the other stores. [#1909]

People often do their serious drinking at home before they go out to a bar or lounge. This is to save money. It costs much less to buy beer and liquor at the liquor store and drink it at home, than it does to buy the same thing in a bar. [#1910]

When you run a garage you see the cheapest side of people. Most people hate to spend money on the upkeep of their car. They think all they should have to do is put gas in it. When you meet people on the street they are pleasant and in good humor. But when they come to a garage because their car isn't working, you can tell by the look on their faces that something is wrong. They feel frustrated and upset and under pressure to get their car working again as soon as possible. Most people are fussy and cheap when their car needs fixing. The majority would rather save their money and spend it on something else. Some people are cheap about everything. One man puts only five dollars of gas in his car each time he comes to the garage and always asks for a receipt. He only gets secondhand parts for his car, never new ones. If he didn't have any income, why does he want receipts to use to file for a tax deduction against his income? Another man and his wife both have very good jobs. When his wife's car was on the hoist I pointed out that the edges of the tires were worn so badly you could see the steel fibers. His response was, "Oh the tires will be fine. They've been like that for a while." The tires weren't suitable for a wheelbarrow, and certainly not for a car. People are less worried about what is wrong with their car than they are with how much it will cost them to fix it. Most of the time people are nearly sick with disgust after they see their bill. Often they put off paying it as long as possible, perhaps hoping we'll forget about it.

Another thing, all your friends, neighbors, and relatives want good deals on car repairs and lots of free favors. They also expect unlimited credit. One neighbor is too cheap to buy a good battery. So every time the temperature falls below freezing, he can't start his car and gives us a call to come start it for him. In winter this happens about twice a week. When we get to his house, he is unavailable and his wife gives us the car keys. He avoids us and doesn't come by the garage because he is scared we would charge him for the boost. Others are backyard mechanics and think that the car is a simple machine that anyone can repair. If they have the right concepts and the right tools they can take something apart. The hard part is to put it back together properly so that it still works. People come to the garage to borrow tools or to get advice. If you are too busy to repair something when they come in they often try to fix it themselves. They want you to tell them what is wrong, how to fix it, and which of your tools to use. Some don't even ask and just walk in and help themselves to tools and equipment. If they break them, you can bet they won't admit they did it. After they finish they don't clean up their mess and they don't offer to compensate you for using your tools, your garage, and your advice. #1911

People ask others for recommendations and they query different companies, such as various movers, house painters, and mechanics, in order to obtain the best service at the best price.

When I needed someone to move my furniture to my new apartment, I called several movers to see what they would charge. One mover wanted $100 an hour for a minimum of four hours. Another one charged only $60 an hour, and didn't require a minimum number of hours. I hired the second one and ended up paying $200 for everything. (Amounts in year 2001 dollars.) #1912

A friend told me to take my car to this mechanic in a nearby town. I did and he's excellent. I feel I can trust him to give me honest repairs. Sometimes he finds that my car needs a minor repair and he charges me just a couple of dollars to replace the part. People come from all over the province to bring him their business. #1913

People also use materials and equipment for their personal use which are supplied at their place of work, rather than pay for them themselves. These include pens, tape, paper, envelopes, stamps, telephones, photocopiers, and computers. In addition, people commonly fix their own meals rather than eat out, walk rather than call a taxi, and shop at garage sales, flea markets, and used clothing stores. People also frequently adopt measures so they will not have to pay for things they are not using. Thus they turn off lights at home when they leave a room and turn down the heat when they are out of the house or in bed. People also attempt to use certain items completely, so they do not have to buy the items as often. For example, they squeeze the toothpaste tube repeatedly to get every bit of toothpaste out, turn shampoo bottles upside down to get out all the shampoo, and add water to "empty" detergent containers to use up all the remaining detergent.

3. Preparing and using protection

People prepare and use various forms of protection in order to reduce the dangers associated with threats. Thus they let people know where they are going and how they can be reached; buy numerous types of insurance; install smoke and intruder alarms; put up fences; prepare storm and bomb shelters; wear seat belts in cars; wear clothing which protects them from the weather; eat proper diets; take vitamin supplements; lock their doors, houses, stores, offices, file cabinets, storage cabinets, desks, lockers, briefcases, cars, suitcases, mailboxes, and dairies; use grounded electrical sockets; use secret passwords to access computers and financial accounts; keep money in bank accounts; use safety-deposit boxes; use traveler's checks, a money belt, and hotel safes when traveling; prevent others from seeing them count money and from knowing their credit-card numbers and telephone numbers; put safety plugs in electrical sockets to protect children; wear helmets and padded clothing when they participate in sports; wear hard hats and safety glasses in construction areas; buy guns and knives for protection; carry personal alarms and chemical sprays for assailants; put up warning signs, such as "Shoplifters will be prosecuted," "No trespassing," and "Beware of guard dog;" install surveillance systems and shoplifting-detection systems; require employees to wear identification cards; and hire security guards or bouncers for their business.

> Before I use a toilet I place a few sheets of toilet paper on the surface of the water in the bowl. That way none of the dirty water in the toilet bowl splashes on me while I am seated on the toilet seat. [1914]

> I keep a list of the books and videos I've loaned other people. That way I'll remember who has them if they aren't returned. [1915]

> When we leave the house in the evening, we turn on a light. We don't want anyone to know the house is empty, because they might consider it a good opportunity to rob us. [1916]

> When I pass a construction team using a jackhammer, I close my eye on the side closest to the jackhammer. This way I'll be less likely to have a particle of concrete fly into it. [1917]

How people take precautions

Have you ever seen those pictures of people with ugly sores and big brown blotches from sitting in the sun too long? Ugh! Now I use a skin lotion which blocks the sun's rays. #1918

I carry condoms in my purse. I don't think of myself as loose, but I'm not a virgin and I want to be prepared if I meet a guy I really like. I don't want to chance getting pregnant or getting something like syph. #1919

Whenever I rent a car I ask for one with air bags. There are so many serious accidents today, it would be stupid not to. #1920

When I'm driving I sometimes see another driver do something that will cause me to have an accident if he doesn't notice me, and I rest my hand over the horn and my foot over the brake pedal. Perhaps he is starting to back out into the street just ahead of me. Normally the other driver sees me and stops, but when he doesn't I'm ready to honk and brake. #1921

I always carry a shovel and a sleeping bag in my car in winter. They really might help if I get stuck or stranded in the snow. #1922

One reason I started working out with weights was that I was tired of being picked on by the bullies at school. I decided I didn't want to be pushed around anymore. #1923

When you join a health club they make you sign a release so you won't sue them if you are injured there. #1924

When my girlfriend told me she was carrying antibodies in her blood for hepatitis B, I went to see my doctor. He suggested I go ahead and get immunizations against the disease just to play safe. I got my first shot last week. #1925

When my husband and I went camping he was worried to death about bears. He carried a pack full of pointed stakes and arranged them around our tent to protect us. #1926

We figured a serious recession was coming. So we saved everything we could and finished paying off the mortgage on our house early. We knew this would put us in a better financial position in case one of us lost our job. #1927

Taking precautions

There is a right and wrong way to plan a party at your house when you don't want your parents to know about it. The most important factor is to tell your friends they shouldn't mention the party around the wrong people. If the wrong people show up and get in, anything from a couple of beer to your best china will disappear by the end of the evening. There are also lowlifes who are likely to become rowdy. When others try to get them to quiet down or leave, they are known to go on a spree of destruction.

Proper timing is also important. If your parents are out of town, there is little problem. You just give the cue and your house is full of people and beer in minutes. However, if your parents are not out of town (perhaps they are working night shift) then you must take very careful precautions. First, you must let everyone know exactly when your parents are leaving in order that none of the guests arrive too early. If it is still daylight, your friends must arrive gradually and not all at once and their alcohol must be properly concealed so the neighbors aren't alerted. If the neighbors have kids the same age as you, it isn't a bad idea to invite them too just to stay on their good side.

One of my friends, Martin, has three or four major parties every year and lots of people go. Aside from the great times we have, the best thing is that there are no major problems. This is due to the careful arrangements that Martin makes. On the day of the party, Martin's closest friends come over and help him prepare the house for that evening. There is a lot of work, but everyone says it is worth it. First of all, they move all the fragile and important things up a long flight of stairs to a neutral bedroom which will be locked that night. This includes plants and expensive smaller furniture, such as antique tables and chairs. Martin labels all of these items in order that he will know exactly where to place them when they are carried back downstairs the next day. For example, if a plant was located on the right side of the television set in the living room, Martin would label the plant R-TV-LR. Similarly, if an antique chair was in the left-hand corner of the den, Martin would label it LC-D. This may seem extreme, but it makes returning things to their proper location a lot easier. It usually takes four or five people two hours to move these items. When the party is underway, Martin and his friends keep a watchful eye on everything and everyone. Everyone has a good time except for one or two who drink more than they can handle. Afterwards, five or six of Martin's friends stay overnight. They awake with hangovers and prepare for the dreaded part of the operation, the cleanup. We usually get up about noon and cleanup starts around one or two o'clock. First of all, the empty bottles are rounded up and Martin takes them to the bottle exchange, where he gets his just reward, or about thirty or forty bucks. By the time he returns from the exchange everyone is up and at it. A couple of guys sweep and vacuum while the others move the furniture and other things back downstairs to their proper locations. Martin makes sure everything is in place. Once this is done some people relax and watch the football game on TV. Those who are worse off go back to sleep or go home. Everyone agrees it was the best party ever, and they can't wait until they have to do the whole thing all over again. #1928

On Prince Edward Island most people take a number of precautions when they plan a trip. "A trip" may be a shopping trip from the country to a major town, such as Charlottetown or Summerside; a trip off the Island to Moncton or Halifax; or simply a day excursion to a provincial park or an afternoon field trip in connection with school.

Most trips are a big deal, rather than a spur of the moment decision of "Let's go right now!" To some extent this is a carry-over from the past when transportation was slow. When my mother was young they had to travel about eighty kilometers from their home to Charlottetown. An entire day would be set aside for the trip. The night before they would set out their clothes, make lunches, and plan the next day's activities. They would plan to get everything they needed done, because they did not know when they would travel to Charlottetown again. The next day they would get up very early and travel by horse and cart to catch the first train to town. Taking a lunch was a must, because you were never certain how long you would be underway. The day in Charlottetown would be quite rushed so that they could run all their errands and catch the late afternoon train and get home before dark.

Even today when my parents travel by car from the country to Charlottetown, they begin to plan their trip a couple of days in advance. They go because they need to do something or buy something, not because they think it would be a fun thing to do. They normally go on a Saturday because it is the only shopping day they are not working. The night before my father fills the car with gas, just to be ready. Although they do not take a lunch with them, they do eat before they leave home. They travel early in the morning so there is enough time to get all their errands done. Each stop in Charlottetown is carefully planned ahead of time in order that "we do not have to run all over town." Then after all the errands are done they go out to eat. Choosing where to eat is an important decision, because they do not eat out very often. When I was younger we usually went to a fast-food restaurant. But now that they are by themselves my parents go to a nice restaurant. After eating they make a quick visit to the relatives. This also involves planning because there are three sets of relatives. They usually visit only one set each trip and then rotate to another set on the next visit in order that no one feels slighted. Then about seven or eight o'clock at night they return home. This amount of preparation and planning is common among local families. Another family I talked to also travels to town on a Saturday. They leave in the morning after milking their cows and return home before the evening milking. Many older people do not travel to Charlottetown unless they have a doctor's appointment. Some people get a relative who is traveling to town to do their errands for them, such as pick up sugar, flour, or butter in Charlottetown when it is on sale.

Islanders are also concerned about being prepared for bad weather. When there is a school field trip most students plan ahead and pack a lunch, even if it is only for the afternoon. Even on a nice day they often take extra clothing in case the weather changes. People also check the weather forecast beforehand. This is a must if you travel in winter. Some even check reports on the weather in Maine so they'll know well in advance what kind of weather is coming. Most Islanders who live in the country will not travel when a storm is expected. If snow is coming they try to avoid travel unless they do not have a choice. Most people in the country and in Charlottetown rush to buy food and get all their errands done before a storm. You never know if you will be storm stayed or without power for several days. Some Islanders try to avoid winter travel altogether. One older lady told me she was very mad at her daughter for making a doctor's appointment for her in Charlottetown during the winter. She said this was crazy, because "you can never depend on winter roads," and she cancelled the appointment.

I think Islanders are very practical. Just as in other aspects of their lives they tend to overprepare and prepare for the worst. This is often to their benefit because when traveling on Island roads anything could happen. In winter you could hit a patch of ice and be stranded in a ditch. In summer you could be stuck in a pothole for days. #1929

People also make mental and physical preparations to protect themselves when they have to deal with others or perform in front of them. They do not want to do or say something which will make them look bad and cause them to be criticized, ridiculed, embarrassed, or punished. Thus they rehearse what they will say and do should certain situations arise, they study for examinations, and they practice beforehand in order that they will perform acceptably. The more they prepare, the better they protect themselves.

> I studied the information thoroughly when I had to take a test to get Canadian citizenship. I didn't want to fail the test and have to go through it all over again. #1930

> My wife and I were scheduled to do a dance demonstration by ourselves in front of an audience. We selected a piece of music, separated it into sections, and decided which sequence of steps to use for each section. Then we practiced the steps repeatedly. The demonstration was quite important to my wife, and I would have felt really bad and guilty if I didn't do my best. #1931

> After my best friend became pregnant, she had no idea what the other kids were saying about her in school. Before she returned to school, I told her what they were saying so she could prepare herself to deal with their questions and comments. #1932

4. Getting training

People also obtain training to deal with possible threats. They may read books on a subject or take formal courses to help them deal with a situation. For example, they may read a book on what to do if an earthquake hits, they may take a first-aid course so they can provide emergency help to family members, or they may take a self-defense course to better protect themselves.

> I bought a book on reducing the risks of getting a heart attack. Now all I need to do is find time to read it. #1933

> My sister was raped and murdered and the possibility of rape is always on my mind. I went and took self-defense lessons. Although I'm still afraid at times, I feel I can handle someone who attacks me. #1934

> This summer my son decided he wanted to get a kayak and paddle around the harbor. He can't swim, so I told him he could get a kayak if he took a swimming course first. He insisted there was no need to take the course because he would wear a life jacket. But I didn't agree. He thinks things will always work out the way he wants them to. However, he might leave

the life jacket at home or take it off if he got hot in the kayak. In any case, he still needs to learn how to swim if he's going to do anything around the water. When he failed to convince me that he didn't need swimming lessons, he dropped the idea of getting a kayak. [#1935]

5. Exerting extra care, attention, and effort

An important way in which people seek to reduce risks is through exerting extra care, attention, and effort. For example, people frequently try to be extra careful in situations when they could be poked in an eye, catch a hand or finger in a machine, get hit by a car, fall down, or have something stolen. When they carry something which can easily be broken or spilled, they hold on with both hands, use containers and lids, walk slowly, take the elevator rather than the stairs, and are very careful when dealing with steps and doors or passing other people. When they pack something fragile, they use protective wrapping, they separate items so they do not rub or bump against each other, and they mark containers so that others will know the contents are fragile.

> When I drop an object in the street, I don't pick it up unless I'm sure no cars are coming. I learned to be careful about this after my mother saw a boy run over by a school bus when he dropped a book in front of the bus and bent over to pick it up. The driver couldn't see him and drove ahead. [#1936]

> I have to walk in the street when there is no sidewalk or when the sidewalk is knee-deep in snow, and I repeatedly look over my shoulder to see if a car is coming from behind me. When a car is coming I get out of the road until it passes. I also try to be careful when I cross a parking lot, because you never know when a car will back into you or strike you from behind. I do something similar when I'm snorkeling. I look back over my shoulder periodically to see if something big, like a shark, is following me. Sharks are known to follow swimmers. [#1937]

> It's really scary when I'm driving and know I shouldn't be because I've been drinking. But what I do is drive real slow and straight, because then I'll never be stopped by the cops. [#1938]

> Most people become supersafe drivers when there is a police car behind them or nearby. They slow down, avoid questionable driving prac-

tices, and try to do everything by the book. "Everyone becomes paranoid when they see a police car. They slow down below the speed limit and put both hands on the steering wheel. You'd think we were in the Soviet Union and the police were the KGB." "When there's a police car waiting to enter the street I let him pull out in front of me. I'd rather have those pigs ahead of me than behind me where they can see everything I do." #1939

When I travel I take all kinds of precautions. If I have several bags I try to remember the exact number, and I count them periodically as I move them in and out of a taxi, on and off a luggage cart, or pick them up at the baggage counter. I often keep my feet pressed against my suitcases while I'm buying my ticket. This way I'll notice if someone tries to take a suitcase while I'm concentrating on something else. When I give my suitcases to the ticket agent at the airport I watch to make sure he puts them on the conveyer belt. Once in Spain a bag of mine fell off the belt behind a desk. If I hadn't seen it happen, the bag would not have been put on my flight. I always make sure my suitcases are locked, and sometimes I put valuable items, such as cameras, in my carry-on bag rather than in my suitcase. This way a baggage handler is less likely to steal them. When I'm sitting waiting with others for a connection and I want to go to the toilet or buy a snack, I ask a person seated nearby to watch my bags for me. If I want to leave the station and don't want to carry the bags with me, I place them in a locker or check them at the baggage window. When I catch a bus I try to see that my bags are actually placed on the bus. Baggage is always being unloaded at bus stops along the route, and I watch from the window to make sure no one takes my bags by intent or mistake. When there are restaurant stops en route I often carry my carry-on bag into the restaurant with me, because it contains things I don't want to lose. During thirty years of travel on my own, the only thing I've had stolen was a carry-on bag which I left in the bus during a restaurant stop. Another thing I do when I go from one location to another is check to make sure I am taking everything with me. So when I get up from a table in a restaurant or climb out of a taxi, I automatically look behind me to make sure I haven't forgotten my briefcase, gloves, umbrella, or something else. Another thing I do when I stand up is touch my back pocket to make sure my wallet hasn't fallen out. #1940

When they feel it necessary, people make special efforts to protect their jobs.

Taking precautions

I had an ongoing disagreement with my principal, and went over his head to the superintendent to have it ended. In the process I embarrassed my principal, and likely made an important enemy. Thereafter I knew I would really have to mind my p's and q's so he wouldn't have an opportunity to have me fired. There were some petty regulations about filing lesson plans that I considered insulting and had ignored. From then on I obeyed the regulations to the letter. #1941

People take extra precautions to maintain access to positive reactions from others. They do so by dedicating considerable time, energy, and money in the pursuit of knowledge, skills, endeavors, objects, and equipment which help them get positive reactions from family, friends, colleagues, acquaintances, and strangers.

My brother Dave and his friends like to race their trucks on a one-mile stretch near home, and Dave usually wins. One of his friends just bought a new truck which may be faster than Dave's, and Dave has already started talking about getting a new truck for himself. #1942

In order to protect relationships, people make special efforts so that they do not alienate their mate, children, parents, friends, and pets. They listen to them; go along with things they want to do; avoid saying and doing things which would hurt them; loan and give them money; give them presents on birthdays, at Christmas, and on other occasions; aid them in a myriad of ways, ranging from helping them with homework to driving them to activities; watch out for their welfare; and act civil to their associates.

I was very much involved with a girl in Toronto and I traveled there frequently. When the relationship broke up I called my best friend, Nancy, from Toronto and told her I really needed to see her when I got back home because I was so upset. Nancy said she would be at the airport to meet me. Now Nancy has been laid up at home with back trouble for the past year. She goes outside some, but she has to take it very easy. That's the kind of friend she is. Despite her back, she was there when I needed her. It's turned out Nancy will have to have an operation on her back. I've let her know I'll be there as much as she needs me. It's only fair. #1943

300

6. Double-checking

People frequently recheck what they have done to make sure they did it correctly. Thus they double-check that they have locked the door to their home, office, store, or car; that they turned the stove or floor heater off; that the safety is on on their gun; that their outgoing mail or their bank deposit actually fell through the chute into the mail box or deposit box; that they did not leave their original or their copies in the photocopying machine; that the correct amount of money was deposited in or subtracted from their bank account; that there are no errors in what they have written; and that no vehicles are coming when they cross the street. The more threatening something is to a person, i.e., the greater the possibility of damage to oneself or one's resources, the more likely a person will double-check.

7. Providing a margin of safety

In order to reduce their risks, people often provide themselves with a margin of safety. Thus they will leave for destinations earlier than necessary in order to minimize the risk of arriving too late. Consequently they are less likely to miss a bus, train, or airplane connection, or to arrive after a movie, play, concert, or lecture has begun. Some people try to fool themselves in order to increase the likelihood they will successfully meet deadlines. They set their watch or alarm clock ahead by perhaps two, five, ten, or fifteen minutes so they will leave early enough to get to work, school, or an appointment on time. People book airline tickets, arrange reservations in restaurants, and buy tickets to performances early, before they are sold out, in order to be certain to get a place and in order to get the place they prefer. People often begin assignments sooner than necessary in order that they will be sure to finish them on time. Many people attempt to get sufficient exercise and rest so they can better withstand health problems if they appear. People also construct objects stronger than necessary so that they will be sure to withstand the stresses they undergo. This is the case with furniture, houses, buildings, bridges, roads, automobiles, boxes, and clothing.

When a new blockbuster movie arrives in town, one that everyone has heard about and is eager to see, you don't dare wait to buy your ticket just before the time the show begins, because they may sell out for days or weeks. What you have to do is go as early as possible, even before the box office opens, and stand in line to get a ticket. Then you have to enter the theater as soon as possible to get a good seat. #1944

It's a real bother worrying that you are about to run out of cash in your checking account. What I've learned to do is to write in my checkbook that each paycheck is less than it actually is. This allows a few unreported dollars to accumulate in the account each pay period, and over time it adds up. Since I've started doing this I've never had a check bounce. #1945

When a teenager in our community was discovered to be pregnant, her parents sent her to Ontario to get an abortion. The family told as few people as possible what was happening. Instead, they told others that their daughter was going on a holiday. The family is highly regarded in the community and did not want their name dragged in the dirt. When their daughter returned from Ontario she attended church every week. Before this she rarely went to church. I think the reason her family sent her to church was because they wanted to encourage her not to get pregnant again and they wanted her to appear to be a very proper girl in case anyone ever heard about the pregnancy and abortion. #1946

People often want to have others with them who provide them with a sense of security. They think they are less likely to be injured or lose resources if other people are present, because other people may help them, may cause a threatening agent to think twice about attacking them, or may provide a barrier.

When I walk across the street at an intersection, I try to make sure there are other people between me and the traffic. If a car doesn't stop, I figure it will hit the other people first, and stop before it gets to me. #1947

My wife likes to sleep on the side of the bed farthest from the bedroom door. She believes that if an intruder enters the room he is likely to get the person closest to the door first. In other words, me. #1948

I sell real estate. I'm a woman and it isn't safe for me to go out in the country to an unoccupied house or farmhouse. Some houses are quite isolated, and you never know what might be lurking about an old place. Even occupied houses may contain a single male who is drinking. I don't like to take chances, so when I don't trust the situation I take one of my teenage children with me. If my children are busy, I get someone else from my office to go with me. It's better to be safe than sorry. #1949

I don't like to go to the movies or to watch television alone. I think the reason for this is that in order to be entertaining, films and TV programs create tense situations and then successfully remove the tension. The more tension they produce and the more successful they are at removing this tension, the better we are entertained. I don't like dealing with tension when I am alone. If someone else is present, I can tolerate tension better. I probably feel safer if someone else is there. #1950

Some people focus on the supernatural when they feel threatened. They may turn to the supernatural for support, or else they may be careful to give the supernatural no reason to punish them or to let something bad happen to them.

When I feel anxious or afraid about facing something unpleasant I try to be on my best behavior. Then I can be sure God will have no reason to harm me. #1951

8. Providing backup

Another means people use to reduce threats is to provide backup. For example, people carry more cash than they need so they will not run out; write their names on possessions they loan others, so that others will be more likely to return them; buy shirts with replacement buttons sewn on them; and buy a larger quantity of items, such as milk, toilet paper, facial tissue, soap, toothpaste, light bulbs, batteries, and cigarettes than they need right away, so they are less likely to run out in the near future.

I always take extra pens to examinations, in case the one I'm using stops working. And I take extra paper too. I've even taken an extra eraser in case I misplace my regular one. #1952

Taking precautions

When we drive long distances, my wife and I make sure we each have a separate set of car keys. Can you imagine what a hassle it would be if you left the keys inside the car and locked yourself out? #1953

Before I give my grade book to my grading assistant, I worry that she might lose it. If she did, then all of the marks that we've recorded for my current students would be lost, and it would be impossible to reconstruct student grades. So I always photocopy the pages with the previously recorded marks first, before I hand her the grade book, and I keep the photocopies in my office. #1954

I'm always scared my cat might not have enough water when we are away for the day or away on a trip. I keep a bowl of water in the kitchen next to his food, a second bowl in the bathroom, and a third bowl outside the back door in case he gets thirsty while he is waiting to get inside. When we go on a trip, I leave a very large metal bowl full of water in case the person who feeds him for us forgets to give him water. Often we've come home from a trip and found his water bowl only half full, which means that the person feeding him has forgotten to give him fresh water. #1955

When I get an idea, I write it down. Then if I forget it later, my notes remind me about it. Sometimes I'll think of a good idea in the middle of the night and get up and go in the bathroom or kitchen to write it down. If I turned on the light next to my bed it would wake my wife. #1956

Yesterday I saw some small personal-safety alarms for sale in a store. They're designed to attract attention if you're attacked. They make a loud, piercing noise after you use the wrist cord to pull out a plug. I bought two for my wife and two for my daughter. That way if they misplace one, they've got another one to use. #1957

When my wife and I are in the car together we watch out for each other, and we warn each other when an accident could happen. I think it would be foolhardy to drive alone in a strange city where you don't know the roads. But even if you're driving in your hometown, you can be watching one thing and fail to notice something else, or you can fail to see an approaching car which is behind a car which blocks your vision. A second person is much more likely to see what you don't see. #1958

If I'm worried about breaking up with my girlfriend, I start to get to know other girls I might be interested in dating. #1959

9. Controlling others

People often seek to reduce threats to themselves and those they depend on by controlling the actions of others. They try to control others by a) providing them with information and rationales, b) restricting the information they give them, c) giving them false information and rationales, d) restricting their access to knowledge and skills, e) refusing to let them do things, f) threatening them, and g) getting them to take their place in facing a threat.

People attempt to reduce threats by providing others with information which will influence their behavior. For example, they may give them written information on avoiding disease or fires, tell them how to handle dangerous objects and substances, and use signs to warn them of guard dogs or electric fences.

> There was an article in the local newspaper on recent attempts to kidnap young boys where I live. I tore out the article and gave it to my son to read so he would take the threat seriously. #1960

> I told my wife that it makes me uneasy when she leaves dishcloths, paper packages, and pieces of plastic wrap on the top of the stove. She replied, "There isn't any danger because none of the burners are on." I said I knew that, but sometimes someone forgets that a burner is on or turns the wrong burner on by mistake. She often forgets she has something cooking in the oven, so she could forget she has a burner on. #1961

> Our son and daughter live on the west coast in an earthquake zone. Last year I gave them two books and a video on what to do in an earthquake. Of course, they are as busy as everyone else, so they didn't read the books or see the video. My son always needs extra money, so I told him I would give him $100 for reading each book and $50 for seeing the video. He did so immediately. My daughter doesn't need money as badly, so I am still trying to figure out what to do with her. Last time I talked to her on the phone she said she thought she could get her boyfriend, who is very well organized, to read her a chapter from one of the books every night. I told her to tell her boyfriend we would be very grateful if he did this. (Amounts in 1999 dollars.) #1962

I attended a native powwow, and one of the elders warned the participants that it was important not to have an eagle feather touch the ground. Despite his warnings, an eagle staff with eagle feathers fell to the ground twice. So they halted the ceremonies and several elders circled the dance area sprinkling tobacco. They wanted to resanctify Mother Earth. #1963

Jane is a business manager. When she attends social functions and out-of-town conferences in her capacity as a manager, her male colleagues often bring their wives with them. Jane has learned that one of the first things she must do is put their wives at ease in order that she can feel comfortable talking to their husbands. Jane is automatically viewed with suspicion because she is divorced and has children. The wives see her as a threat because they think she is in business to get a husband and find a father for her children. Jane tries to appear less threatening by making conversation with the wives and talking with them about their interests. She makes a point of telling them that she is a self-educated hard worker who is very serious about succeeding in the business world. Jane doesn't feel pressured by her colleagues to prove herself because her work speaks for itself. Instead, she wants to avoid becoming the subject of gossip and suspicion by their wives. #1964

In order to reduce threats, people also restrict the information they give others. Such information might damage their reputation, threaten those they depend on, jeopardize their relationships, or endanger their job. For example, at work people frequently hide their shortcuts, moonlighting, sexual relations with members of the organization, and other details of their personal and professional life which might be used against them.

There are people I would never hire in my store, because they are friends of my competitors, and would probably give them information on my business. #1965

I know a sixteen-year-old male who has been taking piano lessons for years and has tremendous ability. But he hasn't told anyone, even his closest friends. He's worried they will tease him about it. #1966

When you are in an office war, you have to be very careful who you tell things to. Often some of the people you trust talk to the other side, and some of the people that the other side trusts talk to you. The ideal situation is when you are able to get information about the other side, while you prevent the other side from learning anything about you. #1967

How people take precautions

In addition, people give others false information in order to better protect themselves from threats.

Students can produce an incredible array of reasons why they don't have an assignment done on time. They do so because they don't want the fact they are late to hurt their grade. I don't doubt many of these reasons are true. But some students use so many excuses for the same course that you start to wonder. It's hard to believe that one student has a car accident, a dead grandfather, and a broken marriage all in the same semester. Sometimes I check it out and find they made the whole thing up. #1968

It is important to teenagers that they wear the current fashions and also that they buy their clothes at the right stores. They want to wear the cool and expensive clothes that the popular kids wear in order that they will be accepted by the in-crowd and be able to get a boyfriend or girlfriend. They don't want to wear anything which will cause them to be made fun of or picked on. If you don't shop at cool stores you'll be considered a geek or loser, and if others find out you buy at a mass-market store you'll be made fun of the rest of the school year. Therefore, unless you are careful where you shop you can easily be put on the spot when people ask you where you got your jeans or tops. In Charlottetown there are trendy stores, such as Esprit, Dalmys, Christopher's Beach Club, Agnew, Dave's Cave, The Loft, Kettle Creek, and Benetton, that sell expensive status brands. In contrast there are department stores and discount stores, such as K-Mart, Zellers, Bargain Harold's, BiWay, and Sears, where many kids wouldn't be caught dead buying clothes because they consider them tacky and tasteless. Linda, a high-school student, said her friends couldn't stop raving about her new jacket. But when they asked where she got it and she told them, "K-Mart," a look of disgust came over their faces and nothing more was said about it. Another girl was leaving Sears carrying a shopping bag, when a friend of hers asked what she had bought. She proudly showed her a new sweater. Her friend said, "It's nice. But personally, I never buy anything at Sears. It looks too much like everyone else's." In my case, a girl told me, "I just love your shoes. I saw them at Agnew and I am going to get a pair." I replied, "As a matter of fact, I got them at Bargain Harold's because they were $25 cheaper." The look on her face was priceless. Often one can find nice original items as well as similar, cheaper items in the department and discount stores. But in order to avoid negative reactions some girls lie about where they buy their clothes. A friend of mine bought an outfit she liked at Zellers. Then she begged us not to tell anyone where she bought it. She said, "Tell them I bought it at The Loft. If they find out where I really got it, they'll turn up their noses at it." #1969

One of my male employees placed some store merchandise on hold until he could pay for it. Later I saw the merchandise was gone and asked the employee about it. He told me he'd paid the money to a female cashier. But when I asked the female cashier, she said he never purchased any merchandise from her. The male employee was lying to hide the fact he had stolen the merchandise. #1970

People engage in numerous coverups to protect themselves from embarrassment, criticism, rejection, punishments, and loss of relationships.

A young man from Prince Edward Island committed suicide in Calgary by shooting himself. His parents are well respected here and they told everyone he had died in an automobile accident. #1971

I was arrested and had to go to jail on a drug offense. My family told the neighbors that a relative of ours had a stroke and I went to help him operate his farm. #1972

People also seek to reduce threats by restricting other people's access to knowledge and skills.

After we gave my older daughter, Jane, a music keyboard, she spent many hours practicing on it and frequently showed us what she had accomplished. My younger daughter was jealous of the attention Jane was receiving. She wanted to get better than Jane at the keyboard and gain this attention for herself. However, Jane tightly restricted the amount of time she let her sister use the keyboard to make sure she wouldn't get very good at it. #1973

We've never talked to our children about sex, because if we don't say anything, they won't be curious about it until they're married. If you don't bring it up, they won't. #1974

Another measure used to reduce threats is to prevent others from doing things which are risky.

I hate being late all the time. When my friends and I get ready to go somewhere, and someone isn't ready, it really makes me upset. However, I have this friend who is never ready on time. Sometimes we call and tell her to be ready half an hour before we actually go pick her up. That way we know she'll be ready. We don't let her do the driving for our group because she'd pick us up so late that we'd never get anywhere on time. Instead we pick her up. #1975

Occasionally pets get lost when they go outside during bad snowstorms. So we won't let our cat out when it's really storming, no matter how much he insists. #1976

Our local hospital has specific times for visitors in order to let the patients rest. It also limits the number of visitors who can be in a patient's room at one time, to avoid overtaxing the patients. When visitors enter the hospital they are greeted at the door by a member of the hospital auxiliary. She helps family and friends locate the patient they want to see and she controls the number of people in the patient's room. #1977

Ruth had known Ernest for four years. Ernest liked Ruth and wanted to go out with her, and one night he drove Ruth home from a dance. The next day Ruth's parents asked who brought her home. When Ruth said Ernest, her parents became upset because Ernest was known to hang out with people who were involved with drugs. Ruth's parents forbade her to see Ernest again, even though Ruth knew Ernest was not involved in drugs. Ruth is a very nice girl, and Ernest lost out because of his reputation. #1978

When we were traveling last summer, the only thing my girlfriend's kids wanted to do was visit amusement parks and go on all the exciting rides. At one park there was a new ride, the Avalanche, which had caused several deaths. The ride had been closed while they made it safer, and had just been reopened. Naturally the kids were eager to try it. However, I talked it over with my girlfriend and we decided the ride hadn't proven safe yet. So we told the kids no. #1979

People also threaten others to stop them from doing things that increase risks or to get them to do things which reduce risks. For example, signs are used to threaten shoplifters, those who litter, and trespassers with fines or prosecution.

My son moved to British Columbia and has lived there several years, but he has never bothered to get a health card. If he needed to go to the doctor or a hospital without a health card he would have to pay a great deal of money. He phones me once a month to ask for some money to help make ends meet. The last time he called, I told him if he didn't get a card, I wasn't going to give him any more money. When he called me again last night, I asked if he had gotten the card. He said he had finally applied for it the day before. I went ahead and sent him the money he asked for. [#1980]

If I ever got my girlfriend pregnant, life would end for me. My father is really old-fashioned and believes in treating a woman right. He's told me if I get a girl pregnant, I can find a new place to live. He said I'd be a disgrace to the family name and would be out on my ass. [#1981]

Another tactic that people use in reducing risks to themselves is to get other people to take the risks for them.

I have back trouble. Do you mind carrying this for me? [#1982]

When I go to bed, I always make sure Mommy and Daddy check my closet and under my bed to see if there are any monsters. I'm always scared one will grab me in the middle of the night and drag me off to Monsterland. My parents have never found any, but I'm still scared. [#1983]

10. Maintaining resources in good working order

People maintain many of their living and nonliving resources in good working order to reduce the threat that they will cease to function. For example, people provide plants with water and sunlight, and children and pets with food, water, and positive reactions.

Our cat always drank from the leaky faucet in our bathtub. After we fixed the leak we had to constantly remind ourselves to pour a bowl of fresh water for him. [#1984]

Possessions such as automobiles are regularly serviced to keep them operating properly.

11. Performing acceptably

People seek to complete their tasks and fulfill social obligations at an acceptable level in order to reduce the risk that they will lose the things that are important to them, such as their job, reputation, and relationships. Jobs are important as a means of obtaining money and status, which are helpful in obtaining other resources, such as food, shelter, stimulation, and positive reactions. Consequently, people take numerous precautions to keep their jobs. Most people arrive and depart work at acceptable times, conform to the dress code, maintain good relations with those they consider important to them, and perform their duties at an acceptable standard.

> During this last summer I was employed as a special supernumerary constable by the Royal Canadian Mounted Police, or RCMP. As a special supernumerary constable you have powers of arrest and search and seizure, and you wear a student badge, but you don't wear a gun. Before I had this job, my friends and I never thought twice about driving around with open liquor in our cars or speeding. But once I got the job, I had to be careful what I did so I wouldn't embarrass the RCMP and hurt my career, and my friends became more concerned about breaking the law. Now when we went out for a night, my friends always made sure there was someone driving who did not drink at all and that there was absolutely no open liquor in the car. During the summer my friends and I usually play baseball every Sunday and go to a bootlegger's establishment afterwards to drink. The first Sunday after I began my job we finished a double-header and took off for the bootlegger's. But just before we got there I realized I couldn't even go in, and I had to tell the guys to have a couple for me. Throughout the summer I constantly had to ask myself, "Should I be doing this?" and make sure I didn't do things which might look bad to other people. #1985

If one fails to complete a task properly, one's resources may be threatened. Normally people remove this risk by completing the task at an acceptable time and level of competence. This includes preparing a speech or presentation, writing a report, studying for a test, delivering goods and services, or getting dinner ready for others.

> If my kids don't do their chores, such as washing dishes or sweeping the floor, they lose the right to watch TV for a week. #1986

311

12. Rectifying a situation

Another means people use to reduce a threat is to attempt to rectify a situation before it becomes worse. For example, they may repair an object, such as a roof, before it deteriorates further; dry an item which has become wet before it becomes water damaged; see a dentist about a toothache or a doctor about a pain before it becomes more serious; search for missing objects, pets, or persons before they become permanently lost; or take steps to prevent further damage to one's reputation. When people have differences with those they are close to, they frequently make special efforts to smooth things over in order to restore their relationship to its previous state.

> When a teenage friend of mine got pregnant she told me, "The thing that was on my mind and worried me the most was what my parents would say. Then came the worry about how my friends would react." When it became widely known that she was pregnant I heard community members speaking badly of her. One man commented, "Did you hear about Andrew's daughter? She finally got herself burnt." After my pregnant friend heard such comments she was too hurt and ashamed to go to local stores. Instead, she traveled to Charlottetown to do her shopping where she wouldn't have to face the local people. Finally, after much pressure from her parents and other community members, she married the father. She didn't love the man, but everyone felt it looked better for her to marry the father of her child. People consider this the moral thing to do. #1987

> Every year we go to Nova Scotia for the yearly indoor-Rugby tournament. There are about 90 teams and 900 players. It is an incredible drunken blast. As one player stated, "If you can't play Rugby drunk, you should play an easier sport." People go to the tournament to party, and to see what stunts the others will pull. Many people get so drunk they can't remember what they did the night before. You usually make an idiot of yourself, but you don't care because everyone else does too. You have a successful weekend as long as you don't puke while you're playing and you don't end up in jail.
> The biggest problem is trying to get your damage deposit back from the hotel when you are ready to go home. A member of one team explained, "On Sunday morning we were running around our room trying to clean it up. We used chewing gum to fasten things back together, put

furniture over the burn marks in the carpet, and tried to get the toilet unclogged. We also borrowed the vacuum cleaner from the cleaning staff. Then when our room was checked they didn't notice that a chair was missing. As long as you don't act like an asshole and are nice to the cleaning staff they'll overlook minor damage. We got our damage deposit back. But other teams weren't as lucky. One team had to pay for a huge hole they'd put in the wall. If the cleaning staff doesn't like you, any little thing will cost you." #1988

Combining actions

Often people use a combination of actions in dealing with threats. In the following example, the person seeks to avoid the threat, to remove it, and to reduce the chance it will occur.

Two weeks ago I was visiting my parents when I saw a mouse. It came out of a vent in the kitchen and I climbed on a cabinet and started screaming. Because I was frightening the mouse, it hid under the cabinet. My sister came in the kitchen and claimed she saw the mouse go back down the vent, but the problem is my family just lie to me. I went and got the cat and the cat killed the mouse under the cabinet. Last night I visited my parents again but hardly slept at all. I worry that when there's one mouse, there are others around too. I kept the whole family up until I was ready to go to bed. When there are people around, mice are likely to stay hidden. Before I went to bed I had my sister kick all the furniture in my room to make sure there was no mouse in it. Then I wedged a mat under the door to seal off the room so no mouse could get in. This morning I waited until others were up before I got out of bed. #1989

Feelings

Nature of anxiety

The feeling that is instrumental in getting people to take precautions is anxiety. The term anxiety is applied here to various degrees of apprehension about events, ranging from concern to fear. It includes worry,

313

stress, nervousness, insecurity, stage fright, dread, and terror. Anxiety involves an increase in tension and is a punishing feeling. It is based on recognizing a threat to one's person or one's resources. The threat may be an immediate one, such as an angry dog, or a distant one, such as the possibility of getting cancer from pesticides sprayed on crops. Whether the threat is real or imaginary is irrelevant. What is significant is that a person feels there is a threat.

Now that there's a hole overhead in the ozone layer, I think it would be a good idea to wear a hat every time I go outside. I haven't done anything about it yet, but I might. #1990

At bingo last night we were playing a game and a woman promptly yelled out "Bingo!" However, when her numbers were checked it was discovered she had made a mistake. She was sitting close to me and I saw her turn about five shades of red from embarrassment. Everyone else had already cleared their cards, so the numbers had to be called all over again. Later on in the evening the same woman did win a game. While the man was checking her card she looked scared to death she might have made an error again. #1991

I've been scared I was pregnant two or three times. Each time I am scared shitless and feel my life is ruined for good. There is no fear like it in the world. It is a sick feeling which just rots your stomach. Normally I dread having my period, but am I ever glad to have it start when I think I'm pregnant. #1992

I work at a hospital. When people are notified that a family member has been involved in an automobile accident, I see them rush through the front door to the front desk with panic-stricken faces, desperate to find out the condition of their relative. #1993

I went on a half-hour flight with my mother, and when we were ready to taxi down the runway, I went into a severe panic. I started screaming I wanted to get off the plane. My mother was embarrassed to pieces. She didn't know how to control me, and the steward sat on my armrest trying to calm me down. I was so scared I couldn't hear what he was saying. I made a complete spectacle of myself, but I didn't care. I got through the flight, but I will not fly again. #1994

Often anxiety is accompanied by physical signs and symptoms. A person who is anxious may fidget, shiver, shake, sweat, stutter, bite their fingernails or lips, feel nauseous, tense up, eat, pace, become hyperactive or flustered, need to eliminate, act quiet and withdrawn, or engage in repetitive movements.

I am nineteen and have always been afraid of bugs. I hate all bugs! The very sight of them gives me goose bumps and sends chills up my spine. [#1995]

Before I call up a girl for a date, I pace the floor trying to get up my courage. When I finally call, I stutter and stammer while I try to talk. I'm always this nervous because I'm afraid she'll turn me down. [#1996]

When I'm with other people I feel nervous and get headaches and sweaty palms. I also blush and trip over things. [#1997]

My sister gets very nervous if she rides in a car when there is any hint of bad weather or when traffic is heavy. She digs her fingernails into the armrest and sits with her face just inches from the window to make sure there won't be an accident. [#1998]

I try to control my worrying, but it's hard. My parents are paying for my tuition at university, so I don't want to let them down and displease them by bombing out. I get discouraged at times when the pressure gets so bad. I hate the thought of not making the dean's list, so I get myself in a turmoil. I get so full of fear around exam time that I have nausea. I really envy other students who can stay cool and calm about school. [#1999]

Before I have to give a public talk or write a major exam, I get extreme gas pains. They are almost crippling and have humiliated me on several occasions. But the pains subside when I get into the situation. Afterwards I feel completely relieved and my stomach returns to normal. [#2000]

I started worrying about being pregnant after my period was a week late. By the time it was two weeks late I was extremely worried and couldn't eat, sleep, or study. I felt lonely and afraid like never before. I must have prayed and cried for seven days solid. My friends wanted to know why I was so depressed and I told them to leave me alone. It was awful. When my period finally started, I felt so good. My boyfriend was even happier than me. #2001

People can become sick with worry. When I was very ill my mother was so physically and emotionally drained by worry that she ended up in the hospital. #2002

When people feel threatened they may run or hide. In other cases they may laugh or giggle, or avoid looking a person who intimidates them in the eyes.

A nineteen-year-old girl told me, "I was walking home from work late one night and came to a bit of woods I always have to walk through. I've always been terrified of walking there, because I think of those TV shows where people get attacked. Anyway, this night I was going through the woods and heard a crackle. Every thought went through my mind. I started walking a lot faster. I heard more crackling, like someone walking fast. Well, I didn't wait for a second. I just ran. And the whole time I thought I was going to be stabbed or something." #2003

When I get nervous I laugh, and sometimes at the most inappropriate times. Recently I was at a funeral home, started laughing, and couldn't stop. I certainly didn't find the situation funny. My nephew also tends to laugh when someone is angry with him or he is in a confrontation. He gets into more trouble because he laughs, and he has a difficult time trying to apologize and explain his behavior. #2004

Tension from anxiety makes it difficult to relax and release one's breath. When a person who feels anxious finally releases his breath, he sighs. Shortness of breath and sighing are indicators that a person is anxious. Anxiety can also cause people to lose sleep, have bad dreams, or feel depressed.

It is easy to become overwhelmed with anxiety when one thinks about everything one has to do. Sometimes I wake up in the middle of the night or very early in the morning and spend an hour or two worrying about all the things I must do. I get terribly discouraged, because it looks so impossible to finish it all. The only way out of this is to tell myself to ignore the big picture and just focus on one specific thing. Sometimes I make a list of things to do, prioritize them, and deal with them one at a time. #2005

Anxiety is produced by inconsistency, or a contradiction, between two models. The first model is what one wants to happen. The second model is concern that something negative could happen that differs from what one wants to happen. For example, one may realize that a specific situation can occur during which one could be injured or killed or lose resources. If one is injured or killed, one is likely to experience pain and to be unable to do the things one wants to do. If one loses resources, it will be more difficult to survive, accomplish one's goals, and keep one's other resources. Individuals want to experience pleasure through well-being and resources, and do not want to experience pain, loss, and failure. The contradiction, or inconsistency, between a) what one wants to happen, and b) what could prevent this, produces anxiety, or tension. See Model 2. The greater this inconsistency, the greater one's anxiety. Also, the more likely and the more immediate the threat that something negative could happen, the greater one's anxiety. When one takes precautions one reduces the risk that a threat will prevent what one wants to have happen. Therefore when one takes precautions there is less inconsistency between what one wants to happen and what could happen. When there is less inconsistency one experiences less anxiety, or tension. People take precautions in order to reduce anxiety. They reduce anxiety by reducing the inconsistency between what they want to happen and what could happen to prevent this. Normally this involves avoiding, removing, or reducing what they do not want to happen.

People's anxieties are related to the situations they are currently in.

I never really think about something happening to me except when I am walking somewhere alone. Then I start hearing things or begin to think someone may be following me. I worry about being beat up, or raped, or having my purse stolen. #2006

I've been a policeman for the past ten years. Back when I entered the force, there weren't as many crimes or as many criminals as there are today. Today I don't only have to worry about being shot by a thief, but also about people on drugs who don't realize what they are doing. There was a period recently when it seemed like people were trying to kill every police officer they saw, and I never knew what to expect each time I walked the streets or answered a call. I worry about who would look after my wife and child if I get killed. #2007

Model 2: The production of anxiety

A. Anxiety is produced by inconsistency between a) what one wants to have happen, and b) concern that something would prevent this from happening

For example, anxiety is produced when one wants to get to work or school on time, but is in a traffic jam that could prevent one from doing so. Anxiety also occurs when one wants to pay rent and buy food, but thinks one will not have enough money to do so.

B. The greater this inconsistency, the greater one's anxiety

The greater the degree of a threat, i.e., the greater the inconsistency with what one wants, the more anxiety one feels. For example, the greater the chance that one will be injured or killed or lose important resources, the more anxiety one feels. Thus one feels more anxiety over being able to pay to repair one's roof when the bill is $5000 than one does when it is $50. Similarly one feels more anxiety when the clothes one is wearing are on fire than when they are getting wet from the rain. One also feels more anxiety when the lump in one's body is diagnosed as a malignant tumor than when the lump is diagnosed as a benign cyst.

C. The greater the likelihood that something will prevent what one wants to have happen, the greater one's anxiety

The more likely that one will be prevented from getting what one wants, the greater one's anxiety. One feels more anxiety when one is actually taken hostage by a terrorist than when one thinks about the possibility that this might happen. One also feels more anxiety when a plague is killing people in one's neighborhood than when it is killing people in another country.

318

D. The more immediate the threat, the greater one's anxiety

The sooner something threatening will happen, the more anxiety one feels. For example, one feels more anxiety if one has to write an important examination tomorrow or give an important talk tonight, than if one has to do so three months from now.

E. The less prepared one is to deal with the threat, the greater one's anxiety

The less prepared one is, the more anxiety one feels. Conversely, the more prepared one is, the less anxiety one feels. When one knows what to do, has planned what to do, has practiced what one will do, has the necessary materials at hand, and/or has obtained the help of others who know what to do, then one is less likely to feel anxiety.

As a person's situation changes, the person's worries are also likely to change.

It was discovered that my father had cancer and would have to have an operation. We all became very worried he might not live through the operation. #2008

A friend of mine had been seeing a guy for three years when she found out she was pregnant. She was only seventeen and in her last year of high school. For five months she couldn't sleep at night worrying about what her parents would say and do when they found out. She was also worried that her grandparents would think less of her and her friends would be angry with her. I and a couple of other close friends tried to help her think of a way to break the news to her parents. I know how worried I was; I can only imagine how worried she was. Finally she told them, and after the shock wore off everyone began to worry. My friend realized she had to grow up a lot in a very short time. She was worried sick because she didn't have a job to support the child. Her boyfriend worried about what his parents would say, and whether her parents would want him around anymore. Now, one year later, my friend has a child, and she has all the worries of a parent. #2009

After I finished university I had a good job, a nice apartment, and many friends I liked to go out with to have a good time. But as I got older, MS (multiple sclerosis) began to change my life. At first I found it hard to walk up stairs or hold on to a glass. I had to use a walker to get around, had to rely on other people to drive me places, and had to move into a new apartment with less stairs. MS gradually confined me to a wheelchair and made it hard for me to use my arms. I couldn't take care of myself, and I quit my job and moved in with my parents. My parents are quite old and I can't rely on them for long. I have to worry about every little ordinary task that I used to be able to do for myself, and I worry about who will help me in the future. #2010

I lost my worries about my children when they became grown, and my worries about my job when I retired. Now I worry about my wife and grandchildren. I also worry about death, because I do not have many years left. #2011

People are more likely to feel anxious when they a) recognize a threat, b) believe something important to them is threatened, c) know

320

that others recognize a threat, and d) do not have higher priorities which occupy their thoughts. Conversely, they are less likely to be anxious when they a) do not recognize a threat, b) believe nothing important to them is threatened, c) do not know that others recognize a threat, or d) have higher priorities which occupy their thoughts. People are likely to feel more anxious, a) as the event which produces anxiety draws nearer in time, and b) the less prepared they are for the event. For example, if they must take a test or give a speech, they are likely to experience more anxiety, a) the sooner the event will occur, and b) the more they still have to do to get ready for it.

Anxiety is an unpleasant feeling. It weighs on one's mind and dominates one's consciousness. Anxiety often interferes with other thoughts and actions, and tends to shake one out of one's normal routines. Anxiety encourages one to act to remove the feeling. Normally, the best way to remove anxiety is to take appropriate precautions against what it is that one fears. Therefore, one is inclined to act and deal with a specific threat in order to get rid of the anxiety. People avoid, remove, and reduce threats to themselves and their resources which produce anxiety. The more serious the threat or the more pressing the threat, the more anxiety one feels. We become anxious because we worry about the consequences if we do not act. As the consequences become more likely, our anxiety increases. Often we act well in advance of an approaching threat in order to stop the anxiety from mounting.

When I'm in a car I don't feel secure unless I have my seat belt on. #2012

When I'm not getting any work done on my research project, or not doing any exercise to protect my health, it bothers me and I feel frustrated. I know the only thing that will get rid of the feeling is to get back to work or start exercising again. As soon as I do so the sense of frustration disappears and I feel really good. #2013

I had a couple of weeks of vacation left and was making a concerted effort to find a new girlfriend before I had to go back to work. Then a female friend who is very interested in me called up from out of town and said she was planning to come visit me. The problem was I didn't feel the same way about her. So I was put in a real bind. I didn't want to be rude to my friend, but if she came to visit I wouldn't be able to go out looking for a girlfriend because it would hurt her feelings. This

321

caused such a conflict in my mind that it kept me awake all night. I went through a real anxiety attack. I felt so frustrated I just felt like climbing the wall and screaming. My anxiety was so severe I finally called up my friend and told her it would be best if she didn't come to visit. Afterwards I felt a lot better because I knew I was free to spend the weekend the way I wanted. #2014

Because anxiety is a punishing feeling, people frequently take precautions to avoid or reduce the occurrence of anxiety in the future.

Whenever I have to get a task done by a specific date or get somewhere on time, I give myself plenty of leeway so I'm sure I won't be rushed. When I'm rushed I get to feeling really stressed out and hyper. I hate the pressure and I know it's not good for my heart. I would much rather arrive early and wait, than have to deal with the anxiety and have to rush around to get somewhere on time. #2015

My wife always wants me to call a taxi well before I'm ready to go somewhere. That way I won't have to waste time waiting for the taxi to come. But this puts me under lots of pressure and makes me rush, because I feel uncomfortable making the taxi driver wait for me. So I always get ready first and then call the taxi. I don't mind waiting as much as I mind worrying that I won't be ready when the taxi arrives. #2016

Taking precautions normally does remove anxieties.

When various brokerage firms started failing, I realized I would be better off if I took the stock my brokerage firm was holding for me and put it in a safety-deposit box. I kept thinking about this until I finally did it. Afterwards, I didn't worry about it anymore. #2017

An elderly friend of mine locks her bedroom door when she leaves home, and her front and back doors when she goes outside in her yard. When I asked why, she explained, "Just watching TV today gives a person a pretty good idea what people are up to. I value everything I have, and it would be terrible to lose them to a thief. If a thief knew an elderly person lives here, he might assume I would be naïve and not lock up. So I'm one step ahead of him. I guess it gives me a sense of security. When I go out, if I know everything is safe, I have peace of mind." #2018

Sometimes a partial precaution will quiet anxieties. For example, when people feel overwhelmed because they have a very large task or a great many tasks to do, if they deal with part of the large task or with a few of the many tasks, often they are able to temporarily relieve their anxiety.

> My biggest fear in life is not being able to succeed. I've set a goal for myself in regard to my career, and I really want to reach it. But sometimes my studies are very hard or I do rotten on an exam. Then the anxiety sets in. I start thinking that I can't do it, or that I'm not smart enough to succeed. At this point I have to give myself a pep talk. I find the best way to avoid the anxiety is to just go day by day and not try to think about my task so deeply. #2019

Once an event or task which generates anxiety has passed or has been completed, people normally lose their anxiety.

Alcohol enables people to ignore their anxieties. It helps people overcome their fear of being criticized and embarrassed. Alcohol plays an important role in bars and clubs by allowing males to overcome their fear of rejection so that they can make social and sexual advances toward females. At the same time it allows females to overcome their fear of getting a bad reputation for being promiscuous so that they can initiate advances toward males and accept advances from them. Alcohol also plays an important part in allowing males to be aggressive and to fight without worrying about the physical and social consequences.

Most people find certain types of anxiety entertaining and stimulating. A popular form of entertainment consists of identifying with characters in films and books or on television who are in situations which involve risks to themselves and/or their resources. Viewers and readers are so sensitive to threats that they easily feel threatened when characters are in risky situations. Threats produce tension (anxiety) in the audience, and the release of this tension produces pleasure. Tension is released when characters successfully avoid, remove, or reduce threats. This is what occurs in most crime dramas, soap operas, and sports, and in romance, science fiction, horror, and adventure stories. Another form of entertainment consists of rides in amusement parks which create the illusion of bodily risks, usually in the form of falling, being thrown, or colliding. Normally, the more anxiety the entertainment produces on the part of the viewer, reader, or participant, the more successful the entertainment. This is because the more tension that one experiences, the more tension one has that one can release. The release of tension is experienced as pleasure, and the more tension one releases, the more pleasure one experiences. People release tension when the causes of tension are removed, when people remember that they are not really at risk, and when tension-producing experiences end safely. Entertainment that fails to produce tension is boring; and entertainment that fails to remove tension fails to generate pleasure. (See the chapter on Seeking Stimulation in a later volume.)

People also take precautions for themselves and for others when these actions are not caused by feelings of anxiety. People may take precautions when they plan ahead, do something meaningful, and act to support their self-image.

> We had reservations to go to Sunday brunch at one o'clock at a nice hotel. It's a real feast and you eat yourself silly. I wanted to leave plenty of room for the meal, so I purposely ate a light breakfast and avoided the snacks that I usually eat before lunch. #2020

Also, people introduce precautions which do not affect themselves personally when they do their jobs as police, social workers, city planners, or traffic engineers.

> I work at a community park with an unusually large playground facility for children. The playground contains elaborate and original equipment for children to climb around and hide in. It's perfect for exercising a child's imagination, but terrible for guaranteeing a child's safety. Even though there is a sign that the park is not supervised, parents often sit in their cars or read a book while their child explores the facility. Children as young as two or three years old wander about on their own or with slightly older children. Often the younger children try out equipment which is much too advanced. I frequently have to guide children to equipment which is more suitable for them. In one case a child just over two years old struggled with high steps and a fireman's pole. I stopped her from descending into a six-foot-high stack of tires and took her to equipment which was more manageable for her. Sometimes parents can't find their children. One man asked if I had seen his two daughters. I had, but not for some time. He said, "Oh, it's not like I'm worried. As long as there aren't any bad men around. You haven't seen any bad men,

have you?" and he walked away laughing. I found the two girls a little later talking quietly in a small hiding place. Children can easily hurt themselves in the park. They have cut themselves on broken glass, fallen off of raised equipment, and tripped over structures at ground level. In one case a child of a year and a half removed his shoes. The floor of the area is covered with wood chips, and although I carried him over most of them, he still got a number of splinters in his feet. So I took him back to his parents. I get upset because so many parents do not supervise their children and trust nothing will happen to them. #2021

How one develops anxieties

One develops specific anxieties by a variety of means. These include the following:

1. Personal experiences
2. Seeing and hearing what happens to others
3. Learning of the concerns of others
4. Exposure to mass media
5. Using one's imagination

1. Personal experiences

As a result of one's own experiences one learns where many dangers to oneself and one's resources lie.

I had a great weekend in Halifax with booze, drugs, and sex. Naturally I didn't get much sleep, and driving home to the Island wasn't easy. When I nearly fell asleep at the wheel it scared the shit out of me. #2022

I had unprotected sex with this guy I was really attracted to. Unfortunately, I barely knew him, and certainly not his sexual history. A few days later I got this really bad genital infection. The doctor said I had caught it from the guy I'd slept with. I really wish I had been more careful. #2023

Often one does not fully comprehend risks until afterwards when one thinks about what might have happened. At that time one frequently resolves not to get into the same situation again. Subsequently, when one is in similar situations one is likely to experience anxiety.

Taking precautions

It bothers me that my apartment might be robbed again. [#2024]

One day when I was ten, I went to school wearing a pair of purple-colored pants. People laughed at me, and I was never so embarrassed. From that point on I always worry about how I look and try to dress in the latest fashions. [#2025]

Once I turned two appliances on at the same time, one with each hand, and got shocked. It's made me careful to only turn on one appliance at a time. [#2026]

I wasn't afraid during my first pregnancy. But the baby almost died during labor. This made me afraid when my second baby was born. [#2027]

My main worry is that something will happen to my mother. My father died three years ago and now I am preoccupied with the thought that my mother is going to die too and I will be all alone. I calculate how old my mother will be as I get older. I envy people who have younger parents than I do and get angry when they don't appreciate them. [#2028]

Often a change in one's situation produces new anxieties.

When there was an escaped criminal in my area I was scared to go home alone in the dark, particularly past any woods. My friends all dared each other to walk home alone, but no one was willing to do so. [#2029]

I used to make fun of Ed all the time. I thought he was crazy waking up at six o'clock every morning to go jogging. But when I developed high blood pressure, I changed my lifestyle. Now I watch what I eat and try to maintain a good exercise program. I do all the things I used to bug Ed about. [#2030]

At times it is the immediacy of an experience which causes one to feel anxious.

Most of the people I know are scared to walk home alone at night after seeing a horror movie. I know it's only make-believe, but I start wondering if all the scientists are wrong and there really is a werewolf, vampire, or monster loose in the community, or if aliens really are about to take over, starting with me all alone in the dark. [#2031]

Often, however, anxieties remain long after an experience has occurred.

> I have a strong fear of deep water where I can't touch bottom. When I was little we were out for a drive and drove out on the wharf. My father walked on the gas and I thought we were going over the edge. Boy, did I cover my eyes. Ever since I've been terrified of deep water. That's the reason I won't go out in small boats. #2032

The previous example illustrates that the specific threat does not have to actually occur in order for a person to develop anxiety. Simply recognizing that there is a real possibility of something happening is enough to produce a lasting fear.

2. Seeing and hearing what happens to others

One is not restricted to one's own personal experiences in learning what one should be anxious about. One also sees and hears about the experiences of others. Sometimes one learns of these experiences by watching and listening to those that the experiences happen to. In other cases one learns third hand from others what they have seen and heard happen to other people.

> When I go on a trip for several weeks or more, I unplug my TV and computer and put objects that could be destroyed by water up on tables. I do this because if lightning struck it would blow out the TV, and if the radiator burst it would flood the place. I don't think these things are very likely, but they have both happened to people I know. #2033

> My mother is afraid of locking the door in strange bathrooms. Once when she flew down to Florida, she had to have the stewardess stand outside the bathroom door so no one else would walk in on her. She's afraid she'll get locked in and not be able to get out. It's never actually happened to her, but it did happen to another member of her family. #2034

> I never really thought about the danger of rape before I went to university, and I like to study in the campus library at night. Then a friend told me about a girl who was raped on campus. It scared me enough so that I no longer study as late as I want. Instead, I leave early so I'll have someone to walk back to the dorm with. #2035

A colleague of mine developed a sore on his foot during a tennis game. He ignored it, it became gangrenous, and there was a long period during which they debated whether or not to amputate his foot. It just makes me go to the doctor all the sooner when something doesn't heal properly. #2036

I worry when my son has the car on a weekend night. He hit a car before and caused a lot of damage. I find myself pacing the floor worrying what he may do next. #2037

When I was in college a friend of mine was killed in a car accident because she didn't have a seat belt on. It's made me extra careful to always wear mine. #2038

I am scared I'm going to screw up in university, because smarter people than me have screwed up in the past. #2039

One of the people where I work was hit and killed by a snowplow when he was walking across a parking lot. Ever since I've been quite wary of snowplows. #2040

My number one phobia is that I'm terrified of any illness, especially in old people. I think this was brought on by watching an elderly lady who was a guest in our house suffer from a severe stroke and die. Ever since I've tried to get away from old people. I feel guilty because there are so many things I could do to help these folks, but they terrify me so I won't even give them a smile or a kind word. I go cold at the sight of someone blind, lame, or in a wheelchair, because I view them as stroke victims. I've had this combination of terror and guilt for over thirty years now. #2041

3. Learning of the concerns of others

Another source of one's anxieties is exposure to the anxieties of other people.

My mother was always worried something might hit me in the eye and put it out. It's made me extra careful anytime I'm near someone with a stick or pole. She also told me stories about kids who lost an arm when they put it outside the vehicle they were riding in. As a result I always keep my arms inside a car or bus. I always notice when others hang their arms outside and feel they are extremely foolish. #2042

My pregnancy was difficult from the start. The doctors expressed concern for my safety, and I became scared I might die during labor. #2043

I have a fear of big animals, especially horses. When I was a young girl, my grandfather used to warn me to stay away from the big horse on his farm because it kicked. I must have generalized this to all horses, because even today I'm scared of horses in parades. #2044

Terri had a mole on her shoulder and didn't give it much thought until her husband noticed it. He asked if it was raised and if it bothered her. When Terri responded that it was raised and sometimes felt itchy, her husband suggested she have a doctor look at it. From that day on Terri was convinced she had cancer. She went to the doctor and had some tests done and the doctor told her he would call her back if necessary. Terri could hardly get through each day, and was terrified of being alone by herself. She insisted her mother spend the day with her, and every time the phone rang Terri would shriek and exclaim, "It's the doctor! I knew it was cancer!" Finally the doctor's receptionist called and Terri was so anxious she couldn't go to the phone. Her mother took the message which was that Terri had left her health-care card at the doctor's office. It turned out Terri was fine and the mole was nothing to worry about. #2045

4. Exposure to mass media

One obtains information from the mass media that one would not other-wise know regarding potential threats and other people's experiences. These experiences often involve a loss of resources or bodily harm, and notify people what they should be apprehensive about and take precau-tions against.

I've always had a great deal of trust in everyone and never had any reason not to. But when I hear all these news reports about rapes I don't know who I can trust. #2046

The lead story in the newspaper today was about a "frail" eighty-one-year-old man who was arrested at the local airport in Charlottetown (*The Guardian*, Charlottetown, October 4, 2001, pp. 1-2.). The man asked a baggage inspector, "Are you looking for a bomb?" when she was examining the contents of his wife's change purse. Because of this question the man was arrested by the city police, photographed and fingerprinted, and charged under the Criminal Code with making bomb threats. Both he and his wife were told they are banned from flying with Air Canada for the remainder of their lives. According to the newspaper he may face a two-year jail sentence. The story makes you realize you'd better never, never, never use the "B-word" in public again. [#2047]

I am a complete basket case on a plane. A million visions run through my mind. I see the engines blowing up or worry the pilot may have worked one too many shifts and is so exhausted he'll push the wrong button or forget to push the right one. The worst part is the takeoff. As the plane leaves the ground I think the tail will hit the pavement. By this time my hands are gripped tightly to the arms of my seat, my teeth are clenched, and my eyes are closed. I always make sure I get an aisle seat by the emergency exit. I also try to get direct flights, so there will be fewer takeoffs and landings. I watch the stewardesses to see if their expressions change drastically, which would signal a problem. It just amazes me that a person would take a job flying every day. When I fly I keep repeating to myself that this flight is made several times a day, every day of the year. I don't think I developed this fear as a child, because when I was young I didn't mind flying. I think it comes from hearing about crashes on the news. A few years back there were a number of plane crashes and I think they had an effect on me. [#2048]

I watched the news on TV and saw the scenes of the deaths caused by a powerful earthquake in India. This made me concerned about the welfare of my children, who live in an earthquake zone in British Columbia. The next time I spoke to my kids on the phone I asked if they knew what to do in an earthquake. [#2049]

I worry about terrorists coming to Canada. The news said they plan to bomb targets in North America next. [#2050]

Many people were concerned about the transition to the year two thousand (2000 AD) and the problems that would be created when flight control, banking, military, and government computers could not handle the calendar change and crashed. These problems were discussed repeatedly in newspapers and on television. One couple I know started major preparations for the end of the world. They built a room in their basement where they stored blankets, food, cat and dog food, and other items. #2051

5. Using one's imagination

People also use their imaginations to foresee possible outcomes in which they would lose resources or experience bodily harm. This can generate considerable anxiety and subsequent precautions. For example, many people feel anxious when they get a long-distance telephone call or a letter, or are called in to see their supervisor before they know why. Often people imagine the worst as they try to prepare themselves for the impact if the worst occurs.

I think one reason I save money is because there is a chance I might lose my job. It's a secure job, but one is never entirely sure about the future. #2052

I think it is so foolish for humans to assume that contact with aliens in space will be peaceful and beneficial. Every species has absolutely no hesitation to completely exploit other species and take their resources for their own purposes. The stronger always take everything the weaker have. A species does not accord another species any rights at all. We act this way with every other species on earth, and will certainly do so with any alien species that is weaker than we are. If you have a wild lot and go to build a house, what do you do? You kill everything there except for a few favorite trees. You replace the existing ecology (a great diversity of species) with a sterile environment (your house) and with a monoculture (your lawn). It's more convenient to kill everything than to live with it. If you tried to move the plants and animals elsewhere, they wouldn't survive. If you move species from your yard to another location you put a great deal of pressure on the members of these species which are already there. All other areas are already fully populated by all the members of each species which can survive there. When other species try to coexist with us, such as mice, roaches, earwigs, skunks, and crows, we do our best to exterminate them. We fuss about the ecological destruction that people carry out in other parts of the world, and we ignore the ecological destruction we carry out on our own property. What we do to the members of other species on our property puts the pogroms of any tyrant or villain in history to shame. We love to blame others; never ourselves.

When we move into a new environment, we go there to take everything for ourselves. It may take us a while to learn how to do so, but we are not about to take second fiddle to anything. Europeans did not move to North and South America to coexist and live with the native peoples there. They moved there to take everything for themselves. We do not move into wild areas to coexist with other species. We go there to take everything for ourselves. We are not going to colonize other planets in order to coexist with alien species. We are going there to take all the resources for ourselves, and to fully exploit every other species we find. Humans are so used to thinking of themselves as the dominant species that it is difficult for them to imagine an existence in which they are not.

At the same time we have this remarkable childlike belief that an alien species which is stronger than we are will not treat us the way we treat other species. Supposedly they will recognize a kinship with us, see our basic goodness and potential, and for ethical reasons will not exploit us or our resources. I mean, dream on. Talk about a double standard. We do anything we want to others, but no one would be so awful as to do the same thing to us? We can't imagine being treated as a slave, food, or pest species.

We think we are so smart. But we are not smart enough to keep quiet about our presence until we know what's out there. If aliens are anything like us, we're in serious trouble. [#2053]

Individual differences in anxieties

There is considerable individual variation in what causes a person to feel anxious. Often any two people experience very different anxieties.

Many teenagers I know get quite nervous before their first major exams. They fidget, get upset stomachs, and are quite hyper. My cousin, on the other hand, is as calm as can be. She says she has no reason to feel nervous, because she is prepared to do the best she can. She thinks writing exams is a fun experience when you know the answers. And she likes the fact it lets her do something that is different from everyday class work. [#2054]

All these cholesterol-free foods are bull. They say they are good for you, but who's to know? Many people worry about cholesterol. But I'd rather stick to eating the same food I've always eaten. I get so sick of all the hype about "free" this and "light" that. #2055

You see people who have smoked all their lives and don't have any problems. I never had anything wrong with me because I smoke. Why should I give up something I enjoy just because people say it's bad for you? I feel fine. #2056

I have a friend who backs away from any situation where he thinks a risk might be involved. For example, he refuses to fly. When I told him I was planning on traveling to the Great Barrier Reef to do a diving course and then going to spend some time in Bali and Thailand, he stated that I must have a death wish. #2057

I'm afraid of letting people get too close to me physically. I hate crowds. I try to avoid crowded elevators and having someone stand too close while carrying on a conversation. If you were to sit down next to me on the couch, I would feel so uncomfortable I would use almost any excuse to move to a chair. #2058

It is easy to see why any two people would have different anxieties, because a) they have had different personal experiences, b) they have seen and heard about different things happening to others, c) they have been exposed to different concerns from others, d) they have encountered different information from the mass media, and e) they have imagined different things happening. Notice in the next two examples that two people have reached opposite conclusions on taking precautions with seat belts as a result of having different personal experiences.

One Saturday night my friend and I were returning from the clubs. I drove my friend's car because I was the only one sober. When I looked in my rearview mirror I saw a car behind us swerving all over the road. I slowed down and pulled over close to the side of the road, hoping he would pass me. The car behind me sped up and I became very scared. It came right up behind us without slowing down. I tried to pull over some more, but before I knew it we were struck from behind. My friend and I were both thrown forward. It turned out the driver who struck us was drunk. If we hadn't been wearing our seat belts we would have probably gone through the windshield and been killed. This experience made me realize that seat belts do save lives. After that night my friend and I always wear our seat belts. #2059

Taking precautions

One day my cousin and I went for a drive in the country. I had a new car and it was a nice day to take it for a spin. As we went around a corner, an oncoming truck lost control and smashed head-on into us. It hit us so hard that my car flew backwards and rolled over into a ditch. I was screaming, but my cousin wasn't making any noise. I kept yelling his name, but he didn't answer. I thought he was unconscious. About ten minutes later the police and an ambulance arrived. I was still calling my cousin's name and getting no response. By this time I was really worried. It took fifteen minutes to get us out of the car. I had a few scratches on me but my cousin didn't survive. What bothered me was that he was wearing a seat belt and I wasn't. I keep asking myself, "Why him and not me?" I have not worn my seat belt since that day and I never will. I will never agree with the saying, "Seat belts save lives," because in my case they didn't. If my cousin hadn't been wearing his, he might be alive today. #2060

In many cases people take precautions which others consider unnecessary or excessive. Others define such precautions as wasted effort, foolish, and even dysfunctional. People usually show little tolerance of another person's anxieties when they differ from their own. However, those who take precautions consider them warranted. As a result of their experiences they assign the threats greater significance than do those who dismiss them.

My wife wants us to travel abroad, but I refuse to fly. You won't catch me in an airplane. When we take vacations, we go places that I can drive to. #2061

I like to travel in the United States, but I won't go to any large cities. My friend thinks I'm silly. However, cities are where you find large concentrations of unemployed Blacks and lots of arson, looting, rape, and murder. #2062

It is also clear that something does not have to be an actual threat for a person to become frightened of it. A person may learn to perceive a non-threat as a threat because of personal experience, seeing what happens to others, learning about the concerns of others, being exposed to the mass media, and/or using his own imagination. As a result one may perceive something as a threat which does not actually threaten him.

I don't like clowns. You never know who they are or what they might do. #2063

What makes people feel secure

Individuals find that various sources provide them with a general sense of security. A source may be a person, place, thing, or money. When people are separated from this source, they are particularly likely to feel anxious and insecure.

I was sitting in the waiting room of a doctor's office watching the children present. I noticed one child was holding a teddy bear, another a security blanket, and a third had a pacifier in his mouth. The third child began to cry, because his pacifier had fallen to the floor. His mother picked it up and put it back in his mouth and he stopped crying. #2064

I was one of the "boat people" who escaped from South Vietnam across the Gulf of Siam to Thailand. With me were my two children. My youngest child, my daughter, was two years old. She had her pacifier, or plastic nipple, with her, but it fell beneath the floorboards into the bottom of the boat where we couldn't retrieve it. I had an extra pacifier in our medical kit, but we were intercepted by the Vietnamese Coast Guard, who confiscated the medical kit when they searched our boat. After my daughter lost her pacifier, she asked for it repeatedly and cried for most of two to three days. I tried giving her food, but it didn't work as a substitute. My daughter was so upset about her pacifier that she bit my shoulder out of frustration several times. It was like an addiction. Gradually she stopped crying for it. A week and a half later, when we were settled in a refugee camp in Thailand, she no longer asked for one. #2065

My sister, who is twenty-four years old, still sucks her thumb when she is really nervous. #2066

Many adults still have their "blankie," or security blanket, even though they are embarrassed to admit it. A friend, who is twenty-one years old, told me, "I still sleep with my baby blanket." Others leave a night light on. It lets them see there is nothing there to harm them. #2067

Even though I am an adult, I refuse to sleep over at someone else's house. I have to sleep in my own bed, where I feel safe and sound. I feel nothing is going to invade my bed and get me. #2068

When my husband is at work at night, I like to turn on the TV. Even if I'm not watching it, it makes me feel I'm not alone at home. #2069

I get nervous when I travel, whether I am in a car or a plane. I feel much safer at home. #2070

I like for Mom to be home, even if I'm not. I get a feeling of security knowing Mom is there or soon will be. When I was a child I caught my arm on a barbed-wire fence. Mom was working that day. It wasn't the blood that terrified me; it was knowing Mom was not there to look after me and tell me I would be OK. Dad kissed my cuts to make them better and bandaged them up. But without Mom's assurance, I thought I was going to die and would never see her again. #2071

I can't sleep well unless I have a back rub from my mom. It helps me sleep safely, and makes me feel secure about my plans for the next day. #2072

I don't even want to think about being without Paul. I've been going out with him since I was fifteen. I don't think I'd feel safe on my own. When you're one half of a couple, men hesitate to attack you. But when you're alone you're unprotected. #2073

Lots of women say they always feel safe with their husband or boyfriend around. I feel the same way about my wife. If anything were to happen to me I know she would do everything she could for me. I am more content and much happier when I am with her. #2074

Many restaurants have both booths and tables for customers. Usually the booths are along the walls and the tables are in the middle of the room. People almost always want to sit in the booths and will only take a table if all the booths are full. Then if a booth is vacated, they often move from their table to the booth. I think this is because the booths seem more secure. You are surrounded on three sides and feel protected. Out in the middle of the room at a table there is nothing separating you from other people. One restaurant I know had both booths and tables. They redecorated, got rid of their tables, and installed nothing but booths. I think people also like to sit in an easy chair with a high back and arm-rests because it makes them feel more protected. #2075

It is important for me to have some money in my wallet. Often this has to be $20 or more. Then I feel no matter what happens I can deal with it. If I need to buy something, like lunch, I can pay for it. If someone asks me for a donation, I can give them money then and there. If I need to go to the hospital, I can take a taxi. When I have less than $20, I feel I need to get some more cash from the bank. #2076

I have my savings invested in stocks. When I buy goods and services I always try to pay for them out of my salary and never out of my savings in stocks. This forces me to keep my purchases at an affordable level. It is so hard to put money aside for savings that it would be almost impossible to replace the savings if I exhausted them. Whenever my wife suggests that I use my savings to pay for some purchases, like a computer or a trip, I become very anxious. My savings are important because they help me feel more secure. Sometimes I wonder what I would do if I lost my job. If I did, my savings would pay for our living expenses and for my retraining to get another job. #2077

Functions

Because of anxiety, people take appropriate precautions in response to threats to themselves and their resources. Anxiety forces people to give threats serious attention. It signals the need to review one's situation, weigh alternatives and consequences, and determine whether one should allocate more resources to deal with specific threats. It pressures people to take precautions. Even when people do not act in response to anxiety, anxiety encourages people to examine their situation and decide that it is not possible, necessary, or in their best interest to act at the time. Recurrent anxiety reminds people that they have not yet dealt adequately with a threat. The knowledge one will have to face recurrent anxiety acts as a goad which pushes people to take the precautions they have been meaning to take.

As a result of taking precautions, people better protect themselves from bodily harm. They protect themselves from injury and death by taking precautions in regard to present and future physical dangers. They avoid potentially injurious situations, such as heights, animals, and fights. They prepare to deal with potentially injurious agents which can not be avoided, such as storms and sharp tools. They engage in preventive precautions, such as eating healthy foods and exercising.

People also take precautions to better protect their resources. They seek to guard their resources from damage and destruction, and take measures to prevent others from taking their resources. Thus, they may build a garage, purchase fire insurance, or install a burglar alarm.

> Because I'm heavily invested in stocks, when there are changes in the stock market and in the prices of my stocks, I get worried and make changes in my portfolio. One genetic engineering stock I was holding increased in value until it represented sixty percent of my portfolio. I stood to lose so much if it fell in price, that I sold half of it. I'm really glad I did, because within a year it fell to one-fifth its previous value. Another time the stock market fell five percent in a day. I had borrowed money from the broker to buy stock on margin and I realized that if the market kept falling I stood to lose most of my holdings. So the next day I sold a thousand shares and used the money to reduce my margin debt with the broker. [#2078]

People's most important resource is other people. People take precautions to guard the welfare of those who provide them with positive reactions, sex, food and water, protection, and other goods and services necessary for their physical well-being. They engage in certain actions and avoid other actions in order to maintain good relations with others. If people do not meet the expectations of others in their social relations and in the workplace, they are likely to jeopardize the resources they receive from others. The anxiety that people feel over losing these resources encourages them to do what others expect of them at the appropriate time.

> Worry keeps employees on their toes. I often worry whether I've finished a task in such a way that I've fully met the expectations of my boss. I leave no stone unturned in trying to do the job right. [#2079]

> When my girlfriend is late for a date I worry I've been dumped. When she shows up I feel relief. I'm happy I haven't been dumped, which was not even on her mind. I become more attentive to her needs out of fear of losing her. [#2080]

People experience anxiety as soon as they become aware of a potential threat. This provides them with a maximum amount of time in which to take precautions to protect themselves and their resources.

People expend a considerable amount of time and energy both worrying about threats and taking precautions. However, this is often outweighed by the amount of time and energy people would have to expend if they did not protect themselves from threats and had to try to regain resources or restore their physical well-being.

Failure to take precautions

People often fail to take precautions. This occurs because a) they lack specific anxieties which encourage them to take relevant precautions, and b) they do not act upon the anxieties they experience.

People fail to develop anxieties to specific threats when they a) do not personally experience these threats to their resources or physical well-being, b) do not see or hear that others experience these threats, c) do not learn that others are concerned about these threats, d) are not exposed to mass media reports about these threats, e) do not imagine these threats occurring, and f) do not believe the threats could happen to them.

At the same time people often fail to act on the anxieties they experience. For example, many people do not use seat belts when riding in automobiles, do not save money for the future, do not exercise regularly, and do not take adequate precautions against venereal disease or pregnancy. There are a number of reasons why this occurs.

Although people would like to minimize their risks, no one has enough time, energy, and other resources to take sufficient precautions to quiet all of their anxieties. Consequently people must be highly selective. Numerous anxieties occur in connection with distant, possible threats rather than immediate, almost certain threats. As a result people give many anxieties and precautions a lower priority relative to the anxieties that they do act on. They frequently take the chance that many of the things they are anxious about will never happen, or at least not happen before they have taken adequate precautions.

Occasionally I think about the need to stock up on food and water in case of a natural disaster. Even though I know this would be a good idea, I don't worry about it much, and I haven't done anything about it. [#2081]

The males in my family usually die of strokes. I know I need to get back into exercising, and I will as soon as I get on top of things at work. Of course, I've been saying that for the past five years. [#2082]

In addition, certain precautions would be so costly to pursue, that one's ability to commit resources to other pursuits would be threatened, and this would generate even greater anxiety. For example, building an adequate personal shelter for use in the event of a nuclear war could prevent one from saving money for one's retirement, having money available to educate one's children, or paying for travel in order to gain stimulation. People constantly make trade-offs, and this is certainly true with anxieties and precautions. Finally, there are numerous threats which people feel they can do little to prevent and therefore do not bother trying. Depending on the individual, these might include natural disasters, environmental destruction, overpopulation, air pollution, recession, inflation, war, death, and taxes.

There are other reasons why people fail to act on their anxieties. Such reasons include a) the fact we often consciously decide to put off dealing with certain anxieties until some time in the future, b) we become too tired dealing with anxieties which are a higher priority to get to the anxieties which are a lower priority, and c) it is easier to continue old routines of behavior than to initiate new ones.

My family always ate lots of roast pork, and fat from the pork was poured over the vegetables to flavor them. When my father was diagnosed as having high cholesterol, he ignored the doctor's warnings and continued to eat his regular diet. He used to say he was going to die someday and intended to do it on a full stomach. He died of coronary disease. [#2083]

Other reasons why people fail to act on their anxieties are that a) particular anxieties drop out of our consciousness as other things capture our attention, and b) current temptations, i.e., the likelihood of pleasurable experiences, often displace our anxieties.

I know I need to lose five pounds, but it's hard to resist nibbling when you are sitting in the kitchen next to a plate or two of goodies. #2084

Sometimes my girlfriend fails to take her birth-control pill for a day or two. I suddenly remember this when we start making love and I mention it to her. Then both of us decide to go ahead anyway. #2085

When I go out to a club, I think about the dangers of catching a disease from a pickup. But after a few beer, I don't think all that straight anymore. I've woken up the next day with some pretty skanky sluts. It's worried me, but hasn't stopped me. #2086

Taking precautions requires effort. People avoid effort because exertion requires mental and physical tension, and tension is experienced as hurt. (See the chapter on Conserving Time and Energy in this volume.) Therefore, when people do not take precautions, they avoid exertion, tension, and hurt. People take precautions when the tension from anxiety is greater than the tension required by the effort to take precautions. People also take precautions when the tension produced by other people, for example, through threats or nagging, is greater than the tension required by the effort to take precautions.

Another consideration is that we often do not act on an anxiety when it first appears. Frequently we need to think about a situation after we have been in it in order to realize how serious the consequences could have been. Often it seems necessary for us to experience a specific anxiety many times before we actually get around to dealing with it by taking a relevant precaution. The reason we finally act may be in order to stop being annoyed by the specific anxiety in the future. Therefore one reason why we do not act on an anxiety is that we have not been annoyed by it often enough.

Because anxiety is an unpleasant feeling, people often focus on anxiety as being the source of their problems, and ignore its relationship to perceived threats to themselves and their resources. Instead of dealing with the causes of their anxiety and trying to remove threats, they deal instead with the symptom, or the feeling of anxiety itself. People complain about being unable to handle stress, or tension, and being overwhelmed by it. Some people take tranquilizers or seek a technique of reducing anxiety which works for them. One technique that is used is meditation. Another is pursuing an activity, such as exercising or playing a game, which focuses one's mind elsewhere.

I find TV helps me take my mind off my worries. #2087

I try to go to sleep to forget about my fears. #2088

I like to go to a movie when I'm worried, or to get involved in a good book, especially one that scares the heck out of me. #2089

When I'm worried, I eat just about anything in sight. Then I feel guilty. I begin to worry about getting fat, the cost of buying bigger clothes, what I am going to look like, and if I will lose my boyfriend. But it sure does take my mind off my first worry. #2090

I find it very hard to stay home alone at night. I'm usually OK until ten o'clock or so, and then I start hearing noises, strange noises. If I'm watching TV, I constantly turn down the volume to listen to some particular noise. I just can't relax. I find it's a good time for me to do housework. I can whiz through it all at an amazing speed. I just whistle while I work hoping time will pass quickly until someone comes home. #2091

Another technique which is commonly used to reduce anxiety is to attribute outcomes to fate, rather than to personal responsibility. Thus many people adopt the attitude that when one's time, or life, is ended, it's ended, regardless of what one might try to do to forestall this.

Why should I stop smoking or wear a seat belt in a car? When your time is up, it's up, and nothing you can do will prevent this. #2092

Excess behavior

Excess behavior is behavior in response to feelings which results in one acting contrary to the purposes the feelings are designed for. Therefore, one loses resources rather than gains or protects them. For example, the feeling of anxiety causes people to take precautions. As a result people protect themselves and their resources. However, there are situations in which people take precautions to such an extent that they actually lose resources. People engage in several kinds of excess behavior in response to anxiety. These include a) taking unnecessary precautions, b) devoting so much effort to taking precautions that they are unable to obtain resources, and c) developing so much anxiety that they are unable to either take precautions or obtain resources. People engage in excess behavior both in regard to themselves and in regard to other people.

People take many unnecessary precautions.

My friend worries about her health constantly. When she gets a mild problem, like a headache or a local rash, she convinces herself there is something terribly wrong with her. She argues she has good reason to worry, because "I really do have poor health." It's amusing watching her swallow numerous vitamin pills and make frequent appointments to see her doctor. When her doctor tries to reassure her, it does little to quell her anxiety. #2093

People are scared of all sorts of things that I think are absurd. Most are frightened of ghosts, which simply don't exist. Others are scared of snakes and bats, and all snakes and bats want to do is escape, because people love to kill them. And mice, if anything is charming it is a mouse. Women react with such fear, I wonder if they are scared the mouse will run up their vagina? #2094

People can also be so concerned with taking precautions that they are unable to obtain resources.

I like to go to clubs to have a good time and to look out for my friends. I think my friends are a little careless when it comes to guys they meet at clubs. When a guy asks me to dance I get scared. I have never left a club or gone on a date with a guy I've met there. I would not want to be raped, and I worry about my friends because they don't seem to care. They think I'm old-fashioned and that this is why I don't have a boyfriend. Maybe I'll never get a boyfriend and get married. #2095

People's anxieties can cause them to prevent others from obtaining resources and living normal lives.

Taking precautions

Even though I'm in university, I still have to call Mom if I'm not coming home right after class or work, so she won't worry that something bad has happened to me. No matter how late I come home at night, she's waiting up for me. In one sense it makes me mad that she worries about me all the time, because I'm not a kid anymore. On the other hand, her worrying shows she really loves me and she wants things to work out well for me. I must admit though, it is kind of embarrassing when I go out with the other guys and have to go to the phone and check in with "Mommy." It makes it hard to play tough and cool, and the guys tease me about it a lot. [#2096]

My grandmother kept a tight hold on her eight children, and kept them around her even after they became adults. When one of her daughters left home to study nursing, my grandmother developed chronic health problems so that her daughter had to move back home and take care of her. She had her children convinced that no other family in the area was good enough for them. As a result seven of her eight children never married. [#2097]

We don't let our cat outside unless he's on a leash. I suppose it would be alright if he stayed in our yard and in the woods next door, but we wouldn't want him to wander off and get lost or hit by a car. [#2098]

Also, people can develop so much anxiety that they are unable to either take precautions or obtain resources.

Sometimes I get so worried about all the things I have to do that I can't sleep at night. I lie in bed for hours just worrying, and because I get so little sleep I'm not good for much the next day. Then there are the times I get so discouraged by how much there is to do that I can't get myself motivated to do anything. By the middle of the afternoon I realize I've wasted the whole day fretting about things, so I give up and watch TV. [#2099]

People are normally so anxious about being criticized and rejected that they are unwilling to take risks, say and do things differently than others, strike out on their own, explore and discover new resources, and stand up and oppose others. As a result they obtain less resources than they might obtain.

Societal precautions

People institute and employ social practices in order to more effectively protect themselves and their resources. These social practices take many forms, including social conventions, informal and formal organizations, and government. As a result, members of the society are coordinated into acting in ways which provide greater security for many members of the society.

Societal precautions become instituted as people become anxious about possible threats to themselves and their family members and solicit the help of others in reducing these threats. Often their anxiety occurs in response to mishaps and near mishaps to themselves and others. For example, when automobile accidents occur repeatedly at a particular location, there is often public pressure to have a warning sign or a traffic light installed at that location. In reaction to specific threats, people frequently group together; form organizations; research, design, and implement countermeasures; or put pressure on existing organizations to do something. Societal precautions provide protection for many people in the society. Thus the use of traffic regulations, such as driving on one side of the road, obeying stop signs and traffic lights, and getting a safety inspection for one's vehicle on a regular basis, result in greater predictability of the movement of others, greater personal safety, less vehicle damage, and less expenditure of time and energy getting from one place to another.

Government consists of superordinate organizations which are instituted to investigate certain threats and legislate and enforce precautions against them. In order to facilitate making and carrying out decisions, government normally uses formal bodies and procedures as well as hierarchies with single individuals assigned specific areas of responsibility. Government decisions are often backed up by investigatory bodies, fines, imprisonment, and armed enforcers. Those who are charged with breaking rules established by a government are also subject to public embarrassment and considerable outlays of time and energy defending themselves. By assigning penalties to certain actions and by determining the severity of the penalties, a government is able to influence the amount of anxiety associated with these actions. The more anxiety produced, the less likely members of the society will engage in these actions.

Examples of societal precautions will be organized below into the following categories:

Personal safety
    1. Health and physical safety
    2. Travel
    3. Sports
    4. Environment
    5. Other people
Protecting the acquisition of resources
Protecting personal resources
    1. Jobs and money
    2. Property
    3. Reputations
    4. Relationships
Protecting models
Protecting groups, organizations, the government, and other public
    resources
Protection from government

Personal safety

Personal safety includes protection from hazards in the areas of health and physical safety, travel, sports, the environment, and other people.

1. Health and physical safety

Various societal precautions are put in place to give individuals better protection from health hazards and physical threats. For example, facilities which process and sell food are required to meet certain standards and are regularly inspected, people are informed of the need for regular medical examinations and exercise, research is conducted on diseases and on the side effects of various foods and drugs, and ingredients are listed on packages of food. Public instruction is also given in how to prepare food, such as pork; on the use of contraceptive devices to prevent venereal disease; and on the dangers of smoking, alcohol, and drugs to oneself and one's fetus. In order to ensure proper nutrition, people are educated concerning desirable diet and weight and the risks associated with certain foods, lunches are provided to school children, and meals are served to patients in hospitals and the elderly in their homes. In order to remove health hazards, chlorine is added to water to kill bacteria, immunization programs are conducted to combat communicable diseases, people with epidemic diseases are isolated, disposable needles and bandages are used to reduce the chance of infection from other people, contaminated and poisoned food is removed from store shelves, smoking is prevented in many public areas, and the use of dangerous drugs and food additives is prohibited. To better control alcohol use, there are detoxification centers, rehabilitation groups such as Alcoholics Anonymous, and laws prohibiting the sale of liquor to minors. In order to counteract health problems, professionals, such as doctors, dentists, and nurses, are trained and certified; facilities, such as clinics and hospitals, are maintained and monitored; and instructions are given to non-professionals on how to deal with emergencies, such as poisoning, heart attacks, drowning, bleeding, blockage of breathing, and shock. In order to facilitate individual survival, the government and other organizations provide unemployment insurance, welfare payments, old-age pensions, retirement programs, medical benefits, disability compensation, paid maternity leave, organ transplants, orphanages, adoption procedures, nursing homes, emergency food rations, food and rent subsidies, price controls, instruction for the illiterate and speech impaired, language instruction for immigrants, special advantages for members of minority groups, equal opportunity requirements in hiring, commissions to investigate violations of human rights, facilities for the handicapped, institutions for the retarded and mentally ill, income tax reductions for elderly and handicapped individuals and those with excessive medical expenses, and aid for political and natural disaster victims. In order to reduce threats to physical safety, wells are covered and doors are removed from discarded refrigerators; excised tissue is examined to determine whether surgery was necessary; signs are erected to notify people not to drink or swim in unsafe water; prescriptions are required to purchase certain medications; substances which cause internal or external injuries are labeled as such; safety features are installed in vehicles to protect people both inside and outside the vehicles; electrical wiring is insulated and grounded and fuses are installed; and construction standards are specified for houses, buildings, and bridges.

2. Travel

Societal precautions are instituted to provide individuals with greater safety when they travel. Pedestrians are provided with sidewalks, traffic lights, crosswalks, right of way, and the removal of snow and ice from sidewalks. Drivers of vehicles are required to pass tests to obtain a license, and must renew their license at regular intervals. To reduce the likelihood of accidents, there are traffic reports; reports on road conditions; standards for road construction and repair; snow removal; school and work cancellations during bad weather; traffic police; speed limits; traffic lights; railroad crossing lights and barriers; stop signs; barriers along edges of cliffs; separate lanes for travel in each direction; markers and islands separating lanes; control of plant growth along the sides of roads; exit warnings; rest stations; emergency telephones on roadways; areas alongside roads where vehicles can pull over and stop; regulations when to stop for school buses; warning sirens and lights on police and emergency vehicles; requirements to allow police and emergency vehicles the right of way; traffic control measures when accidents occur; laws against excessive alcohol consumption and driving; tests for alcohol consumption; and warning signs for curves, bridges, bumps, icy roads, falling rocks, road construction, detours, animal crossings, and steep inclines. In addition, vehicles are equipped with safety equipment, such as driving lights, turning lights, breaking lights, hazard lights, back-up bells, brakes, emergency brakes, horns, safety glass, air bags, safety belts, padded insides, safety tires, and ashtrays. Vehicles are constructed to meet certain safety standards and are recalled to repair defects. In addition, different makes of vehicles are systematically compared and ranked in regard to safety.

In the case of public transportation involving buses, trains, ships, and airplanes, there are traffic controllers; trip cancellations in bad weather; fire extinguishers; alarms and broadcast systems for communication between staff and passengers; barriers to communication between passengers and vehicle operators; investigations of accidents in order to take corrective measures; and reputations of carriers for safety. In the case of ships there are buoys, lighthouses, foghorns, pilots, life preservers, life boats, and life-boat drills. The use of airplanes includes seat belts, emergency exits, emergency oxygen, life preservers, training of staff for flight and medical emergencies, instruction of passengers before flights regarding emergency procedures, smoke alarms to prevent smoking in toilets, metal detectors to deter hijackers, bomb detectors to inspect luggage, the removal of ice from wings, fire trucks and ambulances for emergency landings, and regular safety inspections.

3. Sports

Numerous measures are taken by groups and organizations to protect players of sports from injuries. Each sport is customarily played in such a way as to minimize injury. There are also measures taken by regulatory bodies, equipment manufacturers, and referees to make the sport safer. As a consequence individuals and those they care about are less likely to be injured when they participate.

Normally there is standardized clothing in each sport which allows players ease of movement and better control over their actions. For example, there are shorts, T-shirts, and sneakers in basketball. Standardized clothing often includes items which protect one's body from contact with a) other players, b) equipment, and c) the playing area. This includes helmets, goggles, padding, gloves, specialized shoes, and mouth guards. Often players are expected to remove hard items, such as watches and jewelry, which might cut or otherwise harm other players. In certain sports there are extra precautions to prevent mishaps. These include safety lines for mountain climbers; life preservers for sailors; diving partners, extra air regulators, and quick-release weight belts for scuba divers; backup parachutes for sky divers; life guards and television monitors at swimming pools; and nets to keep sharks from coastal swimming areas. Various restrictions are put on activities which might cause injury, such as descending below a certain depth when one is learning to scuba dive, or tackling players when one is playing football without protective gear. Rules are established and penalties are enacted against actions which could seriously injure another player. These include slugging a football player, hitting a boxer below the belt, spearing with a hockey stick, and using a stranglehold in wrestling. Often there are referees and coaches to carefully monitor play and intercede when injuries occur or appear likely.

For example, a boxing match may be halted because of facial cuts. Safety procedures are commonly used when training, and may include harnesses, nets, catchers, and close supervision. Often there is preliminary instruction in a classroom or safe area. Extra precautions are taken to ensure that players do not overtax themselves. For example, there are regularly scheduled rest breaks between periods of play during many games. Participants may be required to pass a physical examination before engaging in a sport, such as scuba diving; or may be required to stretch, warm up beforehand, and warm down afterwards, as in aerobic and dance classes.

4. Environment

Various societal efforts are made to protect people from environmental hazards. Better protection is provided from dangerous weather by means of weather reports and warnings and evacuations. Efforts are made to protect people from fire by means of lightning rods, fire-resistant fabrics, fire alarms, smoke detectors, fire extinguishers, fire-escape ladders, sprinklers in rooms and hallways, clearly marked exits, directions as to where to go in case of fire, fire drills, fire hydrants, fire departments, and fire trucks. Research is conducted on the effects of pollution and radiation, permissible levels are established, controls are instituted to help ensure that levels are not exceeded, current levels are monitored, and toxic wastes are disposed of in areas which are not inhabited by humans. Obstacles and warnings are used to keep the public out of areas where they might be injured. Thus fences and signs are placed around electrical power stations; animals in circuses and zoos are isolated from the public by cages, walls, and moats; and signs and fences are used in parks to keep people from swimming in dangerous areas, feeding animals, and approaching ledges and other unsafe areas. Animals that might injure humans, such as snakes, sharks, bears, wolves, and rabid animals, are killed or removed.

Safety equipment, such as hard hats, gloves, boots, and goggles, is mandatory in many occupations. Equipment which can cause injury is often designed with safety in mind. For example, chain saws stop automatically when the user releases a pressure switch, and ladders often have nonskid grips at their base. In many buildings and houses, adherence to construction codes reduces the chance of collapse, appliances are electrically grounded, stairways and ledges are enclosed by barriers to prevent falls, revolving doors have rubber edges to prevent injuries, emergency exits are clearly identified, and emergency lighting is turned on when power fails. To reduce the likelihood of personal injury, doors on elevators and subways reopen automatically if a person is caught in them, microwave ovens and washing machines shut off automatically if they are opened in the middle of operation, and obstacles are placed along the islands between escalators to stop people from sliding down the islands. Other measures to protect people include regulations concerning maximum noise levels, the designation of separate smoking and non-smoking areas, and signs on buildings warning of falling snow and ice. In addition, many products are evaluated and redesigned to provide greater safety.

5. Other people

Various social practices are instituted to provide individuals with protection from other people. Laws and punishments are designed to prevent assault, murder, rape, and sexual harassment and abuse. Police investigate crimes involving physical harm and offenders are fined and jailed. In addition, there are security officers in buildings and at concerts, and bouncers in bars and lounges. There are simplified emergency telephone numbers for contacting police, anonymity for informants, legal aid, block-parent associations, and lighting in public areas at night. In order to control violence, guns are licensed and registered and individuals are prohibited from owning certain types of weapons. To better protect children, reports of abuse and neglect are investigated and children are sometimes removed from their parents. Fetuses are better protected through antiabortion laws. Formal training and certification are required to ensure competence on the part of those, such as the police, whose job it is to protect individuals from other people.

Protecting the acquisition of resources

Various societal measures are put in place to facilitate and protect the individual's effort to gain resources. Many services are provided by the government which would be difficult for individuals to provide on their

351

own. Such services include education, disease control, roads, bridges, traffic control, public parking, snow removal, weather reports, clean water, waste and sewage removal, electricity, airports, port facilities, inflation and recession controls, and national defense.

The resources which individuals seek include jobs, money, information, food, physical comfort, stimulation, and positive reactions. To facilitate the acquisition of jobs and money, individuals are provided with public education, professional training, and on-the-job training. Various agencies and services provide help selecting and locating jobs. In addition, there are regulations regarding minimum wages, pay equity, and discrimination in hiring. The ability of individuals and businesses to make employment plans is made easier through the provision of research, indicators, and forecasts regarding the economy, agriculture, natural resources, and the weather. This may be supplemented by trade agreements, trade tariffs, and government subsidies. The development of business is encouraged by means of tax incentives, industrial parks, low-interest loans, shopping centers, and the removal of unsightly objects and people, such as wrecks and derelicts, from shopping areas. Businesses are protected by bankruptcy law. Access to information is provided through libraries, government departments and agencies, and information services. Buildings, displays, presentations, seating, and the removal of disruptive people, make it possible for people to obtain stimulation at museums, art galleries, concerts, and movie theaters. Social groups and gatherings; social facilities, ranging from churches to bars; and personal advertising sections in newspapers enable people to meet others and develop relationships.

Protecting personal resources

Numerous societal measures are taken to protect personal resources, such as jobs, money, property, time, energy, information, entertainment, reputations, and relationships.

1. Jobs and money

Various social organizations and practices help to reduce threats to people's jobs. There are measures which help protect the individual from losing employment. These include unions, tenure, and the need to show just cause for dismissal. Unemployment insurance provides income while one looks for another job, declaration of personal bankruptcy protects one from creditors, and workers' compensation helps one cope with illness or injury. Those with jobs are protected from competition through tariff walls; limits on immigration; and requirements for specialized training, examination, and certification.

Bank accounts, traveler's checks, and police provide individuals with protection from theft, and deposit insurance protects individuals from the collapse of a financial institution. Incorporation provides business owners with personal financial protection in the event of failure of their business. There are also laws to protect the public from chain letters and other attempts to defraud them of their money. Those who experience financial loss have recourse to lawyers, legal aid, lawsuits, hearings, judges, and appeals. There are numerous other social practices which are designed to help protect the individual's money. Examples include laws controlling certain forms of gambling and investment scams.

People receive protection from inflation, monopolies, and financial exploitation through government controls over rate increases for gas, water, electricity, telephone service, cable television, garbage collection, and rent. For consumers there are consumer protection agencies, research reports on products, and controls over truth in advertising. Many businesses have refund policies when customers are dissatisfied with their products. Some businesses seek to compensate clients for personal losses. For example, when there are lengthy delays caused by equipment failure, strikes, or bad weather, transportation carriers may provide free food and lodging to travelers. In addition, people hear reports from others about the service, reliability, and honesty of specific businesses and individuals. This allows people to make better decisions whether or not to deal with them.

2. Property

Society provides a large number of means for individuals to better protect their property from loss or damage. For example, individuals are required to register ownership of certain types of property, such as land and vehicles. External identification is also required on certain forms of property, such as license numbers on vehicles and identification tags on airline luggage. In the event of loss or theft, this identification makes it easier to return the property to the owner. Patents and copyright make it possible to register and protect ownership of inventions, designs, written work, music, and films; and zoning helps people protect property values.

Storm warnings, water drainage systems, and curbstones help people protect their property from wind and water damage. Night lighting in public areas, curfews at Halloween and other times, and numerous laws and punishments help to prevent theft, vandalism, and trespass. Police patrols, police investigations, rewards for information, and jails help to control theft and damage to property. Fire departments, hydrants, and public alarms help control fires.

3. Reputations

Various measures have been adopted by the society to help protect the individual's reputation. Laws, regulations, and professional standards seek to a) prevent libel, b) keep minors who are charged with crimes from being named in the news media, and c) prevent private information about individuals from being revealed by mail handlers, telephone operators, psychological counselors, social workers, medical personnel, stock brokers, the police, bank employees, and the tax department.

4. Relationships

Relationships constitute an important resource because they provide people with positive reactions, sex, and tangible resources. Numerous social measures are in place to ensure the protection of relationships. Relationships are formally announced to the community through ceremonies and the media. Examples include engagement, marriage, and birth notices; marriage and baptism ceremonies; and bridal and baby showers. Socially recognized signs remind others that the relationship exists. Thus wedding rings, titles such as "Mrs.," and the adoption of a common last name, notify others of the relationship and warn them that they are likely to be wasting their time if they try to obtain certain types of resources, such as love, sex, children, or substantial financial aid, from either partner.

Various measures are employed by the society to help protect people's children. Children's physical safety is better guarded by removing sharp points and edges from toys, and putting labels on specific toys which indicate how old a child should be in order to handle them safely. In addition, children are inoculated to protect them from infectious diseases, warnings are put on plastic bags that can cause suffocation, and laws prevent the sale of certain fireworks to children. In order to ensure that children become qualified to find employment, laws require children to go to school. School facilities, teachers, and learning materials are monitored; students are examined and graded on what they have learned; teachers hold meetings with parents to discuss their child's performance; and requirements are established for graduation. Additional measures include a) assigning minors who break the law milder penalties than adults receive, b) requiring financial support for children when parents separate, c) providing adult supervision at social events for children, d) setting up block-parent associations to give refuge to children who are outdoors, and e) organizing community Halloween parties for children to avoid risks associated with trick or treating.

Protecting models

Numerous efforts are made by groups and organizations to protect what is meaningful to their members. Specific models are held by segments of the population, who often seek to have these models adopted by the entire society. For example, certain groups attempt to use legislation and other means to ensure that abortion is halted; the Sabbath is respected; nations disarm; portions of the environment are maintained in a pre-agricultural state; soldiers who died in action are honored; domesticated animals are fed and not beaten; and people are prevented from committing suicide, stealing, using alcohol or drugs, and assaulting and murdering others. Various groups and organizations also seek to ensure that teachers do not teach that God does not exist, Blacks are less intelligent than whites, women are less intelligent and capable than men, capitalism is wrong, Marxism or Communism is right, and the destruction of the Jews in Nazi Germany did not occur. In addition, different groups try to make sure that people do not engage in premarital sex, promiscuity, adultery, or bigamy; that there is no pornography, prostitution, public nudity, sex between close relatives, sex in public, or sexual contact between adults and minors; that crank telephone calls of a sexual nature are prevented; that menstrual products are not advertised; and that people do not swear or use dirty words in front of others. (See the chapter on Establishing Consistency in a later volume.)

Protecting groups, organizations, the government, and other public resources

Numerous organized efforts are made to protect the existence of groups, organizations, and the government. One such effort is gathering funds to pay salaries and to enact policies. Normally dues are collected from the members of each group. In the case of government, members of the society are taxed on various levels. Often there is an elaborate bureaucracy for determining taxes, collecting them, investigating those who fail to pay, and forcing them to do so. The issuance of money is often controlled by the government, and counterfeiting is treated as a serious offense. In many groups and organizations there is an effort to recruit new members to replace those who leave the group. Within the group there are normally well-defined procedures for selecting and replacing leaders and reaching decisions. Such procedures minimize conflict between group members which could threaten the existence of the group. Within a society various approaches are used to develop loyalty to the society and its government. These include instruction of the public by means of the educational system and the mass media to appreciate the advantages of one's own system and the disadvantages of alternative systems. This is supplemented by the use of emotional symbols and exercises, such as flags, songs, parades, oaths of allegiance, stereotypes, and accounts of noble actions (by members of one's own society) and ignoble actions (by members of other societies), which help the populace develop emotional attachments to their society.

In order to protect the society from being invaded and controlled by outsiders, considerable effort is made to maintain a viable military. This often involves supporting a full-time and part-time army; developing a patriotic spirit; conscripting civilians; producing an effective arsenal; planning for military contingencies, including preemptive attacks on enemies; studying military history; collecting political, economic, and military information on potential aggressors; managing news released to the public; controlling travel by civilians to and from enemy areas; and establishing treaties and military pacts with other societies.

Efforts are also made to protect the property of groups, organizations, and the government. There are laws against theft and vandalism, and locks, fences, signs, security guards, and police patrols help support this. In addition there are efforts to prevent environmental damage to public areas, such as parks and wildlife preserves.

Protection from government

Certain measures are instituted to help protect individuals and groups from threats by the government. Often there are limited terms of office for government officials and standardized practices for changing government representatives and leaders. Such practices include selection procedures for candidates, presentations by candidates, voter registration, media campaigns to encourage voting, formal voting procedures, standardized ballots and ballot boxes, official counts of votes, procedures for recounting votes, poll watchers, hearings in regard to the appointment of officials, rules allowing criticism from opposition parties, and procedures for impeachment. In addition, there are often legal limits on the power of government representatives to attack individuals and appropriate their property. There are also various freedoms for the mass media to investigate and criticize government officials and policies, and for individuals to get hearings for their grievances. People frequently decide to change government representatives and leaders when people believe they are doing a poor job protecting their physical well-being and resources.

Environmental impact of taking precautions

Life is inherently risky for an individual and his resources. Individuals are easily injured and killed and frequently lose resources as a result of natural and human agents. Nevertheless, individuals are willing to go to almost any extremes to protect themselves and their resources, and such extremes have considerable impact on the environment.

Taking precautions

In order to protect themselves from unknown contingencies, individuals attempt to accumulate as much wealth and property as possible. The development of human wealth and property is based on the conversion of natural areas and other species into human use. Areas that are converted to human use, such as those occupied by houses, lawns, buildings, farms, factories, roads, and airports, are no longer available for use by a multitude of other species in a natural ecosystem. In addition, people construct fences and walls to protect themselves, their families, and their possessions from other people. Fences and walls prevent the movement and foraging of members of many species and therefore are destructive of ecosystems. Also, people seek to kill off species which they believe can cause them injury or cause them to lose resources. These include wolves, coyotes, foxes, bears, groundhogs, mice, rats, snakes, spiders, termites, ants, wasps, insects that eat crops, sharks, alligators, crocodiles, lions, tigers, and leopards. Humans view human needs and endeavors as the only legitimate ones on earth, and pursue them regardless of their cost to other species. For example, people test and use weapons in order to protect themselves and their resources from other people. Many of these weapons are very destructive of natural habitats and other species. Humans will increasingly take all of the resources required by other species in order to try to ensure human survival and satisfy human feelings and needs.

TRYING TO GET WHAT OTHERS HAVE

Brief contents

Detailed contents

Detailed contents

Introduction

People frequently try to get what others have. This may be positive reactions, possessions, advantages, experiences, relationships, accomplishments, and anything else that others have but they do not. The feeling which motivates people to try to get what others have is envy. Envy motivates people to focus on resources which others have that they do not, and to endeavor to acquire these resources for themselves. They may try to take a resource from the person who has it, get the person to share the resource with them, get those who distribute the resource to give them a share, or find another way to obtain the same resource, such as buying it or making it. The feeling of envy notifies people that someone has succeeded in getting a resource that they would like to have too. Envy encourages people to obtain the same resources that others have and encourages them to exploit the resources that are available. In this discussion, the words "jealous" and "jealousy" are used interchangeably with "envious" and "envy."

What people have that others want

People frequently identify resources that they believe would help them satisfy their feelings and fulfill their needs. Such resources include food and water, comfort, positive reactions, stimulation, and sex, as well as the means to obtain these things. As a result people want to acquire the resources that they recognize as useful. Often they learn of the existence of a resource and how it can be exploited by watching other people use the resource. People show considerable interest in the things that others have. They observe what others have and discuss this among themselves. In addition, others commonly inform them of their acquisitions and accomplishments.

What people have that others want

> My neighbor keeps telling me about his savings accounts. He mentions how much money he makes in interest and how fast his savings are growing. After we talk, I sometimes go in the house and get out the old calculator to see if his savings are more or less than my own. #2100

People are very interested in the things that others have which they do not. They tend to be much less interested in the things that others have which they already have, and in the things that others have which are not as good as what they have.

> I used to have an old out-of-date computer, and was quite jealous of the computer systems used by other people in my office. But I just got a new system with a more powerful processor, larger monitor, faster printer, jazzier keyboard, and better software. It dances circles around everyone else's. Now I don't pay any more attention to their systems and they all tell me they are jealous of mine. #2101

People are quick to notice when someone else has a resource that they do not have, or else has greater access to a resource than they do, i.e., an "unfair" advantage. A person may receive a better grade than they do, be hired instead of them, receive more pay than they do, or get preferential treatment. When this occurs they are likely to get upset.

> Lorraine, who is adopted, gets upset when James gets things and she doesn't. She assumes James is given more because he is a natural child of their parents. When James received a new bike, Lorraine was so angry she ran upstairs, slammed her door, and yelled out her window, "I'm not loved in this house!" #2102

Although people are very concerned about fairness when others have advantages they do not have and when others receive more resources than they do, people are rarely concerned with fairness when they have advantages that others do not have and when they receive more resources than others do. Instances do occur in which people sacrifice an advantage in the interest of fairness to others, such as telling a clerk who wants to wait on them that someone else was there first. However, these are of minor significance compared with what people could do, such as divide their salary or possessions evenly with everyone who has less than they do.

Trying to get what others have

People tend to focus on what another person has that they do not, and ignore what they have that the other person does not. Thus one person may buy a new car, and his neighbor may spend the same amount of money on a trip to Europe, but each may be envious of the other. Neither seems to care that they have spent the same amount of money, just on different things. The person who wants something that another has may even have more and better possessions, experiences, advantages, and relationships than the other person. All that is required is the perception that the other person has something one would like to have too.

I am a single mother with two daughters, Joanne and Sally, who are eleven and nine years old. Yesterday I gave my daughters their allowances and took them out to their favorite cookie shop. I also let my older daughter, Joanne, choose four pieces of material in a fabric store so she can make doll clothes and I bought her a strip of sequins to decorate them with. That evening when my two girls came inside from playing, my boyfriend and I were having some soup. Joanne said she wanted some soup, and I told her to go fix some. Joanne and Sally went into hysterics and remained in this state for the rest of the evening. Joanne denounced me to my face for making soup for my boyfriend but not for them. She said that several weeks before I had asked them, "Who wants some tea?" and they said they wanted some. But then I fixed tea for my boyfriend and myself and none for them. I have rarely seen them this upset before, and Sally cried repeatedly. When I asked Joanne why she doesn't do things for herself, she said she's a child and I am supposed to do these things for her. They wouldn't talk to me for the rest of the evening. Their criticism really hurt, because it is so unjustified. I do so much for them. They forget about all the things I do for them that I don't do for my boyfriend. #2103

People want the same or better resources than others have, and the same or better means of getting them. Thus people want the same or better food and shelter, positive reactions, sex, and stimulation, and the same or better means of obtaining them. They are particularly concerned about the things that others have that they do not. Often their attention is directed at the following:

1. Positive reactions
2. Possessions
3. Advantages

4. Experiences
5. Relationships
6. Accomplishments and success

1. Positive reactions

People are frequently jealous of others who get more positive reactions than they get, or who get types of positive reactions that they do not get. Positive reactions are a limited resource and people compete for them. (See the chapter on Seeking Positive Reactions in Volume One of this series.)

> My best friend is a model and I sometimes feel inferior when I'm with her. I'm bothered that whenever we do things together she's the one who always attracts all the attention. Whenever she has something to say, there's always someone there who'll listen. People consider you more important when you're beautiful. #2104

> I know some hockey players who are very popular in our school. They shouldn't get a second glance, because they aren't good looking. I can't believe those girls who fall all over them just because they're on the hockey team. #2105

> I work at a nursing home, and if one resident gets a cold, the other residents do too. They can't stand to see someone getting more attention than they do. #2106

> My wife complains that our daughter, Janet, listens to me more than to her. She hates it when Janet seeks my advice instead of listening only to her. The other day my wife told Janet she should take ginger pills to settle her stomach. Janet then asked me what I thought. At the time Janet was wearing a pair of sweatpants that had a small hole in one leg. My wife was so furious at Janet for asking my opinion that she grabbed the pants at the hole and ripped the leg half off. #2107

> Few men in rural communities ever compliment their wife's skill in the kitchen. However, after a man has helped out at another man's farm, when he gets home his wife often asks him what the food was like that he ate there. It is considered necessary to feed those who help you with

your farming, and to feed them well. The man normally wouldn't mention the meal at all if his wife didn't bring it up. But if the man praises the other woman's cooking and baking, or a particular dish he liked, his wife is usually quite offended. This was certainly the case with Mom and Dad. Mom would say, "Oh sure, come home telling that story. If you got it home you'd hardly eat it, let alone say it was good." Another thing was that men seldom compliment a woman's appearance. I can remember a couple of times Dad said that so-and-so had a nice dress on. It wasn't said in the sense that Dad was attracted to these women, just that they looked nice. But boy, did Mom get mad. [#2108]

Because siblings compete for positive reactions and other resources from their parents, their rivalry is notorious for jealousy.

Beth has told me how jealous she is of her older sister, Terri. Terri is very pretty and popular and gets good grades in school. Beth feels a lot of pressure to do as well in identical ways, but is unable to do so. She feels very angry at her sister, because as far as she's concerned Terri has everything. [#2109]

I know my parents always loved Rose more than me. Any fight we ever had was always my fault. They would keep asking me why I couldn't get the grades that Rose did and why I couldn't stop eating and be thin like her. I really began to hate her. I tried to make Rose look bad every chance I got. All I ever wanted was for my parents to love me and accept me for what I am. [#2110]

2. Possessions

A person may want the same possessions that another person has, or to have possessions which are better in one or more ways than the other person's. This could be a garage, deck, large-screen television, summer cottage, new car, second car, boat, snowmobile, or new furniture.

On Christmas afternoon when I was a kid, we'd show and tell the other kids in the neighborhood the presents we got and they'd show and tell us what they got. I remember one year being really envious of this kid who got a lot of nice things that I would have loved to get. The thing I still remember was a set of toy soldiers. [#2111]

What people have that others want

I show up in school wearing jeans and a football shirt and I see these fruity-looking guys in their pleated pants and buttoned-down collars and fruit shoes. I don't know why people would bother with such expensive, dressy clothes. I don't know where they get the money on a student's budget. #2112

Preppies wear the latest and most expensive clothes, and many people are jealous of them. "You can always tell a girl is rich by all the little labels on her expensive clothes and by her preppy hairstyle." "If you don't wear the most expensive clothes, you're just not 'with it.'" "People think if you don't wear the expensive brand names, you don't have any style or class." "I wish I was rich so I could buy some really nice clothes. Then I would be 'with it' and everyone would like me." "Preps don't even try to hide how disgusted they are by what I wear. They look me up and down like I'm no good, and from then on they just stare past me like I don't even exist." #2113

In my neighborhood people notice when others own more than they do, have something better, and buy new possessions. Neighbors make comments like "My, my, a new car for them to show off," "They have five telephones in their home. That's stretching convenience a little too far," and "I don't see how they can afford to get the outside of their house refinished. Where are they getting the money? Anyway, the color is absolutely horrid." Neighbors compete to see who has the most trees, the prettiest flowers, and the nicest shrubbery in their yards. They comment, "Why don't they do something with their front lawn. It looks awful," "Oh they're just copying us," and "Well, he's a doctor. He should have nice trees." Everyone tries to prove they are equal to or better than the next fellow. So when one neighbor gets something, the others feel they are falling behind and look bad. Then they do their best to get the same thing or something better. #2114

People are particularly likely to want possessions that others have which carry high status, such as a large modern home, a fur coat, a large boat, a sports car, or expensive jewelry. Few people have these items and those who do win attention from others.

Hugh always wanted his own car. When he saved up enough money he bought a nice secondhand one. He was really proud of it until he saw the brand new sports car his friend bought. Hugh says, "Reggie's car makes mine look like a piece of trash. I wish I could afford something like that." #2115

Status and envy are tied together. The higher an item's status, the more envy it generates. Conversely, the more envy an item generates, the higher its status.

3. Advantages

The advantages that people have are often desired by those who lack them. People are likely to notice any advantage that someone has that they do not have too.

> On Friday and Saturday nights the most popular clubs are filled to capacity, and a line forms in front to wait for people to leave and space to become available. People may wait in line for an hour or more. Although some become impatient and leave, others become resigned and make comments like "There's a good crowd tonight," and "That beer sure is going to taste good." Gradually people feel part of the group that is waiting in line. People joke, someone in the line often provides entertainment, and people are amused by those who have already had too much to drink. Occasionally some individual will try to talk their way to the front of the line, perhaps by saying that their friends are already inside. Those who have been waiting resent this, and someone in the line may call the person back or not let him get by and will usually get the group to back him up. Therefore the individual is forced to go to the back of the line. Often the club allows certain categories of people the privilege of not having to wait in line. One category are club employees on their nights off. Another category are local athletes who frequent the club. Those in the line may express their resentment and make comments like "Some people don't have to wait like everyone else," and "Maybe if I put on my fucking hockey sweater, I'd get in." People in the line tend to forget about this once they get into the club, because their attention is drawn to everything else that is happening. #2116

> I was seated across from two middle-aged women at bingo. They began to talk about a woman named Debbie and the fact she was there again after being there the night before. One said there should be a law against her using the money she gets from welfare to go to bingo. A woman seated next to me interjected that she agreed with them, and

said, "I don't see why they let her do it. I'm on welfare and the money I get barely takes me to bingo twice a week. Debbie comes four times a week, buys twice as many cards as I do, and still has enough to buy pop, chips, and bars. Besides that she smokes a lot. I just don't see that it's fair." I looked over at the woman they were staring at. She was shabbily dressed, was smoking, and had two bottles of pop in front of her. That didn't bother me as much as the fact she was playing six times as many bingo cards as I was. #2117

One of the local bars is in the basement of a large motel. There are "regulars" from the local area who go to this bar, in addition to traveling salesmen, or "travelers," from out of town. Some of the regulars do not like the travelers because they are given special treatment. One complaint is that the travelers do not have to pay their expenses for rooms, meals, and drinks, because their companies pay for them, whereas the regulars have to pay for drinks and meals out of their own pockets. Another complaint is that the manager of the motel comes down to the bar and associates with the travelers, but he rarely does so with the regulars. When the manager drinks with the travelers he drinks a beer from a glass, but when he drinks with the regulars he drinks from a bottle. Another complaint is that the bartender normally serves travelers first, regulars second, and irregulars third. The bartender also checks on travelers more often to see if they need another drink or some food. Regulars feel that the bartender must think that the regulars will wait patiently, and if they do leave they will come back again tomorrow. Regulars note that they tip much better than the travelers do. Regulars resent that they are treated as second-class even though they go to the bar throughout the week, whereas the travelers are treated better even though they are only there half a week. However, motel management knows that if the travelers are not happy, they will inform their companies, and the companies will send them to a different motel. #2118

Some Catholics resent the advantages which they believe priests and nuns have. I know one Catholic man who complains about the priests and nuns living in large communal residences, one of which is nicknamed "the Bishop's Palace." Our Catholic housekeeper, who is relatively poor, criticizes "the rich sisters" for driving around in fancy cars. #2119

Those who do not have advantages frequently complain about the lack of equal opportunity and the absence of "a level playing field."

People desire the advantages that others have, such as a good job or an inheritance. They also resent the disadvantages they have that others do not have, such as a handicap or disease, or having to take care of an elderly relative or fight in a war. They become upset over "double standards" when they believe someone else has more advantages than they do.

> My mother can't stand the loud banging of rock music. But she can listen to classical music going at full blast day in and day out. This really irritates me, because she makes me put on headphones when I want to listen to my "noisy ruckus." But when she wants to listen to her music she can blast it through the whole house. I just want to put on my headphones to get away from it. #2120

> Athletes resent the advantages that other athletes get in other sports. "It's no exaggeration to say that if you play the right sport here, you have got it made. It's very easy to realize that the women's volleyball team and the men's Rugby team are going to have a much tougher time surviving than the men's hockey, basketball, and soccer teams." "Certain teams are given funds to travel to other provinces and the United States when they play. But some teams aren't given any funds at all. We get angry, because we have to pay for all our equipment and all of our trips out of the province." "Even when we win a major competition, we don't get any recognition because our sport isn't considered important here." "Players on certain teams get special privileges, like being able to take fewer courses and easier courses than others. Many of them don't even graduate. But because I play a different sport, I have to work my ass off taking a full load of difficult courses." #2121

People are particularly likely to want the financial advantages that others have. These may be better paying jobs, higher positions at work, more government aid or benefits, greater financial help from relatives, more savings and investments, or lower interest on their mortgage payments. People also frequently wish they were the ones who had won a lottery or received an inheritance. Many who are employed wish they did not have to work, and are jealous of those who are retired or are supported by welfare payments or unemployment benefits. Conversely, those who are unemployed frequently wish they had the jobs and salaries that others have. People are often jealous when others get jobs and they do not. The comment, "Other people need the work more," is common.

What people have that others want

My girlfriend is jealous when I get tax exemptions that she doesn't. #2122

Because my roommate doesn't work during the school year she always has to worry about having enough money for rent, food, and school supplies. Before Christmas she was trying to budget so she could buy gifts while her student loan was dwindling. It was stressful for her and she was critical of other students who were lucky enough to live at home and not pay rent, and who were going to Cuba or Jamaica over the holidays. #2123

Janice never has to worry about money because she uses her credit card and her mother pays the tab. Several of her friends are jealous and make comments like "It must be great to be able to buy whatever you want," and "I wish my mother would give me a credit card." #2124

Many people are jealous of the Island fishermen, because they draw unemployment benefits at the end of the fishing season. People believe they make incredible amounts of money fishing lobsters for a few weeks every year, and then get to spend the rest of the year at home drinking and drawing unemployment benefits. They think fishermen are rich and don't have to work for their money. I come from a fishing community, and I've seen headlines in an Island newspaper which characterized my hometown as "Pogeyville" and stated "Fishermen enjoy great life." Pogey is a term for unemployment insurance benefits. One day when we were in junior high, my brother and I got on the school bus wearing new clothes, and a friend of ours shouted, "You guys hate to show off your money, eh? Lucky thing your father is one of them lazy-ass fishers." Even today one of my good friends frequently says, "You can buy it, you can do it, your father's a fisherman and he's got lots of money." Many of my friends ask why my father doesn't buy me a new car, after all he's a fisherman. #2125

My daughter has a girlfriend, Amy, who is eleven years old, and both her parents have good-paying jobs with the government. They have a nice house in the best part of town, a camper, several video cassette recorders, everything. They give their daughter all kinds of toys and clothes. Amy really doesn't care about such things at all and frequently gives some away to my daughter. The other day my husband went shopping and took my daughter and Amy along. My girl had her allowance of $1.50, but Amy had $20 with her. Amy used her money to buy candy and pop and stuff for herself and my daughter. All the time my husband kept thinking, "The groceries I could buy with $20, and there she is just throwing it away." We resent the fact they can do so much for their daughter and we can't do anything for ours. (Amounts are in 1986 dollars.) #2126

Some people really get upset when they learn that the spouse of a successful person has landed a good-paying job. They feel that others, such as themselves, need the job more. A friend of mine is a teacher, and her husband is a lawyer and owns a successful business too. She had someone tell her that it isn't right for them to have three good sources of income. My friend gets upset by this and says they ignore how hard she and her husband work for their money. #2127

In the summer, university students have to find good jobs so they can pay for their next school year. Looking for a job is often very tedious and frustrating. Each student would like to think he has the same opportunity in the job market as everyone else, but this simply isn't true. When I asked a close friend how he got his summer job, he explained, "I don't know. I didn't even apply to work with the city. But one morning the foreman, who's a friend of my father, came into my bedroom, got me out of bed, and asked if I wanted to go to work. I said, 'Sure,' and started work that very day." Practices like that upset me and make me envy my close friends. Another summer, two friends and I filled out applications to work with the city's recreation department. I was in desperate need of money for university that coming fall. Much to our surprise, the three of us were hired. However, there were two pay levels. Regular workers were paid $7.75 an hour, and workers on the summer project were paid $5.00 an hour. We were paid $5.00, but the foreman's son, who was only fifteen years old and just entering high school, was given a job that paid $7.75 an hour. Here he had no financial obligations and was being paid $2.75 more an hour than we were. It sure made us mad.

One of the major summer employers is the provincial government, but it is very difficult to get these positions without political connections. Normally the jobs go to those whose families have been very active working for the political party that is currently in power. It also helps to have a friend or relative who is an MLA (Member of the Legislative Assembly) or who sits on one of the hiring committees. Last year when I was searching for a job, I asked two friends how they were doing in the job hunt, and they told me they didn't have to look because they were getting positions with the provincial government. This is because both were members of the Young Conservative Party. Another friend of mine had no trouble getting work when the Liberal government was in power because his uncle was on the public-works committee. But now that the Conservative party is in power he does not even bother filling out an application. He knows he no longer has the connections to get a job. My friends and I have spent many summers sitting around making jealous remarks about our other friends who have gotten jobs when we haven't, or who've gotten better jobs than we have because of their connections. #2128

The good-paying summer jobs working for the city go to the kids who play hockey, or who have a dad who makes lots of money or who works for the city. The rest of us get shitty jobs at minimum wages. #2129

A large percentage of the bigger businesses in Vietnam are owned by the Chinese. By Chinese I mean people of Chinese origin who live in Vietnam and maintain their Chinese culture. A common feeling among the Vietnamese is that the Chinese who own businesses charge other Chinese lower prices than they do the Vietnamese and give other Chinese the higher-quality goods. The Vietnamese just hate this. I am Vietnamese and I hate it. Once my relative went into a Chinese medicine shop and asked in Vietnamese for a substance. Unknown to the proprietor, she speaks Chinese. The proprietor told his clerk in Chinese to get her an inferior substitute. My relative stated in Chinese, "No, I want the proper substance." One reason some Vietnamese learn Chinese is so they won't be taken advantage of by Chinese businesses.

Another problem occurs when Vietnamese who have emigrated to other countries, such as myself, go back to visit their relatives in Vietnam. They are charged a much higher admission to public facilities than are local people. If they go to a cultural show or a government exhibit they are often charged three to five times as much as local people. I really resent this. Local Vietnamese can tell we are living in foreign countries because our hairstyles, clothing, and accents are different. In addition we are charged tourist prices in restaurants in Vietnam. #2130

People are also envious of others who they believe have better working conditions than they do.

I work as a cashier in a large grocery store. The cashiers frequently complain about who does their job and who doesn't. Five of the cashiers are rarely at their registers. They are either talking or trying to find something else to do, which really aggravates the rest of us. This causes longer lineups for the cashiers who are at their registers, as well as crankier customers because they have to wait so long. Cashiers also complain about the missing-stock-clerk syndrome. About half the stock clerks spend much of their time away from their job. They often hide out in back and help the grocery department unload trucks or stock shelves. If it is a nice day they wander around outside searching for missing shopping carts. This causes a huge problem for the cashiers, who have to pick up the slack. If the cashier doesn't know the price for a grocery item, she pages a stock clerk. When no stock clerk responds the cashier has to leave her register to go search through the store for the price. While she is in the aisles searching for the price, shoppers ask her for help finding items. Another problem is parcel pick up. If the stock clerks are in back or outside, they don't hear the bell when the cashier needs their help to take a parcel to the pick-up door. As a result the cashier has to take the parcel to the door herself. There is a chain reaction. When cashiers are away from their registers, lines grow longer at the other registers, customers become impatient and angry, and this upsets the other cashiers. #2131

Some nursing students are taking five courses a semester in order to be able to finish as fast as possible. Others take only three courses. "It really ticks me off when I hear some of the other girls (those taking three courses) talking about going to the movies or what they did last night, after I've been up all night studying or doing papers. And then to hear one of them say how hard it is if there is a midterm exam or a paper due. I just want to tell them they have no idea. They have it so easy. All of the nursing courses are hard, but we have two more than they do. They don't have a clue how hard it is." #2132

In a university, members of a department frequently notice, discuss, and try to get the same advantages that the other departments have. This may be more staff; larger offices; newer computers; better furniture; more funds for photocopying, travel, and telephone calls; a larger lounge; more professional journals in the library; and more laboratory space and equipment. #2133

I know a professor at the university who gets intensely jealous of the other professors in his department. This professor likes to give final exams. This means he has to spend a lot of time at the end of each semester grading them. He gets quite peeved at the professors in his department who don't give finals and finish grading well before he does. What he has tried to do is get a regulation passed by the university senate that all professors have to give finals. He doesn't see that he has only himself to blame for the work he has to do. This same professor spends much of his time working in his office, while most of the other professors in the department do their writing at home. He gets upset that they don't spend more time in their offices, and says they are probably home watching TV. #2134

People often get upset when they have to do some work and others do not.

I told my older daughter to take the food from the kitchen to the dining table. She started yelling for her younger sister to come help. She was irate that she had to do it and my younger daughter didn't, even though it only took her two or three trips to carry all the food in. #2135

I am the oldest son in a large family. Because I am oldest I've always been assigned the heavy chores and told, "Well you should do it. You are the oldest." Now, I don't mind working, but it is kind of frustrating to have to cut wood for the winter while my younger brothers are all watching cartoons on Saturday morning TV. When I was their age I had to cut wood on Saturdays and couldn't watch cartoons. Also, before I go to school every morning, I have to do the barn work. I'm expected to do this work without question. As I said before, I do not mind working, but it is kind of frustrating to have to work in the barn while my younger brothers are still in bed. #2136

I'm a member of the choir and I agreed to help serve our Christmas dinner for the choir this year. I couldn't believe how much work a few of us had to do and how little the other members of the choir helped. I am so angry. We had to get everything ready, serve the meal, and then clean up afterwards. We worked like slaves, and they didn't lift a finger to help. #2137

People are jealous of those who contribute less than their share of work or goods. They resent "cheaters" and being exploited by "takers."

Girls don't know how lucky they really are on a date. The guy has to pick them up, drive them around, buy them food and drinks, and pay for the gas. All the girl has to do is enjoy it. #2138

Trying to get what others have

A mature student was complaining that one of the younger students in his course wasn't pulling her weight on their group project. He was clearly flustered and nearly shouting. "Who does she think she is by not helping us? She says she's got a lot to do and doesn't have the time. But I'm busy too. I've got a family. I have to arrange my classes so I can pick up my son at school because my wife has to work until seven o'clock. I help get supper after going to classes all day. I have to study at night, help my son do his homework, and find time to spend with him and my wife before bedtime. I have to shovel snow out of the driveway in order to take my son to school and get here for class at eight thirty in the morning. So I don't believe she doesn't have the time to help with our project. If I can find time with what I have to do, so can she!" #2139

We're scared to go out and all get drunk and then drive home, because we might get caught by the police. It's a lot easier having one person stay sober and drive the rest of us. This means the designated driver can't drink, but the other three can. It's not much fun for the person who has to drive, but it beats hell out of losing your license for six months for impaired driving. The problem is that one of our group, Doug, can't drive. It's not fair that Doug never has to drive and we always have to drive him. So unlike the rest of us, Doug always gets to drink. Me and the other guys have talked about it, but what can we do? Doug doesn't have a license or a car. #2140

However, money and work are not the only advantages which generate envy on the part of others. Envy can be produced by any perceived advantage, including more education, greater popularity, better looks, less gray hair, longer legs, or bigger breasts.

If I see a woman who is in good shape, I get jealous, because I'm not in that great a shape. #2141

God, I wish I looked like that. #2142

Guys whose parents buy them a fancy sports car are much more popular. Girls always want to go out with guys with nice cars. It really doesn't seem fair. Actually, it isn't fair. #2143

I resent it if someone gets to stay in bed when I have to get up. Therefore I try to get my man up before I do. And if this fails, I try to get him up at the same time I get up. #2144

When I leave the bathroom after my shower in the morning, my daughter is usually waiting outside. She often asks, "Is there any hot water left?" in an accusing way. No matter what it is, she wants to make sure she gets as much as everyone else. #2145

Colleen's husband is a truck driver and is home only three days out of every two weeks. Her friends think she has it made, because she has a husband and so much freedom that it's just like being single. They envy her because they think this is a great way to live and she has the best of both worlds. #2146

Every time I talk to a friend of mine, he tells me, "You know you really made the right decision not to have kids. You have all this time to do what you want, but I don't have any time for myself anymore. I can't even read a book because the kids are always interrupting me." #2147

My daughter wanted to eat a mango and brought me three so I could choose the ripest one for her. I selected the two ripest and I decided to cut them up for all of us. I asked her to bring me a knife, but she headed upstairs and said I could get the knife myself. I told her then she would have to cut up her own mango. When she came back downstairs she protested that the remaining mango was the one that was least ripe. She argued that the pieces of the three mangos should be mixed together so she would get an equal share of the riper ones. #2148

A person's advantage may be quite temporary and still produce envy. Thus someone who is working or doing chores may be jealous of another person who is not doing anything, even though the other person may have just finished working or will be working later.

People can also become jealous and upset if their advantages are taken from them and given to others.

I attended a large dinner party at a hotel. Several hundred of us were seated at circular tables, and each table held a maximum of eight people. Instead of serving people at the tables, two separate serving lines were set up. The people at tables closest to the serving lines were notified to join the lines first. After they returned to their tables with their food, those who were at tables slightly further away were notified to join the lines. Our table had only five people at it, and I was worried that we might be overlooked and not get to join the line when we were supposed to. After people at the tables just ahead of us joined the lines, I watched the man closely who was in charge of notifying people that it was their turn. I kept trying to catch his eye, so he wouldn't forget we were there. I was worried that he might not notice our table and let people further away than us go first. If he had, I would have said something to him. This is really foolish if you think about it, because everyone in line was served the same amount of food, there was enough food for everyone, and we would have been served sooner or later anyway. However, I was quite concerned that we be allowed to join the serving lines at the right time, when it was our turn. Fortunately the man did notify us before he notified people at the further tables. As childish as all this sounds, many people notice and comment when other people enter a restaurant after they do and are served first. [#2149]

4. Experiences

People can also desire experiences which others have that they do not. Such experiences include going on a shopping or ski trip, spending a winter vacation in Florida, and traveling to Europe or taking a Caribbean cruise. However, people can desire practically any positive experience that another has.

Our high school band takes a trip once a year, and this year we traveled to Halifax where we competed against other bands. The twelfth-grade students in the band like to have fun and always have some good stories to tell afterwards. The first night we were in Halifax I and the other twelfth graders went to the liquor store and then back to the motel room to drink. Some of the tenth and eleventh graders came to our room and sat around and watched us. It was obvious that they wanted to join in the fun, but none of them had any liquor. So the next day the tenth and eleventh graders brought us their orders so we'd buy them some liquor too when we went back to the store that afternoon. It was quite clear they didn't want to be left out of the fun the second night too. They wanted some stories that they could take home to their friends. [#2150]

The rich kids always have the big parties that only certain people are invited to. To be invited you have to be rich, beautiful, or play sports. "Just once I wish I could go to a big party, like the ones all the hockey players go to, and be the hit of the party and have the guys flirt with me." #2151

My best friend told me that last summer he met these two girls who were tourists and the three of them spent the whole weekend in bed at a motel. All the girls wanted was sex. Jesus, I wish that would happen to me. #2152

I've always wanted to be a bridesmaid at a wedding. When one of my friends got married she had five bridesmaids, but she didn't ask me, even though she knew the others only half as long as she knew me. Not only that but my mother sang at her wedding and my aunt helped at her reception. And I spent two weeks, working eight hours a day, sewing a quilt for her for a wedding present. The least I expected was to be a bridesmaid. Then my own sister was married, and she didn't ask me to be a bridesmaid either. #2153

I've wanted to go to Thailand for years, and I persuaded several friends who were traveling to Asia to go there. Invariably they send me post-cards from Thailand, and I get really jealous when I receive them. I resent the fact that they've gotten to go, but I haven't. #2154

5. Relationships

Another source of jealousy is relationships. People can be jealous of a) the fact others have a relationship, b) the person someone else has a relationship with, and c) the quality of another person's relationship.

In junior high, kids are jealous if you consider someone else a best friend. Barbara and I were best friends. Cindi was another best friend of mine and she was always telling me how much she hated Barbara. Barbara also had a best friend named Noreen, and Noreen would tell Barbara how much she hated me. It was all jealousy. #2155

Single people are jealous when they see couples walking down the street or in clubs. We all want to be loved and it's very depressing when we are left out in the shuffle. #2156

I've never had a boyfriend. But my friends do. I wish I could meet somebody and have what my friends have, but it never seems to work out for me. #2157

I get jealous when someone else is going out with the person I like. #2158

There's this exceptionally pretty blond in town, and every time I see her I wish she went with me. Instead, she goes with this guy who just talks about himself and doesn't have much to offer. #2159

In order to get into my field of work, I had to go to school and get a degree. Unfortunately, I had to do this while I was holding down a regular daytime job. So all my nights and weekends were spent hitting the books. My friends spent that time out socializing and are now married. All I want is to get married too and have a home, but I'm older now and all the good males are taken. Other people get all the breaks, but I never do. #2160

A wife can get jealous when her husband pays more attention to their children than he does to her. #2161

6. Accomplishments and success

People can also want another person's accomplishments and success. They may also be jealous of the accomplishments and success of the other person's family members.

My daughter came home from a dinner for the girls' choir and she was just incensed. Those who have been in the choir for two or more years are planning a trip to Europe to give fourteen performances. This is my daughter's first year in the choir, and at the dinner the director selected one of the first-year girls to go to Europe with them. My daughter was just disgusted with his selection and kept telling us that the girl he chose sings so quietly you hardly notice her. The real reason my daughter was so upset was that she wasn't the one chosen to go. My husband commented that the girl's parents hold good positions in the community and the director was swayed by this. Actually, I'm not surprised at the director's choice, because the girl has a beautiful voice. #2162

A friend of mine and I had equally high grades in university. Then I got a high score on my Graduate Record Examination and was admitted to a very good graduate school. My friend didn't take the exam and didn't apply to graduate school, but she was jealous of my success. #2163

My girlfriend and I are both professional actors and frequently audition for different acting roles. She gets jealous when I get a role and she doesn't. #2164

My neighbor has the perfect marriage; the perfect husband, an engineer; nearly perfect kids; the perfect house with expensive furnishings; a pedigreed dog; a perfectly kept garden; and, of course, perfect status in the community. But I don't have a husband, a garden, a dog, or any status, and I'm poor. I find it rather overwhelming. #2165

Women with families don't show their jealousy as much as younger women do. Women who are married have a certain status and security. But one thing they do get mad about is when their kid says someone else's mom makes better biscuits than they do. #2166

One of the true success stories in town is the guy who obtained a franchise and set up the first McDonald's Restaurant here to sell hamburgers. That restaurant has been incredibly successful, and people frequently mention the guy with the franchise. You can tell they really wish they'd done it themselves and had made all the money he has. #2167

I looked up a man in Who's Who the other day, and was almost floored by how well he's done. He was a Rhodes scholar, has an Oxford degree, and is on the board of directors of a dozen major corporations. He's the best-known person in his field, and he lives wherever he pleases. After I read that, I really craved the same kind of success for myself. For the next two days I just kept thinking about how successful he is, and how much I want to do as well as he has. I also felt discouraged, because in comparison with him I haven't been successful at all. #2168

What others do not want

Nevertheless, people do not want many of the things that others have which they do not. People are not likely to want those things which are not meaningful to them because they would find little use for them. Thus a single person who does not like children is unlikely to want another person's many sons and daughters, and someone who dislikes reading is unlikely to desire a person's large library. People normally want things which they believe would be useful in terms of helping them satisfy their feelings and needs. These include the things which

381

they believe would personally save them time and energy, provide additional positive reactions or stimulation, better protect themselves or their resources, or sustain or enhance their self-image. Items which they believe would not do this are not meaningful to them and therefore hold little interest for them.

> A good friend of mine has a large house with several rental units in it. He just built a deck to barbecue on, and he bought a large refrigerator that dispenses ice cubes through its door. His living room is full of four or five large exercise machines. I wouldn't want any of this. I just would-n't use this stuff, and I wouldn't want his house because it would be too much responsibility and trouble. It just isn't my thing. On the other hand, he has a large-screen TV that I would like to have. It makes watching a movie much more realistic. And he takes several foreign vacations a year to really neat places that I would just love to visit too. #2169

> Some families in our neighborhood are not interested in keeping up with the rest of us. They are viewed as lacking in ambition. Often neighbors don't bother telling them about their latest acquisitions because they know they won't be interested. #2170

In certain cases a person does not want something because he does not know how useful he would find it. Thus people may think they would find a dish-washing machine, microwave oven, video cassette recorder, or computer a waste of money, and sometimes they are mistaken. Another reason why people do not feel much desire for the things others have is that they are not aware of them or reminded of them. It makes a difference whether or not co-workers talk about their expensive antiques, foreign vacation every year, boat at the marina, or large inheritance.

How people act when others have what they want

People respond in a variety of ways when they encounter something that others have that they would like to have too. Their responses include the

382

following:

1. Taking a resource away from the other person
2. Getting the other person to share the resource
3. Getting those who distribute resources to give them a share
4. Finding some other means to obtain the same resource for themselves
5. Running down the other person and what he has
6. Wanting the other person to lose resources
7. Causing the other person to lose resources
8. Rationalizing and compensating
9. Avoiding contact

1. Taking a resource away from the other person

When people see that someone has something they want, they consider how to get it for themselves. The most direct approach is simply to take it away from another person. Often this is the easiest course of action if the other person does not oppose them. However, others are normally willing to put considerable effort into preventing people from taking what they have. Often they employ whatever means necessary to protect their possessions, positions, accomplishments, and relationships, and this can include using violence, getting help from others, dedicating more time and energy to their endeavors, and filing criminal charges and lawsuits. (See the chapter on Protecting Self and Resources in this volume.) Others criticize people who try to take the resources of others, and they are less willing to give them resources. People know this, and this acts as a major deterrent to their simply taking what they want from others. In addition, people are deterred by self-criticism, or guilt, from taking resources from others, particularly when they can see signs that they are hurting others or when they normally receive positive reactions or other resources from them. (See the chapter on Not Hurting Others in Volume One.)

Nevertheless, people do sometimes succeed in taking a resource from another person. Perhaps others are not aware that people plan to take their resource away from them until it is too late. Also, others may not be willing or able to dedicate the time and energy needed to protect their resource. In addition, people may find a way to take the resources of others which appears to be legitimate.

I passed around an envelope for students to put in two dollars each so we could buy some books we needed for the course I was teaching. We didn't have much class time left, so I went ahead and showed a film to the class. At the end of the film I turned the lights back on and the envelope was missing. One of the students had pocketed the money. [#2171]

Shoplifting is a huge problem for local businesses, and most businesses buy expensive security systems to try to control it. One shop owner told me that after he installed a security system many of his best customers quit coming to his store. He realized they had been doing most of the shoplifting during their frequent visits. There is a common belief that because businessmen buy goods for less than they sell them for, businessmen are cheating good people out of their hard-earned money. People never consider the overhead that businesses have to pay, the cutthroat competition between businesses, or how many businesses go under. Many people think that anyone who owns a business is just rolling in wealth. Therefore, it is easy for people to justify shoplifting. [#2172]

As my relatives have become elderly, my brother, who is a lawyer, has convinced them to give him power of attorney over their affairs. Then he has systematically stripped them of their savings by charging them by the hour for administering their affairs. When their savings run out he places them in a nursing home in order that he can sell their homes to get more cash to meet his fees. Placement in a nursing home is so traumatic for them that they die while in transition or soon afterwards. [#2173]

2. Getting the other person to share the resource

Another strategy is to attempt to get the person with the resource to share it.

The boy next door got a new minibike last summer. Day after day the other boys in the neighborhood would gather next door to take turns riding the bike. [#2174]

One tactic people use to is to argue that another person has more than their share of a particular resource. For example, when people are at home and want more access to furniture, food, or the television, they may say such things as "Move over, you've got most of the room," "How come you've got three pillows? I've only got one," "That's right, take the biggest piece," "Leave enough for me," or "You watched what you wanted for the last two hours. Now it's my turn." People also argue that the other person does not need the resource, or that they need it more than the person who has it. People may criticize the person with the resource or try to make him feel guilty, so that he will share it with them. They may also remind the other person that they have shared with him in the past.

I was quite upset with my boyfriend this Christmas. He only spent about $250 on gifts for me, but I must have spent at least twice that on him. The boyfriend of one of my friends took her to Las Vegas for her Christmas present. Another female friend got a 35 millimeter camera and a couple of suits from her boyfriend, even though he earns less than my boyfriend. I tell my boyfriend he's a cheapo and a scrooge. (Amounts in 1984 dollars.) #2175

People in my community get upset when people buy more cars than they need. One family in our community already had three cars and bought a fourth one. Another family has three cars, but only one member of the family drives. One man owns four cars and he's single. And one family built a three-car garage, but they only have two cars. People think such things are a ridiculous waste of money. Many feel they should donate the money to people who are not as fortunate. A friend of my mother becomes very cross about this and thinks they should donate the money to her favorite charity. #2176

After the end of the Vietnam war it was difficult getting foreign goods in Vietnam. At that time I was still living in Vietnam and my husband, who had moved from Vietnam to Canada, sent packages to me occasionally with items such as soap and shampoo. Most of the items were for me and our children, but he often included individual items for his relatives. His relatives repeatedly indicated to me they were jealous that he had sent me so much more than he sent them. One of his relatives argued that I should give her the bottle of skin lotion he sent me. She said that because she was older and living with her husband no one would think badly of her for using skin lotion. I, on the other hand, was younger and my husband was outside the country. Therefore, she claimed, people would think badly of me if I used skin lotion because it would appear I was trying to look attractive to other males. #2177

3. Getting those who distribute resources to give them a share

People will also approach those in charge of distributing resources in order to get a share. Thus children seek resources from parents, employees seek resources from supervisors, students seek resources from teachers, researchers seek resources from granting agencies, and provinces seek resources from the federal government. People often argue that resources are being unfairly distributed and that they should receive the same share that others are receiving. Thus younger children argue that they should receive the same amount of allowance as their older siblings, female employees argue that they should receive the same wages and positions as male employees, professors at a university argue that they should be paid as much as professors at other universities, and representatives of disadvantaged ethnic groups and regions argue that they should receive as much as or more than the prosperous ethnic groups and regions.

Mom, Mike got some pop. Buy me some too. Please, please, Mom! #2178

I sent a package of children's books to my sister's two children. They live in a Vietnamese household in Los Angeles. My niece is seven years old, and my nephew is four. In the package I had four books for my niece and three books for my nephew. My nephew wanted to know, "How come she gets four books and I only get three." He wanted his family to go to the store and buy him an additional book. #2179

When we give something to one of our daughters, whether it's clothing, money, or food, the other daughter becomes jealous. The jealous daughter claims she needs the same thing or something else she would rather have. If we don't give it to her, she accuses us of favoritism, and she stops sitting with us at family meals and when we watch TV together. Sometimes we give in. But if we don't, she eventually gets over it. #2180

My younger sister, Debbie, is often jealous when I get attention. I remember when I got a new dress and Debbie sat there banging her head on the floor. Mom had to take her downtown and buy her a new dress too. Recently when my parents took me shopping to get ready to move to university, I could tell Debbie was feeling left out, because she became quite hostile toward me. To make her feel better, my mother made Debbie's favorite meal and let her have the car to go out with her friends later than usual. #2181

My mother decided to redecorate my sister's bedroom and she put in new drapes, a new carpet, a brass bed, and a dresser. After my sister showed the room to her friends, two of her friends convinced their parents to get their bedrooms redecorated too. #2182

Every year our pictures were taken at school and parents were expected to buy the photographs. Even though we only needed a couple of five-by-seven-inch photos, we pressured our parents to buy the complete package, which included numerous photos of various sizes. We would say, "But Mom, I have to get them. Everyone else is." And the package ended up in a cupboard drawer at home. We used the same arguments to get our parents to pay for school yearbooks, jackets, and graduation rings. #2183

My Vietnamese parents are separated, and my mother lives in California. I invited my mother to join me when I took a trip to Toronto. Subsequently, my father told me he wasn't happy that I hadn't invited him too, and pointed out I had even paid for my mother's airplane ticket. He didn't want to be in Toronto at the same time my mother was. He just wanted a trip too. #2184

A friend I was in school with works in the same profession I do. When I read in our professional newsletter that he'd been promoted, I went and applied for a promotion too. Unfortunately it didn't work for me, because I don't have the list of achievements that my friend has. #2185

It is a lot easier to distribute things evenly in the first place, than to deal with all the carping and whining if you don't. #2186

Attempts to obtain "a fair share" are most successful when those seeking the resources also provide certain resources to those they ask to share or reallocate resources. Thus those dispensing the resources may receive positive reactions, sex, labor, business, or votes from those seeking a share of resources. When others do not provide any resources to those who have what they want, there is often little chance that their requests for resources will be rewarded. People are not willing to provide resources if they can see no reason to do so. When this is the case it is necessary for others to seek different avenues to obtain the resource.

4. Finding some other means to obtain the same resource for themselves

People also try to find a way to get the same resource for themselves other than from the person they are jealous of. A common way is to try to buy it, often by borrowing money to do so. When they can not afford to buy it, they may plan to do so if they have money in the future. However, when the resource is something that cannot be purchased, such as a girlfriend or boyfriend or a promotion, then one may allocate time and energy to try to get it.

> This guy I know eats TV dinners all the time. You just heat the package up, eat the dinner in it, and throw the package away. I often have one when I'm at his place, and they are a lot tastier than anything you'd make for yourself. You'd have to get all these separate ingredients, and it would take an hour or more to fix. Best of all, you don't get any dishes dirty, so you don't have to waste time cleaning up afterwards. When I start making more money, I'm going to buy TV dinners too. #2187

> We decided to buy a dish-washing machine after Diane down the road got one and praised it to the fullest. I told Ed we simply must get one too. Also, since Ed and I both work and regularly go to parties, it's such a bother to have to come home to do dishes. This way we can simply place them in the dishwasher until we have enough dirty dishes to do a full load. #2188

> A woman in our neighborhood started going to a well-known hair-dresser and she told people she would never go anywhere else. Soon other neighbors and their daughters started going to the same hair-dresser. #2189

> It is amazing what we women will do when we see someone we want to look like. We'll spend a great deal of money changing our hair and buying new clothes to match the person we envy. When you think about it, it sounds so stupid. But we all do it. #2190

> I've been working at a taxi company and like most of the drivers I supply my own car. Several of the board members of the company own extra cars and these are driven by drivers who don't have their own cars. Unfortunately, the dispatcher assigns all of the good calls to the

drivers who drive cars owned by the board members. These include calls out of town which frequently charge from $10 to $55, but can run higher. Local calls charge from $4.50 to $5.00. The drivers who own their own cars are assigned the poor calls, such as picking up local passengers with groceries. I went in and told the manager I was getting screwed because I was given so few decent calls. He said if I thought I wasn't making any money before, just wait until I saw what I made over the next month. He was saying he would make sure I got very few calls in the future. So I switched to drive for a different taxi company and I've been making almost twice as much money as I was before. (Amounts in 2001 dollars.) #2191

Last summer I saw a guy driving the most striking sports car I've ever seen. The lines on it were fantastic. I didn't know what it was and I looked in several car magazines until I found out it was a Ferrari. If I ever win the lottery, I'm going to get one too. His was bright yellow, and it looked really good. I never before thought of getting a yellow car, but I think I'd like a yellow one too. I even remember the expression on the driver's face. He sure looked on top of things. #2192

People sometimes seek to find out exactly how the other person obtained the resource, in order that they can get it too.

I read an article about a college student who used his student loan as his original stake and made several million dollars in the stock market. Of course, I wanted to make several million too. So in order to determine just how he did it, I traveled some distance to a business library and got information about the price action of the specific stocks he had bought and sold. Unfortunately, this wasn't enough information to do what he had done. It wasn't until many years later that I developed my own stock-market strategy. Then other people wanted to know precisely what my approach was. #2193

Often people are not content to obtain exactly what another person has, but seek to do one better by getting something better than the other person has, such as a) a possession with more features, b) a better experience, c) a greater advantage, d) a more desirable relationship, or e) a more significant accomplishment. This allows people to reaffirm their self-image, strike back at those who have hurt them by causing them to feel envy, and obtain a bit of breathing space before other people do one even better in return.

Often people do not want to appear to be getting things just because their neighbors have them. They want to avoid negative comments that they are "just keeping up with the Joneses," or that they are "copycats." Instead they want to appear and think that they are above a mundane competition for possessions, that they are quite different from their transparent neighbors, and that they are independent individuals who act for nobler reasons.

> They got their gas barbecue last year, and we used to see them barbecuing in the dead of winter. This year we decided to buy a gas barbecue. They are so much easier to operate and you can use them anytime. We didn't buy our barbecue because of our neighbors. We saw how much they enjoyed using it. Since we like barbecuing so much we just had to have one too. #2194

> I don't care. I'm not the type who has to have everything others have. But take my neighbor, Janice. If Amy gets a new coat, Janice gets a new coat. If Betty gets a new microwave oven, Janice gets a new microwave. The list goes on and on. Lately Janice has been real pleased with herself because she has a brand new living-room carpet. With a person like her, I can't wait to show her what I've ordered for the den. She'll be green. Want to see? #2195

5. Running down the other person and what he has

People often notice and talk to other people about a person's purchases and successes.

> In our community people realized that this one family was buying new furniture even though their existing furniture was less than a year old. Whenever people saw the furniture truck in their driveway they would say, "There they go, trying to keep up with the Joneses." #2196

> There is a running joke in our neighborhood about our next-door neighbor who is forever trading his car in for a new one that is more expensive than his last one. His neighbors laugh about it and say, "We can't even try to keep up with him." #2197

How people act when others have what they want

When someone else has something that people want, people frequently criticize the person and what he has, particularly if they have little hope of getting the same thing. Thus people may state the other person was just lucky; had an unfair advantage, such as a parent's help or a political connection; or used immoral means to win an advantage, such as brown-nosing, cheating, providing sex, breaking the law, or exploiting others.

Few people in the rural areas take a vacation outside the province. If you take one it is considered very bad taste to discuss it with local people, who have little hope of taking one themselves, and are likely to see you as acting big. If you do take a vacation and your neighbor doesn't, he is likely to say something like "Vacation. I don't know from what. He never did a tap all winter. Now he's gone to Florida, mind you. And likely with money he stole from people at that store of his." #2198

My husband has worked very hard all his life and has a successful career in business. After we bought a nice house in a good neighborhood, our friends and relatives started saying we had moved to "snob hill." My husband's parents, brothers, and sisters accuse him of being a crook and belonging to organized crime. They don't want to believe that he could be this successful as a result of hard work. My husband feels quite hurt by this. #2199

There's a girl who works in the same office I do and all the other women despise her. This girl, Annette, uses her body to get ahead. When she first came to work she got as close as she could to her boss. I really don't think there was anything sexual between them, but she pretended to be really interested in him. The rest of us saw through Annette, but her boss didn't. He had her promoted. Afterwards she had nothing more to do with him and turned all her attention elsewhere. She started an affair with her new boss. You'd see the two together after work everywhere, and finally his wife left him. Annette's new boss gave her a promotion, and always gets her a place in special-training programs so she'll be qualified for further promotions. Annette doesn't have much education, isn't very bright, and does poor work, which doesn't endear her to the other employees in the office. She's hated by the other women, and is the most talked about person at work. #2200

Trying to get what others have

People often try to say anything negative they can about someone who is doing better than they are in any regard.

I was sitting in a meeting of the Home and School Association. The woman sitting next to me is a Protestant. She looked up at the podium when they announced the new president of the association, who happens to be a Catholic, and said, "Good heavens, I suppose the Micks are going to take all the public offices now." [This nickname is based on the idea that the Mc's (Micks) are Catholic and the Mac's are Protestant. For example, McD_____ versus MacD_____.] #2201

I was in a casino in Halifax playing a slot machine. The guy next to me won a jackpot of over $200. I felt disgusted. I looked at the guy and said to myself, "This guy is a nothing." I put him down. Then I won a jackpot myself of over $100. After this happened the two of us started talking and joking. We were both happy. #2202

I've been trying for six years to get into the RCMP (Royal Canadian Mounted Police). I know a girl who got in on her first try and I let everybody know just what a bitch she is. #2203

I was in one of the toilet stalls at a club when two girls entered the ladies room and began to talk about me. I had just won a major beauty contest, and one commented, "She has slept with every lifeguard on the beach." #2204

Women in the local small communities put a great deal of time into observing other women. They are quick to notice if a woman is wearing something new and to tell others what they think. Most of their comments are negative. "Did you see the get-up she had on in church? I don't care if it was Ultrasuede, or what it was. I wouldn't wear it to the barn." Some women say that the woman has spent the money unwisely. "Oh yes, she'd have the style all right. Every cent he makes goes right on her back. Personally, I'd rather see it go on the kids. Heavens knows, they look scruffy enough." Or women will say she really couldn't afford it. "Yes, the silks and satins will be all over the place tonight. She'll have to put on the dog for the big show. I guess we could all do that if we wanted to owe every store in the country." Many women will point out that although the woman may look good in public, she doesn't look good at other times. "Yeah, she is always all dolled up with the makeup just so and the clothes all matched to kill. But, let me tell you, if you could see her in the morning, just whenever she falls out of bed, you'd get quite a shock. She must get up awful early to get that load of stuff on her face in time to go to work." In other words, without the makeup and clothes, the woman wouldn't look good at all.

For women, talking about the appearance of other women is serious business. However, if you pointed out they were gossiping, most women would say, "Oh, go 'way! We're just talking." And if you suggested they were jealous of the other woman, they would likely say something to show they didn't care what someone else had on. My mother would reply, "I couldn't care less if she had a dress that was yellow with a pink smell. It wouldn't bother me any. It's just kind of funny that she thinks she looks so grand in it, and everyone knows it's a sight." #2205

People often comment that someone who has something they want is just showing off his wealth, thinks he is better than other people, is a snob, is trying to "act big" or "make himself look big," or can not afford it.

When we interviewed the job candidate, we learned that she had been to a private high school, which is known to be expensive, and she likes to ride horses. On the basis of this information some members of the hiring committee decided she must be a rich, spoiled kid. But really, I was on the hiring committee too and the candidate gave no signs she was spoiled. #2206

They may also criticize the person for being superficial, phony, unpleasant, or lacking important qualities.

Once in a while, I wish I were popular. But those people are so shallow there is nothing to be jealous of. #2207

My best friend is very pretty. So people think she is a bitch who acts like she is nice. But she really is very nice. #2208

People also criticize the things that people have that they would like to have too. They may say that such things are worthless, bad, or a waste of money.

Very few women in our community have dish-washing machines. When one woman bought a dishwasher, the other women in her circle said things like "Now that's definitely the last thing in the world I'd ever buy. What a waste of money. I'm sure it would just make you lazy." #2209

A hairdresser was talking to me about university education. "It really doesn't teach anybody anything useful. It's just a waste of money." #2210

I made plans to go shopping for clothes with two friends, Ann and Sue. Just before I left the house another friend of mine, Gerri, dropped by to see me and I felt I should invite her to go with us. The problem is that Ann and Sue don't like Gerri, because she is thin and tiny and has a great body, while they are a lot larger. Later we were waiting in a clothing shop for a vacant changing room when Gerri came out of a changing room wearing a very short, tight silver dress. She asked how she looked, and as usual she looked great. Ann was quite irritated by this because she was waiting to try on the same dress. Ann remarked that she could never look like that in a dress and moreover she couldn't buy it now because Gerri would have one too. Gerri said she wasn't going to buy the dress, so Ann was free to try it on. Ann snapped back that she would never wear a dress that made someone look so slutty. Gerri returned to the changing room and Ann put the dress she was holding back on the rack. #2211

6. Wanting the other person to lose resources

People also hope that those who have something they want will lose their resources, or that something bad will happen to them.

When a woman is well dressed or looks really spiffy, I frequently hear people say they hope she'll trip and fall. It's just spite. #2212

Some people hold a grudge against those who are much more successful than they are, and make comments such as "Someday I bet his bubble will burst." #2213

The media deal with the financial problems of Island farmers, particularly those operating large-scale farms. They paint a picture of rural communities grieving over the plight of the farmer. However, these reports are misleading. Certainly those who own and work on large-scale farms are concerned about their situation. However, the concern is not universal. Instead, there is a general lack of sympathy felt by many rural Islanders, particularly those who think of themselves as "small farmers."

Many of the small farmers resent the big farmers and their approach to farming. They hope the current crisis will force the government to re-evaluate its support of big farmers and that a renaissance will occur in small farming. "Sooner or later, things are going to have to turn around. Farmers can't be big businessmen. There are too many uncontrollable and unforeseen risks. People have to farm small. There's no way you can win if you don't. A lot of people are just finding that out now. Hell, any of the old people could have told them that years ago. Oh, big ideas, you know, big ideas."

Many local people think that the downfall of many of the big farmers has been caused by a combination of "acting big" and poor management. "They went around thinking they were some big, rich businessmen. Buying anything and everything they liked. Running off to Florida every winter and getting a new car every fall. No one can tell me that there's that kind of money in farming. I don't care how big you go into it. There had to be an end to it sooner or later. They might just as well face up to it first as last."

Small farmers feel a lot of resentment about the financial support that the big farmers receive from the government and the financial institutions. Small farmers often complain that their debts and hardships are just as serious as those of the big farmers, yet the government and financial institutions have no time for them. "I'll tell you what burns me. Every time you turn on the television, there's some damn farmer on telling about hard times. Well we all have seen hard times, but who listens to us. The government is always coming up with some new way of baling them out and the banks go right along with it. Well, if I owe a bill, I damn well have to pay it or face the music. But those lads can carry that big debt year after year and get more money whenever they feel like it. It's not fair. Then they'll get up and tell about how good the big farms are and how the small farms are a thing of the past. Well it's no wonder they are a thing of the past. How could they survive in this situation? How could a little guy ever compete with the big fellow getting all the government subsidies? It really makes me boil to think of it." Small farmers wonder why the banks are so much easier on the big farmers. "I remember when we had to close our grocery store. We weren't making much money but all the debt we had on the store was $2500. That's all, and we thought that was a lot. There was no way the bank would wait or give us one cent more. They wanted the money right then and we had to take out a second mortgage on our house to pay them. Now I hear the same bank is financing Angus for $80,000. Now how can that be? He hasn't made a cent on that farm in the last three years, so how can he get more money every season and still live so high? I'd like to talk to some of those credit managers at the bank. They'd tramp right on the likes of you or me, but some of those big fellows can do just what they like."

Small farmers and those who were forced out of farming when farms "turned big" feel that a day of reckoning has come for those who went at it too big. Many local people find the favoritism awarded the big farmers hard to take. Local people also resent the subsidies and fixes the big farmers have received from the government and lending institutions. While there truly is a crisis in the farming industry, a lot of Islanders think it is a good thing. Many hope it will bring a return of small farms and better community spirit. "This should bring some of them lads down a few pegs. For years they thought they were the wheels around here. Now it looks like a lot of them won't get out with more than enough to cover their arses." #2214

We feel that people who cause us to feel jealous have done us a disservice. When they make us feel envy, they hurt us. They make us look bad by showing they are doing better than we are. Naturally we would like to get back at them for making us look bad and hurting us. We want to run them down and say anything bad we can about them. If we can knock them off their pedestal of success and besmirch them, there is less reason for others to look up to them and for us to envy them. Any indication or gossip that they have suffered a misfortune is music to our ears. We feel they certainly deserve everything bad that happens to them for hurting us.

If others fail then there is less reason to think they are doing better than we are, and there is less reason to envy them. This is particularly true of someone who has more than we have or who is doing better than we are. Their failures and misfortunes show that we do not really need to envy them, and we are not doing so badly after all. This is why negative information about successful individuals is such juicy gossip.

People can even exult over the failures of everyone else. The worse everyone else does, the better one is doing relative to them.

My mother was very pleased to report that a young man in our church was rejected when he applied to seminary. All the man ever wanted to do was to become a priest and my mother said she heard they rejected him because he was too sensitive to others. It must have been a devastating disappointment to him, and it was so mean spirited of my mother to take pleasure in his failure. #2215

7. Causing the other person to lose resources

Another way in which people respond is to try to stop the person from getting the resource. For example, they will often tattle on someone who is getting something they are not.

> I don't like to have my children eat in the living room where the TV set is because they keep spilling food on the furniture and the carpet. The other day I stopped my younger girl, who was headed for the living room carrying a bowl of cereal and milk. When I told her to eat it in the kitchen, she said her sister was already in the living room with a bowl. #2216

Employees frequently tattle on fellow workers who take advantages that they do not take for themselves, such as arriving late and leaving early, spending extra time on lunch or coffee breaks, and talking to friends on the telephone. People sometimes notify authorities of instances of tax evasion, unemployment-insurance fraud, fishing violations, and other illegal activities that they know about.

> Mrs. Smith knows a woman who works and receives welfare too. When Mrs. Smith learned that the woman had bought some new clothes and had taken a trip, she called up the welfare office and complained. Mrs. Smith told them that she was working herself and sure couldn't afford to buy new clothes or take a trip. #2217

Often the purpose of tattling is not to gain a privilege, but to prevent someone else from getting something people are unable to have too. Tattling is common when people know that those in authority would disapprove if they attempted to take the same privilege. The attitude is "If I can't have it, they shouldn't have it either."

Those who are jealous of the success of others, frequently complain and try to prevent their access to resources. For example, university faculty who do not have outside business interests or consulting contracts may lobby to have restrictions placed on "moonlighting."

> I work as a cashier in a large grocery store. Individual cashiers work between fifteen to thirty hours a week, and there is considerable competition for shifts and hours. Cashiers who have worked for the store longer are assigned more shifts and shifts with longer hours. Many

spats occur between the cashiers over the work schedule. Some cashiers can not stand to see anyone get more hours than they do, and there are numerous charges of favoritism and butt kissing. One cashier went to the manager, the owner, our union board, and the government, because another cashier, who had been working six months less than she had, was scheduled to work one hour more that week than she was. She also threatened to quit. As a result she was given an apology and the other employee's hours were reduced. #2218

Darrell and his two older sisters grew up on a farm. His two sisters helped their father with many of the farm chores. But years later when the parents died, Darrell was left with the entire estate. It is a common practice for farm families to leave the farm to the youngest son. However, the two sisters were resentful and bitter. Subsequently they had nothing to do with Darrell, and influenced many other family members to avoid him too. Darrell is not invited to Christmas, birthday, and anniversary celebrations, or to the family reunion which is held every summer. #2219

People may tattle out of spite in order to get someone into trouble, because the person has obtained something that they could not get.

I went out to the local bikers' club with my sister. While we were there we met a good-looking guy. My sister was interested in him, but he offered me a ride home. The next day when my fiancé asked me where we had gone, I didn't mention going there. Then my sister told him we went to the bikers' club and asked me in front of my fiancé, "What time did you get home?" It was after three o'clock in the morning, but I sure didn't want my fiancé to know. My sister was just jealous that the guy was interested in me instead of her. #2220

People may also use physical means to try to remove a privilege others have.

One night my roommate in university stayed up all night studying for a test. She didn't think it was fair that everyone else got to sleep while she had to stay up. So she made her pet guinea pig stay awake too. Every time he would doze off, she would slap him across the head to wake him up. #2221

We can view individuals as a) designed to get and keep resources, and b) engaged in a competition with other individuals for resources.

Those individuals who are better at getting and keeping resources are resented by those who are less successful. It is to the advantage of less successful individuals to attack and weaken individuals who are more successful, because by doing so they improve their own chances of success.

8. Rationalizing and compensating

People frequently state that the things they have compensate for the things others have that they do not.

> I didn't care about her tacky vase from England. But when she showed me that gorgeous settee, I nearly died. I don't care. Wait until she sees what Ronald is bringing me back from New York. #2222

> Right after Christmas there was a competition between me and my classmates in elementary school to see who got the most from Santa Claus. We would ask each other, "What did you get?" and take turns listing things. "I got a _____ , and a _____ , and a _____," and so on. For everything one kid would say, another kid would manage to double it. Then to make up for what she didn't get, the first child would try to make her presents sound extra nice. Eventually some kids felt left behind and hurt. #2223

> One couple in our neighborhood decided they couldn't find original Christmas gifts in Charlottetown and traveled to Montreal to buy their gifts. Afterwards another couple decided they would go to Halifax, which was nearer than Montreal, to do their Christmas shopping. Another neighbor said she had already bought some Christmas gifts when she was in Halifax in October visiting relatives. Satisfied that she was at least partly keeping up with her neighbors, she was content to buy the rest of her presents in Charlottetown. #2224

> If you want to keep up with your neighbors in our community, you should spend your winter vacation in Florida. When in Florida you must stay in a good hotel, not a cheap one, because everyone is bound to ask you what the hotel was like. You should also take excursions and lots of photographs to show others when you get home. One family who was always trying to keep up with their neighbors announced they

were going to Florida too. Later they decided they weren't going and told people they were going to buy a new $1800 couch instead. #2225

People also tell themselves that other people's success is not important and the things that they have are worth more than what other people have.

It doesn't bother us that our neighbors are better off than we are, because we've got a lot more going for us than just money. The whole family is very talented. In fact, Jill just got top honors in conservatory for her singing, and that's a hell of a lot better than I can say for anyone else around here. #2226

I chose to spend my time with my family. I'm glad I did, because it was more important than throwing myself into a career. #2227

In some cases people pretend to get and have things in order to make a favorable impression on others.

At Christmas when one family in our community would show their gifts to visitors, they included things they had given each other the previous Christmas. They hoped their visitors would not remember the items, but of course they did. #2228

9. Avoiding contact

People also try to avoid contact with situations and other people who cause them to feel envy. If they feel they cannot compete, or if they are treated with less respect than they think they should be, they may move to another neighborhood or community. When people avoid contact with those who have what people want, they do not have to deal with their own feelings and the feelings of others that they are inferior.

I think that if a community has several families with rich homes and lots of possessions, the other members of the community look bad and feel inferior. But if the community doesn't have any rich families, people have the same standard of living, there is no one to show them up, and the community is a comfortable place to live in. #2229

People like to have more than others, because it helps them think they are better than other people. I have often heard people in my community talk about two families who went to such extremes trying to get more than others that they ended up poorer than the rest of the community. They had to sell all their luxuries and were so embarrassed that they left the neighborhood. Another family left when they felt out of place. They told Mom that they were going to find a place to live where people weren't as interested in keeping up with the Joneses. #2230

Some people also try to avoid situations in which they feel jealous.

I've been collecting stamps for thirty years now, and a close friend started collecting about a year ago. He's told me he doesn't want me to show him my collection anymore, because it just makes him wish he had the stamps that I do. #2231

When people do not try to get what others have

Even though people employ a number of approaches to get the same resources that others have, there are numerous instances in which they do not make the attempt. Their decision not to try may stem from a) lack of interest in the resource, b) lack of opportunity to take it from the other person, c) fear of the consequences of trying to take it from the other person, d) knowledge that others are unlikely to share or provide the resource if asked, e) lack of knowledge as to how to obtain the resource, f) unwillingness to commit the time and energy required to obtain the resource, g) unwillingness to take the necessary risks, and h) involvement in the satisfaction of other needs.

I regularly lift weights and have done so for several years. I work and work to try to mold myself into the ideal type. However, the longer I work out, the further I seem to be from reaching this goal. I think the odds of the average person achieving the ideal type you see in the mass media are very slim indeed.

A close friend and workout partner of mine decided he would begin to use steroids to speed up muscle growth and asked me to join him. If you lift weights regularly you can add about five pounds of muscle a year. But with steroids my friend added ten pounds in the first month.

401

Others who use the steroids say they feel stronger almost immediately and are able to lift weights they were unable to lift before. Soon my friend looked very good, like the cover of a weight-lifting magazine, with a washboard stomach and huge arms and chest. Everywhere he went he was the center of attention, and he kept telling me how every aspect of his life had improved.

When he asked if I wanted to do it with him, I declined. The health risks are too great. However, when I saw what these miracle drugs were doing for my friend, I was tempted and found them hard to resist. But I decided it wasn't worth risking my health just to improve my physical appearance. There are many negative side effects of taking these drugs. They reduce sperm count, produce impotence, shrink testicles, and cause the development of breasts. Extreme side effects include blood clots, liver damage, and heart attacks. Some steroids carry the warning, "Not intended for animals that will be used for human consumption." Who wants to take drugs that are designed for animals, but are considered unsafe for human consumption? In addition, there are psychological side effects, such as mood swings from euphoria to paranoia.

As my friend's overinflated ego grew, I watched his patience and problem-solving skills deteriorate. Every day he would show us how large his arms had grown. He began the annoying habit of scratching his forehead in order to see his biceps flex. Now I became suspicious of everyone who looked good at the gym. I wondered whether they were sticking needles into their legs in order to gain extra inches on their arms. I noticed that most individuals at the gym with any amount of size seemed to be mysteriously covered with acne and always wore pants. Maybe it was to hide injection marks. I even learned of two males who shared needles, rather than take the trouble to go buy a second needle. In the age of AIDS, how is it possible for people to make such poor decisions? Also I noticed people who underwent sudden massive gains or losses in size. One male that I suspected of using steroids apparently stopped and lost twenty-five pounds of muscle in a few months. People I know who take the steroids claim the risks are minimal. They must think the side effects will happen to someone else. They are just like smokers. They want satisfaction today, but will have to face the consequences tomorrow. #2232

Feelings which encourage people to try to get what others have

The feeling which encourages people to try to get what others have is envy. Envy may involve desire, irritation, resentment, anger, outrage, and/or hatred. Also, when others get and have more than they do, people often feel put down, wronged, demoralized, inferior, worthless, less loved and appreciated, hurt, sorry for themselves, and that they are failures. Such feelings can be quite intense. People speak of being "green with envy."

If we go to a restaurant and the waitress serves me smaller portions than she serves others at the table, I notice and feel slighted. Maybe she puts less soup in my bowl, or gives me a smaller piece of meat or dessert. I feel I've been treated unfairly, even if the others at the table are people I really care about, such as family and friends. However, it never bothers me when she gives me bigger portions than she serves the others. #2233

When I was a teenager I held a grudge because nobody on the street where we lived would walk to school with me except for Janet Taylor. Kelly Simpson, who lived next door to me, said she couldn't walk with me because she had to go with Ann MacDonald, who lived around the corner. What bugged me even more was that unlike Janet, Kelly and Ann were in the same grade and same school as me, which made it an even bigger insult. Thinking about this brings back the same feelings I had as a teenager. #2234

I and my two best friends like to play the stock market, and we watch and buy the same technology stocks. Naturally, we all own different amounts of each particular stock, and we trade actively, so the amounts we own are always changing. When we start talking about a specific stock, one of us frequently asks how much of it the others own. If someone has more shares of that stock than you do, you feel jealous, and if you have more of it than they do, you feel pleased. The fact that you own more or less shares of other stocks than they do is irrelevant at the time. Also, when we buy the same stock, one of the friends always wants to know what I paid for my shares. I think he just wants to gloat if he bought his shares of that stock cheaper than I did, and he feels annoyed if he paid more. #2235

I was in a casino in Quebec and noticed two elderly women who were there together. They were seated next to each other playing slot machines. Then one of them won a jackpot. The other woman slammed her pail of quarters down on the counter, stood up, looked disgusted, and stalked off carrying her pail. #2236

Joe, who is thirty-eight years old, a father of three children, and unemployed, won a large sum of money in a lottery. He immediately began to spend the money. He bought two new cars and redecorated his house. Elizabeth, his neighbor across the street, could barely make ends meet. When trucks delivered goods to Joe's house, Elizabeth would stand in her doorway crying. She couldn't bear to think of the good fortune that Joe and his family were having. #2237

I was at a wedding dance where everyone was drinking heavily when a fistfight broke out between two men. One was a relative of the bride and the other was one of her friends. Both men worked at the same plant and the fight was over the fact that the man who had been working at the plant for twenty years was paid little more than the other man, who had been there for only two years. The grandmother of the bride got really upset and wanted to break up the fight, but the MC (master of ceremonies) cut in and told everyone, "What's a good Irish wedding without a few fights?" Then the MC got the fight stopped. The newlyweds were quite upset and hurt. They soon left for their honeymoon, and the dance continued. #2238

I run a bar in town, and I find one of the major reasons people drink is because someone else is more successful at work than they are. People get quite discouraged when they're passed over for a promotion or something else. #2239

Envy can be directed toward one or more people at a time. It can occur once or many times in relation to a specific object or person. People are most likely to feel envy when they are made aware of, or they are reminded of, something that another person has that they want too.

A person feels envy because he experiences tension, or hurt, as a result of inconsistency between reality and his model. Two forms of inconsistency are involved. In the first type of inconsistency, a person sees that someone else has a resource that he would find useful. He may think that the resource would save him time and energy, or provide him with food, water, comfort, protection, sex, stimulation, or positive reactions. Therefore he realizes that the resource would help satisfy his feelings and needs. His model is that he wants this resource. However, reality is that he does not have the resource. Therefore reality is inconsistent with his model. In the second type of inconsistency, a person realizes that someone else has more of a resource than he has. This is reality. However, the person's model is that he is more worthy than the other person. Therefore he deserves more of the resource than the other person does. Again, reality is inconsistent with his model.

When reality is inconsistent with a person's model, this inconsistency produces tension, or hurt. A person experiences irritation or anger in response to the tension he feels. In order to change reality to be consistent with his model, he can either take the resource away from the other person, or find an alternative means to get the resource. Then reality will be consistent with his model and he will no longer feel tension, or hurt. When it is unlikely that he will be able to take the resource away from the person who has it, and when it is difficult to obtain the resource by other means, he may direct his irritation or anger at the other person.

Because a person experiences this tension firsthand he tries to act to get rid of his own tension. He does not experience the tension that the other person feels. Therefore his own tension is more vivid and immediate, and he frequently does not consider that the other person may be experiencing tension too. Often he does not know how the other person feels about the resource or will feel if he tries to take the resource from him. When other people do not reveal their feelings there is no reason for a person to consider that they have any feelings at all in the matter. But even if a person guesses that the resource is important to the other person, a person experiences his own feelings, not those of the other person, and wants to act in order to alleviate his own feelings. When a person tries to take what the other person has and the other person reveals his feelings, perhaps by acting hurt or angry, it becomes possible to consider the other person's feelings. When the person who wants to take the resource away sees how the other person feels, he may feel guilty or may become anxious that he will be injured, and as a result may stop trying to take the resource away. Therefore, it is very much in the interest of the other person to indicate his feelings to the person who wants to take what he has.

Often a person decides that he is more deserving than the person who has something he wants. Therefore it seems very unfair that the other person has the resource while he does not. Normally a person ignores the effort the other person has made and the risks the other person has taken to obtain the resource. Even if a person is completely unwilling to make the same effort or to take the same risks, he feels he is more deserving than the other person who has what he wants, and he is still jealous.

Envy may also cause a person to doubt his own abilities. When someone else succeeds in getting something that you want but do not have, the implication is that the other person is doing better than you, and is more capable and/or more deserving than you are. When another person gets more resources from other people than you do, the implication is that other people value the other person more than they value you. Therefore, they consider you less deserving. People normally consider the way that others act toward them as indicating their own true worth. Therefore if others treat people unfairly, and give them less than they give to others, then people believe they deserve this. Their self-image is threatened and their self-esteem is lowered. People want to get more than others, because this is evidence to themselves and others that they are superior. They do not want to get less than others, because it is evidence to themselves and others that they are inferior. When a person tries to get the same thing that another has, or to get something better than another has, he is trying to prove his worth, both to himself and others. The phrase, "keeping up with the Joneses," refers to the effort to get as much as one's neighbors have. People do this to prove they are just as good as the neighbors.

> Well, I don't know whether or not you'd call it keeping up with the Joneses. But I do think that if you're going to live in a neighborhood where everybody has a two-car garage, you should have one too. You've got to get respect, and that means being as good as those around you. #2240

> In my community people do not want others to get ahead of them in any way. One man decided to sell his farmhouse and build a new

home nearby. In less than a month, four houses were up for sale and plans were made for four new homes. No one wanted to stay in their old house if the guy down the road was getting a new one. No one wants to appear of lesser means than his neighbor. #2241

When there are wealthy, successful families in the community, other families frequently try to keep up. One man in my community tried so hard, he had a nervous breakdown. When he recovered, he packed up and moved away. Another man actually did work himself to death trying to pay off two extra cars he bought. People say he worked overtime every night and also had a job on Saturdays that no one was supposed to know about. #2242

Our science department hired two new female staff who were still completing their Ph.D. dissertations. They were each told they had a one-year contract, in order to encourage them to hurry up and finish their dissertations and thereby complete their Ph.D.'s. However, during the year the two talked with another woman who had been hired by another department. They learned that the other woman was also still completing her Ph.D. dissertation, but had been given a five-year contract to do so, as well as a higher salary than the two in our department. Our two were quite upset. They felt demoralized and that the effort they were putting into their jobs was not appreciated. They also talked about looking for jobs elsewhere. None of this would have happened if they hadn't compared the terms of their employment with the other woman's. Thank God the person from the other department was a woman. If she had been a man, I think the two in our department would have charged us with sexual discrimination. When the matter was referred to the administration, it was discovered that the contract of our two new female staff also allowed them five years to complete their dissertations, and the salary of one of them was actually higher than the salary of the woman in the other department. #2243

Competition between neighbors

My family lives in a suburban residential area, where the neighbors acquire and display possessions in such a way that it resembles a competition. This competition is conducted on many fronts, but primarily in terms of one's house and yard and the possessions one sees on the premises. One becomes aware of the competition by watching what the neighbors do and when they do it. Often when one neighbor makes an improvement or acquires a new possession, others do the same thing or something comparable almost immediately. Frequently there is a volley. It goes your turn, my turn, your turn, and so on. For example, when our neighbors bought a second car it took us about three weeks to get another one. This was accompanied with comments like "Well, we needed one." After my parents bought their car the neighbors decided that they were going to go on a trip to Mexico. My parents felt they did this because we had bought the car. Our car cost several thousand dollars more than theirs, and the difference in price probably equaled the cost of their trip to Mexico.

Although the expression, "keeping up with the Joneses," is commonly used to refer to this competition, there are more phenomena involved than the expression suggests. Included are a) wanting to have things, b) trying to distinguish yourself favorably from others, c) desiring to tell others about your successes, and d) not wanting to appear less capable than others.

When you become aware that someone has gotten something neat, attractive, or useful, often you'd like to have one too and seriously consider getting it. Frequently the person you know discusses and illustrates the advantages of the new acquisition, and you recognize advantages you weren't aware of before. The more often you see it and hear about it, the more you consider it, and the more likely you are to get one too. Because people tend to have more contact with neighbors than with nonneighbors, they are more likely to see and get the same things the neighbors have. For example, the next-door neighbors put in French doors to create a hallway separating their living room from their entrance way. My parents think it looks nice, and now they're doing it too. Also, our previous neighbors had a skidoo. And since the land behind our houses consists of fields, they could go skidooing for hours. My parents hate the winter and are not active people, but when they saw the skidoo, they bought one too. It cost about $3000 and was a much better model than the neighbors had. I don't think we could afford it, but we got it because the neighbors had one. My parents never used it, but I did. It turned out my parents hated that skidoo, because they didn't like getting cold and wet. When the neighbors eventually sold their skidoo, we sold ours within two weeks, despite my ardent pleas not to.

When you achieve or acquire something which distinguishes you favorably from others, it becomes a sign of accomplishment, a source of identification, and a focus for self-congratulation. It indicates that you are a successful and viable person and it becomes a symbol that you are special. Even if you get what others have, you often try to go one better, perhaps by using better materials or getting a model with more features. If you have done something better than others, you are proud of the fact, and you do not mind having others know about it. People seem to value each of their abilities to excel over others. Because you are constantly in the presence of your neighbors and their possessions, just as you are with certain relatives, they become a primary reference, and you compare yourself to them. This was illustrated by my parents in connection with our lawn and the building of a patio.

Everyone in our neighborhood competes in trying to have the best lawn. In order to have a really beautiful lawn, my parents spent hundreds and hundreds of dollars to purchase a really expensive mixture of grass seed. We put in one type of seed that grew best in the spring, and another that grew best in the fall. During the early part of the season our lawn was fairly nice and quite similar to the lawns of the neighbors. Later in the season, however, the neighbors' grass started to die while our late-blooming strain flourished. As a result our lawn was as green and thick as anything, while everyone else's lawn was yellow. When it was in full growth my parents were always commenting how nice our lawn was compared with others in the neighborhood. Even my grandparents got into the act, saying, "You people have a nicer-looking lawn than everyone else." Then about six months later our next-door neighbors had their lawn dug up and replanted with a mixture of seed similar to ours. My parents were none too pleased. They said, "They might have a nice lawn, but they went and got it done professionally. Ours is just as nice and we didn't have to pay to have it done." However, my parents have since stopped talking about how great their lawn is relative to other people's.

My parents were the first in our area to build a patio on the back of the house. I think it is important to be first, because you don't want people to think you are doing something just because they did it. But then everybody else started talking about putting in a patio and within about a week neighbors on all sides of us started to build theirs. My parents did not appreciate this, and said, "I bet they are doing it just because we built one," and "Now we're going to have patios all the way up the street. We may as well join them together and have a walkway."

People are proud of their accomplishments and want to draw attention to them. Often when they are pleased and enthusiastic about something they have done or gotten, they want to talk to others about it. The newer a possession or achievement, the more enthusiastic they are.

However, they do not want people to think they are showing off or trying to lord it over them. Therefore, they try to be somewhat subtle in letting others know about their successes. For example, neighbors always make sure the other neighbors know when they mix socially with any dignitaries. If they are going to a lunch party with the lieutenant governor or get an invitation to a garden party when a member of the British royal family visits the province, they may try to draw attention to it with a comment to the neighbor that they just don't know what kind of hat they are going to wear. Similarly, our neighbor comes over to tell us where he's going, what he's doing, and when he's doing it. He does it very casually though. "Yeah, in a couple of weeks or so, we're going to go to . . . " When my mother was very depressed about an illness in the family, my father bought her a microwave oven as a surprise. Her first comment was "My God, that's bigger than the neighbor's." However, there is no way she would call the neighbors up and say, "Hey, we bought a new microwave. Come over and see it." Instead I expect her to wait a couple of months and when the subject comes up, say something like "Yes, they really are convenient to have." Normally people are reticent to discuss such things frankly with anyone other than their closest friends and relatives.

Despite people's efforts to be subtle, when neighbors inform you about a new possession or accomplishment you often assume they told you just to show off. A couple of months ago my parents were over socializing with our neighbors, and the neighbors brought up the idea that they should all save for several years and go on a trip to Europe together. My parents said they would think about it, even though they knew deep down that they couldn't afford it. They wanted so badly to be able to go, but when my parents talked about it later, they spoke of it sarcastically and said they would never do anything like that because it was a tremendous waste of money. They were quite offended they had been asked, as if they felt, "How dare you ask us, knowing that we can't do it?" Of course, I'm sure the rich neighbors asked my parents knowing damn well there was no way they could do it. They were telling them, "Guess where we are going?" in a subtle way. The neighbors didn't want to look like they were showing off, but that's exactly what they were doing. And my parents were quite upset that they couldn't act the very same way. I know my parents would love to go, and if they could afford it, they'd make sure the neighbors on the other side of us knew about the trip the very next day.

When someone else does something better than you, you may think you appear less capable or less adequate than the other person, or feel your self-image threatened and question just how successful you really are. This is particularly likely to occur when others achieve something in an area in which you are trying to excel.

One of our neighbors made several improvements to their house all at once. Not only did they build a patio, but they repainted their house a new color, finished their basement, and a month later they built a garage. They just went BOOM! These neighbors went right overboard. If they had just put in the garage and left the house the same color, that'd be fine. But to go bang, bang, bang all of a sudden; it's like wiping out any possible competition for the next two years. Unlike other houses in the neighborhood, the neighbor's house and our house were originally identical, which makes everything they do all the more obvious and challenging. Now all of a sudden, their house looks so much bigger and better than ours because they have this double-car garage sitting on the end of it and the house is painted quite a rich color. Like it looks like a really, really, really nice house. And it makes our house just look so ugh! My dad has wanted a garage from the day we moved into our house. It's the one thing he wants. Seeing the neighbors suddenly construct one was very disheartening to both of my parents. Mom told me she was "suffering from the green-eyed monster," or envy. I think my parents really resent what the neighbors did. I feel it too. My parents have since started talking about building a garage sooner than they had originally planned. I find people don't talk constantly about the possessions of the neighbors. However, an acquisition or improvement by a neighbor tends to set off such talk. When the neighbors do something you've always wanted to do, your talk and plans get speeded up.

Since then these same neighbors have traded their car in on a new one and bought a van for camping. This camper was frigging expensive. It's huge, with a cab like a truck. Also, they travel away every single weekend, flying here and there. They've got a lot of money. But it's a big mystery where their money is coming from. I asked my parents, "Like how in hell can they afford to do this?" And my parents said, "God, we don't know." We do know how much he earns at his job, and his wife doesn't even work. In contrast, my mother and father both work and together earn at least twice what he earns. We think the people next door either won a lottery or he must be getting a sizable disability pension, because he was injured at his previous job. My parents know them well enough to know they didn't have a relative die who left them the money. When the neighbor came over to our house recently, he was talking about his new camper, and my parents asked him how he could afford one. He said, "Just go to the bank, boy. Just go to the bank." But we can't see how the bank would loan him all the money to do the things he does.

Originally my parents socialized frequently with these neighbors. However, since the neighbors have so clearly outstripped my parents in their acquisitions, my parents just barely socialize with them at all. Although my parents wouldn't admit that this is the reason for the change in their relationship, it is the only one I can see. With everything these neighbors have done, my parents now consider them to be at a higher level than we are. Because my parents can't keep up with these neighbors, I expect them to soon change the people they compete with.

Another factor involved is that people do not want to look lax, uncaring, or negligent relative to others. This applies to one's possessions and property, which are viewed as extensions of oneself. Therefore when your neighbors improve the appearance of their property and possessions, you feel compelled to do the same so that it does not become obvious to all that you are less diligent or less responsible than those around you. Often your self-image is tied to the idea that you are fully capable of maintaining proper appearances. But also, you don't want to lose your current position relative to your neighbors. When our neighbors started to repaint their house, my parents had me out painting our house a week later. We had made no plans to do so prior to the neighbors doing so. In my neighborhood neighbors often paint their houses in flurries of about six at a time. Also, practically everyone cuts their lawn on Sunday. Anyone who fails to do this is left with a really ratty-looking lawn, which is obvious every time you drive through the neighborhood. After the neighbors cut their lawn, if our lawn is not cut by the next day, Mom starts to say, "Jeez, our lawn needs cutting." I think if the neighbors on both sides of us never cut their lawns, we would probably cut ours only once every two weeks, rather than once or twice a week as we do now. Another thing is furniture. Refinishing your living-room furniture, or getting new living-room furniture and relegating the old furniture to the family room downstairs, encourages your neighbors to do the same. Currently, several of the families in our neighborhood are refurnishing their living room. People always seem to buy new furniture when others do.

There are good reasons why neighbors are so significant in this competition. Because of proximity, people tend to be much more aware of their neighbors than their nonneighbors, and as a result make more comparisons between themselves and their neighbors. Also, neighbors

412

tend to see and know more about you than do nonneighbors and are in a better position to convey this information about you to others outside the neighborhood.

The degree of involvement in this competition seems to vary according to inclination and available resources. Everyone seems to try to have the best lawn. A number of people have two cars and are replacing their living-room furniture to improve the inside appearance of their house. A few, like my family and the neighbors on one side of us, seem to try to be the best in everything. There are also things that people acquire slowly and not right after a neighbor does, and these tend to be the more expensive items. For example, the neighbors on the other side of us have never put in a patio, but it's something they've hoped for for a long time, and I expect them to do so soon. My parents have always wanted a garage, but it's a major expense and I'm sure they'll get it eventually. One man in our area doesn't seem to be competing at all. He is sixty-five years old and single, and seems oblivious to what is going on. But he does take care of his lawn. In contrast with other neighborhoods, people in our neighborhood do not seem to be concerned with raising the best flower gardens or vegetable gardens, or competing in terms of outside decorations at Christmastime.

Competition with the neighbors is something no one talks about outside of their own household. It is a very hush-hush subject. Competing in this way is considered such a crass activity that one is thought less of when known to be engaged in it. People would be very upset if they were accused of competing and they would certainly not admit to others or in many cases even to themselves that they are participating. Children are absolutely forbidden to mention this activity outside the home. I've been told by my mother, "Don't you tell anybody," after she had just expressed envy over an improvement a neighbor made to his house. Although none of our neighbors talk about competing with each other, I feel sure they are engaged in it. Because I am part of my parents' household, I can see the competition all around me. However, I suspect many of the neighbors may not realize we are competing or at least do not realize how ardently we are doing so.

Children are also very much concerned with possessions and appearances. There is considerable competition between children, and the competition involves the parents, who are required to supply the possessions. Originally my sister's friends all wanted their families to get a game console so they could play video games. Now that they all have the game console, they want a better console, which plays more sophisticated games. Those who don't have the better console yet, compete in terms of who has the largest number of games for the outdated console. You really see the competition between kids at Christmastime. On Christmas afternoon children go to each other's houses to see what presents each received. Often when two kids meet, each rhymes off a list of their gifts. I remember kids saying, "Oh, God, you're so lucky." I didn't mind if other kids got the same kind of things I did, as long as my gifts were a little better than theirs. Most parents are concerned that their children receive at least as much as the other kids, and not feel left behind in this competition. I also remember when I was between thirteen and seventeen years old. I would be hitchhiking home, and I'd tell the driver, "I live here. Just drop me off," and have him let me out at a huge house near where I lived. Then as soon as he drove off, I'd walk out of the driveway and over to my own house. As I got older I would only do this when I got a ride with an attractive girl I wanted to impress.

I think children are a major source of pressure on the parents in the competition with neighbors. I was a major factor behind my parents' decision to get a skidoo. I wanted one very badly and I think it was because of my encouragement that they began to think of getting one. I am presently trying really hard to get my parents to paint the house a color as rich as the one used by the next-door neighbor. I hate the way our house is now, and think it looks gross. The neighbor's house is a golden color and looks really nice, but ours is just a stupid blah green. I've lived in green houses all my life. I told my parents I hate the color of it, and they should do something like the neighbors and paint it another color. My mother asked why, and I said, "Now our house looks cheap compared with all the other houses on the block." My parents even try to forestall pressure from my sister to have us get what the neighbors have. When our next-door neighbors got pay TV, my parents suddenly started running it down, even before they or my sister had seen it. My parents knew my sister would be over watching it at the neighbors' house as soon as she found out they had it, and she'd be saying, "Why can't we have pay TV too?"

I think there is a strong tendency for people to establish their identities in terms of their possessions, and to evaluate their neighbors on the same basis. In my neighborhood you are judged on the basis of what you have. Possessions and achievements enable you and others to make comparisons and determine how successful or unsuccessful you are relative to others. #2244

414

How people deal with envy

People are aware that others are prone to feel envy, and frequently take this into account. As a result they may act in one or more of the following ways:

1. Trying to make others envious
2. Using envy to obtain positive reactions
3. Trying to prevent envy in others
4. Trying to avoid negative reactions from others by preventing envy
5. Protecting oneself from envy

1. Trying to make others envious

On occasion people capitalize on the tendency of others to feel envy, and deliberately try to make them jealous. Having a possession, advantage, experience, or accomplishment that others would like to have too is a way of getting attention from others. People often feel good about themselves when they see signs that others envy them. It means they have successfully acquired something that others have not, and they believe it means they are special, more successful, and better than others.

> My older daughter likes to make her sister jealous. The other day she was visiting a friend in town and called home to talk to me. When my younger daughter answered the phone my older daughter told her the friend had bought her a bottle of pop and a doughnut. She was just trying to make her sister jealous, and she succeeded. #2245

> Many guys like to date girls who are good looking and wear fashionable, coordinated clothes. Guys say, "I like to date a female who makes me look good," "She's just the person I'd love to be seen with on a heavy date," and "I love to go to a club with a classy broad, because I enjoy making my buddies jealous." #2246

> I never really wanted to go to a high-school reunion before. But now that I've been admitted into a top graduate school, I wouldn't mind.

It would be nice to have them know how well I'm doing. But I sure wouldn't volunteer the information that my husband and I are getting a divorce. #2247

You know, as you make progress in your career, there are always some people who cause you grief. They range from those who try to get you in Dutch with your boss to those who can't be bothered replying to your letters. I think one of the real satisfactions of becoming a great success would be just to show these people up. #2248

2. Using envy to obtain positive reactions

People want positive reactions and use numerous tactics to get them. (See the chapter on Seeking Positive Reactions in Volume One of this series.) People frequently acquire possessions and experiences that others do not have and bring them to the attention of others in order to get positive reactions from them. However, these possessions and experiences often produce attention based on envy rather than positive reactions toward the people themselves. When A has a resource that B does not have and wants, B focuses on the resource. The attention and interest that B shows in A's resource is normally interpreted by A as interest in A, and therefore as a positive reaction to A. However, there are significant differences between the feelings a person holds for those he wants positive reactions from, and the feelings he holds for those he feels jealous of. A person frequently feels liking, love, admiration, and respect toward those he seeks positive reactions from, and he gives positive reactions to them in order to get positive reactions from them. In contrast, he often feels irritation, resentment, and anger toward those he is envious of. People consider their possessions and experiences an extension of themselves. Therefore, person A may fail to distinguish between B's efforts to get positive reactions from A, and B's expressions of envy toward what A has. However, B certainly does know the difference between desiring approval from A and feeling envy toward what A has.

When one does not have a better means of getting positive reactions, one can obtain attention by making a person jealous.

3. Trying to prevent envy in others

In other instances people adopt measures to minimize the likelihood that others will feel envy. Often they do not want to cause the other person hurt, or to have the other person's irritation focused on them.

> Christmas is such a commercial success for businesses because everyone has to buy a present for every one of their close relatives and friends. If they don't get a present for a person, that person is likely to feel jealous of those they do get a present for. As a result the person feels left out, rejected, and hurt. Not only does this damage people's relationship with the person that they didn't buy a present for, but people feel guilty that they've hurt the person. #2249

The measures that people use to prevent envy in others include not mentioning things and keeping things out of sight which are likely to produce envy.

> Most people try to avoid eating in front of others who are not eating, because they do not want to share their food. They know that others are likely to want some too, and to feel slighted if they aren't offered any. If people feel they need to go ahead and eat in the presence of others, they often apologize, ask if others mind, and offer to share. #2250

> My wife and I invited two friends over for dinner on Christmas Eve. We had just moved into a new apartment and had a box of nice items we didn't want anymore and were planning to donate to the Salvation Army Thrift Store. We decided to ask the two friends if they wanted any of the items before we took the box to the thrift store. We are very close friends with one of the people who was coming to dinner, Jerry, who always does things for us. We suggested to Jerry that he come early so he could have first choice of the items. He arrived first, found several items he liked, and I placed them in a back room out of sight. We didn't want Rita, the other person invited, to be jealous that we had given the nicer items to Jerry. Rita is a friend of ours, but not nearly as close as Jerry is. Also, when Jerry arrived, he brought a box full of Christmas gifts for us. We had gifts for Jerry too. However, we decided we would not open them that night, because none of the gifts were for Rita. If Rita had not been coming, we would have opened them after

dinner. Instead, we arranged to get together again the next day to open gifts. All of this was arranged before Rita arrived. When Rita got there we offered her the items remaining in the box and she selected several that she wanted. There was no reason to think Rita would be jealous, but we did not want to create the possibility. #2251

When I went on a trip out of town, my daughter wanted me to buy her a stuffed teddy bear, and I bought an absolutely adorable one in a store. However, I wanted to keep it for myself. On my way home at the airport I found another teddy bear on sale and got that one for her. The second one would have fully satisfied my daughter, but it wasn't as nice as the first one I got. All the way home I kept debating what to do and changing my mind about which one to give her. I didn't want her to be jealous of the fact I had the nicer one, and I knew I would feel guilty if I gave her the one that wasn't as nice. What I finally did was give her the second one, but not let her see the first one. She loved the one I gave her. In the meantime I had my boyfriend keep the nicer bear at his place, and several weeks later he "gave" it to me as a Valentine's Day gift. I took it home half covered with gift-wrapping paper so there'd be no question where it came from. I told my daughter that her bear could play with mine whenever she wanted. She had already bonded with her bear, so there was no problem at all. #2252

At times people will say something to or do something for a person in private, to prevent others from witnessing this and feeling jealous.

I wanted to tell my niece that the way she fixed her hair was really lovely, but her friend was with her at the time. I didn't want to make her friend feel unhappy that I wasn't complimenting her hair too. So I didn't say anything until my niece and I were alone. #2253

I was on a cruise in the Caribbean and was so pleased with the service of our steward that I decided I would give him a nice tip at the end of the voyage. However, I didn't do so until I saw him alone, because I didn't want the other ship employees to know how much I was giving him. I tipped the others considerably less, and didn't want to make them feel bad. #2254

When I return to visit Vietnam most of my relatives hope I will bring them gifts, particularly money. When I do give one of them money, I am very careful not to let any of the others see me do it, because they would be jealous and upset. If I do something for one of them in front of the others, I have to do the same thing for everyone there. #2255

People who give gifts to others, may add a gift for someone else who will be present. Thus when one child has a birthday, the parents may give the child's sibling a gift too. Similarly, when a family invites a friend to Christmas dinner, they may include a token gift for the friend under the tree.

People will sometimes help another person at a task, in order that the other person does not resent the fact he is the only one doing the task.

> I've found the best way to get my children to clean up their room is to do it with them. They get upset if they have to do a chore and I don't. They really resent working when I'm not. Also, if I don't help them straighten up, they don't know where to start. #2256

In order to avoid having others feel jealous, people often take meticulous care to treat everyone equally. Thus they often refuse to comply with requests to make exceptions to the rules, because "If I let you do it, everyone else will want to do it, and I'll have to let them do it too."

> I have to be really careful that I don't do more for one of my two children than for the other. Even though they aren't the same age, I give both of them the same amount of allowance each week. As Christmas approaches I keep a total of how much I've spent on gifts so that I'll be sure to spend the same amount on each child. This past Christmas I found I'd already spent more on one, so I made a point of getting the other additional gifts. They know what things cost, so I'd be sure to hear about it if I spent less money on one of them. The same is true of affection. If I spend more time hugging one than I do the other, the one who is hugged less often mentions the fact. #2257

> I bought a box of six ice-cream sandwiches for the family, and when I got them home I told my two boys about them. Jim, my younger boy, ate one, but my older boy didn't because he had to hurry to hockey practice. Jim planned to go over to the rink to skate after the hockey practice, and asked if he could take three ice-cream sandwiches along. One was to be for himself, another for his older brother, and a third for their mutual friend. This was fine with me, except that I was concerned

that my older boy would be jealous that Jim had gotten two of the ice-cream sandwiches. After I explained my concern to Jim, I realized that I could justify giving him two. I told Jim, "If your brother says anything about you getting two, remind him that I bought him some candy last week when just the two of us were together, and you didn't get any." "You bought him some candy and some chips," Jim corrected me. #2258

When I got Christmas presents for my girlfriend and her two children, I really tried to play it safe so no one would feel hurt. I bought the two children identical boxes of candy. Then when I thought about it I went back and got a third box for my girlfriend. She gets jealous too when the children receive things she doesn't. I also decided to buy each of her children a small calculator. I found the ideal model, but when I went to the store with some money I learned they had already sold all but one of that model. I was quite unhappy about this, because I couldn't buy that model for one child and a different model for the other. It would have been inviting trouble, because one child might decide that the other had received the better model. So I shopped some more until I found a different model that the store had two of, even though this model wasn't as useful as the original one. Before I gave these calculators to the children, I showed them to my girlfriend, and later she told me she felt jealous that her children were both getting better models than the one she already owned. But I wasn't stupid. Unknown to her, I'd already bought her a much better model for Christmas. #2259

4. Trying to avoid negative reactions from others by preventing envy

Various tactics are used to try to make sure that people are given an equal opportunity to receive resources in order that they will not criticize or complain that they are being treated unfairly. These tactics include taking turns, providing each person with a vote, giving every person a chance to speak, allotting each person an equal amount of time to speak, flipping a coin, drawing one or more names from a pool which includes everyone, and rotating employees so that no one has to work more of the undesirable shifts than anyone else. In addition, people employ specific operating procedures to minimize envy and conflict. These include the use of "first come, first served" at cash registers and in restaurants; "first come, first choice" in assigning seats at sporting events, concerts, plays, and restaurants; and "first come, first admitted" in the case of educational programs and courses with limited enrollments and also in the assignment of reservations and space in hotels, planes, and restaurants. People will often go to great lengths to "be fair."

My daughter said she wanted some salami for lunch when we were at the store, so I bought a package. When I opened the package at home I counted eight slices, and because there were four of us I announced each person would get two slices when we made our own sandwiches. In the middle of the afternoon my daughter complained that the salami was all gone and she'd only had one slice. No one would admit taking three slices for themselves, so I ended up offering my daughter some money to go buy another package. #2260

The other night I heated up a pizza at home. There were four of us and I divided the pizza four ways. Then it became clear that each person preferred a particular piece because it had more mushrooms, more meat, or more something else. So the best thing to do was to let each person choose the piece they wanted. However, we couldn't all choose at once because two or more of us might have wanted the same piece. There is a very good technique to use when there are just two people involved; one person divides and the other person has first choice. This forces the person dividing to make the pieces as equal as possible. But this time we had four people, not two. Unfortunately I didn't have a deck of cards, some dice, or a calculator with a random-number generator which would let us determine the order in which people could choose their piece. However, I remembered I had a hat in the closet and so I got it, wrote the numbers one through four on some slips of paper, and put them in the hat. I held the hat so no one could see in it, and each person chose a slip. The number on each person's slip determined the order in which they got to choose a piece of pizza. Of course, by the time we'd done all this, the pizza was getting cold. #2261

5. Protecting oneself from envy

People adopt various strategies to protect themselves from the envy of others. Thus many people keep information on their salaries to themselves and discuss their accomplishments only with their closest friends and relatives. By preventing others from feeling envy toward them, they avoid critical and nasty remarks from others.

> I make it a point never to discuss wages with my co-workers. I don't want to know how much they make. And I won't tell them how much I make, because people don't like it if you make more than them. I know I wouldn't like it if somebody was paid better than I was for doing the same work. #2262

> One of the provincial newspapers publishes a list of the salaries of top government employees, and people remember these figures. Some of the government employees are friends of my husband, and one is named Tom. Tom is a nice enough guy, but doesn't do a whole heck of a lot. My husband always says, "Must be great to make $60,000 and do nothing." Well I guess Tom would just as soon no one knew what he earned. #2263

> I was always taught that it is rude to study a platter of food and then deliberately take the biggest piece. People resent this. Instead, what you are supposed to do is take the piece that is closest to you. #2264

Functions of efforts to get what others have

Envy motivates people to try to get a resource that another person has. Sometimes people can take it away from the person who has it. This may involve less effort than obtaining the same resource in another way. Even if they can not easily take it away from the person who has it, the knowledge that the person has obtained the resource brings home the message that the specific resource is available and another person has already obtained it. Envy directs people to go where the resources are. As a result of envy people consider the possibility of obtaining the same thing for themselves, and in many instances attempt to acquire it. If they are not able to obtain it at the time, often they remember that the possibility of getting it exists and they plan to obtain it for themselves if the opportunity presents itself.

My son came home yesterday all excited, because he learned that a father, mother, and daughter in the same family had all won substantial prizes in the national lottery. My son decided he was going to develop his own system so he would win too. #2265

Originally when I entered graduate school, I only planned to get a Master of Arts degree. But the people I hang out with are all getting their Ph.D. degrees. Eventually I said, "If they can do it, I can too." I don't consider them any more capable than I am. #2266

As a consequence of envy people are less likely to neglect available resources within their environment. Envy reduces the chance that individuals will be left out as new resources are exploited.

Excess behavior

Excess behavior is behavior in response to feelings which results in one acting contrary to the purposes the feelings are designed for. As a result, one loses resources rather than gains or protects them. For example, the feeling of envy causes people to try to get what others have. As a result people exploit available resources and obtain more resources. However, there are situations in which people experience envy and try to obtain available resources, but actually lose resources in the process. This occurs when people a) attempt to get resources but do not succeed, b) are damaged when others defend their resources, and c) obtain resources over the short term, but alienate other people in the process, so that over the long term they actually lose resources. In addition, people sometimes try to prevent others from getting resources that they are not getting, rather than try to get the same resources for themselves.

When people attempt to get the resources others have, but do not succeed, they lose resources. At the very least they lose time and energy. However, some attempts can be extremely costly, and result in the loss of many years and a great deal of money. For example, one can repeatedly run for election and lose; one can buy many lottery tickets and never win;

one can invest heavily in real estate or the stock market and lose money; or one can obtain an expensive, lengthy education and then fail to get the job or salary one wants.

> Although I've already graduated from university, I continue going to university trying to get my grades up in my science courses so I can get into medical school. But I never get my grades up high enough and each time I apply to medical school they reject me. #2267

> After I got my Ph.D., I couldn't find a permanent teaching job at a university. I was able to teach an occasional course part-time. But to support myself I have to work as a clerk in local stores at a minimum wage. #2268

The number of top positions and jobs which pay well are quite limited, and only a fraction of the people who try to get them are successful. However, envy encourages people to attempt to get resources when they have little chance of success. Also, if one uses illegal means to try to get what others have, one may be punished and/or ostracized. For example, if one tries to obtain money through embezzlement or by selling drugs, one may be caught and fined, put in jail, and lose relationships with friends and family members.

A person may be physically injured or lose considerable material resources when other people react to his efforts to take their resources from them. This can happen when a person underestimates the willingness or ability of others to defend their resources. Others may respond by attacking him physically, suing him, or getting him fired. Others may tell additional people what he has done and those they tell may be less willing to share their resources with him in the future.

A person may succeed in taking resources from others over the short term, but alienate others in the process, so that over the long term he actually loses more resources than he gains. Thus a person may appear to be so assertive or selfish that people will have little to do with him in the future, and people will no longer be willing to cooperate with him or exchange their resources for his.

The feeling of envy may also cause a person to direct his efforts into preventing others from getting resources that he is not getting, rather than putting his efforts into trying to get the same resources for himself. If he can prevent others from getting resources or cause them to lose their resources, there is no reason for him to feel envy, which is a punishing feeling. Often it takes less effort to remove or destroy another person's resources than it does to do the work necessary to get the same resources for oneself. Although the effort one puts into causing another person to lose resources may help one avoid the feeling of envy, it does not provide one with additional resources. Therefore the time and energy necessary to do this is wasted effort. In addition, it is likely to create lasting enemies. On the other hand, if one can prevent others from getting ahead of oneself, one can maintain one's self-image and one's public image of being as good as or better than others. Therefore by preventing others from getting ahead of oneself, one avoids the loss of positive reactions both from oneself and from others.

Society and efforts to get what others have

Society provides numerous opportunities for people to learn what others have that they do not. Newspapers, magazines, books, films, and television programs portray desirable possessions, advantages, experiences, relationships, and accomplishments of others. Advertisements show other people using specific products and services and enjoying various kinds of pleasure and other advantages with them. The envy that is produced through these media encourages people to try to get the same things for themselves.

> Every time I watch one of those travel ads for the Caribbean, all I want to do is go there too. Perfect deserted beaches, crystal-clear water, beautiful people, tropical drinks, relaxing in beach chairs. It sure would be nice. #2269

> When you buy candy or cigarettes from the place that sells lottery tickets, you see all the pictures they've put up of local people who have won money in a lottery. They want you to think if others who live here can do it, so can you. If they make you jealous, you'll buy tickets too. #2270

Trying to get what others have

Society provides various means a) to prevent people from taking what others have, and b) to help people obtain the same things that others have. People are discouraged from taking things that belong to others by public opinion, laws, courts, police, and punishments, including prison. These help control theft, trespass, vandalism, fraud, and unfair competition. People are aided in obtaining the same things that others have through education, employment services, fair-employment practices, unemployment benefits, welfare, charities, and government-supported health and retirement programs. Other means are used too. At sporting events contestants rotate sides of courts and sides of playing fields to equalize advantages in regard to playing surfaces, wind, and lighting. In order to deal with the envy of those who are less successful, taxes on luxury goods, disproportionate income taxes, and wealth taxes are used to redistribute money from those with more to those with less. In order to provide equal advantages to those who would not otherwise get them, there is preferential placement in training programs, and allocation of scholarships and jobs on the basis of criteria such as sex, race, ethnic group, geographical region, and financial need. However, advantages which are given to those with less produce envy among those who do not qualify for the advantages.

Many people get upset when they see single mothers who receive government assistance for living expenses. When the single mothers have several children, some people say they should be sterilized so they can't have more children. #2271

The native populations of Canada and the United States have been subjected to centuries of genocide while the whites continue to dispossess them of their lands and other resources. Despite this and the obvious signs that the native populations have serious difficulties coping, whites continually criticize any compensation benefits given to native peoples that the whites do not receive too, such as educational support, tax exemptions, and fishing rights. This is illustrated by a nonnative student, who said, "Native people get free tuition and a government allowance to go to university. I know a native student who complains about the course workloads and the way the professors grade his work. I wonder if he would be so quick to complain if he had to pay for his own education. Few students get a free education the way he does, and many

426

students go into debt for untold thousands of dollars to get their degrees. He should show more gratitude for his free education." #2272

Those who do not qualify for advantages constantly criticize and attack the advantages given to others, such as welfare, unemployment benefits, and other help. This forces those who distribute the advantages to become quite strict in trying to ensure that no one can criticize their selection criteria. Concern that the advantages are going to those who do not qualify for them, media reports on "cheaters," and investigations to identify those who do not qualify are common.

Social institutions attempt to deal with envy. Different religions approach envy in different ways. For example, Christianity advocates that people share with those who have less, and informs those with less that they will be the enviable ones in the afterlife while those they envy on earth will be eternally punished. Buddhism, on the other hand, seeks to suppress envy by advocating acceptance and satisfaction with what one has. In addition, there are the politics of envy. Marxists, feminists, and ethnic groups attack those with more, and advocate restructuring society so that others do not have more than they do. Democratic systems seek to minimize feelings of envy by giving each person voting rights, thereby suggesting that each person has equal access to resources.

Numerous social practices attempt to deal with envy. People are taught various models, such as a) it is wrong to feel jealous, b) it is childish to try to "keep up with the Joneses," c) one should be a good sport and accept defeat by a successful competitor, and d) one should not be a tattletale and tell on those who take advantages they are not supposed to have. In order to minimize criticism from people who receive less, those who distribute resources try to use objective means of distribution, such as a single set of rules for everyone, advertisement of positions, objective examinations, admission committees, personnel boards, independent evaluators, and grievance committees. Societies and organizations try to protect themselves from envy, criticism, and loss of resources by trying to appear fair.

Societies and groups within societies are also envious of the resources that other societies and groups have that they wish they had too. This may be territory; a population tax base; a higher standard of living; an oil, coal, or mineral field; an agricultural area; a port; or any other resource that they would like to have too. If they are stronger than those who possess the resource they are often willing to take it from them. In order to reduce criticism and to appear to be "the good guys," they often claim they have legitimate grounds for taking the resource from others. Societies and groups have to have sufficient financial, political, and military strength to protect their resources from the envy of other societies and groups. Societies and groups may also try to obtain the resources that others have by a) persuading them to share their resources with them, b) getting those societies and groups which distribute resources to give them a share, and c) finding ways to obtain the same resources for themselves, such as developing industry or tourism in their own country. They often criticize those who have resources they do not have, and they sometimes act to cause them to lose these resources.

ACKNOWLEDGEMENTS

I most sincerely thank the residents of Prince Edward Island for their patience, openness, and cooperation with this research. Hundreds of people have contributed their time and labor. They have provided information about their families, friends, and neighbors, as well as themselves, for the sole purpose of helping to identify types of behavior. Because of the private nature of much of the information, most of those participating have asked that their names not be mentioned. As a result, I am hesitant to mention the few who indicated they do not care whether I use their names. I certainly would not want these few criticized for information that they did not provide. Therefore, my policy is to identify as few names as possible. If, however, someone wishes to have their name mentioned in connection with specific pieces of information that they provided, I will be happy to do so if this book is reprinted, as long as this does not place others in an embarrassing position.

I wish to single out Sharon Myers, who has been an invaluable assistant in collecting case studies for this research. She gathered excellent information, painstakingly placed this within a proper context, helped me understand the significance of the behavior, answered my numerous questions, and patiently corrected me when I was off base. She has made a significant contribution to our understanding of rural life. I can not thank her enough. Many others have worked for me as research assistants during various stages of this study, and their contribution has been enormous. Regrettably, most have requested that I not mention them by name. I very much thank all of these individuals for the care, attention, and interest they have given this project.

I also greatly thank Hoa Huynh and Llewellyn Watson for their patience and cooperation in serving as sounding boards as I have written up my information and developed my ideas. Often they put aside their own work to listen to me. Their thoughtful comments have helped me deal with certain weaknesses in the study, their examples have clarified the subject matter, and their encouragement has boosted my morale.

I very much want to thank Bill Charlesworth for all of his encouragement and intellectual support for this project.

Acknowledgements

Many other individuals have been extremely helpful in answering specific questions which have arisen during the course of the study. These include Doreley Coll, Satadal Dasgupta, Kay Diviney, Anne Marie Eberhardt, Frank Falvo, Susan Gallant, Egbert Huynh, Joseph Kopachevsky, Frank Ledwell, Brent MacLaine, William Mason, Shannon Murray, Annie Myer, Wayne Peters, John Joe Sark, Barbara Seeber, Charlotte Stewart, Elizabeth Thai, Tien Thai, Linda Trenton, Tom Trenton, Judi Wagner, and David Weale. Thank you very much.

A number of individuals have freely loaned me slides and photographs and have given me a great deal of help understanding their content. Some have also gone to a great deal of trouble to take photographs for me. These include Barbara Currie, Ron Eckroth, Mamdouh Elgharib, Margot Elgharib, Charles Holmes, Hoa Huynh, Thuy Huynh, Vicki Huynh, Amanda MacIntrye, Jean Mitchell, Harold Saint, Charlotte Stewart, Elizabeth Thai, Llewellyn Watson, and Marty Zelenietz. I very much appreciate their help, and know this research would be much poorer without it.

I have also received an enormous amount of technical help. Marc Beland, Dave Cairns, Bruce Ferguson, Nancy Kemp, Scott MacDonald, Evelyn Read, Bonnie Suen, Chris Vessey, and Larry Yeo have provided excellent advice and support with computers and word processing. Donya Beaton, Katie Compton, Shelley Ebbett, Richard Haines, Angela Hughes, and Tom MacDonald have gone far beyond the call of duty and have painstakingly prepared countless outstanding photographs. Glenda Clements-Smith, John Cox, Janos Fedak, Sibyl Frei, Michelle Gauthier, Matthew MacKay, Floyd Trainor, and Mary Ada Upstone have given me excellent advice and a great deal of help with illustrations, layout, and printing. Mary Ada Upstone has created the very useful maps.

I particularly want to thank my wife, Hoa Huynh, who has given me an enormous amount of help and support. It is not possible to express how much this means. She understands how important it is to me to spend so much time on this project.

Although numerous individuals have given freely of their time and help, limitations in the conduct, analysis, organization, and interpretation of this research must be recognized as my own.

SOURCES OF PHOTOGRAPHS

H. H.   Hoa Huynh

H. S.   Harold Saint

E. T.   Elizabeth Thai

M. E.   Margot Elgharib, Mamdouh Elgharib

M. Z.   Marty Zelenietz

The remaining photographs are provided by the author.

INDEX OF NUMBERED EXAMPLES

This index is designed to help those who have read the text to locate specific examples they want to find again. The numbers below refer to the consecutive numbers which follow the indented quotations in the text.

Index of numbered examples

alcohol. *See also* drunk; drunk people
  after I've had a few beer I overlook the danger of catching a disease from a
    pickup, #2086
  avoiding alcohol because it kills brain cells, #1602
  bootleggers, #1851, #1985
  drinking because someone else at work is more successful, #2239
  four girls getting drunk to celebrate end of exams, #1484
  liquor is required to be admitted into party, #1441
  my grandmother sees me drunk with my friends and loses respect for me, #1684
  open liquor in one's car, #1879, #1985
  traveling to a distant liquor store in order to protect his local reputation, #1671
  using a designated driver, #2140
  younger kids in the band getting the older kids to buy them liquor, #2150
aliens, future contact with, #2053
allergies, imagining the worst outcome from one's, #1589
alphabetically arranging items, #1332
amusement park ride, refuse to let their children go on a dangerous, #1979
anger, angry. *See also* the chapter on Protecting Self and Resources; displays of anger;
    violence
  getting over anger before one acts on it, #1513
  women crying when angry, #1562
animals. *See also* animal breeding; pets
  human cruelty to animals, #1419, #1420
ankle, sore. *See* beer
anniversary party, a woman with a bad reputation is not welcome at an, #1870
annoyance, annoyances, annoyed. *See also* TV
  being called the wrong name, #1415
  brother bragging about himself, #1412
  brother with hockey stick and baseball glove, #1403
  caused by others slurping tea, crunching chips, grinding teeth, snapping chewing
    gum, filing nails, chewing bubble gum, pushing against one's chair, singing,
    etc., #1398
  chewing gum, #1491
  colleagues at work dropping in to talk, #1410
  experienced by a housewife, #1338
  girl chewing bubble gum in class, #1491
  hassling a person, #1506
  having to listen to elderly lady on bus, #1408
  leaving used condoms lying around, #1414
  in the library, #1399
  with oneself for not getting anything done, #1598
  others taking one's parking space, #1427
  when others use the shower and bathtub, #1397
  phone interruptions at home, #1409
  produced by sister singing and whistling, #1400

Index of numbered examples

Index of numbered examples

anxiety (*continued*)

      strangers, #1664, #1765, #1766

      terrorists, #2050

      that there is a man with a knife under my bed, #1840

      young son's fear of adult neighbor who had slapped him, #1489

   getting in trouble

      being pregnant, #1992, #2001

      getting a girl pregnant, #1693

      high school parties and drugs, #1788

      if my girlfriend became pregnant, #1833

      meeting with a gym teacher, #1594

      visit from a policeman, #1595

   health, #1589, #1613, #1681, #2093

      AIDS, #1624, #1625

         catching AIDS from patients, #1755

         getting AIDS and having people avoid me, #1799

      alcohol, #1602

      back problems, #1628

      being very sick in Vietnam, #1629

      blood in urine, #1626

      cancer, #1604, #1619, #2045

      car-exhaust fumes, #1609

      chemical spraying of crops, #1604

      cholesterol, #1600, #1601, #1623, #2055

      cigarette smoke, #1608, #1609

      colitis, #1627

      complications during childbirth, #1586, #1618

         I might die during labor, #2043

      coping with multiple sclerosis, #2010

      difficulty breathing, #1589

      dirty hands when eating, #1620

      dying from eating local mussels, #1844

      getting diseases using a public Laundromat, #1842

      getting toxic shock syndrome using tampons, #1841

      gum disease, #1622

      having a stroke, #2082

      having high blood pressure, #2030

      a heart problem, #1623

      medications, #1605, #1606

      not exercising, #1614, #1682, #2013, #2082

      pregnancy scares me to death, #1817

      public washrooms, #1621, #1625

         toilet seats in, #1625

      salmonella poisoning from local cheese, #1844

      sexually transmitted diseases, #1624

         catching a disease from a pickup, #2086

440

Index of numbered examples

Index of numbered examples

Index of numbered examples

Index of numbered examples

Index of numbered examples

anxiety (*continued*)

never put anything in writing, #1865

not allowing a friend who is always late to pick us up, because we wouldn't get where we are going on time, #1975

not allowing her sister the opportunity to use her music keyboard to get attention, #1973

not allowing our pet outside in a storm, so he won't get lost, #1976

not allowing someone who is known to steal into my apartment, #1855

not allowing the family cat outside, #2098

not babysitting again for an exploitative family, #1867

not giving son any more money until he gets a health-care card, #1980

not hiring friends of competitors, #1965

not letting others know I was pregnant, #1871

not locking the door, so people can get to me if I have a heart attack, #1876

not talking to one's children about sex, so they won't be curious about it, #1974

not telling anyone that he (a teenage male) is taking piano lessons, so he won't be teased, #1966

not telling others about your research ideas before you publish them yourself, #1866

not thinking about being unable to succeed, #2019

not turning on two appliances at the same time so won't get shocked, #2026

not using tampons so I won't lose my virginity, #1862

not wearing a seat belt so won't be killed, #2060

parents preventing their daughter from seeing a boy who hangs out with drug users, #1978

parking sports cars away from other cars and at an angle in order to prevent damage, #1858

paying off our house mortgage when we thought a serious recession was coming, #1927

planning a party in such a way that your parents won't know about it, #1928

planning to see the doctor when something doesn't heal properly, #2036

a politician who kicks his brother out of the house because the brother's drinking might ruin the politician's chance of reelection, #1882

practicing repeatedly to be able to demonstrate a dance well, #1931

preventing children from injuring themselves at a large playground, #2021

preventing contact between their husbands and their female friends who have gotten divorced, #1860

preventing glassware from breaking as it dries on the countertop, #1856

providing emotional support when a friend's relationship breaks up, #1943

pushing new desks into locked offices rather than leave them in the hall, #1859

putting cat outside so he won't jump on the dining table to get shrimp, #1878

putting out extra bowls of water for the cat when I go away from home, #1955

450

Index of numbered examples

Index of numbered examples

apple juice. *See* juice

apprehensive. *See* anxiety

architectural book, author upset with publisher over printing of photographs in, #1417

arguing. *See also* fiancée

    with husband over saving money by using a spinner washer, #1201

arranging to meet, husband and wife, #1293

arts courses. *See* courses

assignments. *See* tasks

athlete, athletes

    the big jock stud of the school, #1662

    envious of the advantages given to those who play other sports, #2121

athletic scholarship. *See* procrastinating

attractive, attraction. *See also* appearance

    being seen with an attractive girl, #1686

aunt. *See* family

automatic-dialing telephone, not bothering to reprogram numbers in one's, #1256

automatic teller machines (ATMs), advantages of, #1188

automobile. *See* car

avoiding work (effort), #1156 - #1373

baby

    changing her mind whether to have a baby, #1586

    having a baby in the hospital rather than with a midwife, #1618

babysitter

    breaks up with boyfriend who has gotten another girl pregnant, #1566

    child is upset when left with a new daytime babysitter, #1766

    families that exploit babysitters, #1867

    is wrongly accused of stealing money, #1386

    who steals from family, #1435

back problems, #1943

    laid off work because of back pain, #1628

bag of books, carrying a, #1160

bags for the garbage can, problems finding the right size, #1336

ballet class

    leading and following other students at the barre during, #1313

ballpoint pen, discarding a faulty, #1218

band, bands. *See* band trip

band trip

    drinking, having fun, and getting good stories to tell others, #2150

bank. *See also* bank employee

    advantages of automatic teller machines (ATMs), #1188

    avoiding an incompetent teller, #1321

    delays when dealing with a new teller, #1365

    filling out transaction slips while standing in line, #1198

    selecting a convenient bank, #1317

Index of numbered examples

blood
> reaction to finding blood in one's urine, #1626

blouse. *See* shopping

bomb
> elderly man is arrested for asking a baggage inspector who was examining his wife's change purse, "Are you looking for a bomb?" #2047

book, books. *See also* architectural book; library; publisher
> deciding whether to carry a bag of books upstairs or across campus, #1160
> envy that sister received more books than he did, #2179
> ordering books for a bookstore is mentally exhausting, #1355
> students who underline and dog-ear library books, #1181

book and record club selections
> I avoid looking through them twice, #1234
> not getting around to returning selections you don't want, #1261

book report by students who haven't read the book, #1202

book review, putting off and rushing to do a, #1343

bootlegger, #1985

boss, convincing, to reduce one's workload, #1250

boyfriend. *See also* breakups; cheating; Christmas presents; drugs; girlfriend; revenge; sex
> girl has sex with boyfriend so she won't lose him, #1669
> if she loses her boyfriend she will lose her status with her girlfriends, #1669
> I hope my boyfriend is being faithful, #1691
> I'm bored with my boyfriend, #1700
> is persistent about wanting to have sex, #1690
> I worry whether I'll be able to dump my boyfriend, #1700
> roommate talks constantly about her boyfriend, #1413

bragging
> brother bragging about his good looks and appeal to women, #1412

brakes, not fixing faulty, #1209

bread. *See also* breadmaking machines
> baking on Saturday morning, #1189

breadmaking machines, #1189

breakup, breakups, breaking up. *See also* boyfriend; cheating
> after cheating, #1850
> conflicts after breaking up, #1478, #1485, #1530, #1531, #1560, #1566
> getting to know other girls when one is worried about a breakup with one's girlfriend, #1959
> of his parents because of his mother's adultery, #1720
> I worry that Dad will leave us, #1698
> I worry whether I'll be able to dump my boyfriend, #1700
> my husband left me for another woman, #1697
> providing emotional support when a friend's relationship breaks up, #1943
> ready to give up on boyfriend who is too involved with drugs, #1715
> trying to drive other males away from his ex-girlfriend, #1485
> trying to make his ex-girlfriend jealous, #1695

Index of numbered examples

breasts
> staring at girl with large flopping breasts who walks past trolley stop, #1391

breathing, imagining the worst when I have difficulty, #1589

bridesmaid, always wanting to be a, #2153

bridge (cards), couple kick each other while playing, #1497

brother. *See also* family
> blaming younger brother who is too young to talk, #1549

brushing teeth. *See* teeth

bullies
> at school, #1535
>
> on school busses, #1495

bus trip, forced to talk to elderly lady on, #1408

butt-ended. *See* hockey

buying the best one can afford, #1279

calculators
> buying duplicate calculators as Christmas gifts to avoid envy, #2259
>
> buying several so will always have one available, #1223

campus
> females scared of leaving buildings at night, #1643

cancer. *See also* potatoes
> concern about, #1604, #1619
>
> worries about her brother's cancer, #1705

candy and pop. *See* vending machines

candy machines. *See* vending machines

car, cars. *See also* accident, car; car rentals; car wash; driving; envy; European cars; Japanese cars; parking spaces; tattle; tires
> advantages of having one's own car, #1222
>
> attacks his own car after he causes an accident, #1567
>
> damaging a sibling's car, #1453
>
> disadvantages of depending on others who own a car, #1222
>
> driver blocks path of pedestrian, who then kicks car, #1494
>
> envious responses by people when someone buys more cars than they own themselves, #2176
>
> envy regarding cars owned by others, #2115, #2143, #2176, #2192, #2197
>
> getting rides with a friend who takes driving risks, #1379
>
> girls always want to go out with guys with nice cars, #2143
>
> helping the driver watch for potential accidents, #1958
>
> inconvenience of an older car, #1219
>
> male shouting at a group of guys to keep their hands off his car, #1487
>
> not helping those stuck in the snow, #1307
>
> observer reports a hit and run accident, #1552
>
> opening car door and chipping paint on next car, #1452
>
> problems with getting a car fixed, #1292
>
> putting on makeup or brushing teeth while driving or traveling in a car, #1228

cheating (*continued*)

    in regard to money or property

        brokerage houses assign false prices to market orders, #1446

        dealing with vending machines that don't work properly, #1447

        jeweler switches diamond in ring, #1444

        misleading advertising, #1445

checkbook, not bothering to balance one's, #1258

check from the government doesn't arrive on time, it is upsetting when one's, #1470

checkout counter, minimizing the time spent waiting to pay at a, #1191

chemical spraying, concern about, #1604

chess, playing, blindfolded, #1358

chewing gum. *See also* annoyances

    on an airplane to deal with pressure changes in one's ears, #1572

    sticking it under a desk or seat, #1181

chicken, preparing, to eat in the future, #1233

child, children. *See also* punishment

    asking daughter to make a cup of tea, #1299

    avoiding chores, #1404

    fighting over toys, #1493

    getting son to go to bed on time, #1297

    getting son to put toys away, #1297

    looking in neighbors' windows at night, #1380

    making noise to get attention, #1384

    neighbors take child home who is playing in the road, #1584

    parents threatening noisy children, #1384

    playing "store" with parents' money, #1386

    reaction by parents to attempts to get attention, #1384

    reducing stress dealing with son, #1297

    reminding children not to put garbage in waste baskets, #1273

    repeatedly followed by man in truck, #1848

    resentment over having to do something for a sister, #1311

    telling daughter to get towels herself, #1303

choir

    envy that another girl was chosen to go to Europe with the choir, #2162

    resentment that others do not help with all the work required to serve Christmas dinner to the choir, #2137

cholesterol

    annoyed about public concern over, #2055

    my father ignored his high cholesterol and continued to eat lots of roast pork, #2083

    trying to cut cholesterol out of one's diet, #1600, #1601

    trying to reduce high cholesterol, #1623

chores. *See also* errands; tasks

    children avoiding chores, #1404

    doing a manageable number of, #1171

Index of numbered examples

459

competition between neighbors, #2244

complaint, letters of. *See* taxi driver

complaints. *See* grocery store; taxi driver

computer, computers

    advantages of buying the same model for home that is used at work, #1294

    buying one that will require the least repairs, #1277

    calling the company to find out how to operate software, #1302

    clicking on options before the information finishes loading, #1195

    difficulty giving up old routines, #1327

    envies the better computers that co-workers have, #2101

    not learning to use a, #1327

    not reading the manual, #1302

    printing files, #1373

    as a time saver, #1211

    wanting to replace slow computer, #1200

concentrate and do mentally demanding work, limited ability to, #1161

concentrating, difficulty. *See also* annoyances

    because others are talking, #1406

concern. *See* anxiety

condom, condoms

    finding a hole in one's, #1471

    I carry condoms in case I meet a guy I really like, #1919

    leaving used condoms lying around, #1414

    reason for using, #1624

conflicts. *See* family

con games

    borrowing money for an eye prescription, #1442

    getting tickets for an opera, #1442

    taking money to buy drugs, #1443

    at a youth hostel in Europe, #1442

conscientious objectors. *See* Vietnam War

conserving time and energy, #1156 - #1373

Consumer Reports, #1282

contact lenses, convenience of buying several pairs at the same time, #1231

contest winner. *See* advertising, misleading

contracts. *See* university

convention, beating up fellow student (female) who rejects his advances at a, #1378

cooking. *See also* division of labor

    winging it rather than following a recipe, #1183

copies, filling out nearly identical, #1315

cops. *See* police

courses

    require less mental effort in the arts and social sciences than in the natural sciences, #1185

    wanting to quit working in a course as soon as he has earned a passing grade of 50, #1187

Index of numbered examples

cover up

father falsely claims he, not his son, caused the car accident, #1552

cow, stealing his neighbor's, #1432

criminal, scared to walk home alone because of an escaped, #2029

cruise control, trying to operate, without reading instructions, #1182

cry, cries, crying

when separated from family members, #1766

because sister persuaded her to spend her birthday money on the sister and the sister's friends, #1864

because so upset watching neighbor spend his lottery winnings, #2237

tasks that make one want to cry, #1337

women crying when angry, #1562

curling

teammate's anger at a poor player, #1499

customers

that complain, #1547

dance, dances, dancing. *See also* dance demonstration

boyfriend dances with another girl for an hour, #1553

parents getting son to report on daughter's behavior at teen dances, #1583

dance demonstration, employee turns down lights during a, #1541

dark, fear of the, #1641 - #1643, #1767

date, dates, dating. *See also* appearance

male resents that males have to pay all the expenses on a date, #1476, #2138

male wishes that girls paid their share on, #1476

daughter. *See also* anxiety; family

father criticizes daughter over phone, #1388

deadline, anxiety over approaching, #1334, #1362

Dead Man's Pond, #1650, #1651

dealer, authorized. *See* company

dealer in used goods breaks in line at garage sales, #1430

death, helping those who have a death in the family, #1309

denial. *See* tripping

dentist. *See* root canals

diamond ring. *See* cheating in regard to property

dinner

expects his mom to have dinner ready, #1467

going to bed without, #1382

people who don't reciprocate dinners, #1477

tells his mom when he will be home for dinner, #1467

dirty looks

at girl chomping bubble gum in class, #1491

at rude and difficult customers, #1492

dishes. *See* dish-washing machine; violence; washing dishes

Index of numbered examples

dish-washing machine
> advantages of an electric, #1210
> changes produced in using dishes after getting a, #1230
> deciding to buy one, #2188
> removing similar items when unloading a, #1225
> unloading it in such a way that one won't be asked to do so again, #1267
> women without one running down a woman who bought one, #2209

displays of anger. *See also* anger; the chapter on Protecting Self and Resources
> toward car, #1567
> children and toys, #1493
> on a curling team, #1499
> with ex-girlfriend, #1485
> mom smashes platter on dinner table, #1498

disposable eating utensils at a party, using, #1266

distractions. *See* annoyances

division of labor
> different families drive the same set of kids to or from school, #1305
> girlfriend cooks and boyfriend washes dishes, #1304

divorce, realizing she is ready to get a, #1532

dog, dogs
> fear of, #1644

doing more than one thing at the same time, #1227, #1228

donkeys in the Galapagos, looking for wild, #1289

door
> holding a door open for another person, #1306
> holding heavy door open by bracing one's foot against it and the floor, #1163
> opening door with one hand using a key, #1158

double standards
> my mother gets to play her music at full blast, but she makes me wear earphones
> to listen to my music, #2120

doughnut, daughter takes a bite out of each miniature, #1544

drinking. *See also* alcohol; drunk
> and fights, #1561

drink machines. *See* vending machines

drive-through service window, using businesses with a, #1316

driving, drivers. *See also* accident, car; cars; division of labor; driving license;
> exhausted; traffic fine; traffic light
> anger at delays, other drivers, pedestrians, etc., #1426, #1517
> attacks his own car after he causes an accident, #1567
> being stopped for speeding, #1488
> designated drivers, #2140
> difficulty driving a route for the first time that others have driven you on before,
> #1314
> driving at pedestrians, #1374
> driving away without reporting an accident, #1452, #1552

Index of numbered examples

E-mail
  is less effort than letters and telephone calls, #1184
  not learning to use, #1327
embarrassing, embarrassed, embarrassment
  embarrassing question in a club, #1868
  getting my head shaved as part of our hockey-team initiation, #1785
  when I go out with the other guys and have to check in with Mom, #2096
  when laughed at at school for wearing purple pants, #2025
  not acting on various urges in order to avoid the consequences, #1873
  not using a public toilet because others will hear her, #1673
  saying prayers at a sweat lodge ceremony, #1675
  when sister waves at him when she is last in a race, #1667
  skipping class rather than be seen entering late, #1672
environmental use by humans, #2053
envy, envious. *See also* appearance; sibling rivalry
  efforts to get others to give them resources
    buy me some too. Please, please, Mom! #2178
    why does my sister get four books, but I only get three? #2179
  envy and competition between neighbors, #2244
    a community is a comfortable place to live in if it doesn't have any rich
      families which make people look bad and feel inferior, #2229
    this competition is a hush-hush subject, #2244
    families who couldn't keep up moved away, #2230
    families who do not try to keep up with their neighbors, #2170
    forms of competition
      camping van, #2244
      Christmas presents, #2228, #2244
      French doors, #2244
      garages, #2244
      a gas barbecue, #2194
      house color, #2244
      household furnishings, #2222, #2244
      lawns, #2244
      microwave ovens, #2244
      mixing socially with dignitaries, #2244
      patios, #2244
      possessions, #2244
      ski-doos, #2244
      trip to Europe, #2244
      video-game consoles and games, #2244
      winter vacations in Florida, #2225
    including Christmas gifts from last year when you show visitors what you got
      this year, #2228
    mowing one's lawn when the neighbors do, #2244
    my neighbor has everything, but I have nothing, #2165

Index of numbered examples

Index of numbered examples

Index of numbered examples

Index of numbered examples

Index of numbered examples

Index of numbered examples

Index of numbered examples

Index of numbered examples

husband praising another woman's cooking, #2108
son's resentment over chores, #2136
helping with, #1309
resentment of those operating large-scale farms, #2214
small farmers versus big farmers, #2214
fast-food restaurant
fights at a, #1455
father. *See* family
fatigued. *See* exhausted; tired
fear. *See* anxiety, anxious
federal budget, getting colleague to explain changes in the new, #1301
fiancé. *See* tattling
fight, fights. *See also* hockey; violence
almost happening between two groups of males over "touching" a car, #1487
between baseball teams over near injuries, #1376
between batter and pitcher at a baseball game, #1496
beats up his buddy who deceived him, #1558
between brothers, #1538
with bully on school bus, #1495
the changes one goes through when one fights, #1561
in Charlottetown, #1561
in clubs, #1655
defusing a possible fight, #1487
at a fast-food restaurant, #1455
fistfight at a wedding over salaries, #2238
four males are beaten up and injured by fifteen males, #1377
in hockey, #1539, #1569
males from different towns fighting over girls from their town, #1455
at McDonald's restaurant, #1455
neighborhood gang, #1851
previous bully backs down from fight, #1535
punching guy who is dancing with his ex-girlfriend, #1375
sister rescues younger brother from a fight, #1449
why males didn't run from a fight in which they were seriously outnumbered, #1377
young children fighting over toys, #1493
figure skating
learning to do a one-footed spin, #1325
films. *See* movies; video rental store
finger, giving another person the. *See* taxi driver
fingers, nearly cutting off. *See* snowblower
fire, fear whether will be able to escape a, #1656
fire marshal. *See* revenge
fires an incompetent employee, #1528
fireworks display, viewers trespass on private lawns in order to see a, #1429

473

Index of numbered examples

health problems, imagining the worst in regard to, #1589
heights, fear of
    afraid might jump off, #1637, #1654
    panic reaction on the roof of a church, #1637
helping neighbors, #1309
    resentment over, #1309
helping others, not, #1307
henpecked
    husband upset when wife henpecks him in front of others, #1463
hike, carries bottle of water on, #1570
hiking trip in the Galapagos, #1289
hockey
    badly needs to use the toilet while watching a hockey game, #1673
    chases boys playing street hockey away from his house, #1527
    fans fighting, #1569
    fighters on each team, #1569
    fighting, #1539, #1569
    injuries, #1539, #1569
    popularity of hockey players with girls at school, #2105
    team seeks revenge against opponent who butt-ended their player, #1539
    tough guys, #1569
    worry that will lose game, #1590
homework. *See also* schoolwork; students
    brother falsely blames sister for not giving him the assignment, #1550
    worried that son wouldn't do, #1723
homosexuality
    male tries to avoid the person whom he told that he is interested in other males, #1872
homosexual magazine
    fantasizes sending a subscription to an opponent in an office war, #1509
honking. *See* traffic light
horror movie, fears after seeing a, #2031
houses, outstanding builder of, #1290
humane society called to investigate a supposed pet strangler, #1419
human relations with other species, #2053
humiliated
    when told by wife to get off the phone, #1388
    when wife henpecks him in front of others, #1463
husband. *See* family; wife

ice-cream cone, pretends to have licked, #1544
ice-cream sandwiches, dividing a box of, #2258
ice-making machine. *See* refrigerator
ID (identification) cards. *See also* driving license
    fake IDs, #1484

Index of numbered examples

Index of numbered examples

monsters under my bed, fear of, #1649

morning, sore and tired when get up in the, #1359

motel bar, local regulars are envious of the treatment given to traveling salesmen in a, #2118

mother. *See also* family

    constantly questioning her adult children, #1482

    daughter threatens to move out if mother doesn't stop questioning her, #1482

    not wanting to go get car in order to drive daughter a short distance, #1173

    smashes platter on table when daughter disagrees with her, #1498

mouth. *See* eat

movement. *See* music, moving to

movie, movies

    deciding where to sit in, #1318

    having to go to the toilet during a, #1573

    upset with those breaking into line to see a foreign film, #1568

Mr. Coffee, #1548

multiple sclerosis, trying to cope with, #2010

music. *See also* music, moving to

    listening to. *See* double standard

music cassette. *See* cassette

music, moving to

    switching movements because it is tiring to continue repeating the same movements, #1348

name, dislike being called the wrong name, #1415

nap, telephone calls which interrupt Dad's, #1407

native peoples. *See also* native powwow; sweat lodge ceremony

    envy of whites over benefits received by, #2272

native powwow, #1963

neighbor, neighbors. *See also* envy

    boy's fear of neighbor after being slapped by him, #1489

    competition between neighbors, #2244

    envy between, #2114

    everyone tries to prove they are equal to or better than the next fellow, #2114

    families who are not interested in keeping up with their neighbors, #2170

    helping each other, #1309

    resentment over helping, #1309

    slaps neighbor's child for spitting on him, #1489

    take child playing in the road home, #1584

    telling neighbor how well one is doing saving money, #2100

neighborhoods, avoiding bad, #1851

nervous breakdown, worries that wife will have another, #1718

new issues. *See* stocks

nicknames, #1329

night. *See* rape; walking alone

Index of numbered examples

Index of numbered examples

Index of numbered examples

reciprocation. *See also* division of labor
    between farmers, #1309
    between neighbors, #1309
record clubs. *See* book and record club selections
record store. *See* walk
red light
    man driving ahead before the light changes to green, #1204
referrals
    not buying from a store with a reputation for inferior goods, #1281
    recommending a house builder, #1290
refrigerator with an ice-making machine, convenience of a, #1178
rejection. *See also* bedroom; convention; family; rejection, fear of
    from party if did not bring liquor, #1441
relationship, relationships. *See also* anxiety; boyfriend; breakups; cheating;
        ex-boyfriend; ex-girlfriend; family; females; girlfriends; making up; males
    envy over, #2107, #2155 - #2161, #2220
    fear of not finding the right mate, #1687
    fears about, #1684 - #1700
    feeling loved and unloved, #1310
    giving more than the other person in a, #1310
    an improvement in one's relationship with girlfriend's teenage son, #1581
relatives. *See* family; uncle
remembering something by writing notes for oneself, #1169
rent
    opposition when landlord tries to raise rent by ten percent, #1500
repairs, avoiding the need for, #1277, #1280, #1284
repeat
    not wanting to repeat or explain what you said, #1335
reputation, reputations. *See also* politician; referrals
    not wanting to be late for work or school, #1672
    won't buy liquor at a local store in order to protect his reputation, #1671
research
    problems after hiring student to take photographs, #1434
resentment. *See also* envy
    over having to do something for someone else, #1308, #1309, #1311
restaurants
    getting more business when a restaurant nearby is too busy, #1320
    less effort using a drive-through service window than going inside to eat, #1316
retaliation. *See also* revenge
    retaliation over bean ball in a baseball game, #1376
retarded. *See* mentally retarded
revenge. *See also* retaliation
    attempts to slash girlfriend's tires, #1531
    cheats on boyfriend, #1525
    continues to want to beat up previous school bully, #1535

Index of numbered examples

Index of numbered examples

Index of numbered examples

toilet. *See also* bathroom; toilet, public
    daughter whips her mom with a towel, #1559
    having to go to the toilet during a movie, #1573
toilet, public. *See also* toilet
    concern about getting AIDS from a toilet seat, #1625
    not using one because others will hear her, #1673
    using a paper towel to turn off a faucet and open the door, #1621
toilet paper, using one or two hands to try to tear off, #1156
toothbrush, can not find new, #1438
toothpaste. *See* advertising, misleading
towel, towels
    daughter whips her mom with a, #1559
    telling daughter to get them for herself, #1303
toys. *See* fights
toy soldiers, #2111
traffic. *See* driving
traffic accidents, #1374
    fatalities, #1374
traffic fine for speeding, #1488
traffic light. *See also* red light
    Mom upset that a driver honked at her in order to get her to drive ahead at the
        wrong time, #1510
train
    people standing up in the aisle before reach destination, #1196
trash, cleaning basement and spilling, #1207
travel, travels. *See also* trips
    taking everything one may need while one, #1288
    taking measures so that one does not lose baggage and other items when traveling,
        #1940
    taking precautions in case documents are lost or stolen or one's glasses are
        broken, #1578
travel shots, delay getting a booster for, #1238
tree
    his son breaks limb off his uncle's tree, #1448
trip, trips. *See also* travel
    difficulties when visiting relatives in Alberta, #1387
    Prince Edward Islanders taking precautions when planning a trip, #1929
tripping a boy and then denying that he did it, #1383
trouble maker, trouble makers
    in a department, #1865, #1883
    family with reputation for being, #1869
tutoring girlfriend in statistics, #1308
TV (television). *See also* family
    conflict over loan of television set, #1479
    parents interfering with children watching TV, #1405, #1406

taking what one wants to eat and drink while one watches, #1287
TV dinners, #2187
typewriter, typewriters, electric
    not switching to a computer from an, #1327
    selecting them for student use, #1284

uncle
    uncle upset because relatives are not there in time for his birthday party, #1387
    visiting difficult uncle in Alberta, #1387
unemployment benefits, quitting government project to draw, #1371
unemployment check. *See* check from the government
university. *See also* anxiety; education; envy; graduate school; group project;
        homework; mentally retarded; professor; students
    dropping out to become a kung-fu master, #1368
    envy over differences between faculty contracts, #2243
    it's just a waste of money, #2210
    worried that son will decide not to go to, #1724
upsetting, it is
    when you run out of household supplies or the equipment in your house doesn't
        work properly, #1599
urges and inclinations that people do not act on, #1873

vacation, vacations
    finishing chores before going on, #1887
    resentment over doing chores for those who have left on, #1309
    response to those in rural areas who take, #2198
VCR (video cassette recorder)
    convenient features on a, #1199
    problems with an older model, #1220
VCR tapes
    cataloging the content of recorded VCR tapes, #1272
    comparison in *Consumers Reports*, #1282
    different formats in England versus Canada, #1296
vegetables. *See* steamer
vending machines
    dealing with machines that cheat you, #1447
    getting coins ready when walking to, #1194
verbal abuse. *See* teasing
veteran's benefits, sailor in merchant marine injured in World War II and still trying to
    get his, #1469
video cassette recorder. *See* VCR
video rental store, difficulties dealing with a, #1322
Vietnam, Vietnamese
    being careful not to cause envy when she distributes gifts and money to relatives
        in, #2255

Index of numbered examples

SUBJECT INDEX

See also a) the tables of contents and tables of detailed contents for the individual chapters, and b) the index of numbered examples.

jealousy. *See* trying to get what others have

language, 20 - 22

mind, 28 - 30
models, 18 - 19, 24 - 26
    and behavior, 18 - 19
    the production of anxiety, 318 - 319
    whether or not one engages in an activity, 112 - 116

neighbors. *See* competition between neighbors

orientations, 26 - 28

photographs are between pages 230 and 231
physical discomfort. *See* removing physical discomfort
protecting self and resources, 137 - 209

removing physical discomfort, 211 - 217

sources of photographs, 433
study of behavior, 31 - 33

taking precautions, 219 - 358
tension and release, 16 - 17
threats. *See* taking precautions
trying to get what others have, 359 - 428

volume one, 1
volume two, 3

worry. *See* taking precautions